Early Language Development

Trends in Language Acquisition Research

As the official publication of the International Association for the Study of Child Language (IASCL), TiLAR presents thematic collective volumes on state-of-the-art child language research carried out by IASCL members worldwide.

IASCL website: http://iascl.talkbank.org/

Volume 5

Early Language Development. Bridging brain and behaviour
Edited by Angela D. Friederici and Guillaume Thierry

Early Language Development

Bridging brain and behaviour

Edited by

Angela D. Friederici
Max Planck Institute for Human Cognitive and Brain Sciences

Guillaume Thierry
Bangor University

John Benjamins Publishing Company
Amsterdam / Philadelphia

The paper used in this publication meets the minimum requirements of
American National Standard for Information Sciences – Permanence of
Paper for Printed Library Materials, ANSI z39.48-1984.

Library of Congress Cataloging-in-Publication Data

Early language development : bridging brain and behaviour / edited by Angela D.
          Friederici and Guillaume Thierry
     p.   cm. (Trends in Language Acquisition Research, ISSN 1569-0644 ; v. 5)
     Includes bibliographical references and index.
          1. Language acquisition. 2. Neurophysiology.
     P118 .E22   2008
     401/.93--dc22   2007038185
     ISBN 978 90 272 3475 9 (Hb; alk. paper)

John Benjamins Publishing Co. · P.O. Box 36224 · 1020 ME Amsterdam · The Netherlands
John Benjamins North America · P.O. Box 27519 · Philadelphia PA 19118-0519 · USA

Table of contents

List of contributors

Josiane Bertoncini
Laboratoire Psychologie de la Perception, CNRS – Université Paris 5, France

Barbara T. Conboy
University of Washington, Seattle, WA, USA

Anne Cutler
Max Planck Institute for Psycholinguistics, The Netherlands

Scania de Schonen
Laboratoire Psychologie de la Perception, CNRS – Université Paris 5, France

Ansgar Endress
Scuola Internazionale Superiore di Studi Avanzati (SISSA), Italy

Angela D. Friederici
Max Planck Institute for Human Cognitive and Brain Sciences, Germany

Judit Gervain
Scuola Internazionale Superiore di Studi Avanzati (SISSA), Italy

Galina Iakimova
Laboratoire Psychologie de la Perception, CNRS – Université Paris 5, France

Elizabeth K. Johnson
Max Planck Institute for Psycholinguistics, The Netherlands

Valesca Kooijman
F.C. Donders Centre for Cognitive Neuroimaging, Radboud University, The Netherlands; Max Planck Institute for Psycholinguistics, The Netherlands

Patricia K. Kuhl
University of Washington, Seattle, WA, USA

Claudia Männel
Max Planck Institute for Human Cognitive and Brain Sciences, Germany

Jacques Mehler
Scuola Internazionale Superiore di Studi Avanzati (SISSA), Italy

Debra L. Mills
Department of Psychology, Emory University, USA

Sylvain Mottet
Laboratoire Cognition et Comportement, CNRS – Université Paris 5, France

Thierry Nazzi
Laboratoire Psychologie de la Perception, CNRS – Université Paris 5, France

Marina Nespor
University of Ferrara, Italy

Regine Oberecker
Max Planck Institute for Human Cognitive and Brain Sciences, Germany

Akira Omaki
Department of Linguistics University of Maryland College Park, USA

David Poeppel
Department of Linguistics University of Maryland College Park, USA

Elizabeth A. Sheehan
Department of Psychology, Emory University, USA

Maritza Rivera-Gaxiola
University of Washington, Seattle, WA, USA

Josette Serres
Laboratoire Psychologie de la Perception, CNRS – Université Paris 5, France

Juan Silva-Pereyra
Universidad Nacional Autónoma de México, Mexico

Guillaume Thierry
School of Psychology, Bangor University, UK

Marilyn May Vihman
School of Psychology, Bangor University, UK
Language and Linguistics, The University of York, UK

Preface

The present volume is the fifth in the series 'Trends in Language Acquisition Research' (TiLAR). As an official publication of the *International Association for the Study of Child Language* (IASCL), the TiLAR Series publishes two volumes per three year period in between IASCL congresses. All volumes in the IASCL-TiLAR Series are invited edited volumes by IASCL members that are strongly thematic in nature and that present cutting edge work which is likely to stimulate further research to the fullest extent.

Besides quality, diversity is also an important consideration in all the volumes and in the series as a whole: diversity of theoretical and methodological approaches, diversity in the languages studied, diversity in the geographical and academic backgrounds of the contributors. After all, like the IASCL itself, the IASCL-TiLAR Series is there for child language researchers from all over the world.

The four previous TiLAR volumes were on bilingual acquisition, sign language acquisition, language development beyond the early childhood years, and on the link between child language disorders and developmental theory. We are particularly pleased to present the current volume on neurological and behavioural approaches to the study of early language processing. We are very grateful to the volume editors, Angela D. Friederici and Guillaume Thierry, for their willingness to take on the task of preparing a volume on this exciting research. Dr. Friederici's superb keynote at the IASCL conference in Berlin in July 2005 has set the tone for the state-of-the-art collection of high quality chapters in the present volume. Top researchers in the field provide overviews of the main techniques, theoretical issues and results pertaining to the research carried out in their laboratories.

We are proud to have this important and cutting-edge work represented in the TiLAR series so that child language researchers from all different backgrounds worldwide have the opportunity to become acquainted with it or get to know it better. Because of the wide readership, and the often quite technical nature of the subject matter, we have closely worked together with the editors to try and make sure that the volume is sufficiently accessible, also for non-specialists. Occasionally this means that particular techniques and lines of reasoning are explained more than once. Rather than limit such overlaps, we have welcomed them. An increase in clarity can only help towards making sure that also our uninitiated readers feel ready to 'dive in'. We thank the editors for working with us in achieving as much clarity as possible. Novice readers are advised to start by reading the first 'tutorial' chapter by Claudia Männel. In reading the rest of the book, the glossary at the beginning that explains a number of terms and techniques not covered in the tutorial and the extensive subject index at the end can help readers to find their way through some of the more technical aspects of the book.

Finally, we would like to thank Seline Benjamins and Kees Vaes of John Benjamins Publishing Company for their continued trust and support. We also thank the TiLAR Advisory Board consisting of IASCL past presidents Jean Berko Gleason, Ruth Berman, Philip Dale, Paul Fletcher and Brian MacWhinney for being our much appreciated 'sounding board'.

Antwerp, August 2007

Annick De Houwer and Steven Gillis
The General Editors

Introduction to early language development

Bridging brain and behavior

Guillaume Thierry and Angela D. Friederici

This book is an attempt to build a bridge between a traditional and highly respected method of research, namely, experimental psychology, and the younger but promising methodology of event-related potentials (ERPs), in order to demonstrate how the two approaches complement one another and together provide new routes to exploring the early stages of human language development.

Both behavioral and electrophysiological measures have been substantially used to investigate early language development. However, studies which have used the two approaches in parallel and which have tried to quantify and exploit the link between the two types of measures are only now starting to appear in the literature. The present volume provides compelling evidence that the two approaches are remarkably complementary. On the one hand, behavioral observations of infants and toddlers have been made for over thirty years and have offered invaluable insight into language development based on overt, observable responses. Measures such as high amplitude sucking, visual habituation / dishabituation, or looking time in the head turn procedure, for instance, have revealed that infants have astonishing linguistic abilities very soon after birth. More recently, non-invasive electrophysiological techniques such as electroencephalography and, to a lesser extent, functional brain imaging (e.g., functional magnetic resonance imaging and near infra-red spectroscopy) have proved powerful in establishing language-dependent patterns of brain activity. Such techniques that more or less directly measure the activity of the infant brain independently of overt behavioral manifestations have become widely available, creating unprecedented opportunities towards the understanding of the mechanisms of mental development in general and language acquisition in particular.

To demonstrate the potential of bridging the two approaches in the study of early language development, this volume brings together experimental psychologists and electrophysiologists, but also experimental psychologists who have begun to discover the possibilities offered by electrophysiology, and electrophysiologists who have started to implement protocols inspired by the ingenuity of behavioral designs, as well as researchers well acquainted with both methodological domains. The contributors, each in their own way, provide a review of the context (behavioral, electrophysiological or both) in which their research has flourished, present findings from their own research team, and share their vision of how the field might evolve taking into consideration recent methodological and theoretical developments.

In Chapter 1, Männel provides a general introduction to ERP methodology and considers various issues arising in infant studies. The biological basis of electroencephalography is introduced and the principles of ERP data processing are explained. After reviewing methodological precautions and limitations in the testing of infants, the author provides a synthetic overview of the key ERP components used in studies of cognitive development. Overall this chapter is a very useful tutorial for readers of the present volume, and, more generally, for researchers who intend to start conducting developmental ERP research.

In Chapter 2, Conboy, Rivera-Gaxiola, Silva-Pereyra and Kuhl present a comprehensive overview of key ERP studies investigating phonemes, words and sentences processing during language development. First, they discuss behavioral and ERP results of studies on phoneme processing in early infancy and report data from their research which show that between the age of 7 and 11 months infants tune in towards the phoneme repertoire of their target language. Furthermore, they demonstrate the early predictive power of ERP measures for language skills observed in the second year of life. Then, they present ERP and behavioral studies on word learning conducted both with infants growing up in a monolingual and in a bilingual environment. Finally, they provide an integrative overview of ERP studies on semantic and syntactic processing during the third, fourth and fifth year of life.

In Chapter 3, Nazzi, Iakimova, Bertoncini, Mottet, Serres and de Schonen focus on the infants' ability to segment words from the continuous auditory speech stream, a prerequisite for language learning. They start out from behavioral work on word segmentation in French and extend their report to initial ERP results on this topic. Evidence regarding the key role of stress in English and the importance of the syllable as a unit in French supports the view of a rhythmic-based approach to word segmentation. The combined findings from behavioral and ERP experiments conducted by their own team suggest that word segmentation in French-learning infants is indeed based on the infants' ability to segment syllabic components in the auditory input.

In Chapter 4, Kooijman, Johnson and Cutler also focus on the problem of word segmentation which needs to be solved by the infant as an initial step to language. First, they provide a well-structured overview of behavioral studies on word segmentation. Then, after discussing the advantages and disadvantages of behavioral measures, they present a study of their own research team in which they used behavioral and ERP measures in parallel with the goal to uncover the processes underlying word segmentation. While there is no behavioral effect indicating that word segmentation is in place at 7 months, ERP results suggest that the neural basis for such behavior is already present at that age.

In Chapter 5, Thierry and Vihman give an overview of a cross-sectional investigation addressing the onset of word form recognition in English and Welsh infants based on behavioral measures (HPP – Headturn Preference procedures) collected in parallel with electrophysiological measures (ERPs) in the same individuals. Thierry and Vihman show that ERP and behavioral measures are consistent with one another but shed a slightly different light on the issue of untrained word form recognition. While HPP measures reveal significant word familiarity effects at 11 months in English, ERPs already detect significant neurophysiological differences at 10 months. Thierry and Vihman also reflect on differences between English and Welsh and show how behavioral and ERP data allow deeper interpretation than is possible based on one type of measure alone.

In Chapter 6, Friedrich shows how ERPs can provide fundamental insight into the ontogenesis of the semantic system between 12 and 14 months. Using a picture – word priming paradigm, she introduces electrophysiological markers indexing the integration of word form and word meaning in the infant's mind. Interestingly, the author shows that the two markers develop in stages, with only word form effects at 12 months and effects of both phonological form and word meaning at 14 months. These findings allow Friederich to make inferences regarding the relative development of lexical expectations and semantic integration shortly after the end of the first year of life. In addition, the author discusses the results of a longitudinal study showing that language advances at 30 months can be related to the sensitivity of semantic integration markers at 19 months.

In Chapter 7, Sheehan and Mills offer a rich account of the phonological, prosodic and semantic processing of single words in children between the ages of 3 months and 3 years as indexed by electrophysiology. Based on the relationship between word familiarity effects on ERPs and infant vocabulary size at a later age, the authors propose that chronological age is less relevant than language proficiency in shaping ERP response patterns. Sheehan and Mills depict striking topographical shifts for ERP differences elicited by words that are being acquired versus words that have already been learned, a phenomenon which is found at various stages of development. The authors also discuss interesting results from priming experiments showing that significant gesture-picture priming effects found at 18 months transitorily disappear at 26 months while word-picture priming is found at both ages.

In Chapter 8, Mehler, Endress, Gervain and Nespor make a strong case for experimentation to be grounded in cognitive theory and give an elegant demonstration of the ingenuity which characterizes the behavioral approach. The authors show how experiments contrasting familiarization with artificial grammars and test phases in infants and adults allow a number of key hypotheses regarding the fundamental processes of syntax acquisition to be tested based only on overt measures of participants' attention to a stimulus stream. Based on such observations Mehler *et al.* propose that, in addition to established statistical mechanisms thought to be at work in grammar learning, two elementary processes or perceptual primitives may intervene at a global or "Gestalt" level: a process that keeps track of repetitions or identity relations in language input and a process of edge detection capable of inferring boundaries.

In Chapter 9, Friederici and Oberecker describe ERP patterns elicited by phrase structure violations in 24- and 32.5-month-olds and compare them to those of adult listeners. They show that syntactic aberrations such as phrase structure violations are already detected by 24 months, even though only the late ERP modulations observed in adults can be found at this age. Interestingly, by 32.5 months children display a pattern of response that is qualitatively similar to that of adults, suggesting that the syntactic parsing system is already advanced and capable of early automatic detection of grammatical errors. These observations lead the authors to hypothesize that the transition from 2 to 2.8 years is accompanied by important maturation of syntactic abilities. Friederici and Oberecker then discuss the implications of their findings for quantitative and qualitative aspects of language development.

The rich and synthetic overviews presented in chapters 1 to 9 are followed by a vibrant discussion written by Poeppel and Omaki (Chapter 10).

CHAPTER 1

The method of event-related brain potentials in the study of cognitive processes

A tutorial

Claudia Männel

1 The field of cognitive neuroscience

In the field of cognitive neuroscience, researchers aim for a better understanding of the relationship between behavior and its corresponding brain mechanisms. For example, it is of interest to know whether different brain circuits are involved when people communicate in their native language versus a foreign language. This finding may improve the understanding of why many people do not attain high proficiency in speaking a foreign language as compared to their native language. To bridge the ostensible gap between the cognition that guides behavior and its neural bases, suitable research tools are needed that directly capture the brain's responses to specific events, such as language input. For this reason, various methods from neurology, neuropsychology and computer science have been adapted to deliver convergent evidence not only about the anatomical, but first and foremost about the functional characteristics of the human brain. Thus, all of these methods address temporal and/ or spatial aspects of human information processing in the brain. Here, electroencephalography (EEG[1]) and magnetoencephalography (MEG) measure electrical and magnetic brain signals, respectively, while positron emission tomography (PET), functional magnetic resonance imaging (fMRI), and near-infrared spectroscopy (NIRS) utilize metabolic parameters.

Similar to cognitive neuroscience, developmental cognitive neuroscience focuses on the relation between brain development and cognitive development. In language acquisition, for example, the age at which infants understand the meaning of a word (i.e., when the brain mechanisms for the processing of word meaning are

---

1. In the current tutorial, the abbreviation EEG refers to both the recording method of electroencephalography as well as the result of this recording, the electroencephalogram.

present/functional) is of interest, even if the infants are not yet able to show an according verbal response. In developmental research, the most frequently applied measures are event-related brain potentials (ERPs[2]), which are derived from EEG recordings. The use of NIRS and fMRI has only recently become more prominent.

The following tutorial will give a brief introduction to ERPs as a powerful research tool for the study of cognitive processes as they occur in the brain. First, we explain the method at hand, sketching the way from the EEG to the ERP signal. Then, we briefly illustrate how to look at and interpret the derived ERPs. Here, we point out some methodological considerations that should be kept in mind in the evaluation of ERPs obtained from infants and young children. Then, we address some of the advantages as well as the disadvantages of the ERP method compared to behavioral and other neuroscience methods. We highlight the characteristics that become especially relevant when working with developmental populations. Finally, we will demonstrate the use of the ERP method by introducing some ERP components observed in language processing, which in turn have been utilized in ERP studies of language acquisition.

2   Electroencephalography and event-related brain potentials

The human brain constantly produces electrical activity. This activity is associated with a wide range of brain states and functions, such as various states of activation, relaxation, tiredness, and engagement in cognitive tasks. Electrical brain activity originates from both neurons' action potentials and their postsynaptic potentials (for more detail see Creutzfeldt and Houchin 1974; Lopes da Silva 1991; Speckmann and Elgar 1993). These electrical signals are minute and only recordable at the scalp when large populations of spatially aligned neurons are simultaneously active, so that in sum they are large enough to be measured. The timing characteristics of action potentials (lasting only 1–2 ms), inter alia, restrict the effect of summation so that resulting currents are not measurable at larger distances (only within a few μm). In contrast, the slower postsynaptic potentials tend to sum up in neighboring neurons and produce macrocellular currents that are able to reach the surface of the scalp. The conductance characteristics of the brain tissue, skull, and scalp enable the current flow and summed postsynaptic potentials to be registered by electrodes placed on the scalp. The EEG continuously records electrical brain activity by measuring the voltage changes that arise from the difference in potentials

---

2.   In the current tutorial, the abbreviation ERP refers to both the averaging of EEG epochs as well as the result of the averaging technique, the derived waveform with the particular ERP components.

between the recording electrodes and the reference electrodes (see Figure 2 later on). The EEG is either recorded from single electrodes or an array of electrodes implemented in an electrode cap (for further information on the use of electrode caps, see Sheehan and Mills, this volume).

EEG recordings deliver a global picture of the brain's electrical activity. However, in cognitive neuroscience, we are interested in voltage fluctuations that are time-locked to specific sensory or motor events. The detection of those evoked responses in the global EEG signal is complicated, since they are relatively small and masked by the ongoing background EEG activity unrelated to specific events[3]. To study the processing of events of interest, these events must be repeatedly presented and the EEG signal in response to these events must be subsequently averaged so that brain activity unrelated to processing the stimulus cancels out across a sufficient number of repetitions. In this way, an average electrical brain response to a specific stimulus can be obtained.

In an example experimental procedure, subjects listen to tones of different pitch (Figure 1, A1) while an EEG is recorded. The brain signal generated by the subject is recorded over the course of the experiment and, given its low amplitude, is amplified before being stored on a hard drive (Figure 1, B). Importantly, while the experimental computer is delivering the acoustic stimuli, it is simultaneously sending a trigger to the recording computer, marking the onset of each tone in the ongoing EEG (Figure 1, A2). After the EEG recording (Figure 1, C), filtering and artifact rejection/correction can be applied to the EEG raw data to remove artifacts caused by eye movement, perspiration, etc. (Figure 1, D). Filtering describes the removal of certain frequencies from the EEG signal that are sufficiently different from the frequencies that contribute to the ERP waveform (for more detail on filtering techniques, see Edgar, Stewart and Miller 2005). To increase the signal-to-noise-ratio, artifacts are often eliminated by simply rejecting contaminated trials. Alternatively, especially for artifacts stemming from eye movement, the artifact portion that contributes to the EEG signal can be calculated and subtracted without losing the affected trials (for an overview on artifact estimation and removal, see Talsma and Woldorff 2005 and Brunia, Möcks, van den Berg-

---

3.   The background EEG unrelated to the events of interest contains, in addition to artifacts (which are mainly attributable to eye/body movement, technical equipment, etc.), rhythmic activity (oscillations) that is also functionally interpretable (indicating deep sleep, drowsiness, relaxation, engagement in various cognitive tasks, etc.). This rhythmic activity is defined by the number of sinus waves per second (Hz) and is divided into five main frequency bands (e.g., Alpha 7-12 Hz; Gamma 30-80 Hz). In the case of ERP analyses this activity is noise by definition, since it is not the measure of interest, but could likewise be the actual signal when (event-related) oscillations are analyzed.

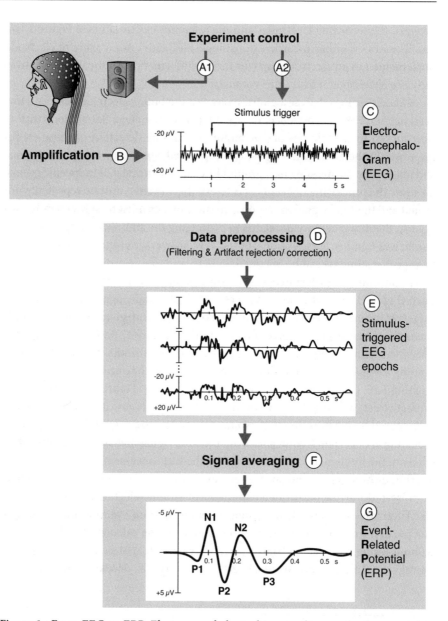

Figure 1. From EEG to ERP. Electroencephalographic recordings and subsequent data processing reveal event-related brain potentials. A1) Experiment computer generates acoustic stimuli. A2) Experiment computer sends stimulus trigger to the ongoing EEG recording. B) Amplification of the scalp-measured EEG signal. C) Ongoing EEG recording. D) Optional preprocessing of EEG raw data. E) Extraction of time-locked epochs from the EEG signal. F) Averaging of time-locked EEG epochs. G) Resulting event-related brain potentials in response to acoustic stimuli

Lenssen, Coelho, Coles, Elbert, Gasser, Gratton, Ifeachor, Jervis, Lutzenberger, Sroka, Blokland-Vogelesang, van Driel, Woestenburg, Berg, McCallum, Pham, Pocock and Roth 1989). Following the preprocessing of the EEG data, time-locked epochs triggered by the onset of each tone (i.e., EEG data in a defined time window) are extracted (Figure 1, E). These temporally aligned EEG epochs are averaged following the assumption that the effect of random noise distributed by each of the single trials is reduced, while the event-related brain response remains (Figure 1, F). Consequently, a sufficient number of artifact-free trials, usually between 50–100, is required for averaging to gain a high signal-to-noise-ratio. Data processing and subsequent trial averaging ideally produce a smooth curve of changes in electrical activity that represents the average processing of a stimulus over time, the event-related brain potential (Figure 1, G).

In sum, the EEG method represents a non-invasive measurement of summed post-synaptic electric potentials at the scalp that are generated by similarly aligned and simultaneously firing pyramidal cells in the neocortex. The subsequent averaging of stimulus-triggered EEG epochs delivers a direct measure of the temporal course of changes in electrical activity, so-called ERPs that correspond to neuronal information processing.

3   ERP components and their interpretation

The schematic ERP waveform in Figure 1 (G) displays a sequence of positive-going and negative-going voltage changes. The designation of these changes as waves, deflections, peaks, or positivity/negativity primarily refers to their physical appearance, while the term component additionally accounts for their functional significance. In other words, ERP components are considered to be indicators of various sensory, motor and cognitive processes that reflect covert and overt information processing. The components of ERPs can be described and defined by four parameters: amplitude/polarity, latency, scalp distribution/topography and functional significance.

Amplitude (plotted on the y-axis in µV, see Figure 1, G) specifies the extent to which neural activity is generated in response to an experimental stimulus. Dependent on the pole orientation of the measured electric field, the *polarity* of this response varies, resulting in positive or negative deflections. These deflections are sometimes called a 'positive-going event', a 'negative-going event' (Nazzi *et al.* this volume) or a 'negative-going ERP' (Kooijman *et al.* this volume). Note that negativity is plotted upward in most figures by convention, but some laboratories plot negativity downward. Amplitude measures can be given by calculating the mean amplitude in a defined time window (mean amplitude measures) or the corresponding peak within this time window (peak amplitudes measures), both relative to the average voltage in a prestimulus period (baseline). Regarding the experimental value of amplitude measures, a decrease of the amplitude of a certain ERP component across experimental conditions may be related to a reduction in the processing demands or efficiency.

Latency (time course plotted on the x-axis in ms, see Figure 1, G) indicates the point in time at which ERP components occur relative to stimulus onset. Both the amplitude/polarity parameter and latency parameter contribute to an ERP component's particular name. Waves with a negative-going deflection are labeled with N, waves with a positive-going deflection with P. The time (in ms) from stimulus onset to certain wave peaks is indicated by a number. The N100 component, for example, refers to a negativity that can be observed around 100 ms after stimulus onset. Note, however, that components are often labeled according to the order of their appearance during stimulus processing (e.g., P1, N1, P2, N2), rather than just in terms of the actual time of their occurrence. This holds for the so-called early components (from 100 ms to about 200 ms), which usually have a relatively fixed latency. So-called late components (from about 300 ms on) are subject to the specific experimental conditions to a much greater degree. For example, the latency of the P300 component varies between 300 ms and 700 ms post-stimulus, depending on the degree of discrimination difficulty, stimulus complexity, and task demands (e.g., Katayama and Polich 1998; Daffner, Scinto, Calvo, Faust, Mesulam, West and Holcomb 2000). Generally, a latency increase of a specific ERP component across experimental conditions can be attributed to a slowing down of a specific cognitive process. Here, latency measures can denote the approximate onset of a component or the time of maximal amplitude in a defined time window (peak latency measure).

Scalp distribution or *topography* (denoted by electrode positions or according to anatomical descriptions, see Figure 2) describes a component's voltage gradient over the scalp at any point during stimulus processing. An ERP component's label can include information about its topography, thus referring to a defining feature of this component, e.g., ELAN for Early Left Anterior Negativity (see later in this chapter). As can be seen from Figure 2, the longitudinal line between nasion (Nz) and inion (Iz) divides the schematic two-dimensional scalp into the left and right hemispheres, while the latitudinal line between the left and right pre-auricular points separates the anterior and posterior brain regions. Thus, the ELAN refers to a negative ERP component that occurs relatively early, at around 200 ms post-stimulus onset, and can be primarily observed at left anterior regions. Furthermore, some ERP components occur with a central focus in their scalp distribution (e.g., N400; see later in this chapter), while others exhibit a more posterior distribution (e.g., P600; see later in this chapter). Thus, the evaluation of the ERP signal across electrode sites delivers some restricted spatial information about the underlying neurophysiological mechanisms and allows conclusions about the lateralization to one hemisphere or the distribution over posterior brain regions. Topographic maps display the voltage difference between two conditions distributed over the scalp (i.e., negativities or positivities over particular regions). However, conclusions about the exact location of the neural generators of ERP components cannot be drawn by relying on topographic information only. To achieve valid localization statements, source localization methods should be applied that estimate the location of the neural generators based on the scalp-recorded potential (for more detail, see Pascual-Marqui 2002; Pascual-Marqui, Michel and Lehmann 1994 on the minimum norm-based technique LORETA and Scherg, Vajsar and Picton 1989; Scherg and von Cramon 1986 on the BESA technique).

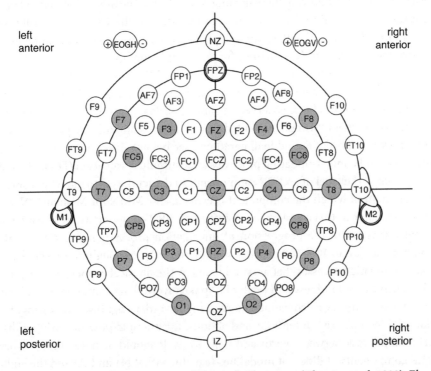

Figure 2. International 10–10 System of Electrode Placement (Chatrian et al. 1988). Electrode positions are defined by letters and numbers: Letters depict anatomical terms; F=frontal, C=central, T=temporal, P=parietal, O=occipital, FP=fronto-polar, AF=anterior frontal, FC=fronto-central, CP=centro-parietal, TP= temporo-parietal, PO=parieto-occipital. Even numbers refer to right hemisphere electrode locations, odd numbers to left hemisphere electrode locations. Additionally, numbers indicate the distance from the midline as zero point (z), with larger numbers indicating greater distance. Gray electrode positions give an example recording configuration. Framed electrode positions indicate reference electrodes (M=mastoid). In addition to the EEG signal, an Electrooculogram (EOG) is recorded to monitor horizontal (EOGH) and vertical eye movement (EOGV)

The recording positions of electrodes are standardized and defined by international conventions. The most common electrode naming and placing system is the 10–20 system (Jasper 1958), where electrodes are located at distances of 10% or 20% along the longitudinal line and the latitudinal line across the head. Electrode positions are denoted by letters that refer to anatomical terms, such as F for frontal, C for central, T for temporal, P for parietal, O for occipital, etc. (see Figure 2). In addition, numbers indicate the distance of lateral positions, from the midline as the zero point (z), with larger numbers indicating greater distance. Even numbers refer to right hemisphere positions, while odd numbers name left hemisphere positions. From this, it follows that the ERP signal, for example plotted for single electrodes only, can be easily allocated by following these naming conventions. The original placement system can be extended to the 10-10 system (according to the 10% distance rule) so that an EEG is recorded with lower or higher density, dependent on the number of electrodes that are used (see Figure 2 for an example configuration).

Regarding their *functional significance*, specific ERP components are known to be elicited under certain experimental conditions or paradigms. For instance, the P300 component has been observed in various oddball paradigms in response to deviant (infrequent) stimuli presented in a series of standard (frequent) stimuli (for an explanation of the oddball paradigm, see below). This component reflects memory- and context-updating processes after stimulus evaluation (Donchin and Coles 1988). The label of an ERP component can depict the particular experimental paradigm in which the component is evoked, e.g., MMN for Mismatch Negativity (see later in this chapter). As pointed out, ERP components are considered to be indicators of the progression of information processing over time. Early components (up to 100–200 ms after stimulus onset) are thought to reflect essentially automatic processes that are modulated by the physical properties of a stimulus, such as the loudness and pitch of a spoken word. Late components (300 ms and beyond) are regarded as indicators of higher-order cognitive processing, influenced by a person's intentions and actions, for example present during a discrimination task between words and non-words. It should be noted that sensory ERP components of different modalities (e.g., the visual N1 and P2 and the auditory N1 and P2) do not usually refer to the same underlying mechanisms, but are specific to the input modality, whereas late components (e.g., the P300) are more modality-independent. Also note that the idea of sequentially occurring ERP components as indicators of successive processing stages is certainly a simplification, as it takes neither parallel processing nor the possible temporal overlap of activation from different neuronal generators into consideration. Nevertheless, this highly simplified model has proven itself in practice. For more detail and a discussion of the functional significance of particular ERP components, see the section on language-related ERP components (later in this chapter) and reviews by

Coles and Rugg (1995); Donchin, Karis, Bashore, Coles and Gratton (1986); Regan (1989); and Rugg and Coles (1996).

The evaluation and interpretation of ERP components in infants and young children call for some additional considerations. The enormous physiological changes of the developing brain with regard to synaptic density, myelination, skull thickness and fontanel state profoundly affect the ERP outcome in developmental populations at different age levels. For instance, the reduced synaptic density in infants yields a greater slow wave activity. This may explain why infant ERPs do not exhibit as many well-defined peaks as adult ERPs (Nelson and Luciana 1998). Infant ERPs usually feature larger amplitudes than adult data, which is possibly attributable to differences in skull thickness. Also, infant ERPs usually show longer latencies than adult ERPs. This most likely means that more time is needed for a particular process. Both amplitude and latency measures gradually decrease with increasing age (e.g., Jing and Benasich 2006; Kushnerenko, Ceponiene, Balan, Fellman, Huotilainen and Näätänen 2002). Those maturational changes should be considered when ERP components across different age groups are compared to each other. First, the younger the children, the smaller the age range of children grouped in one ERP average (e.g., five months +/- one week, four years +/- one month), so that valid statements about specific developmental states are obtained. Second, paradigms used in infant ERP experiments should be used in adults as well. In this way, target adult ERP patterns can be achieved with which developmental comparisons can be made.

4   Advantages and disadvantages of the ERP method

In a nutshell, the ERP method is an online brain measure of sensory, motor and cognitive processes that features an excellent temporal resolution, while the spatial resolution is comparably poor. The evaluation of a method's advantages and disadvantages allows the selection of research questions that can be answered by applying this particular method. The following section will discuss the benefits and shortcomings of ERPs as compared to other methods by considering methodological and pragmatic issues.

4.1   General methodological considerations

Behavioral methods measure overt responses by evaluating response speed and accuracy. These parameters allow for the formulation of conclusions about the direct effect of experimental manipulations on the resulting behavior, for instance, task difficulty resulting in slowed responses. The obvious functional significance of a behavioral response is a definite advantage of these methods. However, since behavioral techniques only capture the end product of the processing of a given stimulus, they do not deliver any information about the cognitive processes involved. This is where the ERP method has a distinct advantage, since it can be used for monitoring the actual online cognitive processes that yield the observed behavior. Consequently, the continuous ERP measure between stimulus input and response output enables investigation of each processing step. This allows, for instance, determination of whether a slow down due to task difficulty stems from slowed perceptional processes or slowed response processes. Here, eye-tracking methods likewise deliver online parameters of the ongoing information processing. Nonetheless, these measures are only indirect indicators of the underlying brain mechanisms. In contrast, electrophysiological and hemodynamic measures directly reflect the online stages of information processing in the brain.

In the realm of neuroscience methods, the ERP method features excellent temporal resolution, as it provides information about the time course of brain responses in millisecond accuracy. In this way, ERPs deliver a mental chronometry, i.e., an exact temporal sequencing of information processing (see Coles, Smid, Scheffers and Otten 1996). In comparison to neuroimaging techniques, such as fMRI and PET, the spatial resolution for the identification of the neural generators of the obtained signal is relatively poor, since maximal amplitude measures at certain electrode sites only provide information about where neural activity, evoked by certain stimuli, arrives at the scalp's surface. As pointed out before, there are source localization techniques that calculate the location of the neural generators of the ERP signal by either postulating distributed current sources as neural origins (e.g., the minimum norm-based technique LORETA; Pascual-Marqui 2002; Pascual-Marqui et al. 1994) or equivalent current dipoles (e.g., the BESA technique; Scherg et al. 1989; Scherg and von Cramon 1986). Nonetheless, these measures deliver only estimations of the location of neural generators, even if highly probable, and cannot compete with the actual spatial marking of hemodynamic changes in the brain in millimeter accuracy.

4.2   Pragmatic considerations regarding developmental research

In working with infants and young children, researchers are confronted with certain limitations that make the experimental procedure much more challenging than in adults. In particular, abbreviated attention span, limited verbal and motor skills, frequently occurring hunger and tiredness necessitate short experiments that work without instructions and do not require motor responses. Given these restrictions, one immense benefit of the ERP method becomes readily apparent. For EEG recordings, no overt responses are necessary since an EEG directly measures brain activity evoked by specific stimuli, thus considerably facilitating developmental research. The fact that ERP components are direct indicators of the underlying brain processes implies not only that no task assignments are necessary, but also that brain processes evoked by certain stimuli might be detectable before there is a behavioral correspondence observable at a specific developmental stage. Although behavioral methods used in infant research such as the headturn paradigm, the preferential looking paradigm and eye-tracking techniques require a less complicated set-up and can be performed in a more natural setting, these methods are more prone to external interferences. Imaging techniques also have some limitations in work with infants and young children (but see Hebden 2003; Meek 2002 on optical imaging in infants). In PET, the invasiveness of the application of small doses of a radioactive marker bars its use in developmental research. In fMRI, movement restrictions during brain scanning make it rather difficult to work with children. Furthermore, there is still an ongoing discussion regarding whether the BOLD signal in adults is comparable to the one in children and whether the applied adult models are appropriate for infant research (for discussion, see Anderson, Marois, Colson, Peterson, Duncan, Ehrenkranz, Schneider, Gore and Ment 2001; Marcar, Strassle, Loenneker, Schwarz and Martin 2004; Martin, Joeri, Loenneker, Ekatodramis, Vitacco, Henning and Marcar 1999; Rivkin, Wolraich, Als, McAnulty, Butler, Conneman, Fischer, Vajapeyam, Robertson and Mulkern 2004; Schapiro, Schmithorst, Wilke, Byars Weber, Strawsburg and Holland 2004). As pointed out, maturational changes have to be similarly considered in electrophysiological techniques, since changes in synaptic density, cell density, cortex folding and so forth are likely to affect ERP outcomes in infants, children and adults.

In addition to the evaluation of quality and quantity differences and the practicability of various methods, it is important to consider that these different methods deliver different kinds of information. Thus, the decision to use a specific method should be based on the kind of question to be answered and, thus, the kind of information sought: the neuronal correlates of information processing in their spatial and/or temporal resolution, or the behavioral consequences that follow from these processes.

5   ERP components in language processing

The most important cognitive phenomenon, the human ability to process and produce language, has been a prominent object of research throughout the centuries. Over the last decades, a great deal of adult ERP studies have revealed that the processing of different aspects of linguistic information can be clearly distinguished by means of different ERP components. These studies have described five functionally different components that are associated with phonetic and phono-logical processing (the MMN), prosodic processing (the Closure Positive Shift; CPS), semantic processing (the N400) and syntactic processing (the ELAN and the P600). In the following paragraphs we will briefly introduce these ERP compo-nents and, in addition, refer the reader to recent reviews (Friederici 2002; 2004; Kutas and Federmeier 2000).

The *Mismatch negativity (MMN)* (see Figure 3) refers to a negative deflection in the ERP that occurs at around 100–250 ms post-stimulus onset and is largest at frontal and central midline electrode sites. Functionally, the MMN can be de-scribed as a pre-attentive electrophysiological response to any discriminable change in repetitive auditory stimulation (Näätänen 1990). This discrimination response is usually studied in a so-called *mismatch paradigm* or *passive oddball paradigm*, where two classes of stimuli are repeatedly presented, with one stimulus occurring relatively frequently (standard) and the other one relatively rarely (devi-ant or oddball). The mismatch response in the ERP is the result of the brain's auto-matic detection of the deviant among the standards and, thus, becomes especially apparent in the ERP subtraction wave, i.e., the ERP response to deviant stimuli minus the ERP response to standard stimuli (Figure 3, right panel). In language processing, the MMN has been observed during the discrimination of phoneti-cally different stimuli (e.g., Opitz, Mecklinger, Cramon and Kruggel 1999) and has been found to be modulated by language experience (Winkler, Kujala, Tiitinen, Sivonen, Alku, Lehtokoski, Czigler, Csépe, Ilmoniemi and Näätänen 1999).

In infants, the *mismatch response (MMR)* has either been observed as negativ-ity or positivity in the ERP. There are several reasons that may contribute to this differential outcome: first, differences in the infants' alertness state (Friederici, Friedrich and Weber 2002); second, methodological differences such as the use of different filters (Trainor, Mc Fadden, Hodgson, Darragh, Barlow, Matsos, and Son-nadara 2003); and third, the coexistence/overlap of two types of mismatch re-sponses (He, Hotson and Trainor 2007; Morr *et al.* 2002). In general, one can ob-serve a developmental transition in the infants' MMR from a positivity to an MMN-like negativity. This transition may be dependent upon the maturation of the human brain (Paus, Collins, Evans, Leonard, Pike and Zijdenbos 2001).

The *Closure Positive Shift (CPS)* (see Figure 4) is a positive-going shift in the ERP with a centro-parietal distribution. As the component's name indicates, it is associated with the closure of prosodic phrases by intonational phrase (IPh) boundaries (Pannekamp, Toepel, Alter, Hahne and Friederici 2005; Steinhauer, Alter, and Friederici 1999). Thus, the CPS marks the processing of phrase-level prosodic cues since IPh boundaries are defined by particular parameters, such as pitch change, syllable lengthening and pause. As can be seen from Figure 4, when subjects are, for instance, listening to sentences that contain one IPh boundary versus sentences that comprise two IPh boundaries, the ERP average for each sentence type shows positive shifts that start with a latency of 500 ms to their corresponding boundary.

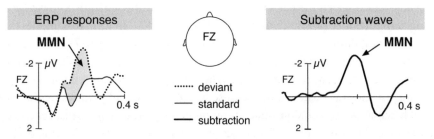

Figure 3. Mismatch Negativity (MMN). Left panel: In a passive auditory oddball paradigm, rarely occurring stimuli (deviant or oddball) are presented among frequently occurring stimuli (standards). Gray shading indicates the difference between the two stimulus conditions. Right panel: The subtraction wave depicts the brain response to deviant stimuli minus the brain response to standard stimuli. Figures are modified with permission from Elgevier from Kujala and Näätänen (2001).

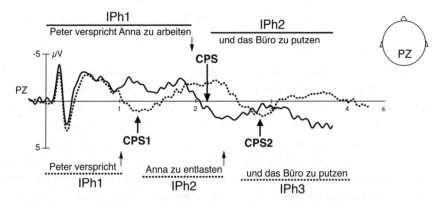

Figure 4. Closure Positive Shift (CPS). Positive shifts in the ERP in correlation to sentences with one intonational phrase (IPh) boundary (solid line) [Peter verspricht Anna zu arbeiten und das Büro zu putzen/Peter promises Anna to work and to clean the office] and with two IPh boundaries (dotted line) [Peter verspricht Anna zu entlasten und das Büro zu putzen/Peter promises to help Anna and to clean the office] are displayed. Small arrows indicate the IPh boundary in the sentence. Large arrows indicate the CPSs that follow the IPh boundaries. Figures are modified from Steinhauer *et al.* (1999)

The *N400* (see Figure 5) describes a centro-parietally distributed negativity that occurs at around 400 ms post-stimulus onset. The N400 has been intensely studied and is known to indicate lexical-semantic processes at both the word level (Holcomb and Neville 1990) and the sentence level (Kutas and Hillyard 1980; 1983). The N400 marks the effort to integrate an event into its semantic context and is more pronounced the more semantically unfamiliar, unexpected, or non-matching an event is, given the current semantic context or the semantic knowledge in long-term memory (for more details see Holcomb 1993). In turn, this implies that the N400 amplitude is inversely related to the expectation triggered by the semantic context, a process called semantic priming, which results in a reduction of semantic integration efforts. The N400 has been studied in various *semantic priming paradigms* and was observed in response to both words and pictures that do not match semantic expectation built up by previously presented words, sentences, pictures and picture stories (Friederici, Pfeifer and Hahne 1993; West and Holcomb 2002). In lexical processing, ERP studies have shown that the N400 amplitude is larger for pseudowords than for real words, whereas nonwords do not evoke an N400 response (Bentin, Mouchetant-Rostaing, Giard, Echallier and Pernier 1999; Holcomb 1993; Nobre and McCarthy 1994). Thus, pseudowords, but not nonwords, are treated as likely lexicon entries as they follow phonotactic regularities, the rules that define how phonemes may be legally combined to words in a given language. In studies on sentence processing, use of the *semantic violation paradigm* revealed N400 responses for sentences with semantically unexpected sentence endings versus semantically expected endings (Friederici *et al.* 1993; Hahne and Friederici 2002).

The *ELAN* (see Figure 5) designates a negativity in the ERP at around 150–350 ms post-stimulus onset that can primarily be observed at left anterior electrode sites. The ELAN is associated with highly automatic phrase structure building processes (Friederici *et al.* 1993; Hahne and Friederici 1999). Thus, when syntactically correct and incorrect sentences that contain phrase structure violations are presented in a *syntactic violation paradigm*, the ELAN occurs together with the P600 component in response to incorrect sentences. This ERP pattern has been observed for both passive as well as active sentence constructions (Friederici *et al.* 1993; Hahne and Friederici 1999; Hahne, Eckstein and Friederici 2004; Rossi, Gugler, Hahne and Friederici. 2005). A left anterior negativity (*LAN*) that occurs between 300–500 ms post-stimulus onset has been reported for morphosyntactic violations for languages with inflectional morphology (for a recent review, see Friederici and Weissenborn 2007). The LAN is followed by a P600 as well.

The *P600* (see Figure 5) refers to a centro-parietal positivity in the ERP between 600–1000 ms post-stimulus onset, sometimes called Syntactic Positive Shift (SPS) (Hagoort, Brown and Groothusen 1993). As mentioned, the P600 occurs together with the ELAN or the LAN in response to syntactic violations (Friederici *et al.* 1993; Hahne and Friederici 1999; Osterhout and Mobley 1995). The P600 is taken to reflect controlled processes of syntactic reanalysis and integration that are initiated after the detection of syntactic errors (ELAN/LAN). This ERP pattern is often called 'biphasic', as the negativity (negative phase) is followed by a positivity (positive phase). The P600 component has not only been observed for the processing of syntactic violations, but also for syntactically complex sentences and syntactically non-preferred garden-path sentences that require a high degree of syntactic integration as well as syntactic reanalysis and repair (Friederici, Hahne and Mecklinger 1996; Hagoort, Brown and Groothusen, 1993; Kaan, Harris, Gibson and Holcomb 2000; Osterhout and Holcomb 1992; 1993; Osterhout, Holcomb and Swinney 1994).

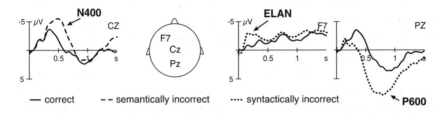

Figure 5. N400. Processing of lexical-semantic information – ERP responses to semantically incorrect and correct sentences in a semantic violation paradigm. ELAN & P600. Processing of syntactic violations – ERP responses to syntactically incorrect and correct sentences in a syntactic violation paradigm. Figures are modified from Friederici (2002)

As discussed, the ERP method represents a highly suitable research tool for developmental populations since it places virtually no demands on children's behavior and delivers online measures of the brain mechanisms underlying cognitive development in infancy and childhood. Given the described language-related ERP components in adults, these components may in turn serve as templates to describe the neurophysiological mechanisms of the language acquisition process as children develop their perceptive language skills. In this way, ERPs not only provide information regarding whether there are specific ERP indicators of particular language processes in infants and children, but, in addition, they allow sketching of the hallmarks of the language acquisition process.

Figure 6 provides an overview of ERP research on the different landmarks of language acquisition and their associated ERP components during the first three years of life. The time course of the outlined developmental stages of auditory language perception is based on the available ERP literature in infant research and is therefore only an approximation of the actual time course of language acquisition. The developmental stages can be viewed as interrelated phases during which already acquired linguistic knowledge serves as a basis for the derivation of new information from the language input.

In detail, the mismatch response (apparent in a positive or a negative MMR) that reflects discrimination of phonological features is present even in newborns (Kushnerenko, Cheour, Ceponiene, Fellman, Renlund, Soininen, Alku, Koskinen, Sainio and Näätänen 2001). Thus, from early on, infants are able to distinguish between different speech sounds (Cheour, Ceponiene, Lehtokoski, Luuk, Allik, Alho and Näätänen 1998; Friederici *et al.* 2002; for a review see Kuhl 2004) and native and non-native word stress patterns (Friederici, Friedrich and Christophe 2007), which is essential for the identification of content and function words in a sentential context at a later point in infant development. Furthermore, infants' early ability to process prosodic information at the sentence level as present in intonational phrase boundaries supports the detection of syntactic phrase boundaries later on. Here, the CPS has been observed in 8-month-old infants (Pannekamp, Weber and Friederici 2006) and, recently, even in 5-month-olds (Männel, Neuhaus and Friederici 2007). These phonological/ prosodic processes eventually allow for the extraction of syntactic rules from speech input, a process called prosodic bootstrapping. The N400 component that indicates lexical-semantic processes in adults has been registered in 14-month-olds, although not yet in 12-month-olds, who, however, showed effects of acoustic-phonological processing (word form) (Friedrich and Friederici 2005a). Thus, the N400 component can be utilized in early childhood to examine: (1) phonotactic knowledge (Friedrich and Friederici 2005a); (2) word recognition (Friedrich and Friederici 2004; 2005a; 2005b; see also Mills *et al.* 1993; 1994; 2004, who report an early negativity between 200–400 ms for 14- and 20-month-olds; and Thierry, Vihmanand, Roberts 2003, who report an early negativity between 170–240 ms for 11-month-olds); and (3) lexical-semantic relations between verbs and their arguments in sentences (Friedrich and Friederici 2005c; see also Silva-Pereyra, Klarman, Lin and Kuhl 2005, who report an anterior negativity between 500–800 ms for 30-month-olds). For the processing of structural dependencies within phrases, an adult-like ELAN-P600 pattern has been found in 32-month-old children, but not yet in 24-month-olds, who show only a P600 response (Oberecker *et al.* 2005; 2006; see also Silva-Pereyra *et al.* 2005, who report a fronto-centrally distributed late positivity for 30-month-olds). This developmental pattern thus characterizes the progress in the processing of local phrase structure and interphrasal relationships, the most complex rule systems infants have to acquire.

Although we are still far from a detailed illustration of the language acquisition process that accounts for all of its single steps, the described results demonstrate the use of the ERP method in the study of language development from very early on. Thus, ERP parameters derived from adult studies are a promising measure that in combination with other methods will enable researchers to obtain a more fine-grained picture of language acquisition and its neurophysiological basis.

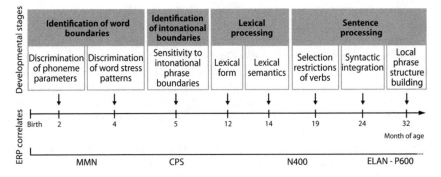

Figure 6. Developmental stages of language acquisition and their related ERP components. Figures are modified from Friederici (2005)

6   Summary

The aim of the current tutorial was to demonstrate the use of the ERP method for the online study of cognitive processes from a developmental perspective. We have illustrated how ERPs are obtained from the scalp-recorded EEG and how they are utilized to sketch the mental chronometry of information processing in the brain. Importantly, the discussion of advantages and shortcomings of the ERP method points to its preferable research application, namely temporal aspects of overt and covert information processing. Furthermore, we have demonstrated the use of the ERP method by introducing ERP components observed during language processing in adults, which in turn can be applied in developmental research to describe the neurophysiological basis of the language acquisition process.

In summary, the ERP method is proving to be a useful research tool in the field of developmental cognitive neuroscience. Despite the advantages and the fast advancements of methods in cognitive neuroscience, this research field considerably benefits from the groundbreaking information provided by behavioral researchers. Thus, convergent evidence should be sought, since different research areas using different methods all deliver single pieces towards the description and understanding of cognition, thus bridging the gap between brain and behavior.

References

Anderson, A.W., Marois, R., Colson, E.R., Peterson, B.S., Duncan, C.C., Ehrenkranz, R.A., Schneider, K.C., Gore, J.C. and Ment, L.R. 2001. "Neonatal auditory activation detected by functional magnetic resonance imaging." *Magnetic Resonance Imaging* 19: 1–5.

Bentin, S., Mouchetant-Rostaing, Y., Giard, M.H., Echallier, J.F. and Pernier, J. 1999. "ERP manifestations of processing printed words at different psycholinguistic levels: time course and scalp distribution." *Journal of Cognitive Neuroscience* 11 (3): 235–60.

Brunia, C.H.M., Möcks, J., van den Berg-Lenssen, M.M.C., Coelho, M., Coles, M.G.H., Elbert, T., Gasser, T., Gratton, C., Ifeachor, E.C., Jervis, B.W., Lutzenberger, W., Sroka, L., Blokland-Vogelesang, A.W., van Driel, G., Woestenburg, J.C., Berg, P., McCallum, W.C., Pham, D.T., Pocock, P.V. and Roth, W.T. 1989. "Correcting ocular artifacts in the EEG: a comparison of several methods." *Journal of Psychophysiology* 3: 1–50.

Chatrian, G.E., Lettich, E. and Nelson, P.L. 1988. "Modified nomenclature for the "10%" electrode system." *Journal of Clinical Neurophysiology* 5(2): 183–6.

Cheour, M., Ceponiene, R., Lehtokoski, A., Luuk, A., Allik, J., Alho, K. and Näätänen, R. 1998. "Development of language-specific phoneme representations in the infant brain." *Nature Neuroscience* 1: 351–3.

Coles, M.G.H. and Rugg, M.D. 1995. "Event-related potentials: An introduction." In *Electrophysiology of mind*, M.D. Rugg and M.G.H. Coles (eds.), 1–26. Oxford: Oxford University Press.

Coles, M.G.H., Smid, H.G.O.M., Scheffers, M.K. and Otten, L.J. 1996. "Mental chronometry and the study of human information processing." In *Electrophysiology of mind. Event-related brain potentials and cognition*, Bd. 25, 86–131. Oxford: Oxford University Press.

Creutzfeldt, O. and Houchin, J. 1974. "Neuronal basis of EEG waves." In *Handbook of electroencephalography and clinical neurophysiology* (Vol. 2, Part C), A. Rémond (ed.), 5–55. Amsterdam: Elsevier.

Daffner, K.R., Scinto, L.F.M., Calvo, V., Faust, R., Mesulam, M.M., West, W.C. and Holcomb, P. 2000. "The influence of stimulus deviance on electrophysiologic and behavioral responses to novel events." *Journal of Cognitive Neuroscience* 12 (3): 393–406.

Donchin, E. and Coles, M.G.H. 1988. "Is the P300 a manifestation of context updating?" *Behavioral and Brain Sciences* 11: 357–74.

Donchin, E., Karis, D., Bashore, T.R., Coles, M.G. H. and Gratton, G. 1986. "Cognitive psychology and human information processing." In *Psychophysiology. Systems, Processes, and Applications*, M.G.H. Coles, E. Donchin and S.W. Porges (eds.), 244–67. New York, NY: The Guilford Press.

Edgar, J.C., Stewart, J.L. and Miller, G.A. 2005. "Digital filters in ERP research." In *Event-related potentials: A methods handbook*, T.C. Handy (ed.), 85–113, Cambridge, MA: The MIT press.

Friederici, A.D. 2002. "Towards a neural basis of auditory sentence processing." *Trends in Cognitive Science* 6: 78–84.

Friederici, A.D. 2004. "Event-related brain potential studies in language." *Current Neurology and Neuroscience Reports* 4: 466–70.

Friederici, A.D. 2005. "Neurophysiological markers of early language acquisition: from syllables to sentences." *Trends in Cognitive Sciences* 9: 481–8.

Friederici, A.D., Friedrich, M. and Christophe, A. 2007. "Brain responses in 4-month-old infants are already language specific." *Current Biology* 17(4): 1208–11.

Friederici, A.D., Friedrich, M. and Weber, C. 2002. "Neural manifestation of cognitive and precognitive mismatch detection in early infancy." *NeuroReport* 13: 1251–4.

Friederici, A.D., Hahne, A. and Mecklinger, A. 1996. "Temporal structure of syntactic parsing: early and late event-related brain potential effects." *Journal of Experimental Psychology: Learning, Memory, and Cognition* 22: 1219–48.

Friederici, A.D., Pfeifer, E. and Hahne, A. 1993. "Event-related brain potentials during natural speech processing: effects of semantic, morphological and syntactic violations." *Cognitive Brain Research* 1: 183–92.

Friederici, A.D. and Weissenborn, J. 2007. "Mapping sentence form onto meaning: The syntax-semantic interface." *Brain Research* 1146: 50–8.

Friedrich, M. and Friederici, A.D. 2004. "N400-like semantic incongruity effect in 19-month-olds: Processing known words in picture contexts." *Journal of Cognitive Neuroscience* 16: 1465–77.

Friedrich, M. and Friederici, A.D. 2005a. "Phonotactic knowledge and lexical-semantic priming in one-year-olds: Brain responses to words and nonsense words in picture contexts." *Journal of Cognitive Neuroscience* 17 (11): 1785–802.

Friedrich, M. and Friederici, A.D. 2005b. "Lexical priming and semantic integration reflected in the ERP of 14-month-olds." *NeuroReport* 16 (6): 653–6.

Friedrich, M. and Friederici, A.D. 2005c. "Semantic sentence processing reflected in the event-related potentials of one- and two-year-old children." *NeuroReport* 16 (6): 1801–4.

Hagoort, P., Brown, C. and Groothusen, J. 1993. "The syntactic positive shift (SPS) as an ERP measure of syntactic processing." *Language and Cognitive Processes* 8 (4): 439–83.

Hahne, A. and Friederici, A.D. 1999. "Electrophysiological evidence for two steps in syntactic analysis. Early automatic and late controlled processes." *Journal of Cognitive Neuroscience* 11: 194–205.

Hahne, A. and Friederici, A.D. 2002. "Differential task effects on semantic and syntactic processes as revealed by ERPs." *Cognitive Brain Research* 13: 339–56.

Hahne, A., Eckstein, K. and Friederici, A.D. 2004. "Brain signatures of syntactic and semantic processes during children's language development." *Journal of Cognitive Neuroscience* 16: 1302–18.

He, C., Hotson, L. and Trainor, L.J. 2007. "Mismatch responses to pitch changes in early infancy." *Journal of Cognitive Neuroscience* 19: 878–92.

Hebden, J.C. 2003. "Advances in optical imaging of the newborn infant brain." *Psychophysiology* 40: 501.

Holcomb, P.J. 1993. "Semantic priming and stimulus degradation: Implications for the role of the N400 in language processing." *Psychophysiology* 30: 47–61.

Holcomb, P.J. and Neville, H.J. 1990. "Auditory and visual semantic priming in lexical decision: A comparison using event-related brain potentials." *Language and Cognitive Processes* 5: 281–312.

Jasper, H.H. 1958. "The ten-twenty electrode system of the international federation." *Electroencephalography and Clinical Neurophysiology* 10: 371–5.

Jing, H. and Benasich, A.A. 2006. "Brain responses to tonal changes in the first two years of life." *Brain & Development* 28 (4): 247–56.

Kaan, E., Harris, A., Gibson, E. and Holcomb, P. 2000. "The P600 as an index of syntactic integration difficulty." *Language and Cognitive Processes* 15: 159–201.

Katayama, J. and Polich, J. 1998. "Stimulus context determines P3a and P3b." *Psychophysiology* 35 (1): 23–33.

Kuhl, P.K. 2004. "Early language acquisition: Cracking the speech code." *Nature Reviews Neuroscience* 5 (11): 831–43.

Kujala, T. and Näätänen, R. 2001. "The mismatch negativity in evaluating central auditory dysfunction in dyslexia." *Neuroscience & Biobehavioral Reviews* 25: 535–43.

Kushnerenko, E., Cheour, M., Ceponiene, R., Fellman, V., Renlund, M., Soininen, K., Alku, P., Koskinen, M., Sainio, K. and Näätänen, R. 2001. "Central auditory processing of durational changes in complex speech patterns by newborns: An event-related brain potential study." *Developmental Neuropsycholgy* 19 (1): 83–97.

Kushnerenko, E., Ceponiene, R., Balan, P., Fellman, V., Huotilainen, M. and Näätänen, R. 2002. "Maturation of the auditory event-related potentials during the first year of life." *NeuroReport* 13: 47–51.

Kutas, M. and Federmeier, K.D. 2000. "Electrophysiology reveals semantic memory use in language comprehension." *Trends in Cognitive Science* 4: 463–70.

Kutas, M. and Hillyard, S.A. 1980. "Reading senseless sentences: Brain potentials reflect semantic incongruity." *Science* 207: 203–5.

Kutas, M. and Hillyard, S.A. 1983. "Event-related brain potentials to grammatical errors and semantic anomalies." *Memory & Cognition* 11 (5): 539–50.

Lopes da Silva, F. 1991. "Neural mechanisms underlying brain waves: From neural membranes to networks." *Electroencephalography and Clinical Neurophysiology* 79: 81–93.

Männel, C., Neuhaus, C. and Friederici, A.D. 2007. "5-month-olds get it: ERP components of phrase structure processing in language and music" (Abstract). Paper presentation at the Conference Language and Music as Cognitive Systems. Centre for Music & Science and Research Centre for English & Applied Linguistics, University of Cambridge, May 11–13, 2007, Conference Booklet, 35.

Marcar, V.L., Strassle, A.E., Loenneker, T., Schwarz, U. and Martin, E. 2004. "The influence of cortical maturation on the BOLD response: An fMRI study of visual cortex in children." *Pediatric Research* 56 (6): 967–74.

Martin, E., Joeri, P., Loenneker, T., Ekatodramis, D., Vitacco, D., Henning, J. and Marcar, V.L. 1999. "Visual processing in infants and children studied using functional MR." *Pediatric Research* 46 (2): 135–40.

Meek, J. 2002. "Basic principles of optical imaging and application to the study of infant development." *Developmental Science* 5 (3): 371–80.

Mills, D.L., Coffey-Corina, S.A. and Neville, H.J. 1993. "Language acquisition and cerebral specialization in 20-month-old infants." *Journal of Cognitive Neuroscience* 5: 317–34.

Mills, D.L., Coffey-Corina, S.A. and Neville, H.J. 1994. "Variability in cerebral organization during primary language acquisition." In *Human Behavior and the Developing Brain*, G. Dawson and K.W. Fischer (eds.), 427–55, New York: Guilford Press.

Mills, D.L., Prat, C., Zangl, R., Stager, C.L., Neville, H.J. and Werker, J.F. 2004. "Language experience and the organization of brain activity to phonetically similar words: ERP evidence from 14- and 20-month-olds." *Journal of Cognitive Neuroscience* 16: 1452–64.

Näätänen, R. 1990. "The role of attention in auditory information processing as revealed by event-related potentials and other brain measures of cognitive function." *Behavioral and Brain Sciences* 13: 201–88.

Nelson, C.A. and Luciana, M. 1998. "Electrophysiological studies II: Evoked potentials and event-related potentials." In *Textbook of pediatric neuropsychiatry*, C.E. Coffey and R.A. Brumback (eds.), 331–56. Washington, DC: American Psychiatric Press.

Nobre, A.C. and McCarthy, G. 1994. "Language-related ERPs: Scalp distributions and modulation by word type and semantic priming." *Journal of Cognitive Neuroscience* 6 (33): 233–55.

Oberecker, R. and Friederici, A.D. 2006. "Syntactic event-related potential components in 24-month-olds' sentence comprehension." *NeuroReport* 17 (10): 1017–21.

Oberecker, R., Friedrich, M. and Friederici, A.D. 2005. "Neural correlates of syntactic processing in two-year-olds." *Journal of Cognitive Neuroscience* 17: 407–21.

Opitz, B., Mecklinger, A., Cramon, D.Y. and Kruggel, F. 1999. "Combining electrophysiological and hemodynamic measures of the auditory oddball." *Psychophysiology* 36: 142–7.

Osterhout, L. and Holcomb, P.J. 1992. "Event-related potentials and syntactic anomaly." *Journal of Memory and Language* 31: 785–804.

Osterhout, L. and Holcomb, P.J. 1993. "Event-related brain potentials and syntactic anomaly: Evidence on anomaly detection during perception of continuous speech." *Language and Cognitive Processes* 8: 413–37.

Osterhout, L., Holcomb, P.J. and Swinney, D.A. 1994. "Brain potentials elicited by gardenpath sentences: Evidence of the application of verb information during parsing." *Journal of Experimental Psychology: Learning, Memory, and Cognition* 20: 786–803.

Osterhout, L. and Mobley, L.A. 1995. "Event-related brain potentials elicited by failure to agree." *Journal of Memory and Language* 34: 739–73.

Pannekamp, A., Toepel, U., Alter, K., Hahne, A. and Friederici, A.D. 2005. "Prosody-driven sentence processing: An event-related brain potential study." *Journal of Cognitive Neuroscience* 17: 407–21.

Pannekamp, A., Weber, C. and Friederici, A.D. 2006. "Prosodic processing at the sentence level in infants." *NeuroReport* 17: 675–8.

Pascual-Marqui, R.D. 2002. "Standardized low resolution electromagnetic tomography (sLORETA): technical details." *Methods & Findings in Experimental & Clinical Pharmacology* 24: 5–12.

Pascual-Marqui, R.D., Michel, C.M. and Lehmann, D. 1994. "Low resolution electromagnetic tomography: a new method for localizing electrical activity in the brain." *International Journal of Psychophysiology* 18: 49–65.

Paus, T., Collins, D.L., Evans, A.C., Leonard, G., Pike, B. and Zijdenbos, A. 2001. "Maturation of white matter in the human brain: A review of magnetic resonance studies." *Brain Research Bulletin* 54 (3): 255–66.

Regan, D. 1989. *Human brain electrophysiology: Evoked potentials and evoked magnetic fields in science and medicine*. New York, NY: Elsevier.

Rivkin, M.J., Wolraich, D., Als, H., McAnulty, G., Butler, S., Conneman, N., Fischer, C., Vajapeyam, S., Robertson, R.L. and Mulkern, R.V. 2004. "Prolonged T*[2] values in newborn versus adult brain: Implications for fMRI studies of newborns." *Magnetic Resonance in Medicine* 51 (6): 1287–91.

Rossi, S., Gugler, M.F., Hahne, A. and Friederici, A.D. 2005. "When word category information encounters morphosyntax: an ERP study." *Neuroscience Letters* 384: 228–33.

Rugg, M.D. and Coles, M.G.H. (eds.). 1996. *Electrophysiology of mind. Event-related brain potentials and cognition*. (Bd. 25). Oxford: OUP.

Schapiro, M.B., Schmithorst, V.J., Wilke, M., Byars Weber, A., Strawsburg, R.H. and Holland, S.K. 2004. "BOLD fMRI signal increases with age in selected brain regions in children." *NeuroReport* 15 (17): 2575–8.

Scherg, M. and von Cramon, D. 1986. "Evoked dipole source potentials of the human auditory cortex." *Electroencephalography and Clinical Neurophysiology* 65: 344–60.

Scherg, M., Vajsar, J. and Picton, T.W. 1989. "A source analysis of the human auditory evoked potentials." *Journal of Cognitive Neuroscience* 1: 336–55.

Silva-Pereyra, J., Klarman, L., Lin, L.J. and Kuhl, P.K. 2005. "Sentence processing in 30-month-old children: An event-related potential study." *NeuroReport* 16: 645–8.

Speckmann, E.-J. and Elger, C.E. 1993. "Neurophysiological basis of the EEG and of DC potentials." In *Electroencephalography. Basic principles, clinical applications and related fields*, E. Niedermeyer and F. Lopes Da Silva (eds.), 15–26. Baltimore-München: Urban & Schwarzenberg.

Steinhauer, K., Alter, K. and Friederici, A.D. 1999. "Brain potentials indicate immediate use of prosodic cues in natural speech processing." *Nature Neuroscience* 2: 191–6.

Talsma, D. and Woldorff, M.G. 2005. "Methods for the estimation and removal of artifacts and overlap in ERP waveforms." In *Event-related potentials: A methods handbook*, T.C. Handy (ed.), 115–48. Cambridge, MA: The MIT press.

Thierry, G., Vihman, M. and Roberts, M. 2003. "Familiar words capture the attention of 11-month-olds in less than 250 ms." *NeuroReport* 14: 2307–10.

Trainor, L., Mc Fadden, M., Hodgson, L., Darragh, Barlow, J., Matsos, L. and Sonnadara, R. 2003. "Changes in auditory cortex and the development of mismatch negativity between 2 and 6 months of age." *International Journal of Psychophysiology* 51: 5–15.

West, W.C. and Holcomb, P.J. 2002. "Event-related potentials during discourse-level semantic integration of complex pictures." *Cognitive Brain Research* 13: 363–75.

Winkler, I., Kujala, T., Tiitinen, H., Sivonen, P., Alku, P., Lehtokoski, A., Czigler, I., Csépe, V., Ilmoniemi, R.J. and Näätänen, R. 1999. "Brain responses reveal the learning of foreign language phonemes." *Psychophysiology* 36 (5): 638–42.

CHAPTER 2

Event-related potential studies of early language processing at the phoneme, word, and sentence levels

Barbara T. Conboy, Maritza Rivera-Gaxiola, Juan Silva-Pereyra and
Patricia K. Kuhl

1   Introduction

The use of event-related potentials (ERPs) in studies of language processing in infants and children is increasing in popularity. The high temporal resolution of ERPs makes them ideally suited for studying the fine-grained, temporally ordered structure of spoken language, and ERP experiments can be completed without overt participation from subjects, thereby reducing the cognitive demands inherent in behavioral paradigms. Thus the use of ERPs in child language research will most likely continue to grow over the next several years, and findings from such studies will become increasingly important for building theories of early language development.

In this chapter we discuss three ways in which ERPs have been applied to the study of child language development. In the first section we review behavioral studies of cross-linguistic phoneme processing during the first year of life, and how ERP studies of infants have elucidated the effects of language experience on speech perception beyond what was known from the behavioral studies. We discuss the similarities and differences between results obtained from ERP and behavioral experiments using the same stimuli. In the second section we review ERP studies of word processing in toddlers, and what these show about the effects of differential language experience on word learning. In the third section we review ERP studies of sentence processing in 2-, 3- and 4-year-old children, which have revealed both similarities to and differences from ERP studies of sentence processing in adults.

2   Phoneme processing in the first year [1]

2.1   Insights from behavioral studies

Several decades of research on infant speech perception have shown how infants process phonetic information that either is or is not phonologically contrastive in their native language. More than 30 years ago, Eimas and colleagues used a non-nutritive high-amplitude sucking technique to show that infants as young as 1 – 4 months of age discriminate stop consonants in a categorical manner (Eimas, Siqueland, Jusczyk, and Vigorito 1971). Since then, research on infant speech perception has employed a variety of behavioral techniques. These have included: *high-amplitude sucking* (e.g., Bertoncini, Bijeljac-Babic, Jusczyk, Kennedy and Mehler 1988; Eilers and Minifie 1975; Eimas 1974, 1975; Jusczyk, Copan and Thompson 1978; Kuhl and Miller 1982; Morse 1972; Streeter 1976; Swoboda, Morse and Leavitt 1976; Trehub and Rabinovich 1972); *heart rate measures* (e.g., Lasky, Syrdal-Lasky and Klein 1975; Leavitt *et al.* 1976; Miller and Morse 1976; Miller, Morse and Dorman 1977; Moffitt 1971); *visual habituation/dishabituation paradigms* (e.g., Best, McRoberts, LaFleur and Eisenstadt 1995; Miller and Eimas 1996; Polka and Werker 1994); and *conditioned (operant) head turn testing* (e.g., Anderson, Morgan and White 2003; Aslin *et al.* 1981; Eilers, Wilson and Moore 1977, 1979; Kuhl 1991, 1993; Liu, Kuhl and Tsao 2003; Polka and Bohn 1996; Tsao, Liu and Kuhl 2006; Werker, Gilbert, Humphrey and Tees 1981; Werker and Tees 1984a). These behavioral techniques have revealed differences in discrimination of contrasts that are phonemic in the language infants are exposed to (native language) versus those that are phonemic in a nonnative language (Best *et al.* 1995; Best and McRoberts 2003; Eilers, Gavin and Wilson 1979; Eilers, Gavin and Oller 1982; Kuhl *et al.* 1992, 2005, 2006; Pegg and Werker 1997; Polka and Werker 1994; Werker and Lalonde 1988; Werker and Tees 1984a).

From the behavioral research has emerged the now widely accepted tenet that infants are born with general auditory perceptual abilities that are subsequently shaped by listening experience in the first year of life. Language experience produces changes in infants' performance on native and nonnative contrasts. Recent studies show that performance on native contrasts shows a statistically significant increase while performance on nonnative contrasts shows a decline, but one that is not statistically significant, and remains above chance (Kuhl *et al.* 2006; Tsao *et al.* 2006). For example, the /r/ and /l/ phonemes are used to contrast meaning in the English words "rock" and "lock", but are not used contrastively in Japanese and

---

1.   The term "phoneme processing" is used in this chapter to refer to the differential processing of speech sound contrasts that are phonemic in the listener's language vs. those that are not phonemic.

several other Asian languages. Infants raised in Japanese-speaking homes discriminate the English /r/ from /l/ at 6–8 months but their discrimination declines by 10–12 months (Kuhl *et al.* 2006). The pattern of a decline in nonnative contrasts, first documented by Werker and Tees using Hindi and Nthlakampx syllables as nonnative stimuli (1984a), is mentioned in virtually every introductory textbook on child language development, and has stimulated the lay public's enthusiasm for exposure to foreign languages during infancy. Yet the mechanisms underlying the shift from broad perceptual abilities to more selective ones that are more and more attuned to the native language remain in question. Early proposals that infants possessed innate linguistic information that was either maintained or lost based on their language experience (e.g., Eimas 1975; Liberman and Mattingly 1985) were revised based on the finding that adults could behaviorally detect various nonnative contrasts under sensitive test conditions (Carney, Widin and Viemeister 1977; Werker and Logan 1985; Werker and Tees 1984b) or after phonetic training (Jamieson and Morosan 1986,1989; Logan, Lively and Pisoni 1991; McClaskey, Pisoni and Carrell 1983; McClelland, Fiez and McCandliss 2002; Morosan and Jamieson 1989; Pisoni, Aslin, Perey and Hennessy 1982; Tees and Werker 1984). It has become clear that a variety of patterns of developmental change exist; current studies are focusing on relating the timeline of developmental change for individual speech sounds to mechanistic models that purport to explain this variance.

Recent studies of the early transition in speech perception have shown that discrimination of native and nonnative speech sound contrasts may be influenced by a host of factors including the acoustic/perceptual salience of the stimuli (Burnham 1986; Polka 1991, 1992; Polka, Colantonio and Sundara 2001), the relationship of the stimuli to phoneme categories in the native language (Anderson *et al.* 2003; Best 1994; Best and Roberts 2003; Best McRoberts and Sithole 1988; Best *et al.* 1995; Kuhl *et al.* 2006; Polka 1991, 1992), the extent to which infants have advanced in native phoneme discrimination (Kuhl 2000a,b; Kuhl *et al.* 2005, 2006; Kuhl, Conboy, Coffey-Corina, Padden, Rivera-Gaxiola and Nelson, 2007), and infants' other cognitive abilities (Conboy, Sommerville and Kuhl, submitted; Lalonde and Werker 1995). The decline in discrimination of nonnative contrasts is not immutable: even at 8–10 months, when the decline in perception of nonnative sounds is well underway, infants can discriminate contrasts from another language after 5 hours of naturalistic, conversational exposure (Kuhl, Tsao and Liu 2003) and can discriminate contrasts from within a native language category after only a few minutes of structured laboratory exposure (Maye, Werker and Gerken 2002; McMurray and Aslin 2005). In addition, infants do not simply maintain perception of all native phonetic contrasts given experience with language. For example, infants with simultaneous exposure to two languages from birth have been shown to display a temporary decline in perception of contrasts that are phonemic in one of their languages (Bosch and Sebastián-Galles 2003). Infants have shown improvement in discrimination of native contrasts from 7 to 11 months (Kuhl *et al.* 2006), and difficulty discriminating some native contrasts even at 12 months of age (Polka *et al.* 2001).

2.2   Insights from ERP studies

2.2.1 *ERP indices of phonetic processing*
The use of the ERP technique in infant speech perception research is resulting in another restructuring of ideas regarding how shifts in native vs. nonnative phoneme processing unfold over the first year. ERPs can be described as a more sensitive technique for studying phonetic processing than behavioral methods. They provide a non-invasive neurophysiological measure of processing, and have a high temporal resolution, on the order of milliseconds, that makes them ideal for studying the time course of speech processing. Passive ERP tasks can be completed without overt participation from participants, and thus reduce the cognitive demands of behavioral paradigms. ERP studies of speech perception in adults have revealed discrimination of nonnative phonetic contrasts in the absence of behavioral responses to the same stimuli (Rivera-Gaxiola, Csibra, Johnson and Karmiloff-Smith 2000a,b; Tremblay and Kraus 2002; Tremblay, Kraus and McGee 1998). As will be described in the next section, a similar picture is emerging from ERP studies of infants.

ERP studies of speech perception typically employ the auditory "oddball paradigm", which has been shown to elicit a P300 when the participant is required to respond overtly to the stimuli (see Picton *et al.* 2000) and a preattentive "Mismatch Negativity" (MMN), (Näätänen, Lehtokoski, Lennes, Cheour, Huotilainen, Iivonen, Vainio, Alku, Ilmoniemi, Luuk, Allik, Sinkkonen and Alho 1997). In the auditory oddball paradigm, subjects are presented with a background or "standard" stimulus (e.g., a tone, click, or syllable), repeated with a high frequency of occurrence (typically, 85% of the time), and a "deviant" stimulus (a tone, click, or syllable differing from the standard stimulus on one or more acoustic parameters such as frequency, intensity, or duration) that is randomly presented with a lower frequency of occurrence (e.g., 15% of the time). In speech perception studies, the difference between the standard and deviant is a single phonetic feature in the consonant or vowel of a syllable that results in a minimal pair (e.g., the English pair /pa/ vs. /ta/ involves acoustic cues that signal a difference in the place of articulation feature). The ongoing electroencephalogram (EEG) is time-locked to the onset of presentation of each stimulus (syllable). Epochs of the EEG for each stimulus type (standards and deviants) are digitized and averaged off-line, after trials with artifact from muscle and eye movement have been removed. Auditory ERPs are typically characterized by a series of positive and negative waveforms peaking within the first few hundred ms after stimulus onset and reflecting different sensory, perceptual, and cognitive processes. The term "Mismatch Negativity" or MMN refers to a negative component observed when the responses to the standard are subtracted from the responses to the deviant, presumably reflecting the brain's "automatic change-detection response" (Näätänen *et al.* 1997; Näätänen, Gaillard and Mäntysalo 1978). Generators in both auditory and frontal cortex are believed to underlie the MMN, reflecting the formation of traces in auditory sensory memory and subsequent involuntary preattentional switches to the deviant stimulus, respectively (Näätänen 2001). There is evidence that the MMN can reflect long-term memory traces such as the representation of phonemes, and that the sources of the MMN elicited by minimal phoneme pairs are neural generators in the left auditory cortex (Näätänen *et al.* 1997; Rinne, Alho, Alku, Holi, Sinkkonen, Virtanen, Bertrand and Näätänen 1999). Thus, the MMN is well suited to studying language-specific phonetic representations (see Cheour, Leppanen and Kraus 2000 and Näätänen 2001, for reviews). However, it is important to note that the MMN is not the only ERP effect elicited by passive listening to phonetic contrasts. For example, differences in the ERPs to deviants vs. standards have been noted in the N1-P2 auditory complex and as a "Late Positive Deflection" in addition to the MMN in adults (Rivera-Gaxiola, Csibra, Johnson and Karmiloff-Smith 2000a).

2.2.2 ERP studies of phoneme processing in infants
Using a habituation/dishabituation ERP paradigm, Dehaene-Lambertz and Dehaene (1994) provided the first ERP evidence of a CV-syllabic "mismatch" response in infants, a recovery of ERP amplitude reflecting discrimination of a phonetic contrast. In their study of 2- to 3-month-old infants they presented trains of 5 syllables with the 5th syllable being either the same or different from the previous 4. Infants displayed a left posterior positivity to the new syllable (/ga/) compared to the previous 4 standard syllables (/ba/), at around 400 ms. A later negative effect was also noted, with a bilateral frontal distribution. Cheour and colleagues reported that a component resembling the MMN could be elicited in infants by presenting phonetic contrasts in an oddball paradigm (Cheour-Luhtanen, Alho, Kujala, Sainio, Reinikainen, Renlund, Aaltonen, Eerola and Näätänen 1995). In that research, ERPs were recorded from sleeping newborns who were presented with a vowel contrast. The deviant elicited a larger amplitude negative component than the standard, peaking at approximately 200–250 ms after stimulus onset. Subsequent studies have shown increased negativity in similar time windows to the deviant vs. standard throughout the first year. This increased negativity has been found for vowel contrasts (Cheour-Luhtanen, Alho, Sainio, Sainio, Rinne, Reinikainen, Pohjavuori, Renlund, Aaltonen, Eerola and Näätänen 1996; Cheour,

Alho, Sainio, Reinikainen, Renlund, Aaltonen, Eerola and Näätänen 1997; Cheour, Alho, Ceponiene, Reinikainen, Sainio, Pohjavuori, Aaltonen and Näätänen 1998; Cheour, Ceponiene, Lehtokoski, Luuk, Allik, Alho and Näätänen 1998; Friederici, Friedrich and Weber 2002, and consonant contrasts (Dehaene-Lambertz and Baillet1998; Kuhl *et al.* 2007; Pang, Edmonds, Desjardins, Khan, Trainor and Taylor 1998; Rivera-Gaxiola, Klarman, García-Sierra and Kuhl 2005; Rivera-Gaxiola, Silva-Pereyra and Kuhl 2005). However, the MMNs reported for the infants in those studies had longer latencies and different scalp distributions than those reported for adults (for a review, see Cheour, Leppanen and Kraus 2000).

ERPs have also been used to study changes in the brain's response to phonetic units that arise from experience with language over the first year (Cheour, Ceponiene *et al.* 1998; Kuhl *et al.* in press; Rivera-Gaxiola, Silva-Pereyra and Kuhl 2005). For example, Cheour, Ceponiene and colleagues (1998) recorded ERPs to Finnish and Estonian vowel contrasts in Finnish infants at 6 and 12 months and in Estonian infants at 12 months. Results indicated that the ERPs of 6-month-old infants showed a discriminatory response to both vowel contrasts, that is, regardless of language experience, whereas the ERPs of 12-month-old infants were attenuated for the contrast that was nonnative.

Rivera-Gaxiola and colleagues conducted a series of studies of consonant processing in infants from monolingual English-speaking homes in the U.S. and monolingual Spanish-speaking homes in Mexico using a double-oddball paradigm. Two "deviants," the coronal stop-initial syllables [da] and [tʰa], were contrasted with a single standard syllable, [ta], that represents phonetic features occurring in the subjects' ambient native languages, English or Spanish, as well as in their nonnative language. The phonetic feature that was contrasted across the three syllables was voice onset time, i.e., the timing of onset of vocal fold vibration relative to the burst portion of the stop consonant. For the English-learning infants, native and nonnative contrasts were English /da/ – /ta/ and Spanish /ta/ – /da/, respectively. The standard stimulus, unaspirated [ta] (VOT= +12 ms), was identified as /da/ by adult English speakers and as /ta/ by adult Spanish speakers. The native voiceless aspirated [tʰa] (VOT=+46 ms) was identified as /ta/ by native English speakers, and the nonnative prevoiced [da] (VOT=-24) as /da/ by native Spanish speakers. Both these deviants differed from the standard on voice onset time by the same amount. The standard was presented approximately 80% of the time, a total of 700 trials, and each deviant was presented approximately 10% of the time, a total of 100 trials each. During testing, each infant sat on his or her parent's lap in a sound attenuated test booth and watched moving puppets, toys, or silent videos.

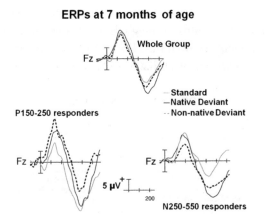

ERPs at 7 months of age

Figure 1. ERPs to native and nonnative deviant syllables (English aspirated [tʰa] and Spanish prevoiced [da]) and a standard syllable (voiceless unaspirated [ta]) recorded in a double-oddball passive discrimination paradigm (frontal-central site displayed, positive plotted upwards). At the group level, 7-month-old infants show larger negativities to both the native and nonnative deviant compared to the standard (top of figure), but individual infants responded to the native and nonnative contrasts with either a positivity (P150–250-responders, bottom left) or a negativity (N250–550-responders, bottom right) (adapted with permission from Rivera-Gaxiola, M., Silva-Pereyra, J. and Kuhl, P.K. (2005), Brain potentials to native and non-native speech contrasts in 7- and 11-month-old American infants. *Developmental Science, 8,* 162–172)

In the first study (Rivera-Gaxiola, Silva-Pereyra and Kuhl 2005) infants were tested longitudinally, at 7 months and again at 11 months of age. Group results were consistent with the behavioral literature. At 7 months, infants showed evidence of discrimination for both the native and nonnative contrasts, whereas at 11 months, they showed a significant discriminatory effect only for the native contrast (Figure 1). However, when individual infants' ERPs were further examined, two subgroups emerged, and indicated that even at 11 months, some infants showed evidence of above-chance discrimination of the nonnative contrast (see also Cheour, Ceponiene *et al.* 1998). One subgroup, labeled the "N250-550 responders" (henceforth, N-responders), evidenced an enhanced negativity to both the native and the nonnative deviants compared to the standard syllable in the negative-going portion of the wave between 250–550 ms. The other group, labeled the "P150–250 responders" (henceforth, P-responders), showed an enhanced positivity to both the native and the nonnative deviants in the earlier positive deflection occurring between 150 and 250 ms (Figure 1). Interestingly, at 11 months, the infants who were P-responders at 7 months continued to be P-responders to the nonnative deviant, but showed an N response to the native deviant. The infants who were

N-responders at 7 months continued to show an N response to both the nonnative and native deviant at 11 months, although the effect was smaller for the nonnative contrast. Thus, all infants showed the N250–550 ERP effect for their native contrast by 11 months of age, an effect that is probably analogous to a late MMN.

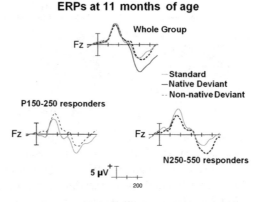

Figure 2. ERPs to native and nonnative deviant syllables (English aspirated [tʰa] and Spanish prevoiced [da]) and a standard syllable (voiceless unaspirated [ta]) recorded in a double-oddball passive discrimination paradigm (frontal-central site displayed, positive plotted upwards). At the group level, 11-month-old infants show a larger negativity only to the native deviant (top of figure), but individual infants responded to the nonnative sound with either a positivity (P150–250-responders, bottom left) or a negativity (N250–550 -responders, bottom right) (adapted with permission from Rivera-Gaxiola, M., Silva-Pereyra, J. and Kuhl, P.K. (2005), Brain potentials to native and non-native speech contrasts in 7- and 11-month-old American infants. *Developmental Science, 8*, 162–172)

In a second study (Rivera-Gaxiola, Klarman *et al.* 2005), a larger sample of infants was tested at 11 months and the pattern of a negative ERP effect for the native contrast and either a P or an N response for the nonnative contrast was replicated (Figure 2). These results indicate that infants continue to exhibit sensitivity to nonnative phonetic contrasts at 11 months, but many do so in the early positive component rather than the later negativity that is thought to index processing at a linguistic level. Also, the infants who continue to show a negativity to a nonnative contrast at 11 months do so to a lesser extent than for a native contrast. Using the same stimuli and testing procedures, Rivera-Gaxiola and colleagues also encountered P- and N-responders in a sample of 10–13 month-old Mexican infants learning Spanish in monolingual households (Rivera-Gaxiola, Silva-Pereyra, Klarman, García-Sierra, Lara-Ayala, Cadena-Salazar and Kuhl, 2007).

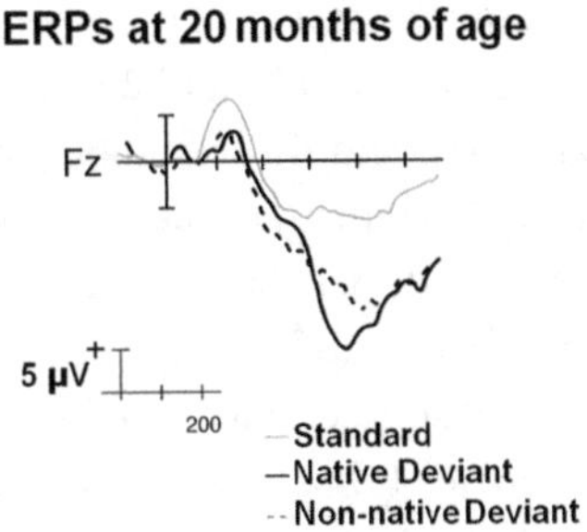

ERPs at 20 months of age

Figure 3. ERPs to native and nonnative deviant syllables (English aspirated [tʰa] and Spanish prevoiced [da]) and a standard syllable (voiceless unaspirated [ta]) recorded in a double-oddball passive discrimination paradigm (right fronto-polar site displayed, positive plotted upwards). At the group level, all 20-month-old infants show larger negativities to both the native and nonnative deviants compared to the standard

Finally, Rivera-Gaxiola and colleagues (in press) found that at 20 months of age, all participants were N-responders to both native and nonnative contrasts; however, the negativity to the native deviant was stronger and had a larger amplitude than that to the nonnative deviant (Figure 3). The P150–250 and the N250–550 were also found to differ in scalp distribution across ages. Rivera-Gaxiola and her colleagues argued that these are two distinct discriminatory components that differ in polarity, latency, scalp distribution, developmental pattern, and have different implications for later language development (see next section).

Two recent behavioral studies using either an English /r/-/l/ contrast with infants from monolingual Japanese-speaking homes (Kuhl *et al.* 2006) or a Mandarin alveolo-palatal affricate-fricative contrast with infants from monolingual English-speaking homes (Tsao *et al.* 2006) have also indicated that nonnative discrimination remains above chance levels at this age, at the group level. However, behavioral methods do not provide adequate temporal precision for distinguishing between levels of processing in the same way that ERP methods do. Thus the use of ERPs may help determine whether there are differences in the perceptual and cognitive processes involved in the discrimination of native and nonnative contrasts during infancy.

2.2.3 ERP phoneme processing measures as predictors of early language development

One important question regarding changes in speech perception during the first year is how these shifts relate to other aspects of language acquisition. Do these shifts in speech sound perception facilitate subsequent language learning? Do they constitute a step in a continuous process in language acquisition? Early speech perception abilities may underlie the ability to recognize and segment words from ongoing speech (Jusczyk 1993, 1994, 1997; Kuhl 2000a; Mehler, Dupoux, and Segui 1990; Werker and Yeung 2005), and those abilities may in turn facilitate other aspects of language acquisition (Newman, Ratner, Jusczyk, Jusczyk and Dow 2006; Weber, Hahne, Friedrich and Friederici 2004). Continuity across domains of language learning has previously been shown in the relationships between early expressive lexical development and subsequent expressive grammatical development (e.g., Bates, Bretherton and Snyder 1988; Bates and Goodman 1997), and between early expressive phonological and lexical development (Locke 1989; MacNeilage and Davis 2000; MacNeilage, Davis and Matyear 1997; McCathren, Yoder and Warren 1999; McCune and Vihman 2001; Oller, Eilers, Neal and Schwartz 1999; Stoel-Gammon 1989; Vihman 1993; Vihman, Ferguson and Elbert 1986). Models of early word acquisition have suggested links between the development of language-specific phonetic representations and the formation of lexical representations (Jusczyk 1993, 1994, 1997, 2003; Werker and Curtin 2005; Werker and Tees 1999; Werker and Yeung 2005).

Few studies have linked early phonetic perception to later language outcomes. Molfese, Molfese and colleagues (Molfese 2000; Molfese and Molfese 1985, 1997; Molfese, Molfese and Espy 1999) recorded ERPs to syllables shortly after birth and showed that these measures predicted language scores at 3, 5, and 8 years and reading disabilities at 8 years. In addition, maturation of the ERP response to speech and nonspeech stimuli from 1 to 8 years was related to reading scores at 8 years (Espy, Molfese, Molfese and Modglin 2004). That research was retrospective in that children were classified according to language or reading ability at later ages and this classification was then linked to previous ERP results. Prospective studies more directly test whether ERPs recorded at an early age have predictive value for later outcomes.

In order to prospectively investigate the association between native and nonnative phoneme processing and later language functioning, Rivera-Gaxiola, Klarman, Garcia-Sierra and Kuhl (2005) obtained parent reports of expressive vocabulary development using the MacArthur-Bates Communicative Development Inventory (CDI; Fenson *et al.* 1993) at 18, 22, 25, 27, and 30 months in the same infants from whom they had recorded ERPs at 11 months (see previously). Recall that at 11 months all infants showed a negative ERP effect for the native contrast, but for the nonnative contrast they either showed a negative (N250–550) or a positive (P150–250) effect. Results indicated that the infants who at 11 months showed a larger P150–250 to the nonnative deviant than to the standard had larger vocabulary sizes at every age than the infants who showed a larger N250–550 to the nonnative deviant compared to the standard. Topographical analyses further indicated that the P150–250 and N250–550 responses differed in scalp distribution. The P150–

250 amplitudes were largest over frontocentral sites, while the N250–550 amplitudes were largest over parietal sites. These different scalp distributions support the hypothesis that the P150–250 and N250–550 effects reflect different neural processing of the nonnative contrast, which are associated with different rates of subsequent vocabulary learning (Rivera-Gaxiola *et al.* 2007). Using the same sample of children, Klarman, Rivera-Gaxiola, Conboy, and Kuhl (2004) elaborated further on how the CDI language scores of P- and N-responders developed beyond word production. N-responders consistently showed lower scores for the Mean of the Three Longest Utterances (M3L), which is a measure of a child's longest reported utterances in morphemes, compared to P-responders. N-responders also showed lower sentence complexity scores compared to P-responders.

Using different stimuli and a different analysis technique, Kuhl and colleagues (2005) recorded ERPs in monolingual English infants at 7.5 months and collected CDIs at 14, 18, 24, and 30 months. ERPs were recorded to a native place contrast (standard /ta/ – deviant /pa/) and one of two nonnative contrasts: a Spanish prevoiced-voiceless unaspirated contrast (standard /ta/ – deviant /da/) or a Mandarin fricative-affricate contrast (standard /ɕi/ – deviant /tɕʰi/). Infants were tested in two separate auditory oddball sessions, one for the native and one for the nonnative contrast. Testing was conducted on the same day, and the contrast order was counterbalanced. For each session, the standard stimulus occurred 85% of the time and the deviant occurred 15% of the time. Mismatch responses were calculated for the native and nonnative contrasts in the negative-going portion of the waveform between 300 and 600 ms. Results indicated a significant negative correlation between the size of the mismatch response (negativity to the deviant vs. the standard) for the native and nonnative contrasts, regardless of whether the Mandarin nonnative or the Spanish nonnative contrast was tested. Infants with more negative amplitudes for the native /ta/-/pa/ contrast tended to have less negative values for the nonnative contrast (either Mandarin or Spanish). Infants' MMN-like responses for the native and nonnative contrasts were differentially associated with language skills between 14 and 30 months. A larger native-language MMN-like response at 7.5 months was associated with a larger number of words produced at 18 and 24 months, greater sentence complexity scores at 24 months, and a longer M3L at 24 and 30 months. The opposite pattern of associations was observed between infants' mismatch responses for the nonnative contrast and their future CDI scores. A more negative amplitude effect for the nonnative contrast was associated with a smaller number of words produced at 24 months, lower sentence complexity scores at 24 months, and a shorter M3L at 30 months. The rate of growth over time in expressive vocabulary size from 14 to 30 months was also related to the native and nonnative contrast mismatch responses. A larger native-contrast MMN-like response at 7.5 months was linked to larger vocabulary sizes at 24 months and a steeper slope in vocabulary growth from 14 to 30 months. The opposite pattern was obtained for the nonnative-language contrast: a larger nonnative-contrast MMN-like response at 7.5 months was related to smaller vocabulary sizes at 24 months and slower growth in vocabulary size.

In sum, recent ERP studies using two different types of speech sound contrasts have revealed that infants' neural responses to speech sounds during the first year of life predict subsequent achievements in language development over the next two years. Infants who respond to a native phonemic contrast with a strong negative ERP effect at 7.5 months show an advantage in later vocabulary development over infants who either do not show this effect or show a weaker effect to that contrast. Infants who respond to nonnative contrasts with a negative ERP effect at 7.5 or 11 months show slower subsequent growth in vocabulary and grammatical development than infants who do not show this negativity to nonnative contrasts at that age. Further research is needed to determine whether early attunement to the relevant features of speech sounds for the infant's native language serves as a bootstrapping mechanism for learning at the word and sentence levels, or if the relationships between rates of learning in each of these domains derive solely from other factors, such as amounts and types of input and more general cognitive abilities.

2.2.4 Behavioral phoneme processing measures and language outcomes

The Kuhl et al. (2007) and Rivera-Gaxiola, Klarman, Garcia-Sierra and Kuhl (2005) studies indicate that ERPs reflect the shifts in speech sound processing during the first year of life that have been reported in the behavioral literature. Additionally, ERPs capture important individual variability in brain activity that is linked to future advances in language acquisition. Of interest is whether ERPs and behavioral methods capture similar patterns of individual variability. Three behavioral studies from our research group have linked phonetic discrimination scores during the first year to later vocabulary and/or utterance length and complexity. In the first study, Tsao, Liu, and Kuhl (2004) tested 6 month-old infants from monolingual English-speaking homes on a native vowel contrast using the conditioned head turn paradigm, and subsequently followed the infants using the CDI at 4 time points between 14 and 30 months. The results indicated that the 6-month head turn scores positively correlated with later vocabulary size, utterance length, and utterance complexity. In a second study, Kuhl and colleagues (2005) tested 7.5 month-old monolingual English infants on the native English /ta/-/pa/ contrast and the nonnative Mandarin fricative-affricate /ɕi/-/tɕʰi/ contrast using head turn, and subsequently administered the CDI at 4 time points between 14 and 30 months. In striking similarity to the ERP study described above in which the same phonetic contrasts were used, the head turn scores for the native contrast were positively correlated with later language scores, and head turn scores for the nonnative contrast at 7.5 were negatively correlated with later language scores. In addition, in this study, native and nonnative contrast discrimination were negatively correlated, indicating that as infants improve in native language skills, they attend less to information that is irrelevant for that language. In a third study, Conboy, Rivera-Gaxiola, Klarman, Aksoylu, and Kuhl (2005) conducted a double-target conditioned head turn test with 7.5 and 11 month-old infants from monolingual English backgrounds using the same English and Spanish stimuli used by Rivera-Gaxiola, Silva Pereyra and Kuhl and Rivera-Gaxiola, Klarman, Garcia-Sierra and Kuhl (2005). At the group level, the 7.5 month-old infants performed at similar levels for the English and Spanish contrasts, whereas the 11 month-old infants performed at higher levels on the English than on the Spanish contrast. Because the infants were tested on both contrasts simultaneously, performance factors such as fatigue and inattentiveness would be expected to affect both contrasts equally. Thus the design controlled for such factors. At both ages there were individual differences in performance across contrasts, and these were linked to 11-month vocabulary size. Infants who displayed a larger difference between scores for the native (English) and nonnative (Spanish) contrasts tended to have higher receptive vocabulary sizes as measured by the CDI.

The finding that better language skills are linked to better discrimination of native contrasts and worse discrimination of nonnative contrasts seems to reflect infants' ability to attend to acoustic cues that are relevant for the language they are acquiring while disregarding irrelevant or misleading cues. Conboy, Sommerville and Kuhl (submitted) hypothesized that this ability may involve more general developing cognitive skills which would also be evident in infants' performance on nonlinguistic tasks (see also Lalonde and Werker 1995). To explore this, Conboy and colleagues administered the double-target head turn test, a detour-reaching object retrieval task (based on Diamond 1990), and a means-ends object-reaching task (based on Sommerville and Woodward 2005) to a group of 11-month-old infants. These cognitive tasks required infants to inhibit attention and motoric responses to irrelevant, misleading information in the visual domain. Parent reports of receptive vocabulary were obtained using the CDI. The head turn results replicated those of the previous study, showing better discrimination of the native vs. the nonnative contrast. Discrimination of the native contrast was positively associated with CDI receptive vocabulary size. In addition, discrimination of the nonnative contrast was negatively associated with performance on each of the nonlinguistic cognitive tasks, but not related to vocabulary size. We can conclude that the low head turn responses to the nonnative target were not due to a general reduction in attention during the testing for two reasons. First, because we used a double-target design, fatigue and other factors would be expected to affect performance in both languages, but this was not the case. Second, low head turn performance for the nonnative contrast was associated with *higher* performance on the cognitive tasks, in keeping with previous findings reported by Lalonde and Werker (1995). Thus, advances in cognitive control abilities that allow infants to ignore irrelevant information may also influence the extent to which infants tune out phonetic information that is not relevant for their ambient language. Ongoing research is exploring whether ERP responses to these stimuli are linked to the same cognitive tasks (Conboy, Sommerville and Kuhl, submitted). Because ERPs can tap preattentive processes, we are interested in whether they are linked to performance on the cognitive tasks in the same way as the head turn scores, reflecting shifts in processing of irrelevant information across domains (Conboy, Sommerville and Kuhl, unpublished data; Kuhl *et al.* 2007).

2.3   Future directions for phoneme processing studies using ERPs

Taken together, these studies suggest that infants who show earlier attunement to the features of speech sounds that signal phonemic differences in their native language, and relatedly, earlier *tuning out* of nonnative contrasts that are not relevant for the native language, show faster growth in early language development. The same overall pattern of association between the native vs. nonnative contrast have been obtained using behavioral and ERP methods, across different sets of stimuli. However, the ERP findings further elucidate differences in the neural processes involved in sensitivity to the native vs. nonnative contrast. An important area for future research is the use of direct comparisons of ERP and head turn responses to native and nonnative contrasts in the same infants. Such studies will provide a better understanding of the functional significance of ERPs elicited by a variety of phonetic contrasts. One study that used behavioral and ERP measures with the same group of infants from monolingual English-speaking homes has already shown significant correlations between the ERP mismatch effect and head turn sensitivity scores for both native and nonnative contrasts (Kuhl *et al.* 2005; see also, Kuhl *et al.* 2007).

Studies across a wider range of populations and language learning environments would be useful for determining how these ERP effects are linked to experience with language. In addition, longitudinal studies of phoneme processing throughout the period of early lexical development are needed for determining how the emerging use of contrastive phonology in words affects the brain's responses to speech sounds, and to determine the predictive power of individual ERPs to speech sounds recorded during the first year and later language achievements.

Finally, ERP phoneme processing studies of infants exposed to two or more languages during the first year of life will help us understand how the auditory-perceptual space is shaped in the bilingual brain and allow us to test specific hypotheses regarding neural commitment to language arising from individual variation in language experience. Our group has been conducting ERP studies of bilingual infants from two different language backgrounds (Spanish/English, Mandarin/English). We predict that by 11 months of age infants exposed to both Spanish and English will respond with larger N250–550s to both the Spanish and English contrasts used in the studies described above, reflecting the linguistic relevance of both contrasts. Differences in the latencies, scalp distributions, and amplitudes of these effects may arise with respect to the specific language dominance of each infant. An analogous pattern would be expected for the Mandarin/English infants. Of interest would be to test them in a third language that they have not heard. Will they show the expected pattern of decline for perception of the nonnative contrast over the first year, or will their systems remain more flexible or "open" to nonnative contrasts as a result of their experience with two languages?

3   Word processing in the second year

3.1   Insights from behavioral studies

An important aspect of early language acquisition involves the ability to recognize words in the speech stream and to link those words to meaning. Infants are faced with the challenge of segmenting words early on; it has been estimated that more than 90% of the speech addressed to 6 to 9 month-old infants consists of multiword utterances (van de Weijer 1998). Behavioral experiments have revealed shifts in strategies for segmenting words from connected speech in the input between 6 and 12 months, from an initial focus on familiar prosodic and sequential cues to increasing integration of prosodic, segmental, and statistical cues (e.g., Bortfield, Morgan, Golinkoff and Rathbun 2005; Christophe, Dupoux, Bertoncini and Mehler 1994; Friederici and Wessels 1993; Goodsitt, Morgan and Kuhl 1993; Houston, Santelmann and Jusczyk 2004; Johnson and Jusczyk 2001; Jusczyk, Hohne and Bauman 1999; Jusczyk, Houston and Newsome 1999; Mattys and Jusczyk 2001a,b; Mattys, Jusczyk, Luce and Morgan 1999; Morgan and Saffran 1995; Saffran, Aslin and Newport 1996). In addition to this ability to segment words from ongoing speech, behavioral experiments have shown that infants retain long-term memory for new words. For example, using a head turn preference procedure, Hallé and de Boysson-Bardies (1994) found that by 11 months, infants prefer words that are frequent in the input over less frequent words. Using a similar procedure, Jusczyk and colleagues have shown that by 7.5 months infants listen longer to passages containing word forms they have previously heard either in passages or as isolated words, compared to passages containing words to which they have not been previously exposed (Jusczyk and Aslin 1995; Jusczyk and Hohne 1997). Even by 4.5 months, infants show recognition of their own names, as measured by a preference for listening to those names over other words (Mandel, Jusczyk and Pisoni 1995).

Other behavioral techniques have shown that some ability to map word forms to meaning is in place by the first months of the second year, and possibly earlier. These techniques include parent reports of infants' reliable responses to words (e.g., Fenson *et al.* 1993, 1994), naturalistic observations of appropriate responses to verbal commands (Benedict 1979), and visual attention to and/or manipulation of objects or pictures that are labeled during experimental tasks (e.g., Hollich, Hirsch-Pasek and Golinkoff 2000; Oviatt, 1980; Pruden, Hirsh-Pasek, Golinkoff and Hennon 2006; Schafer 2005; Waxman and Booth 2003; Waxman and Braun 2005; Werker, Cohen, Lloyd, Stager and Casasola 1998; Woodward, Markman and Fitzsimmons 1994). Using a preferential looking paradigm, Tincoff and Jusczyk (1999) showed that infants as young as 6 months of age comprehended highly familiar words associated with animate beings (i.e., "mommy" and "daddy").

In spite of these early advances in word learning, infants' lexical processing skills are limited. For example, Hallé and de Boysson-Bardies (1996) reported that 11-month-old infants preferred to listen to nonsense words that were phonetically similar to real, highly frequent words over dissimilar nonsense words, leading to the suggestion that early word representations are phonetically underspecified. Stager and Werker (1997) found that at 14 months, infants were able to link two dissimilar nonsense words to different referents (e.g., "leef" and "neem"), but not two similar sounding nonsense words that they could easily tell apart in a discrimination task (e.g., "bih" and "dih"), suggesting they treated the two word forms as instances of the same label during the more cognitively demanding word-learning task (see also Pater, Stager and Werker 2004). However, by 14 months infants with larger vocabulary sizes succeeded on this task (Werker, Fennell, Corcoran and Stager 2002). By 17 – 20 months infants easily map phonetically similar nonsense words to different referents (Bailey and Plunkett 2002; Werker *et al.* 2002), except when the minimal difference is in a vowel rather than a consonant (Nazzi 2005), and by 14 months they can map similar sounding words to different referents when both words are highly familiar (e.g., "doll" and "ball") (Fennell and Werker 2003). At both 18–23 (Swingley 2003; Swingley and Aslin 2000) and 14–15 months (Swingley and Aslin 2002), infants are slower to fixate visually to a picture of a familiar object (e.g., baby) vs. a foil in a looking preference task when they hear a mispronunciation of that word (e.g., "vaby") compared to when they hear a correct pronunciation of that word. Also, at 14 months infants look longer to pictures matching correct pronunciations of novel words compared to foils, but not mispronunciations of those target words (Ballem and Plunkett 2005). Finally, there is evidence that even younger infants can access phonetic detail in their representations of words: Jusczyk and Aslin (1995) found that 7.5 month-old infants showed a listening preference for familiarized words (e.g., "cup") over unfamiliarized words, but not when the initial consonant of the familiarized word was changed ("tup"); Stager and Werker (1997) reported that 8-month-old infants succeeded in detecting a switch from "bih" to "dih" in a single sound-object pairing, a task at which 14-month-old infants failed; Swingley (2005) showed that 11-month-old infants preferred correct pronunciations to word-onset (but not word-offset) mispronunciations of familiar words, although they did not prefer onset or offset mispronunciations of the familiar words to nonwords; and Vihman and colleagues reported that changing the initial consonants of the accented syllables of familiar words blocked recognition of those words in 11-month-old infants, whereas changing the initial consonants of the unaccented syllables of those same words did not block recognition, but did delay recognition of the words (Vihman, Nakai, De Paolis and Hallé 2004). It has been suggested that the results with younger infants are tapping into simple recognition of word forms rather than the more difficult process of mapping of word form to meaning (Hallé and de Boysson-Bardies 1996; Pater *et al.* 2004; Stager and Werker 1997; Werker and Curtin 2005).

Taken together, the behavioral research on early word processing suggests that phonetic detail is available to infants in their earliest word representations, but due to limited cognitive resources, more holistic representations may be used when mapping words to meaning in demanding word-learning and processing tasks (Fennell and Werker 2003; Pater, Stager and Werker 2004; Stager and Werker 1997; Werker and Tees 1999). This explanation has also been extended to account for phonological errors in the early stages of word production (Fikkert 2005).

Throughout the second year, infants become more efficient at learning, producing, and processing words. Evidence of this is also found in fine-grained analyses of eye movements during looking preference tasks, which have reflected increases in the efficiency of lexical access during the second year (Fernald, Perfors and Marchman 2006; Fernald, Pinto, Swingley, Weinberg and McRoberts 1998; Fernald, Swingley and Pinto 2001; Zangl, Klarman, Thal, Fernald and Bates 2005).

3.2   Insights from ERP studies

3.2.1 *Infants growing up with one language*
Given these early advances in word segmentation, recognition, and comprehension, words with which infants have had repeated experience from their language input would be expected to elicit different neural responses than unfamiliar words. In a series of ERP studies, Molfese and colleagues showed that brain responses reliably discriminated between known and unknown words that infants passively

listened to as young as 12 -16 months (Molfese 1989,1990; Molfese and Wetzel 1992; Molfese, Wetzel and Gill 1993). Molfese, Morse and Peters (1990) additionally showed that ERP effects linked to the acquisition of names for novel objects could be obtained as young as 14–15 months.

Mills, Coffey-Corina and Neville (1993, 1997) reported different brain responses for children as young as 13–20 months of age to words that parents reported to be known words, unknown words, and known words that were played backwards. Additionally, they found that the scalp distributions of these effects varied according to vocabulary size, with higher vocabulary children showing more focal ERP effects (an enhanced negativity to known vs. unknown words between 200 and 400 ms), only at left temporal and parietal electrode sites, compared to lower vocabulary children who showed more symmetrical, broadly distributed effects. More recently, ERPs have been shown to differentiate familiar from unfamiliar words by 250 ms in infants as young as 11 months (Thierry, Roberts and Vihman 2003), and as young as 9–11 months in infants who have high CDI receptive vocabulary scores (Sheehan and Mills, this volume). The finding that ERPs linked to word familiarity and meaning are modulated by experience with individual words was further demonstrated by Mills, Plunkett, Prat, and Schafer (2005). In that research, ERPs were recorded in 20 month-old infants as they listened to known and unknown words, and nonwords that were phonotactically legal English words. ERPs were then recorded during a brief training session in which half of the nonwords were presented with an unknown object referent, and the other half were simply repeated without any pairing of word to referent. Subsequently, ERPs were recorded to all 4 word types, without any pairing of word form to a visual referent. The amplitude and distribution of the ERPs to the nonwords that had been paired with a referent were strikingly similar to those of the previously known words and different from the ERPs to the nonwords that had not been paired to a referent. These results indicate that short-term learning of new word forms may be encoded in the same neural regions as words that were previously learned.

To investigate whether phonetic specificity in words is reflected in ERP known-unknown word effects, Mills and colleagues recorded ERPs to words that children knew, phonetically similar words, and dissimilar words (Mills, Prat, Stager, Zangl, Neville and Werker 2004). The results indicated that ERPs are sensitive to shifts from holistic to phonetically specific lexical representations between 14 and 20 months. At 14 months, infants displayed the ERP effect that has previously been shown to index word meaning, an enhanced negativity between 200 and 400 ms (N200–400), to known vs. dissimilar nonsense words (e.g., "bear" vs. "kobe"), but not to known vs. phonetically similar nonsense words ("bear" vs."gare"). Moreover, they showed the N200–400 effect to words that were similar to the known words vs. dissimilar words ("gare" vs. "kobe"), suggesting that they processed mispronunciations of known words in the same way as correct pronunciations. By 20 months, there was an N200–400 effect to known vs. dissimilar words and known vs. similar words, but no effect in the ERPs to words that were similar to known words vs. dissimilar words (i.e., "gare" vs."kobe"). These results are consistent with the behavioral literature reviewed above indicating that novice word learners have difficulty attending to phonetic detail in words under processing conditions in which they link the words to meaning.

3.2.2 Infants growing up with two languages

Infants raised bilingually provide a natural test case for examining the effects of experience with language on the brain activity elicited by known and unknown words. Of interest is whether similar ERP effects are noted for known vs. unknown words in each of the bilingual child's languages, and whether the timing and distribution of these effects vary according to single-language vocabulary size or the child's total vocabulary size. To investigate these questions, Conboy and Mills (2006) recorded ERPs to known and unknown Spanish and English words in 19- to 22-month-olds who received naturalistic input in both Spanish and English on a regular basis, starting within the first 6 months of life. Following the procedure of Mills *et al.* (e.g. 1993, 1997, 2004), known words were determined by asking parents to rate a list of words in each language on a 4-point scale, with a rating of 1 indicating that the parent was absolutely certain the child did not understand the word and a 4 indicating the parent was very certain the child understood the word. The words on this list were selected based on normative data from studies of early language acquisition in English (Fenson *et al.* 1993) and Spanish (Jackson-Maldonado *et al.* 1993). Each child's individualized known stimulus word list was made up of 10 English and 10 Spanish words that received ratings of 3 or 4 for that child, and the unknown words were low frequency words in each language reported as unfamiliar to the child and matched in syllable structure to the known words. In addition, a picture-pointing task was used to ensure that infants comprehended the particular word forms used in the ERP task, rather than derived forms (e.g., the dimunitive form *carrito* for *carro*). No two words on any child's list were translation equivalents. All words were recorded in the same voice by a female bilingual speaker, and presented in a randomly mixed order during testing.

Expressive vocabulary sizes were obtained using the CDI and its Spanish language counterpart, the Inventario del Desarrollo de Habilidades Comunicativas (Jackson-Maldonado *et al.* 2003). These scores, along with parent reports of children's ability and preference for each language, were used to determine the language of dominance for each child. Approximately equal numbers of children were English- and Spanish-dominant. In addition, a conceptual vocabulary score was calculated by summing the total number of words in both languages and then subtracting out the number of times a pair of conceptually equivalent words (e.g., "water" and "agua") occurred across the two languages. This conceptual score was used to divide the group into two subgroups, a higher and a lower vocabulary group. Mean conceptual vocabulary sizes were 212 words for the higher producers and 66 words for the low producers.

Across the entire group of 30 children, ERP differences to known and unknown words in the dominant language occurred as early as 200–400 and 400–600 ms, and were broadly distributed over the left and right hemispheres, resembling the pattern observed for 13- to 17-month-old monolingual children (i.e., Mills *et al.* 1997). However, ERP differences for words in the nondominant language of the same children were not apparent until late in the waveform, from 600 to 900 ms. For the dominant language the known-unknown word effect was larger over right hemisphere anterior sites (Figure 4).

These ERP effects were modulated not only by experience with each individual language, but also by overall experience with both languages. When children were divided into higher and lower groups based on their conceptual vocabulary sizes, differences in the timing of ERP known-unknown word effects were noted for the nondominant language. For the higher producers, the ERP effects occurred by 200–400 ms, consistent with the latency observed for the dominant language of the same children, and with that observed in monolingual children at the same and younger ages. For the lower producers, there was no difference in the negativity to known-unknown words at 200–400 or 400–600 ms, but the difference was significant at 600–900 ms.

Different scalp distributions of the ERP known-unknown word effect were also noted in the bilingual 20-month-old children in this study. For the dominant language, N200–400 known-unknown word effects were larger over right frontal regions, in contrast to the left temporal-parietal distribution of this ERP effect in monolingual 20-month-olds. In the bilingual study the stimuli switched randomly between Spanish and English, and this language switching may have elicited more frontal activation than the monolingual testing conditions. Switching between languages has been linked to frontal activation in studies of bilingual adults using fMRI (Hernández, Dapretto, Mazziotta and Brookheimer 2001; Hernández, Martínez and Kohnert 2000) and ERPs (Jackson, Swainson, Cunnington and Jackson 2001; Moreno, Fedemeier and Kutas 2002). Moreover, switching may have engaged the right hemisphere to a greater degree, given that the right hemisphere has been shown to be involved in integration of information across domains (Goldberg and Costa 1981). The effects of switching were thus investigated by testing a group of ten 19–22 month-old bilingual toddlers on the same stimuli, but in alternating blocks of 50 English and 50 Spanish trials (Conboy 2002). The children in this group were matched for total conceptual vocabulary size and approximate English and Spanish vocabulary sizes to 10 infants from the group of 30 toddlers

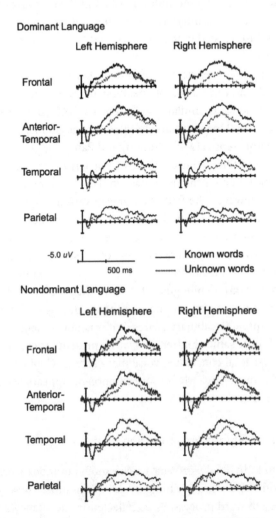

Figure 4. ERPs to known and unknown words in a group of 30 19–22 month-old Spanish-English bilingual toddlers (negative plotted upwards). At the group level, children show greater negativity to known compared to unknown words in both their languages (N200–400, N400–600, and N600–900 effects), The earlier negative effects (N200–400 and N400–600) occur only for the dominant language, whereas the later effects (N600–900) occur for both languages. When the group is subdivided into higher and lower vocabulary groups, children in the higher group show the N200–400 and N400–600 effect for both languages (adapted with permission from Conboy, B.T. and Mills, D.L. (2006). Two languages, one developing brain: Event-related potentials to words in bilingual toddlers. *Developmental Science, 9*(1), F1-F12)

who heard the stimuli in a randomly switched presentation. As predicted, the children in the blocked condition did not show the right frontal asymmetry for their dominant language shown by the children tested in the language-switched group. All other ERP effects were similar across groups, but latencies for all effects were shorter for the children tested in the blocked condition than for those tested in the switched condition.

One ERP component elicited by auditory words in infants as young as 6 months is the P100, an early positivity peaking at approximately 100 ms (Neville and Mills 1997). Due to its similarity to a sensory ERP component observed in adults, the P50, the P100 in infants and toddlers is thought to index a sensory stage of processing auditory words (Mills, Conboy and Paton 2005). In studies of monolingual infants and toddlers, this component was larger over the left vs. the right hemisphere, for both known and unknown words (Mills *et al.* 1997; Mills, Conboy and Paton 2005). However, the P100 asymmetry varied as a function of a child's percentile rank on the MacArthur-Bates CDI. Across studies, the P100 to words was larger in amplitude at left vs. right electrode sites in children who scored above the 50th percentile, but this asymmetry was not present for children with slower vocabulary development, including late talkers as old as 30 months of age (Mills, Conboy and Paton 2005). In bilingual 20-month-olds, the left over right P100 amplitude asymmetry was noted for the dominant language of the children with higher total conceptual vocabulary scores, but was not present for the nondominant language of those same children, nor was it present for either language of the children with lower total conceptual vocabulary scores (Conboy and Mills 2006). Thus, the distribution of this early sensory component appears to be modulated by experience with particular words.

3.3   Future directions for word processing studies using ERPs

ERPs recorded to individual words have been shown to index word familiarity as young as 9 months and word meaning by 13–17 months. These studies suggest that the efficiency of word processing, as reflected in the latency and distribution of ERP effects, is linked both to general language experience and to experience with particular words. Further work is needed to compare the brain's responses to words under different listening conditions, those that may slow processing and those that make processing more efficient, and to investigate the nature of lexical representations tapped by ERPs. In a study of 14–15 month-old infants, Molfese and colleagues (1990) found distinct ERPs to nonsense words that matched objects that the infants had been trained to associate with the words, vs. nonsense words that did not match. Using a different type of cross-modal design, two research groups have reported distinct ERPs to words that are congruous with pictures of objects vs. those that are incongruous, in 14- and 19-month-olds (Frie-drich and Friederici 2004, 2005a, 2005c) and in 13- and 20-month-olds (Mills, Conboy and Paton 2005). In addition, Friedrich and Friederici (2005c) have shown that ERPs reflect phonotactic familiarity and semantic priming effects as early as 12 months (2005c). Additional work using ERPs in cross-modal designs will help reveal the nature of infants' earliest word representations.

4   Sentence processing in the third, fourth, and fifth years

4.1   ERP effects associated with semantic and syntactic processing in adults and school-age children

The processing of semantic and morphosyntactic information in sentences has also been studied in young children using ERPs. These studies have exploited the well-known finding that in adults, semantic and syntactic anomalies elicit ERP components with distinct latencies and scalp distributions. The ERP effect elicited to a word that renders a sentence semantically anomalous is a negative wave oc-curring between 250 and 500 ms post stimulus onset, peaking around 400 ms and largest over right posterior sites (known as the N400; Kutas 1997; Kutas and Hill-yard 1980). In contrast, words that render a sentence syntactically anomalous typically elicit a late positivity beginning around 500 ms with a parietal distribu-tion, known as the P600 (for reviews, see Friederici 2002; Hagoort, Brown and Osterhout 1999). In addition, many studies have reported a negative wave between 300 and 500 ms that is largest over left frontal sites (known as the "left anterior negativity" or LAN; e.g., Friederici 1995, 2002; Münte, Heinze and Mangun 1993) in response to both syntactic and morphological violations, an even earlier left anterior negativity (ELAN) occurring between 150 and 250 ms in response to phrase structure violations (Friederici, Hahne and Mecklinger 1996; Münte and Heinze 1994), and more centrally-distributed frontal negative effects in the same approximate time ranges to morphological violations although this latter effect has been linked to working memory processes, and may not necessarily be specific to morphosyntactic processing (Coulson, King and Kutas 1998a; King and Kutas 1995; Kluender and Kutas 1993a,b). Thus in adults, distinct neural systems are in place for semantic vs. grammatical levels of language processing. This has led re-searchers to ask how early these ERP effects are noted in children.

In one of the first developmental ERP sentence processing studies, the N400 semantic anomaly effect was replicated in children from 5 years through adoles-cence, and it was further shown that the peak latency of this component was as long as 620 ms in the youngest children and decreased steadily with age (Holcomb,

Coffey and Neville 1992). Since then, several studies have documented sentence-level N400 effects in school-age children, and in many cases reported longer latencies for these effects than those reported for adults (González-Garrido, Oropeza de Alba, Riestra Castaneda, Riestra Castaneda, Perez Avalos and Valdes Sosa 1997; Hahne, Eckstein and Friederici 2004; Neville, Coffey, Holcomb and Tallal 1993). Adult-like ERP effects to syntactically anomalous sentences have also been replicated in children; both an ELAN and P600 by 13 years and a P600 by 7–13 years (Hahne, Eckstein and Friederici 2004).

4.2 ERP effects associated with semantic and syntactic processing in pre-school-age children

Several recent studies have also addressed sentence processing in preschool-age children. Harris (2001) provided ERP evidence of semantic and syntactic processing in 36–38 month-old English-speaking children. In the first study, semantic violations in sentences elicited a larger negativity, but in contrast to the N400 reported for adults, this negative ERP effect was largest over posterior regions of both hemispheres. Phrase structure violations elicited a larger positivity for syntactic anomalies from 500–1500 ms, bilaterally, which resembled the adult P600 in its latency but not in its scalp distribution. In contrast to the P600 in adults, this slow positive shift was largest at anterior sites. In this study there was no evidence of a LAN, which has been interpreted as a component that reflects automatic processing. Thus it was concluded that children this age do not yet use syntactic information in the same ways as adults. However, in the second study, Harris (2001) reported that a different type of phrase structure violation elicited a bilateral negativity between 300 and 600 ms. In addition to the differences in phrase structure violation type, there were differences in how the sentences were produced across these two studies (with pauses between words in the first study, and in a natural, continuous voice in the second), which may have influenced the results. Friedrich and Friederici (2005b; 2006) provided evidence of a prolonged, centroparietal N400-like effect to semantic anomalies in sentences in 19- and 24-month-old German-speaking children. Oberecker, Friedrich, and Friederici (2005) reported both an early negativity and a late positivity to phrase structure violations in 32-month-old German-speaking children, whereas Oberecker and Friederici (2006) observed only a P600 to the same stimuli in 24-month-old children.

Silva-Pereyra, Rivera-Gaxiola, and Kuhl (2005) recorded ERPs to sentences with syntactic and semantic anomalies in 36- and 48-month-old English-speaking children. In order to ensure that children were familiar with the lexical material used in the stimuli, the sentences were constructed using words from the MacArthur-Bates CDI lexical database (Dale and Fenson 1996). Morphosyntactic anomalies were created by adding the grammatical inflection "-ing" to the verb in the control sentences (i.e., *My uncle will watch +ing the movie*), and sentences with semantic anomalies were created by changing the verb so that it was incongruous with the last word of the sentence (i.e., *My uncle will blow the movie*). Each sentence had the same syntactic structure. All of the sentences were recorded using the same female speaker and were presented via loudspeaker while the child watched a puppet show. For syntactically anomalous sentences, the ERPs were time-locked to the verb, whereas for semantically anomalous sentences, they were time-locked to the sentence-final word (noun). For the control sentences, ERPs were time-locked to both the verb, to serve as a comparison for the syntactically anomalous sentences, and to the final word, as a comparison for the semantically anomalous sentences.

Results indicated different effects for each sentence type at both ages (Figure 5). For the semantically anomalous sentences, there were two negative-going waves that were larger in amplitude than those elicited by the control sentences. In the 36-month-old children, the first of these (N400 effect) started at 400 ms after the onset of the critical word, and peaked at approximately 550 ms. A second negative effect (N600 effect) began at 550 ms, and peaked at 650 ms. In the 48-month-old children, the first negative (N400) effect occurred earlier, beginning at approximately 200 ms and peaking at around 400 ms, and the second negativity (N600) peaked at 600 ms. A third negative effect, from 800–1200 ms (N800 effect), was evident only in the 36-month-olds. For the grammatically anomalous sentences, both age groups displayed a positive wave from 300–600 ms after the onset of the critical word (the verb with the "-ing" inflection), peaking at approximately 400 ms (P400 effect). This effect was broadly distributed across electrode sites but largest at anterior electrode sites. A second positivity from 600–1000 ms (P800 effect) peaked at approximately 800 ms. The effects were more clearly defined at 48 than at 36 months.

In a follow-up study, Silva-Pereyra, Klarman, Lin, and Kuhl (2005) used the same stimuli as in the previous study but with 30-month old children. Similar to the results obtained with 36- and 48-month old children, these younger children displayed anterior negativities to semantically anomalous sentences, but at a longer latency, from 600–800 ms. They also evidenced a broadly distributed late positive shift to morphosyntactic violations from 600–1000 ms (P800 effect), but the earlier frontal positivity (P400 effect) observed in 36- and 48-month-old children was not observed in these younger children (Figure 5).

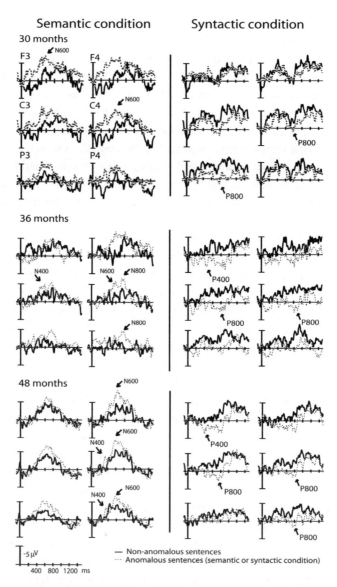

Figure 5. ERPs elicited by anomalous and non-anomalous sentences at 30, 36, and 48 months of age (negative plotted upwards). In the semantic condition all 3 groups show greater negativity to the semantically anomalous sentences compared to non-anomalous sentences (N400 and N600 effects, left side of figure). In the syntactic condition all 3 groups show greater positivity to the syntactically anomalous sentences compared to non-anomalous sentences (P800 effects, right side of figure) (adapted with permission from Silva-Pereyra J., Rivera-Gaxiola M. and Kuhl P. (2005). An event-related brain potential study of sentence comprehension in preschoolers: Semantic and morphosyntactic processing. *Cognitive Brain Research, 23,* 247–258

The results of these two studies indicate that both semantic and syntactic processing mechanisms in young children share many similarities with those reported for adults. Anterior concept-relevant brain areas that are active during spoken sentence processing appear very early in development and are identifiable as specific electrical responses to semantic anomalies. Similar to the longer latencies in the younger children studied by Holcomb and colleagues, the N400-like component in these young children had a longer latency than that reported for adults, suggesting slower rates of processing.

The late positive effects elicited by syntactic anomalies were in the same general time range as the adult P600 component, which has been hypothesized to reflect evaluation and repair processes specific to language processing (Friederici 2002). Silva-Pereyra and colleagues considered a possible interpretation for the presence of the early frontal positivity in preschool children. This effect could reflect attentional processes that were enhanced by the lower probability of the anomalous sentence types during the experiment, similar to the P300 effect that has been linked to probability and expectancy in adults (Coulson, King and Kutas 1998a,b). Although no LAN was observed, it is possible that a LAN-like effect overlapped with the early positivity. Alternatively, the LAN may not have been observed because the automatic mechanism it is believed to index may not yet be developed in children this young. The positive effect to morphosyntactic anomalies was more broadly distributed in 30- and 36-month-old children than in 48-month-old children. This increasing anterior-posterior specialization reflects a move in the direction that is more typical of responses at later stages in development and may reflect the fact that the specialization of brain mechanisms continues to mature until the mid-teen years (Bates, Thal, Finlay and Clancy 2003; Huttenlocher 2003). Such developmental specialization is also reflected in the latency of this effect, which was longer than that reported for the 6-year-old children previously studied by Hahne *et al.* (2004).

It is interesting to note that Oberecker and colleagues (2005) reported both LAN and P600 effects to phrase structure violations in 32-month-old children. In that study, children displayed a late positivity, resembling a P600, with a centro-parietal positivity, but starting somewhat later than in adults. Also observed was a LAN between 300 and 600 ms. The peak of this effect, however, was later in the children (513 ms) than in adults (400 ms). Due to its similar distribution, Oberecker and colleagues interpreted this negativity as a child-specific precursor to the ELAN component. The reasons for the discrepancy between the results of this study and the studies of Silva-Pereyra and colleagues are unclear, but it is noteworthy that LAN effects have not been reported in all studies of morphosyntactic violation processing in adults (see Kim and Osterhout 2005). Furthermore, Oberecker and Friederici (2006) failed to observe an early negativity in 24-month-old children. In a recent study, Silva-Pereyra, Conboy, Klarman and Kuhl (2007) examined ERP responses to phrase structure violations in 36-month-old children. There were two positive ERP effects elicited by the syntactically anomalous vs. non-anomalous real English sentences. The first positivity began at 500 ms and was observed only at left frontal, temporal and posterior temporal electrode sites. The second, later, positive effect was significant only at the left temporal site. While similar to those reported for morphosyntactic violations in 30-, 36-, and 48-month-old children (Silva-Pereyra, Klarman *et al.* 2005; Silva-Pereyra, Rivera-Gaxiola and Kuhl 2005), these results for phrase structure violations showed a more clearly left-lateralized distribution. In contrast, the late positivity to phrase structure violations reported by Oberecker and colleagues (2005) was more right-lateralized.

4.3   ERP effects associated with syntactic processing in the face of reduced lexical-semantic information

In the results reviewed thus far, morphosyntactic anomalies were presented in real sentences that contained intact lexical-semantic information. Of interest is whether preschool-age children show similar syntactic processing effects under conditions of greatly reduced semantic content, or if lexical-semantic information modulates these morphosyntactic effects. Children of preschool age may comprehend word order and other syntactic information in sentences not only because of purely syntactic processing mechanisms but because they also make use of lexical-semantic, pragmatic, and prosodic cues (Hirsh-Pasek and Golinkoff 1996). To this end, Silva-Pereyra and colleagues (2007) recorded ERPs in 36-month-old children to phrase structure violations in "jabberwocky" sentences (i.e., sentences in which content words were replaced with pseudowords while grammatical functional words were retained). Children listened to real English sentences with and without phrase structure violations (as described above) and their jabberwocky counterparts, which contained no cues to sentence meaning other than regular past-tense inflections on pseudoverbs and intact closed class words (determiners and prepositions). The pseudowords differed from the canonical words by only a few phonemes (e.g., My uncle watched a movie about my family / *My macle platched a flovie about my garily*). Certainly, this kind of sentence provides some semantic information, but not complete lexical information. ERPs were time-locked to the final noun phrase, as that was the point at which the phrase structure violation would be detected in the syntactically anomalous sentences (e.g., * *My macle platched about a flovie MY GARILY*).

    Silva-Pereyra and colleagues observed two negative effects to the anomalous vs. non-anomalous jabberwocky sentences over the left hemisphere, from 750–900 ms and from 950–1050 ms. Thus the positivities noted to phrase structure viola-tions in real sentences in these same children were not noted in the jabberwocky sentence condition. One possible explanation for this result is that the children did not note any syntactic anomaly because they were interpreting the final noun phrase as the beginning of a reduced relative clause (as in the construction, "My uncle talked about a movie *my family was in*"). However, P600-like positive effects have not been consistently reported for grammatical violation processing in jab-berwocky studies with adults (Canseco-Gonzalez 2000; Münte, Matzke and Jo-hannes 1997), and Hahne and Jescheniak (2001), who did report a P600 effect for jabberwocky stimuli, have hypothesized that such effects depend on the presence of very early syntactic effects (i.e., an ELAN). In all three studies of jabberwocky processing in adults, negative effects were reported, although at a much shorter latency than those observed in 36-month-old children. In addition, a study by Harris (2001) using jabberwocky sentences with preschool-age children also re-ported negative (but no positive) effects, which were bilateral but largest at left anterior electrode sites. As described above, the longer latency of the effects noted in the children studied by Silva-Pereyra and colleagues may be due to their under-developed language processing systems. It is also possible that these negativies in children reflected different processes than those observed in adults. Specifically, the children may have been attempting to extract meaning at the level of the pseu-dowords rather than at the sentence level. Late negativities, albeit with a right-hemisphere distribution, have been reported in ERP studies of word processing in 13–17 month-old infants, 20-month-old toddlers with delayed expressive lan-guage development, and 20-month-old bilingual toddlers, and appear to reflect the use of attentional resources during more effortful processing (Mills, Conboy and Paton 2005).

4.4   Future directions for sentence processing studies using ERPs

Together, the studies reviewed above indicate that sentence processing mechanisms develop early in life, but are less efficient in young children compared to adults, as reflected by longer latencies and in some cases, broader distributions of ERP ef-fects. Studies of sentence processing in children have been conducted in English and German; a more complete picture would be obtained through studies of sen-tence processing across a wider range of typologically distinct languages. In addi-tion, longitudinal studies might be undertaken to determine how the mechanisms involved in grammatical processing develop with age and language experience.

5   Conclusions

The ERP studies reviewed in this chapter suggest that early language processing mechanisms undergo important changes during the first few years of life. ERPs recorded to syllables have shown that within the same infants, the neural mechanisms involved in processing both native and nonnative phoneme contrasts change between 7 and 11 months, and that these early patterns are predictive of later language learning in the second and third years. ERPs recorded to words in the second year have suggested important links between the experience of learning and using words and the neural activity elicited by those words. ERPs recorded to sentences in the third and fourth years suggest that although adult-like semantic and syntactic processing mechanisms are noted at these ages, there are differences in the latencies and scalp distributions of these components between children and adults. Further research using ERPs with infants and young children will complement behavioral approaches by providing a means of observing how changes in brain systems give rise to and are shaped by advances in early language development.

References

Anderson, J.L., Morgan, J.L. and White, K.S. 2003. "A statistical basis for speech sound discrimination." *Language and Speech* 46 (2–3): 155–82.
Aslin, R.N., Pisoni, D.B., Hennessy, B.L. and Perey, A.J. 1981. "Discrimination of voice onset time by human infants: New findings and implications for the effects of early experience." *Child Development* 52: 1135–45.
Bailey, T.M. and Plunkett, K. 2002. "Phonological specificity in early words." *Cognitive Development* 17: 1265–82.
Ballem, K.D. and Plunkett, K. 2005. "Phonological specificity in children at 1;2." *Journal of Child Language* 32: 159–73.
Bates, E., Bretherton, I. and Snyder, L. 1988. *From first words to grammar: Individual differences and dissociable mechanisms.* New York NY: CUP.
Bates, E. and Goodman, J.C. 1997. "On the inseparability of grammar and the lexicon: Evidence from acquisition, aphasia, and real-time processing. *Language & Cognitive Processes*" 12: 507–84.
Bates, E., Thal, D., Finlay, B. and Clancy, B. 2003. "Early language development and its neural correlates." In *Handbook of Neuropsychology, Vol. 6, Child Neurology (2nd edition)*, I. Rapin and S. Segalowitz (eds.). Amsterdam: Elsevier.
Benedict, H. 1979. "Early lexical development: Comprehension and production." *Journal of Child Language* 6: 183–200.
Bertoncini, J., Bijeljac-Babic, R., Jusczyk, P.W., Kennedy, L.J. and Mehler, J. 1988. "An investigation of young infants' perceptual representations of speech sounds." *Journal of Experimental Psychology: General* 117 (1): 21–33.

Best, C.T. 1994. "The emergence of native-language phonological influences in infants: A perceptual assimilation model." In *The development of speech perception: The transition from speech sounds to spoken words* J.C. Goodman and H.C. Nusbaum (eds.), 167–224. Cambridge, MA: The MIT Press.

Best, C.T., McRoberts, G.W., LaFleur, R. and Silver-Isenstadt, J. 1995. "Divergent developmental patterns for infants' perception of two nonnative consonant contrasts." *Infant Behavior & Development* 18 (3): 339–50.

Best, C. and McRoberts, G. 2003. "Infant perception of non-native consonant contrasts that adults assimilate in different ways." *Language & Speech* 46: 183–216.

Best, C.T., McRoberts, G.W. and Sithole, N.M. 1988. "Examination of perceptual reorganization for non-native speech contrasts: Zulu click discrimination by English-speaking adults and infants." *Journal of Experimental Psychology: Human Perception and Performance* 14 (3): 345–60.

Bortfeld, H., Morgan, J.L, Golinkoff, R.M., Rathbun, K. 2005. "Mommy and me: familiar names help launch babies into speech-stream segmentation." *Psychological Science* 16 (4): 298–304.

Bosch, L. and Sebastián-Gallés, N. 2003. "Simultaneous bilingualism and the perception of language-specific vowel contrast in the first year of life." *Language and Speech* 46: 217–43.

Burnham, D.K. 1986. "Developmental loss of speech perception: Exposure to and experience with a first language." *Applied Psycholinguistics* 7: 207–40.

Canseco-Gonzalez, E. 2000. "Using the recording of event-related brain potentials in the study of sentence processing." In *Language and the Brain: Representation and processing*, Y. Grodzinsky, L. Shapiro and D. Swinney (eds.), 229–266. San Diego, CA: Academic Press.

Carney, A.E., Widin, G.P. and Viemeister, N.F. 1977. "Noncategorical perception of stop consonants differing in VOT." *Journal of the Acoustical Society of America* 62: 961–70.

Cheour, M., Alho, K., Ceponiene, R., Reinikainen, K., Sainio, K., Pohjavuori, M., Aaltonen, O. and Naatanen, R. 1998. "Maturation of mismatch negativity in infants." *International Journal of Psychophysiology* 29 (2): 217–26.

Cheour, M., Alho, K., Sainio, K., Reinikainen, K., Renlund, M., Aaltonen, O., Eerola, O and Näätänen, R. 1997. "The mismatch negativity to changes in speech sounds at the age of three months." *Developmental Neuropsychology* 13 (2): 167–74.

Cheour, M., Ceponiene, R., Lehtokoski, A., Luuk, A., Allik, J., Alho, K. and Näätänen, R. 1998. "Development of language-specific phoneme representations in the infant brain." *Nature Neuroscience* 1: 351–3.

Cheour, M., Leppanen, P. and Kraus, N. 2000. "Mismatch negativity (MMN) as a tool for investigating auditory discrimination and sensory memory in infants and children." *Clinical Neurophysiology* 111: 4–16.

Cheour-Luhtanen, M., Alho, K, Kujala, T., Sainio, K., Reinikainen, K., Renlund, M., Aaltonen, O., Eerola, O. and Näätänen, R. 1995. "Mismatch negativity indicates vowel discrimination in newborns." *Hearing Research* 82: 53–8.

Cheour-Luhtanen, M., Alho, K., Sainio, K., Rinne, T., Reinikainen, K., Pohjavuori, M., Renlund, M., Aaltonen, O., Eerola, O. and Näätänen, R. 1996. "The ontogenetically earliest discriminative response of the human brain." *Psychophysiology* 33:478–81.

Christophe, A., Dupoux, E., Bertoncini, J. and Mehler, J. 1994. "Do infants perceive word boundaries? An empirical study of the bootstrapping of lexical acquisition." *Journal of the Acoustical Society of America* 95 (3): 1570–80.

Conboy, B.T. 2002. Patterns of language processing and growth in early English–Spanish bilingualism. PhD dissertation, UCSD and San Diego State University, 2002. *Dissertation Abstracts International, B: The Sciences & Engineering,* 63 (11-B), (UMI No. 5193).

Conboy, B.T. and Mills, D.L. 2006. "Two languages, one developing brain: Event-related potentials to words in bilingual toddlers." *Developmental Science* 9 (1): F1-F12.

Conboy, B., Rivera-Gaxiola, M., Klarman, L., Aksoylu, E. and Kuhl, P. 2005. "Associations between native and nonnative speech sound discrimination and language development at the end of the first year." In *Supplement to the Proceedings of the 29th Boston University Conference on Language Development* A. Brugos, M.R. Clark-Cotton and S. Ha (eds.), http://www.bu.edu/linguistics/APPLIED/BUCLD/supp29.html.

Conboy, B.T., Sommerville, J. and Kuhl, P. K. submitted. "Cognitive control and the transition to native-like speech perception at 11 months."

Coulson, S., King, J. and Kutas, M. 1998a "Expect the unexpected: event-related brain response to morphosyntactic violations." *Language and Cognitive Processes* 13: 21–58.

Coulson, S., King, J. and Kutas, M. 1998b. "ERPs and domain specificity: Beating a straw horse." *Language and Cognitive Processes* 13 (6): 653–72.

Dale, P.S. and Fenson, L. 1996. "Lexical development norms for young children." *Behavior Research Methods, Instruments and Computers* 28: 125–7.

Dehaene-Lambertz, G. and Baillet, S. 1998. "A phonological representation in the infant brain." *Neuroreport: An International Journal for the Rapid Communication of Research in Neuroscience:* 1885–8.

Dehaene-Lambertz, G. and Dehaene, S. 1994. "Speed and cerebral correlates of syllable discrimination in infants." *Nature* 370: 292–5.

Diamond, A. 1990. "Developmental time course in human infants and infant monkeys, and the neural bases, of inhibitory control in reaching." *Annals of the New York Academy of Sciences* 608: 637–76.

Eilers, R.E., Gavin, W.J. and Oller, D. K. 1982. "Cross-linguistic perception in infancy: Early effects of linguistic experience." *Journal of Child Language* 9 (2): 289–302.

Eilers, R.E., Gavin, W. and Wilson, W.R. 1979. "Linguistic experience and phonemic perception in infancy: A crosslinguistic study." *Child Development* 50 (1): 14–18.

Eilers, R.E. and Minifie, F.D. 1975. "Fricative discrimination in early infancy." *Journal of speech and Hearing Research* 18: 158–67.

Eilers, R.E., Wilson, W.R. and Moore, J.M. 1977. "Developmental changes in speech discrimination in infants." *Journal of Speech and Hearing Research* 20 (4): 766–80.

Eilers, R.E., Wilson, W.R. and Moore, J.M. 1979. "Speech discrimination in the language-innocent and the language-wise: A study in the perception of voice onset time." *Journal of Child Language* 6 (1): 1–18.

Eimas, P.D. 1974. "Auditory and linguistic processing of cues for place of articulation by infants." *Perception and Psychophysics* 16: 513–21.

Eimas, P.D. 1975. "Auditory and phonetic coding of the cues for speech: Discrimination of the /r-l/ distinction by young infants." *Perception and Psychophysics* 18: 341–7.

Eimas, P.D., Siqueland, E.R., Jusczyk, P. and Vigorito, J. 1971. "Speech perception in infants." *Science* 171: 303–6.

Espy, K.A., Molfese, D.L., Molfese, V.J. and Modglin, A. 2004. "Development of auditory event-related potentials in young children and relations to word-level reading abilities at age 8 years." *Annals of Dyslexia* 54 (1) 9–38.

Fennell, C.T. and Werker, J.F. 2003. "Early word learners' ability to access phonetic detail in well-known words." *Language and Speech* 46: 245–64.

Fenson, L., Dale, P.S., Reznick, J.S., Bates, E., Thal, D.J. and Pethick, S.J. 1994. "Variability in early communicative development." *Monographs of the Society for Research in Child Development* 59: 1–173.

Fenson, L., Dale, P.S., Reznick, J.S., Thal, D., Bates, E., Hartung, J.P., Pethick, S. and Reilly, J.S. 1993. *The MacArthur Communicative Development Inventories: User's guide and technical manual.* San Diego, CA: Singular.

Fernald, A., Perfors, A. and Marchman, V.A. 2006. "Picking up speed in understanding: Speech processing efficiency and vocabulary growth across the second year." *Developmental Psychology* 42: 98–116.

Fernald, A., Pinto, J.P., Swingley, D., Weinberg, A. and McRoberts, G.W. 1998. "Rapid gains in speed of verbal processing by infants in the second year. *Psychological Science* 9: 72–75.

Fernald, A., Swingley, D. and Pinto, J.P. 2001. "When half a word is enough: Infants can recognize spoken words using partial phonetic information." *Child Development* 72: 1003–15.

Fikkert, P. 2005. "Getting sounds structures in mind. Acquisition bridging linguistics and psychology?" In *Twenty-first century psycholinguistics: Four cornerstones*, A.E. Cutler (ed.), 43–56. Mahwah, NJ: Lawrence Erlbaum Associates.

Friedrich, M. and Friederici, A.D. 2004. "N400-like semantic incongruity effect in 19-month-olds: Processing known words in picture contexts." *Journal of Cognitive Neuroscience* 16: 1465–77.

Friedrich, M. and Friederici, A.D. 2005a. "Lexical priming and semantic integration reflected in the ERP of 14-month-olds." *NeuroReport* 16: 653–6.

Friedrich, M and Friederici, A.D. 2005b "Semantic sentence processing reflected in the event-related potentials of one- and two-year-old children." *Neuroreport* 16: 1801–4.

Friedrich, M. and Friederici, A.D. 2005c. "Phonotactic knowledge and lexical-semantic processing in one-year-olds: Brain responses to words and nonsense words in picture contexts." *Journal of Cognitive Neuroscience* 17: 1785–802.

Friedrich, M. and Friederici, A.D. 2006. "Early N400 development and later language acquisition." *Psychophysiology* 43 (1): 1–12.

Friederici, A.D. 2002. "Towards a neural basis of auditory sentence processing." *Trends in Cognitive Sciences* 6: 78–84.

Friederici, A.D. 1995. "The time course of syntactic activation during language processing: a model based on neuropsychological and neurophysiological data." *Brain and Language* 50: 259–81.

Friederici, A.D., Friedrich, M. and Weber, C. 2002. "Neural manifestation of cognitive and precognitive mismatch detection in early infancy." *Neuroreport: For Rapid Communication of Neuroscience Research* 13 (10): 1251–4.

Friederici, A.D. and Wessels, J.M.I. 1993. "Phonotactic knowledge of word boundaries and its use in infant speech perception." *Perception & Psychophysics* 54: 287–95.

Goldberg, E. and Costa, L. D. 1981. "Hemisphere differences in the acquisition and use of descriptive systems." *Brain and Language* 14: 144–73.

González-Garrido, A.A., Oropeza de Alba, J.L., Riestra Castaneda, R., Riestra Castaneda, J.M., Perez Avalos, M.C. and Valdes Sosa, M. 1997. "Event related brain potentials to semantically incongruent words in children of different ages." *Archives of Medical Research* 28: 109–13.

Goodsitt, J.V., Morgan, J.L. and Kuhl, P.K. 1993. "Perceptual strategies in prelingual speech segmentation." *Journal of Child Language* 20: 229–52.

Hagoort, P., Brown, C.M. and Osterhout, L. 1999. "The neurocognition of syntactic processing."
In: *The neurocognition of language,* C.M. Brown and P. Hagoort (eds.), 273–316. New York,
NY: OUP.

Hahne, A., Eckstein K. and Friederici, A.D. 2004. "Brain signatures of syntactic and semantic
processes during children's language development." *Journal of Cognitive Neuroscience* 6:
1302–18.

Hahne, A. and Jescheniak, J.D. 2001. "What's left if the Jabberwock gets the semantics? An ERP
investigation into semantic and syntactic processes during auditory sentence comprehension." *Cognitive Brain Research* 11: 199–212.

Hallé, P. and de Boysson-Bardies, B. 1994. "Emergence of an early lexicon: Infants' recognition
of words." *Infant Behavior and Development* 17: 119–29.

Hallé, P. and de Boysson-Bardies, B. 1996. "The format of representation of recognized words in
infants' early receptive lexicon." *Infant Behavior and Development* 19: 435–51.

Harris, A.M. 2001. "Processing semantic and grammatical information in auditory sentences:
Electrophysiological evidence from children and adults." PhD dissertation, University of
Oregon, 2001. *Dissertation Abstracts International: Section B: The Sciences & Engineering,*
61 (12-B), (UMI No. 6729).

Hernández, A.E., Dapretto, M., Mazziotta, J. and Bookheimer, S. 2001. "Language switching and
language representation in Spanish–English bilinguals: an fMRI study." *NeuroImage* 14:
510–20.

Hernández, A., Martínez, A. and Kohnert, K. 2000. "In search of the language switch: An fMRI
study of picture naming in Spanish–English bilinguals." *Brain and Language* 73 (3): 421–31.

Hirsh-Pasek, K. and Golinkoff, R.M. 1996. "A coalition model of language comprehension." In
The origins of grammar: Evidence from early language comprehension, K. Hirsh-Pasek and
R.M. Golinkoff (eds.), 150–203. Cambridge MA: The MIT Press.

Holcomb P.J., Coffey S.A. and Neville H.J. 1992. "Visual and auditory sentence processing: A
developmental analysis using event-related brain potentials." *Developmental Neuropsychology* 8: 203–41.

Hollich, G., Hirsh-Pasek, K. and Golinkoff, R. 2000. "Breaking the language barrier: An emergentist coalition model for the origins of word learning." *Monographs of the Society for Research in Child Development* 65 (3, Serial No. 262).

Houston, D.M., Santelmann, L.M and Jusczyk, P.W. 2004. "English-learning infants' segmentation
of trisyllabic words from fluent speech. *Language and Cognitive Processes* 19 (1): 97–136.

Huttenlocher P.R. 2003. "Basic neuroscience research has important implications for child development." *Nature Neuroscience* 6: 541.

Jackson, G.M., Swainson, R., Cunnington, R. and Jackson, S.R. 2001. "ERP correlates of execu-
tive control during repeated language switching. *Bilingualism: Language and Cognition* 4
(2): 169–78.

Jackson-Maldonado, D., Thal, D., Marchman, V., Bates, E. and Gutiérrez-Clellen, V. 1993. "Early
lexical development of Spanish-speaking infants and toddlers." *Journal of Child Language*
20: 523–49.

Jackson-Maldonado, D., Thal, D., Marchman, V., Fenson, L., Newton, T. and Conboy, B. 2003. *El
Inventario del Desarrollo de Habilidades Comunicativas: User's guide and technical manual.* Baltimore, MD: Paul H. Brookes Publishing.

Jamieson, D.G. and Morosan, D.E. 1986. "Training non-native speech contrasts in adults: Acquisition of the English /θ/-/ð/ contrast by francophones." *Perception & Psychophysics* 40: 205–15.

Jamieson, D.G. and Morosan, D.E. 1989. "Training new, nonnative speech contrasts: A comparison of the prototype and perceptual fading techniques." *Canadian Journal of Psychology* 43 (1): 88–96.

Johnson, E.K. and Jusczyk, P.W. 2001. "Word segmentation by 8-month-olds: When speech cues count more than statistics." *Journal of Memory and Language* 44: 548–67.

Jusczyk, P.W. 1993. "From general to language-specific capacities: The WRAPSA model of how speech perception develops." *Journal of Phonetics* 21 (1–2): 3–28.

Jusczyk, P.W. 1994. "Infant speech perception and the development of the mental lexicon." In *The development of speech perception: The transition from speech sounds to spoken word*, J.C. Goodman, and H.C. Nusbaum (eds.), 227–27. Cambridge, MA: The MIT Press.

Jusczyk, P. W. 1997. *The discovery of spoken language*. Cambridge, MA: The MIT Press.

Jusczyk, P.W. 2003. "The role of speech perception capacities in early language acquisition." In *Mind, brain, and language: Multidisciplinary perspective*, M.T. Banich and M. Mack (eds.), 61–83. Mahwah, NJ: Lawrence Erlbaum Associates.

Jusczyk, P. W. and Aslin, R.N. 1995. "Infants' detection of sound patterns of words in fluent speech." *Cognitive Psychology* 29, 1–23.

Jusczyk, P.W., Copan, H. and Thompson, E. 1978. "Perception by 2-month-old infants of glide contrasts in multisyllabic utterances." *Perception & Psychophysics* 24 (6): 515–20.

Jusczyk, P.W. and Hohne, E.A. 1997. "Infants' memory for spoken words. *Science* 277 (5334): 1984–6.

Jusczyk, P.W., Hohne, E.A. and Bauman, A. 1999. "Infants'sensitivity to allophonic cues for word segmentation." *Perception & Psychophysics* 61: 1465–76.

Jusczyk, P.W., Houston, D. and Newsome, M. 1999. "The beginnings of word segmentation in English-learning infants." *Cognitive Psychology* 39: 159–207.

Jusczyk, P.W., Luce, P.A. and Charles Luce, J. 1994. "Infants' sensitivity to phonotactic patterns in the native language." *Journal of Memory and Language* 33: 630–45.

Kim, A. and Osterhout, L. 2005. "The independence of combinatory semantic processing: Evidence from event-related potentials." *Journal of Memory and Language* 52 (2): 205–25.

King, J.W. and Kutas, M. 1995. "Who did what and when? Using word- and clause related ERPs to monitor working memory usage in reading." *Journal of Cognitive Neuroscience* 7: 378–97.

Klarman, L., Rivera-Gaxiola, M., Conboy, B. and Kuhl, P.K. 2004. "Event-related potentials to speech: Individual variation and vocabulary growth." Poster presented at the Society for Neuroscience Annual Meeting, San Diego, October 23–27, 2004.

Kluender, R. and Kutas, M. 1993a. "Bridging the gap: Evidence from ERPs on the processing of unbounded dependencies." *Journal of Cognitive Neuroscience* 5 196–214.

Kluender, R. and Kutas, M. 1993b. "Subjacency as a processing phenomenon." *Language and Cognitive Processes* 8: 573–633.

Kuhl, P.K. 1991. "Human adults and human infants show a 'perceptual magnet effect' for the prototypes of speech categories, monkeys do not." *Perception & Psychophysics* 50 (2): 93–107.

Kuhl, P.K. 1993. "Infant speech perception: A window on psycholinguistic development." *International Journal of Psycholinguistics* 9 (1): 33–56.

Kuhl, P.K. 2000a. "A new view of language acquisition. *Proceedings of the National Academy of Sciences, USA* 97: 11850–7.

Kuhl, P.K. 2000b. „Language, mind, and brain: Experience alters perception." In *The new cognitive neurosciences, 2nd edn,* M. Gazzaniga (ed.), 99–115. Cambridge, MA: The MIT Press.

Kuhl, P.K., Conboy, B.T., Coffey-Corina, S., Padden, D., Rivera-Gaxiola, M. and Nelson, T. 2007. "Phonetic Learning as a Pathway: New Data and Native Language Magnet Theory-expanded (NLM-e)." *Philosophical Transactions of the Royal Society B.*

Kuhl, P.K., Conboy, B.T., Padden, D., Nelson, T. and Pruitt, J. 2005. "Early speech perception and later language development: Implications for the 'critical period'". *Language Learning and Development* 1: 237–64.

Kuhl, P.K. and Miller, J.D. 1982. "Discrimination of auditory target dimensions in the presence or absence of variation in a second dimension by infants." *Perception and Psychophysics* 31 (3): 279–92.

Kuhl, P.K., Stevens, E., Hayashi, A., Deguchi, T., Kiritani, S. and Iverson, P. 2006. "Infants show a facilitation effect for native language phonetic perception between 6 and 12 months." *Developmental Science* 9: F13-F21.

Kuhl, P.K., Tsao, F.M. and Liu, H.M. 2003. "Foreign-language experience in infancy: Effects of short- term exposure and social interaction on phonetic learning." *Proceedings of the National Academy of Science* 100 (15): 9096–101

Kuhl, P.K., Williams, K.A., Lacerda, F., Stevens, K.N. and Lindblom, B. 1992. "Linguistic experience alters phonetic perception in infants by 6 months of age." *Science* 255: 606–8.

Kutas M. 1997. "Views on how the electrical activity that the brain generates reflects the functions of different language structures." *Psychophysiology,* 34: 383–98.

Kutas, M. and Hillyard, S.A. 1980. "Reading senseless sentences: Brain potentials reflect semantic incongruity." *Science* 207: 203–20.

Lalonde, C. and Werker, J. 1995. "Cognitive influence on cross-language speech perception in infancy." *Infant Behavior and Development* 18: 495–475.

Lasky, R.E., Syrdal-Lasky, A. and Klein, R.E. 1975. "VOT discrimination by four to six and a half month old infants from Spanish environments." *Journal of Experimental Child Psychology* 20: 215–25.

Leavitt, L.A., Brown, J.W., Morse, P.A. and Graham, F.K. 1976. "Cardiac orienting and auditory discrimination in 6-wk-old infants." *Developmental Psychology* 12 (6) 514–23.

Liberman, A.M. and Mattingly, I.G. 1985. "The motor theory of speech perception revised." *Cognition* 21: 1–36.

Liu, H.-M., Kuhl, P.K. and Tsao, F.-M. 2003. "An association between mothers' speech clarity and infants' speech discrimination skills." *Developmental Science* 6(3): F1-F10.

Locke, J.L. 1989. "Cognitive influence on cross-language speech perception in infancy.Babbling and early speech: Continuity and individual differences." *First Language* 9 (26, Pt 2): 191–205.

Logan, J.S, Lively, S.E. and Pisoni, D.B. 1991. "Training Japanese listeners to identify /r/ and /l/: A first report." *Journal of the Acoustical Society of America* 89 (2): 874–86.

MacNeilage, P.F. and Davis, B.L. 2000. On the origin of internal structure of word forms. *Science* 288 (5465): 527–31.

MacNeilage, P.F., Davis, B.L. and Matyear, C.L. 1997. "Babbling and first words: Phonetic similarities and differences." *Speech Communication* 22 (2–3): 269–277.

Mandel, D.R., Jusczyk, P.W. and Pisoni, D.B. 1995. "Infants' recognition of the sound patterns of their own names." *Psychological Science* 6: 315–18.

Mattys, S. L. and Jusczyk, P. W. 2001a. "Do infants segment words or recurring contiguous patterns? *Journal of Experimental Psychology: Human Perception and Performance* 27: 644–55.

Mattys, S.L. and Jusczyk, P.W. 2001b. "Phonotactic cues for segmentation of fluent speech by infants." *Cognition* 78: 91–121.

Mattys, S., Jusczyk, P., Luce, P. and Morgan, J. 1999. "Phonotatic and prosodic effects on word segmentation in infants." *Cognitive Psychology* 38: 465–94.

Maye, J., Werker, J.F. and Gerken, L. 2002. "Infant sensitivity to distributional information can affect phonetic discrimination." *Cognition* 82: B101-B111.

McCathren, R.B., Yoder, P.J. and Warren, S.F. 1999. "The relationship between prelinguistic vocalization and later expressive vocabulary in young children with development delay." *Journal of Speech, Language, and Hearing Research* 42 (4) 915–24.

McClasky, C.L., Pisoni, D.B. and Carrell, T.D. 1983. "Transfer of training of a new linguistic contrast in voicing." *Perception and Psychophysics* 34: 323–30.

McClelland, J.L, Fiez, J.A. and McCandliss, B.D. 2002. "Teaching the /r/-/l/ discrimination to Japanese adults: Behavioral and neural aspects." *Physiology & Behavior* 77 (4–5): 657–62.

McCune, L. and Vihman, M.M. 2001. "Early phonetic and lexical development: A productivity approach." *Journal of Speech, Language, and Hearing Research* 44 (3): 670–84.

McMurray, B. and Aslin, R.N. 2005. "Infants are sensitive to within-category variation in speech perception." *Cognition* 95: B15-B26.

Mehler, J., Dupoux, E. and Segui, J. 1990. "Constraining models of lexical access: The onset of word recognition." In *Cognitive models of speech processing: Psycholinguistic and computational perspectives*, G.T.M. Altmann (ed), 236–62. Cambridge, MA: The MIT Press.

Miller, J.L. and Eimas, P.D. 1996. "Internal structure of voicing categories in early infancy." *Perception and Psychophysics* 58: 1157–67.

Miller, C.L. and Morse, P.A. 1976. "The heart of categorical speech discrimination in young infants." *Journal of Speech & Hearing Research* 19 (3): 578–89.

Miller, C.L., Morse, P.A. and Dorman, M.F. 1977. "Cardiac indices of infant speech perception: Orienting and burst discrimination." *Quarterly Journal of Experimental Psychology* 29 (3): 533–45.

Mills, D., Coffey-Corina, S. and Neville, H. 1993. "Language acquisition and cerebral specialization in 20-month-old infants." *Journal of Cognitive Neuroscience* 5: 317–34.

Mills, D., Coffey-Corina, S. and Neville, H. 1997. "Language comprehension and cerebral specialization from 13 to 20 months." *Developmental Neuropsychology* 13 (3): 397–445.

Mills, D., Conboy, B.T. and Paton, C. 2005. "How learning new words shapes the organization of the infant brain." In *Symbol use and symbolic representation* L. Namy (ed.), 123–53. Mahwah, NJ: Lawrence Erlbaum Associates.

Mills, D., Plunkett, K., Prat, C. and Schafer, G. 2005. "Watching the infant brain learn words: effects of language and experience." *Cognitive Development* 20: 19–31.

Mills, D., Prat, C., Stager, C., Zangl, R., Neville, H. and Werker, J. 2004. "Language experience and the organization of brain activity to phonetically similar words: ERP evidence from 14- and 20-month-olds." *Journal of Cognitive Neuroscience* 16:1452–64.

Moffitt, A.R. 1971. Consonant cue perception by twenty- to twenty-four-week-old infants. *Child Development* 42: 717–31.

Molfese, D.L. 1989. Electrophysiological correlates of word meanings in 14-month-old human infants. *Developmental Neuropsychology*, 5 (2–3): 79–103.

Molfese, D.L. 1990. "Auditory evoked responses recorded from 16-month-old human infants to words they did and did not know.: *Brain and Language*, 38 (3): 345–63.

Molfese, D.L. 2000. "Predicting dyslexia at 8 years of age using neonatal brain responses." *Brain and Language* 72: 238–45.

Molfese, D.L. and Molfese, V.J. 1985. "Electrophysiological indices of auditory discrimination in newborn infants: The bases for predicting later language development?" *Infant Behavior & Development* 8 (2): 197–211.

Molfese, D.L. and Molfese, V. 1997. "Discrimination of language skills at five years of age using event-related potentials recorded at birth." *Developmental Neuropsychology* 13: 135–56.

Molfese, D.L., Molfese, V.J. and Espy, K.A. 1999. "The predictive use of event-related potentials in language development and the treatment of language disorders." *Developmental Neuropsychology* 16 (3): 373–7.

Molfese, D.L., Morse, P.A. and Peters, C.J. 1990. "Auditory evoked responses to names for different objects: Cross-modal processing as a basis for infant language acquisition." *Developmental Psychology* 26 (5): 780–95.

Molfese, D.L. and Wetzel, W.F. 1992. "Short- and long-term auditory recognition memory in 14-month-old human infants: Electrophysiological correlates." *Developmental Neuropsychology* 8 (2–3): 135–60.

Molfese, D.L., Wetzel, W.F. and Gill, L.A. 1993. "Known versus unknown word discriminations in 12-month-old human infants: Electrophysiological correlates." *Developmental Neuropsychology* 9 (3–4): 241–58.

Moreno, E., Federmeier, K. and Kutas, M. 2002. "Switching languages, switching palabras (words): An electrophysiological study of code switching." *Brain and Language* 80 (2): 188–207.

Morgan, J.L. and Saffran, J.R. 1995. "Emerging integration of sequential and suprasegmental information in preverbal speech segmentation." *Child Development* 66 (4): 911–36.

Morosan, D.E. and Jamieson, D.G. 1989. "Evaluation of a technique for training new speech contrasts: Generalization across voices, but not word-position or task." *Journal of Speech & Hearing Research* 32 (3): 501–11.

Morse, P.A. 1972. "The discrimination of speech and nonspeech stimuli in early infancy." *Journal of Experimental Child Psychology* 14 (3): 477–92.

Münte, T.F., Heinze, H.J. and Mangun, G.R. 1993. "Dissociation of brain activity related to syntactic and semantic aspects of language." *Journal of Cognitive Neuroscience* 5: 335–44.

Münte, T.F., Matzke, M. and Johannes, S. 1997. "Brain activity associated with syntactic incongruencies in words and pseudo-words." *Journal of Cognitive Neuroscience* 9: 318–29.

Näätänen, R. 1999. "The perception of speech sounds by the human brain as reflected by the mismatch negativity (MMN) and its magnetic equivalent (MMNm)." *Psychophysiology* 38: 1–21.

Näätänen, R., Gaillard, A. W.K. and Mäntysalo, S. 1978. "Early selective-attention effect on evoked potential reinterpreted." *Acta Psychologica* 42: 313–29.

Näätänen, R., Lehtokoski, A., Lennes, M., Cheour, M., Huotilainen, M., Iivonen, A.,Vainio, M., Alku, P., Ilmoniemi, R.J., Luuk, A., Allik, J., Sinkkonen, J. and Alho, K. 1997. "Language-specific phoneme representations revealed by electric and magnetic brain responses." *Nature* 385: 432–4.

Nazzi, T. 2005. "Use of phonetic specificity during the acquisition of new words: Differences between consonants and vowels." *Cognition* 98: 13–30.

Neville, H.J., Coffey, S.A., Holcomb, P.J. and Tallal, P. 1993. "The neurobiology of sensory and language processing in language-impaired children." *Journal of Cognitive Neuroscience* 5: 235–53.

Neville, H.J. and Mills, D.L. 1997. "Epigenesis of language." *Mental Retardation & Developmental Disabilities Research Reviews* 3: 282–92.

Newman, R., Ratner, N.B., Jusczyk, A.M, Jusczyk, P.W. and Dow, K.A. 2006. "Infants' early ability to segment the conversational speech signal predicts later language development: A retrospective analysis." *Developmental Psychology* 42 (4): 643–55.

Oberecker, R. and Friederici, A.D. 2006. "Syntactic event-related potential components in 24-month-olds' sentence comprehension." *Neuroreport* 17 (10): 1017–21.

Oberecker, R., Friedrich, M. and Friederici, A.D. 2005. "Neural correlates of syntactic processing in two-year-olds." *Journal of Cognitive Neuroscience* 17 (10): 1667–78.

Oller, D.K., Eilers, R.E, Neal, A.R., Schwartz, H.K. 1999. "Precursors to speech in infancy: The prediction of speech and language disorders." *Journal of Communication Disorders* 32 (4): 223–45.

Oviatt, S.L. 1980. "The emerging ability to comprehend language: An experimental approach." *Child Development* 51: 97–106.

Pang, E., Edmonds, G., Desjardins, R., Khan, S., Trainor, L. and Taylor, M. 1998. "Mismatch negativity to speech stimuli in 8-month-old infants and adults." *International Journal of Psychohysiology* 29: 227–36.

Pater, J., Stager, C. and Werker, J.F. 2004. The perceptual acquisition of phonological contrasts. *Language* 80: 361–79.

Pegg, J.E. and Werker, J.F. 1997. "Adult and infant perception of two English phones." *Journal of the Acoustical Society of America* 102: 3742–53.

Picton, T.W., Bentin, S., Berg, P., Donchin, E., Hillyard, S.A., Johnson, R., Miller, G.A., Ritter, W., Ruchkin, D.S, Rugg, M.D. and Taylor, M.J. 2000. "Guidelines for using human event-related potentials to study cognition: recording standards and publication criteria." *Psychophysiology* 37: 127–52.

Pisoni, D.B., Aslin, R.N., Perey, A.J. and Hennessy, B.L. 1982. "Some effects of laboratory training on identification and discrimination of voicing contrasts in stop consonants." *Journal of Experimental Psychology: Human Perception and Performance* 8: 297–314.

Polka, L. 1991. "Cross-language speech perception in adults: Phonemic, phonetic, and acoustic contributions." *Journal of the Acoustical Society of America* 89 (6): 2961–77.

Polka, L. 1992. "Characterizing the influence of native language experience on adult speech perception." *Perception & Psychophysics* 52: 37–52.

Polka, L. and Bohn, O.S. 1996. "A cross-language comparison of vowel perception in English-learning and German-learning infants." *Journal of the Acoustical Society of America* 100: 577–92.

Polka, L. Colantonio, C. and Sundara, M. 2001. "A cross-language comparison of /d/-/ð/ perception: Evidence for a new developmental pattern." *Journal of the Acoustical Society of America* 109: 2190–201.

Polka, L. and Werker, J.F. 1994. "Developmental changes in perception of non-native vowel contrasts." *Journal of Experimental Psychology: Human Perception and Performance* 20: 421–35.

Pruden, S.M, Hirsh-Pasek, K., Golinkoff, R.M., and Hennon, E.A. 2006. "The birth of words: Ten-month-olds learn words through perceptual salience." *Child Development* 77 (2): 266–80.

Rinne, T., Alho, K., Alku, P., Holi, M., Sinkkonen, J., Virtanen, J., Bertrand, O. and Naatanen, R. 1999. "Analysis of speech sounds is left-hemisphere predominant at 100–150 ms after sound onset." *Neuroreport: For Rapid Communication of Neuroscience Research* 10 (5): 1113–7.

Rivera-Gaxiola, M., Csibra, G., Johnson, M.H. and Karmiolff-Smith, A. 2000a. "Electrophysiological correlates of cross-linguistic speech perception in native English speakers." *Behavioral Brain Research* 111:13–23.

Rivera-Gaxiola, M., Csibra, G., Johnson, M.H. and Karmiolff-Smith, A. 2000b. "Electrophysiological correlates of category goodness." *Behavioral Brain Research* 112: 1–11.

Rivera-Gaxiola, M., Klarman, L., Garcia-Sierra, A. and Kuhl, P.K. 2005. "Neural patterns to speech and vocabulary growth in American infants." *NeuroReport* 16: 495–8.

Rivera-Gaxiola, M., Lara-Ayala, L., Cadena-Salazar, C., Jackson-Maldonado, D. and Kuhl, P.K. submitted. "Neural correlates of discrimination of voice-onset time speech contrasts in Mexican infants."

Rivera-Gaxiola, M., Silva-Pereyra, J., Klarman, L., Garcia-Sierra, A., Lara-Ayala, L., Cadena-Salazar, C. and Kuhl, P. K. in press. "Principal component analyses and scalp distribution of the auditory P150–250 and N250–550 to speech contrasts in Mexican and American infants." *Developmental Neuropsychology* 31: 363–78.

Rivera-Gaxiola, M., Silva-Pereyra, J. and Kuhl, P.K. 2005. "Brain potentials to native and nonnative speech contrasts in 7- and 11-month-old American infants." *Developmental Science* 8: 162–72.

Saffran, J.R., Aslin, R.N. and Newport, E.L. 1996. "Statistical learning by 8-month old infants." *Science* 274: 1926–8.

Schafer, G. 2005. "Infants can learn decontextualized words before their first birthday." *Child Development* 76: 87–96.

Silva-Pereyra, J., Conboy, B.T., Klarman, L. and Kuhl, P.K. 2007. "Grammatical processing without semantics? An event-related brain potential study of preschoolers using jabberwocky sentences." *Journal of Cognitive Neuroscience* 19 (6): 1050–65.

Silva-Pereyra, J., Klarman, L., Lin, L.J.F. and Kuhl, P.K. 2005. "Sentence processing in 30-month-old children: An event-related brain potential study." *NeuroReport* 16: 645–8.

Silva-Pereyra J., Rivera-Gaxiola M. and Kuhl P. 2005. "An event-related brain potential study of sentence comprehension in preschoolers: Semantic and morphosyntactic processing." *Cognitive Brain Research* 23: 247–58.

Sommerville, J.A. and Woodward, A.L. 2005. "Pulling out the intentional structure of action: The relation between action processing and action production in infancy." *Cognition* 95 (1): 1–30.

Stager, C.L. and Werker, J.F. 1997. "Infants listen for more phonetic detail in speech perception than in word-learning tasks." *Nature* 388: 381–2.

Stoel-Gammon, C. 1989. "Prespeech and early speech development of two late talkers." *First Language* 9: 207–24.

Streeter, L.A. 1976. "Language perception of 2-month-old infants shows effects of both innate mechanisms and experience." *Nature* 259: 39–41.

Swingley, D. 2003. "Phonetic detail in the developing lexicon." *Language and Speech* 46: 265–94.

Swingley, D. 2005. "11-month-olds' knowledge of how familiar words sound." *Developmental Science* 8 (5): 432–43.

Swingley, D. and Aslin, R.N. 2000. "Spoken word recognition and lexical representation in very young children." *Cognition* 76: 147–66.

Swingley, D. and Aslin, R.N. 2002. "Lexical neighborhoods and the word-form representations of 14-month-olds." *Psychological Science* 13: 480–4.

Swoboda, P.J., Morse, P.A. and Leavitt, L.A. 1976. "Continuous vowel discrimination in normal and at risk infants." *Child Development* 47 (2): 459–65.

Tees, R.C. and Werker, J.F. 1984. "Perceptual flexibility: Maintenance or recovery of the ability to discriminate nonnative speech sounds." *Canadian Journal of Psychology* 38: 579–90.

Thierry G., Vihman M. and Roberts M. 2003. "Familiar words capture the attention of 11-month-olds in less than 250 ms." *Neuroreport* 14: 2307–10.

Tincoff, R. and Jusczyk, P.W. 1999. "Some beginnings of word comprehension in 6-month-olds." *Psychological Science* 10 (2): 172–5.

Trehub, S.E. 1973. "Infants' sensitivity to vowel and tonal contrasts." *Developmental Psychology* 9: 91–6.

Trehub, S.E. and Rabinovitch, M.S. 1972. "Auditory-linguistic sensitivity in early infancy." *Developmental Psychology* 6: 74–7.

Trehub, S.E. 1976. "The discrimination of foreign speech contrasts by infants and adults." *Child Development* 47: 466–72.

Tremblay, K.L. and Kraus, N. 2002. "Auditory training induces asymmetrical changes in cortical neural activity." *Journal of Speech, Language, and Hearing Research* 45 (3): 564–72.

Tremblay, K., Kraus, N. and McGee, T. 1998. "The time course of auditory perceptual learning: Neurophysiological changes during speech-sound training." *Neuroreport: An International Journal for the Rapid Communication of Research in Neuroscience* 9 (16): 3557–60.

Tsao, F.M., Liu, H.M. and Kuhl, P.K. 2004. "Speech perception in infancy predicts language development in the second year of life: A longitudinal study." *Child Development* 75: 1067–84.

Tsao, F. M., Liu, H.M. and Kuhl, P.K. 2006. "Perception of native and non-native affricate-fricative contrasts: Cross-language tests on adults and infants." *Journal of the Acoustical Society of America* 120 (4): 2285–94.

Van de Weijer, J. 1998. Language input for word discovery. PhD dissertation, University of Nijmegen.

Vihman, M.M. 1993. "Variable paths to early word production." *Journal of Phonetics* 21 (1–2): 61–82.

Vihman, M.M., Ferguson, C.A. and Elbert, M. 1986. "Phonological development from babbling to speech: Common tendencies and individual differences." *Applied Psycholinguistics* 7 (1): 3–40.

Vihman, M.M., Nakai, S., DePaolis, R.A. and Halle, P. 2004. "The role of accentual pattern in early lexical representation." *Journal of Memory and Language* 50: 336–53.

Waxman, S.R. and Booth, A.E. 2003. "The origins and evolution of links between word learning and conceptual organization: New evidence from 11-month-olds." *Developmental Science* 6 (2): 130–7.

Waxman, S.R. and Braun, I. 2005. "Consistent (but not variable) names as invitations to form object categories: New evidence from 12-month-old infants." *Cognition* 95 (3): B59-B68.

Weber, C. Hahne, A., Friedrich, M. and Friederici, A.D. 2004. "Discrimination of word stress in early infant perception: electrophysiological evidence." *Cognitive Brain Research* 18: 149–61.

Werker, J.F., Cohen, L.B., Lloyd, V., Stager, C. and Casasola, M. 1998. "Acquisition of word- object associations by 14-month-old infants." *Developmental Psychology* 34: 1289–309.

Werker, J.F. and Curtin, S. 2005. "PRIMIR: A developmental model of speech processing." *Language Learning and Development* 1: 197–234.

Werker, J.F., Fennell, C.T., Corcoran, K.M. and Stager, C.L. 2002. "Infants' ability to learn phonetically similar words: Effects of age and vocabulary." *Infancy* 3: 1–30.

Werker, J.F. and Lalonde, C. 1988. "Cross-language speech perception: Initial capabilities and developmental change." *Developmental Psychology* 24: 672–83.

Werker, J.F and Logan, J.S. 1985. "Cross-language evidence for three factors in speech perception." *Perception and Psychophysics* 37: 35–44.

Werker, J. and Tees, R. 1984a. "Cross-language speech perception: Evidence for perceptual reor-
    ganization during the first year of life." *Infant Behavior and Development* 7: 49–63.
Werker J.F. and Tees R.C. 1984b. "Phonemic and phonetic factors in adult cross-language speech
    perception." *Journal of the Acoustical Society of America* 75: 1866–78.
Werker, J.F. and Tees, R.C. 1999. "Influences on infant speech processing: toward a new synthe-
    sis." *Annual Review of Psychology* 50: 509–35.
Werker, J.F. and Yeung, H.H. 2005. "Infant speech perception bootstraps word learning." *Trends
    in Cognitive Sciences* 9 (11): 519–27.
Woodward, A.L., Markman, E.M. and Figzimmons, C.M. 1994. "Rapid word learning in 13- and
    18-month-olds." *Developmental Psychology* 30: 553–66.
Zangl, R., Klarman, L., Thal, D., Fernald, A. and Bates, E. 2005. "Dynamics of word comprehen-
    sion in infancy: Developments in timing, accuracy, and resistance to acoustic degradation."
    Journal of Cognition and Development 6 (2): 179–208.

CHAPTER 3

Behavioral and electrophysiological exploration of early word segmentation in French

Distinguishing the syllabic and lexical levels

Thierry Nazzi, Galina Iakimova, Josiane Bertoncini, Sylvain Mottet, Josette Serres and Scania de Schonen

The present chapter deals with issues relating to the acquisition of the sound patterns of individual words in a cross linguistic perspective but with a special emphasis on French. The aim is to specify how the mechanisms allowing the retrieval of these sound patterns emerge during development. Although it will become clear that almost all the data on this issue have so far been gathered using behavioral methods, we argue for the need of an approach integrating behavioral and electrophysiological evidence.

The learning of sound patterns is a requirement for the acquisition of the lexicon, given that each word corresponds to the association of a sound pattern with its appropriate concept/meaning. But access to individual sound patterns is also crucial for the acquisition of syntax, given that most theories of syntax acquisition assume that infants process sentences as sequences of individuated words.

Although some learning of individual sound patterns has to have happened by the first birthday, as attested by emerging word comprehension and word production abilities, this sound pattern learning is no trivial task. A first difficulty comes from the fact that the linguistic input addressed to infants (like that addressed to adults) consists of fluent speech rather than isolated word forms. The presence of isolated word forms in the input has been investigated in a few studies of infants acquiring English (Aslin 1993; Brent and Siskind 2001) and in a study of a Dutch/German bilingual infant (van de Weijer 1998). In these studies, infant-directed speech was found to consist mainly of multiword utterances, with words spoken in isolation accounting for no more than 10% of all the words present in the analyzed samples. Therefore, infants will not be able to directly access most of the words they hear.

Could lexical acquisition rely solely on these few words appearing in isolation in the input? Some support for this comes from a study showing that the frequency with which a word is presented in isolation (rather than the total frequency of that word) partly predicts whether it will be produced several months later (Brent and Siskind 2001). Therefore, acquisition of a given word seems to be facilitated by the fact that it sometimes appears in isolation. However, van de Weijer (1998) has pointed out another difficulty for the acquisition of sound patterns: not every type of word appears in isolation (e.g., grammatical words), and many of the words that appear in isolation correspond to fillers ("yes," "hmm," …), vocatives ("baby's name") and social expressions ("hi!,"…). It therefore appears that the learning of individual word patterns will have to rely on speech segmentation abilities (and abilities to phonologically represent the segmented word forms) that extract word patterns from fluent speech.

This proposal of a reliance on segmentation abilities in order to extract individual word patterns from fluent speech raises the issue of the markings of word boundaries in fluent speech. While in many writing systems boundaries are marked by blank spaces between the consecutive words making up a sentence, no equivalent obvious markings of word boundaries have been found in the speech signal: there are no obvious pauses between words in connected speech, and no clear and systematic markings of word boundaries at the acoustic level (Cole and Jakimik 1978, 1980; Klatt 1979, 1989). As can be seen on Figure 1 representing the waveform of the French sentence "Il y a un lapin dans le jardin" (There is a rabbit in the garden), none of the seven word boundaries in the sentence are marked in the signal. The only moment in which the energy is null corresponds to the closure preparing the realization of the "p" in the word "lapin" (rabbit). Similar phenomena can be found in all languages. Given the lack of an obvious acoustic marking of word boundaries, the plausibility of the proposal that infants use segmentation abilities in order to learn the sound pattern of words relies on evidence showing that there are in fact more subtle markings of word boundaries in the signal, and that infants are able to use those markings to segment speech.

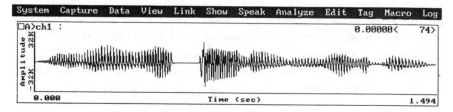

Figure 1. Waveform of the sentence "Il y a un lapin dans le jardin"

In the present chapter, we will first review data that specify the time course of the emergence of segmentation abilities in English-learning infants and that highlight some of the segmentation cues these infants are using. Based on this review we will raise some crosslinguistic issues and propose some bootstrapping hypotheses as well as some original ideas about the development of language-specific segmentation procedures. We will then present some work on French that has started to test these hypotheses. In the last section, we will argue that the research in this domain, which has so far been conducted using behavioral methods, would greatly benefit from the use of brain imaging techniques, in particular the technique of ERPs, which is the easiest to use with infants.

1   The emergence of segmentation abilities in English-learning infants

As stated above, the proposal that infants need segmentation abilities in the early acquisition of sound patterns requires the presence in the speech signal of subtle cues to lexical boundaries which can guide infants in their segmentation. This implies that the acoustic signal should not be as poor as it might seem at first sight. Many studies have recently explored this proposal, which falls within the classic bottom-up, phonological bootstrapping theoretical framework (Jusczyk, Houston and Newsome 1999; Saffran, Aslin and Newport 1996). This proposal has been explored using experimental paradigms which together form the three steps needed to address it:

(1)   the specification of the cues in the signal marking word boundaries;

(2)   a demonstration of infants' sensitivity to these cues; and

(3)   the establishment of the fact that infants use these cues for segmentation.

In the following, we present in more detail the data addressing these three steps. Most of the data pertain to English, and to infants acquiring English.

In a first step, several cues have been found to partly correlate with word boundaries or to partly mark the cohesion of consecutive sounds within words. One such cue has to do with the prosodic level cues, and more precisely with how stress and pitch information are affected by their position within words. For example, there is ample evidence for a stress-initial bias at the lexical level in English (Cassidy and Kelly 1991; Cutler and Carter 1987; Kelly and Bock 1988), while word-final syllables tend to be lengthened in French (Nazzi, Iakimova, Bertoncini, Frédonie and Alcantara 2006). Other cues are related to the phonetic level (phonemes or sequences of phonemes). On the one hand, some phonemes are realized differently according to their position within words or syllables (allophonic variations); for example, in English, the phoneme /p/ tends to be realized as aspired at the onset of a word, but is often not aspired when it occurs intervocalically (Hohne and Jusczyk 1994). On the other hand, there are some constraints on the sequences of phonemes that are allowed within words (phonotactic constraints); for example, in English, the sequence /kn/ cannot occur in syllable onsets, while in Dutch this is perfectly fine (Jusczyk, Friederici, Wessels, Svenkerud and Jusczyk 1993). For English, clear bimodal distributions have been found based on the probabilities for pairs of consecutive phonemes to either appear at a word boundary or within a word. This suggests that if accessed, such information could be used to predict word boundaries (Hockema 2006).

Finally, the syllabic level also appears to provide cues to segmentation. There is emerging evidence that there are higher transitional probabilities between syllables-within-words than between syllables-between-words (Curtin, Mintz and Christiansen 2005). This supports the proposal that statistical/distributional information regarding consecutive syllables might be used for segmentation (Saffran, Aslin and Newport 1996).

At this point, two elements regarding this marking are worth underlining. First, none of these cues systematically mark word boundaries or could allow an error-free segmentation of the signal on their own. However, there is evidence that using them in conjunction would provide sufficiently precise information for successful segmentation (Christiansen, Allen and Seidenberg 1998). Second, the specific way in which each of these cues potentially marks word boundaries will differ across languages, as evident from the evidence presented in the paragraph above. Some acquisition of language-specific properties is therefore required before these cues can be used for segmentation.

In a second step, several studies have established that young English-learning infants are sensitive to the cues discussed above. The early acquisition of certain prosodic properties is suggested by the emergence of a preference for words with the predominant English strong-weak stress pattern (e.g., *porter*) over less frequent weak-strong words (e.g., *report*) between 6 and 9 months (Jusczyk, Cutler and Redanz 1993; Turk, Jusczyk and Gerken 1995). A sensitivity to allophonic differences was found in infants as young as 2 months of age (Hohne and Jusczyk 1994), as attested by their ability to discriminate between pairs such as *nitrate* and *night rate* (in *nitrate*, the /t/ is retroflexed and the /r/ devoiced, which signals word internal segments). Infants appeared to become sensitive to phonotactic properties between 6 and 9 months of age, as shown by the emergence of a preference for pseudowords made up of "legal" or frequent sequences of phonemes in their native language (e.g., *chun*) compared to pseudowords made up of "illegal" or infrequent ones (e.g., *yush*) (Jusczyk, Friederici, Wessels, Svenkerud and Jusczyk 1993; Jusczyk, Luce and Charles-Luce 1994; Mattys, Jusczyk, Luceand Morgan 1999; see also

Friederici and Wessels 1993, for similar data on Dutch-learning infants, and Sebastián-Gallés and Bosch 2002, for Catalan-learning infants).

In a third step, on the basis of this sensitivity, many studies have investigated infants' use of these various linguistic cues for segmentation by exploring whether and how they segment multisyllabic words from fluent speech. The methodology used for the majority of these studies is the same as what was used in the seminal study by Jusczyk and Aslin (1995), which established that English-learning infants start segmenting monosyllabic words between 6 and 7.5 months of age. In this paradigm, infants are first familiarized with two target words (or, in some conditions looking at multisyllabic word segmentation, two syllables extracted from two target words). Then they are presented with passages containing the familiarized/target words and with passages that do not. Evidence for segmentation is demonstrated by longer orientation times to the passages containing the familiarized words (alternatively, infants may first be presented with the continuous passages, and then with the words in isolation. Familiarization is then attested by a preference for the words that were embedded in the passages).

From the studies on English-learning infants emerges the following developmental pattern. At about 7 to 8 months of age, infants use prosodic information to segment fluent speech into sequences of syllables that begin with a strong syllable, i.e., trochaic units (Jusczyk, Houston and Newsome 1999; for further evidence, see also Curtin, Mintz and Christiansen 2005; Echols, Crowhurst and Childers 1997; Houston, Santelmann and Jusczyk 2004; Johnson and Jusczyk 2001; Morgan and Saffran 1995; Nazzi, Dilley, Jusczyk, Shattuck-Hufnagel and Jusczyk 2005). Given that most English bisyllabic words have a strong-weak stress pattern (Cassidy and Kelly 1991; Cutler and Carter 1987; Kelly and Bock 1988), this prosodic segmentation procedure (similar to the metrical segmentation strategy used by adults, c.f. Cutler, Mehler, Norris and Segui 1986; Cutler and Norris 1988; McQueen, Norris and Cutler 1994) would allow English-learning infants to appropriately segment most bisyllabic words from a very young age. Indeed, Jusczyk, Houton and Newsom (1999) found that English-learning infants segment trochaic (strong-weak) nouns (e.g., *candle*) appropriately by 7.5 months of age, but missegment iambic (weak-strong) nouns (e.g., *guitar*) at that age: they place a boundary between the initial/weak syllable and the final/strong syllable (e.g., *gui / tar*) and so appear to segment that final syllable on its own (Jusczyk, Houston and Newsome 1999). Finally, note that the proposal of this prosodic segmentation procedure is compatible with the data on monosyllabic word segmentation (Jusczyk and Aslin 1995) given that these words were strong syllables.

Distributional regularities concerning the ordering of syllables (henceforward, syllabic order information) in the speech signal were also found to be a crucial cue for early segmentation. For example, 7.5-month-olds tested on passages containing strong-weak words such as *doctor* were found to show a segmentation effect when they were familiarized with the whole words, but not when they were familiarized with their initial syllables, e.g. *doc* (Jusczyk, Houston and Newsome 1999). Moreover, in an artificial language paradigm in which infants were presented with a continuous sequence made up of randomly ordered repetitions of four trisyllabic pseudo-words, 8-month-olds were found to group syllables into cohesive word-like units on the basis of the transitional probabilities between consecutive syllables (Saffran, Aslin and Newport 1996; see Perruchet and Vinter 1998, for an alternative interpretation of these results, and Brent and Cartwright 1996, Dahan and Brent 1999, for an alternative model).

Importantly, the data obtained using the Jusczyk and Aslin (1995) paradigm suggest that English-learning infants first segment speech according to prosodic information and then use syllabic order information within the prosodically-defined units (Jusczyk, Houston and Newsome 1999). Indeed, the prosodic boundary placed between the two syllables of a weak-strong word (e.g., *guitar*) appears to block 7.5-month-olds' use of syllabic order information (the fact that *gui* and *tar* always appeared consecutively), resulting in the segmentation of the sole strong syllable. Similarly, if a weak-strong word is always followed by the same prosodically weak syllable (e.g., *guitar_is*), 7.5-month-olds place a word boundary between the first two syllables (via prosodic information) and group the last two syllables together. This results in the segmentation of an incorrect word pattern with a prosodically predominant stress pattern (e.g., *gui / taris*). These findings suggest that English-learning 7.5-month-olds use prosody to perform a first-pass parsing of continuous speech into smaller units that constitute the basis of further analyses of the signal.[1]

Later in development, the role of prosody and/or the relation between the use of prosodic and other segmentation cues appears to change. Evidence for this comes from findings that 10.5-month-olds can segment weak-strong words correctly and do not incorrectly segment strong-weak units across word boundaries when presented with a weak-strong word that is consistently followed by a weak syllable (Jusczyk, Houston and Newsome 1999). This could reflect that at that age, the final product segmentation is less dependent on prosodic patterns. This could be a consequence of the use of syllabic order information to detect the cohesiveness of two consecutive syllables even when they cross a prosodically-placed boundary. Alternatively, it could also reflect the fact that 10.5-month-olds have started to use additional word boundaries such as allophonic (Jusczyk, Hohne and Bauman 1999), phonotactic (Mattys and Jusczyk 2001a), and phonological phrase

---

1.   However, see the debate between Johnson and Jusczyk (2001) and Thiessen and Saffran (2003) regarding data on this issue obtained with the artificial language paradigm.

boundary (Gout, Christophe and Morgan 2004; Nazzi et al. 2005) cues. Finally, note that other cues have been found to influence segmentation: coarticulation at 8 months (Johnson and Jusczyk 2001) and, between 8 and 13 months, the nature (consonant vs. vowel) of the initial phoneme of the word (Mattys and Jusczyk 2001b; Nazzi et al. 2005) and pitch accent information (Nazzi et al. 2005).

In summary, the studies described in this section support a bottom-up, phonological bootstrapping account of the early acquisition of word forms. They trace, for English, the picture of the development of a combination of segmentation abilities during the first year of life. Prosody and syllabic order regularities are used as early as 8 months, with evidence that infants use a prosody-based segmentation procedure in their initial parsing of the signal (through the segmentation of trochaic units) and then use syllabic order information within the prosodically-defined units. By 10.5 months, the relative weight of these two cues has changed, and infants have started using additional (e.g., phonotactic, allophonic) cues. Finally, there is recent experimental evidence suggesting that infants are able to use segmentation procedures that rely on top-down, rather than bottom-up, information. Indeed, English-learning infants have been found to be able to segment unfamiliar words as early as 6 months of age if these words followed highly familiar words, such as their own name and the word "mommy" (Bortfeld, Morgan, Golinkoff and Rathbun 2005). Such effects, though marginal when lexical acquisition begins, probably become more important as the size of infants' vocabulary increases.

2 Crosslinguistic issues

The developmental pattern outlined in the previous section was established for English-learning infants. Given that the prosodic, phonotactic and allophonic cues used to segment speech are language-specific, and therefore signal word boundaries differently across different languages, it is likely that the pattern of emergence of segmentation abilities will differ across languages. Descriptions of the acquisition patterns for different languages are therefore needed.

Such descriptions will help specify the impact of crosslinguistic phonological differences on language acquisition for each individual segmentation cue. For example, when it comes to phonotactic constraints, it could be that the acquisition of the language-specific constraints follows different chronological paths, possibly as a consequence of differences in the strength of the relation between phonotactic patterns and lexical boundaries, or of the relative salience of these cues in the signal. Moreover, these descriptions should help us understand the complex relationship between the emergence of the combined use of these different segmentation cues during development, which cannot be done by studying only one language.

Maybe even more importantly, acquisition data from different languages should help us understand the mechanisms that allow infants to use these different cues for segmentation. Indeed, although the work on English has undoubtedly allowed the identification of some of the cues used for segmentation, research so far has left open the following crucial question: how can it be that infants are able to start segmenting words using properties such as stress patterns, phonotactic constraints and allophonic variations that are defined at the lexical level?

Several tentative answers to this question have been proposed. Some have suggested that infants might learn these properties by analyzing the few words that they hear in isolation, and might then use their knowledge of these properties to segment multisyllabic utterances (Brent and Siskind 2001; Johnson and Jusczyk 2001). Although this proposal is appealing for its simplicity, its claim is weakened by the fact that the presence of few isolated words in the input has been used to argue for the need of segmentation procedures in the first place. A second proposal has been that infants actually start off by doing a statistical analysis of the input that allows them to compute and specify prosodic, allophonic and phonotactic regularities in the signal (Saffran, Aslin and Newport 1996; Thiessen and Saffran 2003). Because statistical analysis processes might be domain general, this proposal seems, at first sight, to solve the issue of prior phonological acquisition. However, one should note that these mechanisms would have to operate on phonological representations specific to the language in acquisition (if only to resolve the question of the normalization of the acoustic realization of the phonemes), hence the need for some prior acquisition. Moreover, the earlier use of statistical information, although supported by some of the research on artificial language acquisition (Thiessen and Saffran 2003; though see Johnson and Jusczyk 2001) does not seem to hold when it is applied to the processing of more varied and complex speech stimuli (Jusczyk *et al.* 1999). In these experimental situations, the evidence rather suggests that prosodic information is used before distributional information.

On the basis of this evidence of an anteriority of the use of prosodic information, and given research on linguistic rhythm and its impact on processing, a third solution has been offered to the question of how infants might use, at the onset of segmentation, cues that appear to be defined at the lexical level. This phonological bootstrapping proposal states that if prosodic information plays a crucial role at the onset of segmentation abilities, it is due to the fact that rhythmic/prosodic information relevant to the lexical level can be learned through an early sensitivity to the global rhythmic pattern of one's native language (Mehler, Dupoux, Nazzi and Dehaene-Lambertz 1996; Nazzi, Bertoncini and Mehler 1998; Nazzi, Jusczyk and Johnson 2000). This proposal is based on a series of facts suggesting (a) the existence of rhythmic cues in the signal influencing speech processing in adulthood that (b) appear to be perceived by infants as early as birth and (c) would lead to the acquisition of language-specific segmentation structures.

Regarding the first point, it has been suggested many decades ago that languages can be classified into different rhythmic classes, in particular the stress-, syllabic-, and mora²-timed language classes (Abercrombie 1967; Pike 1945). The rhythm in these different kinds of languages relies, respectively, on the trochaic unit, the syllable and the mora (see Ramus, Nespor and Mehler 1999 for more details). Recently, many linguistic studies have started providing evidence in support of this classification (Arvaniti 1994; den Os 1988; Fant, Kruckenberg and Nord 1991; Nazzi 1997; Shafer, Shucard and Jaeger 1999; Ramus, Nespor and Mehler 1999). Moreover, these rhythmic classes have proved useful for explaining crosslinguistic differences in the way adults process speech, by suggesting a link between the adults' segmentation and lexical access abilities and the global rhythmic properties of their native language. In particular, the syllable has been found to be the basic segmentation unit for adults speaking French (Mehler, Dommergues, Frauenfelder and Segui 1981; Peretz, Lussier and Béland 1998; but see Content, Meunier, Kearns and Frauenfelder 2001), Spanish and Catalan (Sebastián-Gallés, Dupoux, Segui and Mehler 1992), while the trochaic stress unit appeared to be used in English (Cutler *et al.* 1986; Cutler and Norris 1988; McQueen *et al.* 1994) and Dutch (Vroomen, van Zon and de Gelder 1996).

Evidence supporting infants' sensitivity to these rhythmic properties comes from studies showing that infants as young as 2 days of age discriminate languages according to how they fall within rhythmic classes (Nazzi *et al.* 1998, 2000; Nazzi and Ramus 2003; Ramus *et al.* 2000). Given the adequacy of the rhythmic and segmentation units in the languages previously investigated, it has been proposed that this bias to attend to global rhythmic patterns allows the emergence of the prosodic/rhythmic segmentation procedure appropriate to the (rhythmic class of the) native language (Nazzi *et al.* 1998, 2000; see also Mehler *et al.* 1996). Although still unknown, the mechanisms that could allow infants to exploit rhythmic differences for specifying the segmentation unit appropriate to their native language are currently under investigation (see current research based on an adaptive dynamical model, McLennan 2005).

In the more straightforward version of this rhythmic-based acquisition framework, we predict that the trochaic stress unit should be the unit of early prosodic segmentation in stress-based languages, and the syllable should be the unit of early

---

2. Note that these three rhythmic units are in a hierarchical relation: the stress unit is made up of syllables that are themselves made up of morae. In Japanese, the mora can be either syllabic or subsyllabic. Indeed, CV syllables with long vowels and syllables with final nasals (like the first syllable in "Honda") or final geminate consonants (like the first syllable in "Nissan") have two morae.

prosodic segmentation in syllable-based languages. In other words, we predict that the product of prosodic segmentation, observable when segmentation abilities emerge, will be multisyllabic sequences starting with a stressed syllable in stress-based languages such as English, while it will be isolated syllables in syllable-based languages such as French. Is there any evidence from the developmental literature supporting this proposal?

On the one hand, the early trochaic segmentation bias found in English-learning infants (Jusczyk, Houston and Newsome 1999) fits into this framework. However, on the other hand, most of the few studies that have investigated early word segmentation in languages other than English do not allow an evaluation of our predictions given that they have mainly focused on establishing the ages at which infants are able to segment different types of words. With respect to stress-based languages, Dutch-learning infants were found to start segmenting strong-weak words between 7.5 and 9 months of age (Houston *et al.* 2000; Kooijman, Hagoort and Cutler 2005; Kuijpers, Coolen, Houston and Cutler 1998), while German-learning infants appeared to start segmenting monosyllabic words between 6 and 8 months of age (Höhle and Weissenborn 2003). Recently though, preliminary evidence has been reported of an early strong-weak segmentation bias in German similar to that found for English in this other stress-based language (Höhle and Weissenborn 2005). In the following, we review data obtained for French, the only syllable-based language in which segmentation issues have been studied so far.

3   Testing the rhythmic-based early segmentation hypothesis: the case of the syllable in French

Three studies have recently explored the emergence of word segmentation in French, two with Parisian infants (Gout 2001; Nazzi, Iakimova, Bertoncini, Frédonie and Alcantara 2006) and one with French-Canadian infants (Polka and Sundara 2003). The two earliest studies (Gout 2001; Polka and Sundara 2003), which were mostly interested in establishing the time course of segmentation abilities in French and were not designed to test the hypothesis of early syllabic segmentation, offer contrasting results.

The data on Canadian-French learning infants showed segmentation of bisyllabic words as early as 8 months of age (Polka and Sundara 2003). In this study, infants were familiarized with two bisyllabic words, and then presented with two passages containing the familiarized words and two passages containing novel words. The stimuli were pronounced using highly exaggerated infant-directed speech intonation, and were recorded either by a Canadian-French speaker or a Parisian-French speaker. Similar segmentation results were obtained in both cases, that is, there was a preference for the passages containing the familiarized bisyllabic words. This study thus suggests that Canadian-French infants segment whole bisyllabic words as early as 8 months of age.

The above results on Canadian-French infants are in contradiction with data on Parisian-French learning infants. Indeed, in a first study, no evidence could be obtained for the segmentation of bisyllabic words by Parisian-French learning infants between 7.5 and 11 months of age, although there was evidence of monosyllabic words segmentation at 7.5 months of age (Gout 2001). Following this, and given the rhythmic-based hypothesis presented above, Nazzi *et al.* (2006) investigated whether the null results obtained by Gout (2001) could be a consequence of the fact that French-learning infants start segmenting the two syllables of bisyllabic words individually, as predicted by the syllable-based segmentation hypothesis, before segmenting bisyllabic words as whole units.

To test the prediction that the syllable is the unit of early prosodic segmentation in syllable-based French, Nazzi *et al.* (2006) explored the segmentation of bisyllabic words embedded in fluent passages. They predicted that at the onset of speech segmentation, the infants' prosodic segmentation procedures would place boundaries between every two consecutive syllables, and that no other information (e.g., syllabic order information) would be used to group these two syllables together (as consistent with Jusczyk, Houston and Newsome 1999, results on English). As a consequence, French-learning infants would not be expected to initially segment whole bisyllabic words from fluent speech; rather, they would be expected to segment both syllables of bisyllabic words as individual, independent units. A few months later in development, the importance of the use of prosodic information for segmenting fluent speech was expected to have diminished in comparison to other cues, and the segmentation of bisyllabic words as a whole was expected to be observed as a result of infants' use of other cues (e.g., syllabic order or phonotactic cues).

To investigate this proposed developmental scenario, infants were tested on four passages containing target bisyllabic words (each passage was made up of 6 sentences that each contained one instance of the target word). Two of the passages matched the two items previously presented during familiarization, which differed according to the experiments: the familiarization items were either two bisyllabic words (e.g., *putois* and *toucan*), their final syllables (e.g., *tois* and *can*) or their initial syllables (e.g., *pu* and *tou*).

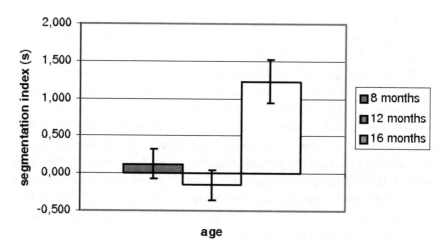

Figure 2. Segmentation effects following familiarization with the whole word (positive values indicate a preference for the passages containing the familiarized words)

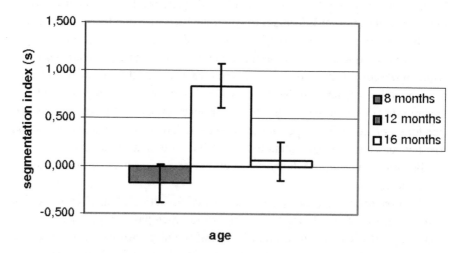

Figure 3. Segmentation effects following familiarization with the final syllables of the target words (positive values indicate a preference for the passages containing the target words)

For the first two types of familiarization items (whole word and final syllable, all recorded in isolation), infants were tested at three ages: 8, 12 and 16 months. Figure 2 for whole-word segmentation and Figure 3 for final syllable segmentation give segmentation indexes, that is, the difference in orientation times between the passages matching and those not matching the familiarization items The results in these figures supported our predictions. At 8 months, no evidence of segmentation was found for either whole words or final syllables. At 12 months, a segmentation effect was found, but only for the final syllable condition. Finally, at 16 months, the opposite pattern was found: there was no more evidence of final syllable segmentation, but only of whole word segmentation.

For investigating initial syllable segmentation infants were only tested at 12 months (the age at which they showed an effect for the final syllable). Two experiments were conducted, one in which infants were familiarized with initial syllables recorded in isolation (as done for the other familiarization types) and one with initial syllables spliced-out from the test passages. Evidence of segmentation was found in the spliced-out condition, reinforcing the conclusion that French-learning infants are segmenting on a syllabic basis at 12 months. But they failed to show segmentation evidence in the isolation condition. This suggests (1) that infants are sensitive to the acoustic distance between the familiarization and test items (as further supported by acoustic analysis), and (b) that young French-learning infants are somewhat sensitive to word level accentuation (see Figure 4).

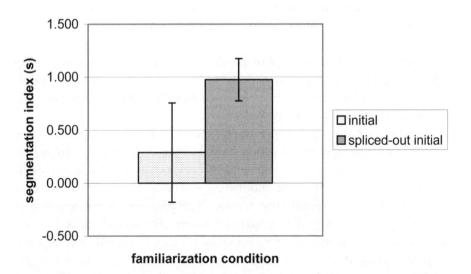

Figure 4. Segmentation effects following familiarization with the intial syllables (isolated or spliced-out forms) of the target words (positive values indicate a preference for the passages containing the target words)

Although further evidence is needed, the study by Nazzi *et al.* (2006) together with earlier work on linguistic rhythm sensitivity (Nazzi *et al.* 1998, 2000) supports the proposal, that similarly to English-learning infants' initial reliance on the rhythmic unit of English (the trochaic unit), French-learning infants initially rely on the rhythmic unit of French (the syllable) to segment continuous speech. Indeed, effects of syllabic segmentation were found at 12 months, but were no longer observable by 16 months of age, when effects of whole word segmentation were found. Finally, note that although the results on Canadian French 8-month-olds might seem in contradiction with Nazzi *et al.* (2006), syllabic segmentation was not in fact tested by Polka and Sundara (2003). The possibility thus remains that Canadian-French infants also recognize individual syllables in bisyllabic words at that age, or at an earlier age. This will have to be tested in the future.

At this point, the results by Nazzi *et al.* (2006) raise an intriguing question: what happens to the syllabic segmentation procedure after 12 months, given that one piece of data motivating the rhythmic-based segmentation proposal was the finding that French-speaking adults do seem to rely on the syllable to segment and access words (Mehler *et al.* 1981; Peretz *et al.* 1998)? This issue is further discussed in the next section.

4   Using ERPs to further explore the relationship between syllabic and whole-word segmentation during development

The absence of a syllabic effect at 16 months needs to be further explored, in the light of the results showing syllabic effects at 12 months (with the same methodology) and in adulthood (with a different experimental method). At least two radically different explanations are possible.

On the one hand, a possible reason for the fact that syllabic segmentation is not used by infants at 16 months might be that infants at that age segment speech relying on the sole use of other segmentation cues such as transitional probabilities, allophonic and phonotactic information as is evident from the data on English. According to this perspective, the use of syllables for the segmentation of French is part of a U-shaped developmental pattern. Alternatively, the syllabic effects found at 12 months and those found in adulthood may not be related and might result from different mechanisms relying on different neural networks.

On the other hand, French-learning 16-month-olds might in fact still be using syllabic information in the process of segmenting speech, but they might be doing so in conjunction with other segmentation cues such as transitional probabilities, allophonic and phonotactic information. Given that, as mentioned earlier, no segmentation cue allows in and of itself the error-free segmentation of an utterance, this second hypothesis appears more likely to us, even though the lack of evidence for the use of syllabic information at 16 months in the Nazzi *et al.* (2006) study does not really support it. Nevertheless, it should be noted that there are limits as to what the behavioral method used by Nazzi *et al.* (2006) can reveal. In particular, this method is not very efficient at revealing graduated effects. This might be due to the fact that many mechanisms are implicated in the behavioral task: besides segmenting, infants need to represent the sound patterns, memorize them, and match the representations extracted during the familiarization and test phases. This last point also highlights the fact that the behavioral method does not provide an online measure of perceptual processing; Instead, the global orientation times measured are more likely to reflect the availability of the final product of perceptual processes rather than intermediate representations. Therefore, the absence of a syllabic effect at 16 months using a behavioral method might be due to the fact that at this age the final product of segmentation, using all available cues, is the whole word and not its individual syllables.

What evidence could be collected to support this second line of reasoning? All behavioral methods available for studying infant perception and cognition will run into similar difficulties, as they all investigate the product of a given perceptual/cognitive process. However, because event-related potentials (ERPs) provide a continuous, online measure of processing, time-locked to the onset of a given event, they constitute a method that should be able to provide information regarding the time course of the combined use of different segmentation cues (see Thierry 2005, for a review of the interest in ERPs for studying development). In order to specify what such information would look like, below we review the few studies so far that have used ERPs for investigating word segmentation.

A series of experiments has explored whether ERP components marking the detection of the onset of words presented in continuous speech can be observed in English-speaking adults (Sanders and Neville 2003a, 2003b; Sanders, Newport and Neville 2002). Previous studies had shown that the onsets of sentences preceded by a silence elicit components described as P50 and N100 (see Sanders and Neville 2003a, for a review). However, there has been a debate in the literature as to whether or not the onset of words in fluent speech would also elicit such responses, given the absence of silences between consecutive words in fluent speech. Sanders and Neville (2003a) systematically explored this issue by presenting sentences in which target syllables were embedded in sentences, and measuring the ERPs elicited by the onset of similar-sounding syllables (same onset phonemes, same accentuation level) according to whether these syllables constituted the onset of a word (e.g., dangerous) or not (e.g., pedestrians). The syllables either belonged to real words (e.g., bottles) or to pseudowords (e.g., * bokkers).

The results first showed that syllable onsets elicit P50/N100 complexes. Second, they revealed that although the P50 response was not modulated by the position of the syllable within the word, the N100 was. Indeed, the mean amplitude of the N100 was larger for word-initial than word-medial syllables at midline and medial electrode sites for pseudowords, while the amplitude difference between the P50 and N100 was larger for word-initial than word-medial syllables at midline and medial electrode sites for real words. Such effects were not replicated when the same stimuli were presented to Japanese late-learners of English (Sanders and Neville 2003b). This confirms the existence of limitations in the acquisition of procedures for the segmentation of words in a foreign language with a different rhythmic pattern (Cutler, Mehler, Norris and Segui 1986), or even in the acquisition of more than one type of segmentation procedures by bilinguals speaking two rhythmically distinct languages (Cutler, Mehler, Norris and Segui 1992). The fact that the N100 word onset component was found for English-learning adults when they were presented with sentences in which the target words were replaced by pseudowords (Sanders and Neville 2003a), or in a segmentation task involving the learning of new "English" pseudowords (Sanders, Newport and Neville 2002), suggests that this N100 ERP component is not limited to real, well known words.

To our knowledge, there is only one study that has explored the ERP signature of word onsets in infants (Kooijman, Hagoort and Cutler 2005). This study was conducted with Dutch-learning 10-month-old infants, and used a paradigm inspired by the one used in the behavioral studies on early word segmentation (e.g., Jusczyk, Houston and Newsome 1999). In this study, infants were presented with blocks of stimuli. Each block consisted of 10 repetitions of a target strong-weak bisyllabic word (isolated items), followed by eight sentences presented in random order: four sentences containing the target/"familiar" word, and four sentences containing another strong-weak bisyllabic word (the "unfamiliar" word). Infants heard up to 20 blocks.

An analysis of the ERPs first revealed an effect of repetition during the presentation of the target words in isolation: the positivity that developed on the anterior part of the scalp in the 200–500 ms window after word onset was larger for the first repetitions, and had almost totally disappeared by the time of the last two repetitions. The difference between the first and last repetitions of the words became statistically significant in the latency range of 160–190 ms after word onset, suggesting that it takes no more than 200 ms for infants to detect the familiarity of the target words when presented in isolation. Second, an effect of segmentation was obtained by comparing ERPs to familiar and non-familiar words embedded in the sentences. The ERPs were more negative to the familiar words in the 350–500 ms window, but only in the left hemisphere. This effect was already significant in the first 50 ms of this time window. This effect suggests that it takes about 300/400 ms for 10-month-old infants to segment from sentences and recognize words previously heard in isolation. Given the duration of the target words (about 700 ms), these results suggest that recognition has begun by the end of the first syllable of the bisyllabic words. The comparison of the neural responses to the presentation of the words in isolation versus embedded in sentences further suggests that the neural networks underlying both processes are at least partly different, as attested by different latency and scalp distribution characteristics.

Given the above studies, how could ERPs be used to study the relationship between syllabic and whole-word segmentation in French? The idea is that syllabic and whole-word segmentation might be marked by ERPs differing in their signature, in particular in scalp distribution and latency. As a consequence, before the onset of whole-word segmentation (thus up to 12 months of age according to Nazzi *et al.* 2006), one should observe ERPs corresponding to syllabic segmentation, which should therefore be obtained for both syllables (time-locking the analyses to the onset of each syllable) and should show a specific latency and scalp distribution.

Predictions for infants who are already able to segment whole words (that is from 16 months of age onwards according to Nazzi *et al.* 2006) and adults would differ according to whether syllabic segmentation is still used at that age or not. If syllabic segmentation is not used any more, then we should observe ERP effects only for the word-initial syllable. These word-initial ERPs most likely will have a different latency and scalp distribution than those obtained for syllabic segmentation, given age/maturation differences in the infants tested (see Mills, Coffey-Corina and Neville 1997; Mills, Prat, Zangl, Stager, Neville and Werker 2004; Rivera-Gaxiola, Silva-Pereyra and Kuhl 2005, for evidence of similar developmental changes in language related tasks) and probable differences in the neural networks involved in syllabic versus whole-word segmentation (with the latter involving the processing of cues other than syllabic information).

Alternatively, if syllabic segmentation is still present after 16 months of age, a hypothesis we favor, and if its non-observation by Nazzi *et al.* (2006) was due to limitations of the behavioral method used, then one should observe ERP effects for both word-initial and non-initial syllables. However, these effects, contrary to the effects predicted if only syllabic segmentation is available, would most likely be different for the two syllables. This would be the consequence of the fact that while probably only syllabic processing underlies the effects time-locked to the non-initial syllable, the ERPs time-locked to the initial syllable will most likely result from the combined response of different neural networks that are responding to syllabic information but also to other segmentation cues responsible for whole-word segmentation at this age.

At this point, we have conducted a first study on 20 French adults using a paradigm somewhat similar to that used by Kooijman *et al.* (2005). In our study, four words were selected (cagoule, dorade, perruque and guitare), and 60 sentences were constructed in which each target word appeared, either in sentence-initial, -medial or –final position (20 sentences per position). A native speaker of French recorded the stimuli. During testing, participants were presented with 5 experimental blocks. Each block comprised four familiarization/test phases, one for each of the four target words presented in random order. In this design, the same words appeared at different familiarization/test phases in both familiarized and non-familiarized conditions for each subject. For each phase, ten different occurrences of a target word were presented, followed by 12 sentences: 6 containing the familiarized word and 6 containing another word (in each condition, 2 sentences for each position). ERPs were measured continuously using a 64-channel Geodesic EEG system, and will be analyzed time-locked to two different events in the sentences: the onset of the initial syllable, and the onset of the medial syllable.

Preliminary analyses have been conducted for initial syllables only. An inspection of the data for anterior electrodes (see Figure 5) shows a positive-going event that peaks around 100 ms after onset (P1), followed by a negative-going event peaking around 140 ms (N1). It is followed by another positive event in the 180–280 ms window (P2), followed by another negative event in the 300–400 ms window (N2). This pattern was most clear on frontal/fronto-central median/medial electrodes. As found previously in studies looking at continuous speech processing, the mean amplitudes of these components are relatively small, that is, for the N1, between .5 and 1 µv (Hagoort and Brown 2000; Sanders and Neville 2003a).

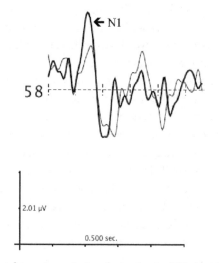

Figure 5. ERPs over a right centro-anterior electrode site (58) showing a more negative N1 response for the new words (dark line) than for the familiar words (light line)

Analyses of a "familiarity" effect on the peak amplitude of the different ERP components were conducted on a subset of 32 electrodes. Distributional effects (see Figure 6) were assessed by dividing the electrodes into 16 regions according to hemisphere (left versus right), laterality (medial versus lateral) and the anterior-posterior axis (prefrontal versus frontal versus central versus parietal). No significant effects involving "familiarity" were found for the P1, P2 and N2 components. However, for the N1 peak amplitude, the condition x hemisphere interaction was significant, $(F(1,19) = 4.28, p = 0.05)$. Planned comparisons revealed that the peak amplitude difference between familiarized and non-familiarized words was significant for the right hemisphere (M = -.66 μv vs. M = -.83 μv respectively, $F(1, 19) = 8.98, p =.007$) but not for the left hemisphere (M = -.80 μv vs. M = -.81 μv respectively, $F(1, 19) < 1$, n.s.). Moreover, significant hemisphere differences were found for the familiarized words ($F(1, 19) = 7.73, p =.012$) but not for the non-familiarized words ($F(1, 19) < 1$). Taken together, these effects indicate that the "familiarity" effect is due to a decrease in response to the familiarized words observed on centro-frontal electrodes at the level of the right hemisphere. Finally, position effects were observed ($F(3, 57) = 7.08, p =.0004$), revealing that responses were more negative on frontal and central electrodes than on prefrontal and parietal electrodes.

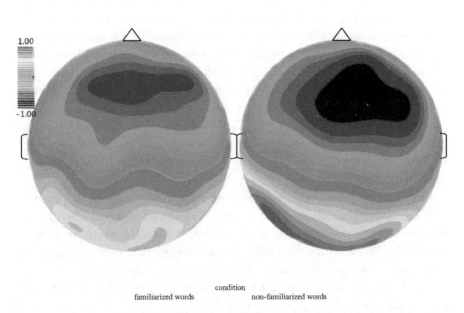

condition

familiarized words   non-familiarized words

Figure 6. Topographic map at 140 ms after target onset, showing both the frontal distribution of the N1 component and the less pronounced N1 response for the familiarized words relative to the non-familiarized ones over the right hemisphere

These first analyses confirm that ERPs to the onset of words embedded in sentences can be observed in adults. Thus, previous findings on English (Sanders and Neville 2003a, 2003b; Sanders *et al.* 2002) are extended to French. They further show that the negative component peaking around 140 ms after the onset of the word (N1) is sensitive to the induced "familiarity" of the target words. Familiarity thus influences the earliest stages of word segmentation and recognition, possibly by facilitating the phonological processing of the familiarized words, as attested by the amplitude reduction of the N1 onset effect to familiarized words in the right hemisphere (see Friedrich and Friederici 2005, for early phonological effects in adults tested on a word recognition task in a picture context). Given that the initial syllables of the target bisyllabic words in the sentences were about 170 ms long, this suggests that in this experimental context recognition has started by the end of the first syllable, thus before the unambiguous identification of the target words (which was the last phoneme for all 4 target words). Note that at this point it is unclear why this early familiarity effect in the French data was more pronounced on electrodes located over the right hemisphere than over the left hemisphere. Right hemisphere effects have however been reported in other studies on adult speech/language processing, suggesting for example the involvement of the right hemisphere in prosodic processing (Pannekamp, Toepel, Alter, Hahne and Friederici 2005; Wioland, Rudolf, Metz-Lutz, Mutschler and Marescaux 1999) or syllable discrimination (Wioland, Rudolf, Metz-Lutz, Mutschler, Kurtz and Marescaux 1996), or some processes of integration of the lexical and sentential levels (Coulson, Federmeier, van Petten and Kutas 2005). However, note that several left posterior electrodes showed ERP activity reversed in polarity compared to the right centro-frontal electrodes, with an apparent difference between the two familiarization conditions. This suggests that the neuronal networks responsible for the observation of these two opposite effects at the scalp level are located somewhere on the diagonal between these two scalp locations, and might therefore not be located in the right hemisphere.

In a follow-up of the present report, we will conduct analyses of our data to explore whether induced "familiarity" effects can also be observed when we analyze the data time-locked to the onset of the second syllable, which would signal that in French, and contrary to English, N1 effects mark syllable onsets rather than lexical onsets (given attested effects of syllables in speech segmentation in French). Moreover, further studies will test infants on the same stimuli and in the same experimental design, using the adult data as comparison point to evaluate the level of maturity of the infant electrophysiological responses at different ages (for other studies using this comparative approach, see, e.g., Weber, Hahne, Friedrich and Friederici 2004; Friedrich, Kotz, Friederici and Alter 2004).

5   Conclusions

In the present chapter, we have reported data regarding the emergence of the abilities to segment words from continuous speech. Given the evidence of the importance of the use of prosodic cues in early word segmentation in English, and given the evidence of the impact of rhythmic properties on perception/processing in both infants and adults, we proposed a developmental scenario according to which infants start segmenting speech according to the rhythmic unit of their native language. Behavioral evidence from stress-based English and syllable-based French was presented that provides support for the rhythmic-based proposal. We then discussed certain limitations of the behavioral data, stressing the fact that they do not provide an online measure of segmentation processes. The specific familiarization/test design used in studies of early word segmentation depends a lot on the "phonological" relation between the familiarized word form and the segmented word form. Moreover, observation of segmentation effects rely heavily on the end-product of segmentation, which prevents the observation of intermediate processing steps and the use of intermediate units. In this context, the ERP technique, which provides a continuous measure of brain activity time-locked to the onset of specific events, should help us understand the temporal sequence of the different sub-processes implicated in speech segmentation in a context in which various segmentation cues are available in the signal. Accordingly, ERP studies should contribute to providing answers to some of the issues we raised on the basis of our behavioral data regarding the relation between syllabic and whole-word segmentation in French-learning infants of various ages.

References

Abercrombie, D. 1967. *Elements of general phonetics.* Edinburgh: EUP.

Arvaniti, A. 1994. "Acoustic features of Greek rhythmic structure." *Journal of Phonetics* 22: 239–68.

Aslin, R.N. 1993. "Segmentation of fluent speech into words: Learning models and the role of maternal input." In *Developmental neurocognition: Speech and face processing in the first year of life,* B. de Boysson-Bardies *et al.* (eds.), 305–15. Dordrecht: Kluwer.

Bortfeld, H., Morgan, J.L., Golinkoff, R.M. and Rathbun, K. 2005. "Mommy and me: Familiar names help launch babies into speech-stream segmentation." *Psychological Science* 16: 298–304.

Brent, M.R. and Cartwright, T.A. 1996. "Distributional regularity and phonotactic constraints are useful for segmentation." *Cognition* 61: 93–125.

Brent, M.R. and Siskind, J.M. 2001. "The role of exposure to isolated words in early vocabulary development." *Cognition* 81: B33-B44.

Cassidy, K.W. and Kelly, M.H. 1991. "Phonological information for grammatical category assignments." *Journal of Memory and Language* 30: 348–69.

Christiansen, M.H., Allen, J. and Seidenberg, M.S. 1998. "Learning to segment speech using multiple cues: A connectionist model." *Language and Cognitive Processes* 13: 221–68.

Cole, R.A. and Jakimik, J. 1978. "Understanding speech: How words are heard." In *Strategies of information processing*, G. Underwood (ed.), 67–116. New York, NY: Academic Press.

Cole, R.A. and Jakimik, J. 1980. "How are syllables used to recognize words?" *Journal of the Acoustical Society of America* 67: 965–70.

Content, A., Meunier, C., Kearns, R.K. and Frauenfelder, U.H. 2001. "Sequence detection in pseudowords in French: Where is the syllable effect?" *Language and Cognitive Processes* 16: 609–36.

Coulson, S., Federmeier, K.D., van Petten, C. and Kutas, M. 2005. "Right hemisphere sensitivity to word- and sentence-level context: Evidence from event-related brain potentials." *Journal of Experimental Psychology: Learning, Memory and Cognition* 31: 129–47.

Curtin, S., Mintz, T.H. and Christiansen, M.H. 2005. "Stress changes the representational landscape: Evidence from word segmentation." *Cognition* 96: 233–62.

Cutler, A. and Carter, D.M. 1987. "The predominance of strong initial syllables in the English vocabulary." *Computer Speech and Language* 2: 133–42.

Cutler, A., Mehler, J., Norris, D. G. and Segui, J. 1986. "The syllable's differing role in the segmentation of French and English." *Journal of Memory and Language* 25: 385–400.

Cutler, A., Mehler, J., Norris, D. G. and Segui, J. 1992. "The monolingual nature of speech segmentation by bilinguals." *Cognitive Psychology* 24: 381–410.

Cutler, A. and Norris, D. 1988. "The role of strong syllables in segmentation for lexical access." *Journal of Experimental Psychology: Human Perception and Performance* 14: 113–21.

Dahan, D. and Brent, M.R. 1999. "On the discovery of novel wordlike units from utterances: An artificial-language study with implications for native-language acquisition." *Journal of Experimental Psychology: General* 128 (2): 165–85.

den Os, E. 1988. *Rhythm and tempo of Dutch and Italian: A contrastive study.* Utrecht: Drukkerij Elinkwijk BV.

Echols, C.H., Crowhurst, M.J. and Childers, J.B. 1997. "The perception of rhythmic units in speech by infants and adults." *Journal of Memory and Language* 36: 202–25.

Fant, G., Kruckenberg, A. and Nord, L. 1991. "Durational correlates of stress in Swedish, French and English." *Journal of Phonetics* 19: 351–65.

Friederici, A.D. and Wessels, J.M.I. 1993. "Phonotactic knowledge and its use in infant speech perception." *Perception & Psychophysics* 54: 287–95.

Friedrich, C.K. and Friederici, A.D. 2005. "Phonotactic knowledge and lexical-semantic processing in one-year-olds: Brain responses to words and nonsense words in picture contexts." *Journal of Cognitive Neuroscience* 17: 1785–802.

Friedrich, C.K., Kotz, S.A., Friederici, A.D. and Alter, K. 2004. "Pitch modulates lexical identification in spoken word recognition: ERP and behavioral evidence." *Cognitive Brain Research* 20: 300–8.

Gout, A. 2001. Etapes précoces de l'acquisition du lexique. [Early steps in lexical acquisition]. PhD dissertation, Ecole des Hautes Etudes en Sciences Sociales, Paris, France.

Gout, A., Christophe, A. and Morgan, J.L. 2004. "Phonological phrase boundaries constrain lexical access II. Infant data." *Journal of Memory and Language* 51: 548–67.

Hagoort, P. and Brown, C.M. 2000. "ERP effects of listening to speech: Semantic ERP effects." *Neuropsychologia* 38 (11): 1518–1530.

Hockema, S.A. 2006. "Finding words in speech: An investigation of American English." *Language Learning and Development* 2: 119–46.

Höhle, B. and Weissenborn, J. 2003. "German-learning infants' ability to detect unstressed closed-class elements in continuous speech." *Developmental Science* 6: 122–7.

Höhle, B. and Weissenborn, J. 2005. "Word segmentation in German-learning infants." Paper presented at the international workshop: Early word segmentation: a crosslinguistic approach taking advantage of Europe's linguistic diversity, Paris, France, February 25–26.

Hohne, E.A. and Jusczyk, P.W. 1994. "Two-month-old infants' sensitivity to allophonic differences." *Perception & Psychophysics* 56: 613–23.

Houston, D.M., Jusczyk, P.W., Kuijpers, C., Coolen, R., Cutler, A. 2000. "Cross-language word segmentation by 9-month-olds." *Psychonomics Bulletin & Review* 7: 504–9.

Houston, D.M., Santelmann, L.M. and Jusczyk, P.W. 2004. "English-learning infants' segmentation of trisyllabic words from fluent speech." *Language and Cognitive Processes* 19: 97–136.

Johnson, E.K. and Jusczyk, P.W. 2001. "Word segmentation by 8-month-olds: When speech cues count more than statistics." *Journal of Memory and Language* 44: 1–20.

Jusczyk, P.W. and Aslin, R.N. 1995. "Infants' detection of the sound patterns of words in fluent speech." *Cognitive Psychology* 29: 1–23.

Jusczyk, P.W., Cutler, A. and Redanz, N. 1993. "Preference for the predominant stress patterns of English words." *Child Development* 64: 675–87.

Jusczyk, P.W., Friederici, A.D., Wessels, J., Svenkerud, V.Y. and Jusczyk, A.M. 1993. "Infants' sensitivity to the sound patterns of native language words." *Journal of Memory and Language* 32: 402–20.

Jusczyk, P.W., Hohne, E.A. and Bauman, A. 1999. "Infants' sensitivity to allophonic cues for word segmentation." *Perception & Psychophysics* 62: 1465–76.

Jusczyk, P.W., Houston, D.M. and Newsome, M. 1999. "The beginning of word segmentation in English-learning infants." *Cognitive Psychology* 39: 159–207.

Jusczyk, P.W., Luce, P.A. and Charles-Luce, J. 1994. "Infants' sensitivity to phonotactic patterns in the native language." *Journal of Memory and Language* 33: 630–45.

Kelly, M.H. and Bock, J.K. 1988. "Stress in time." *Journal of Experimental Psychology: Human Perception and Performance* 14: 389–403.

Klatt, D.H. 1979. "Speech perception: A model of acoustic-phonetic analysis and lexical access." *Journal of Phonetics* 7: 279–312.

Klatt, D.H. 1989. "Review of selected models of speech perception." In *Lexical representation and process,* W. Marslen-Wilson (ed.), 169–226. Cambridge, MA: The MIT Press.

Kooijman, V., Hagoort, P. and Cutler, A. 2005. "Electrophysiological evidence for prelinguistic infants' word recognition in continuous speech." *Cognitive Brain Research* 24: 109–16.

Kuijpers, C., Coolen, R., Houston, D. and Cutler, A. 1998. "Using the head-turning technique to explore cross-linguistic performance differences." *Advances in Infancy Research* 12: 205–20. Stamford, CT: Ablex.

Mattys, S., Jusczyk, P.W., Luce, P.A. and Morgan, J.L. 1999. "Phonotactic and prosodic effects on word segmentation in infants." *Cognitive Psychology* 38: 465–94.

Mattys, S. and Jusczyk, P.W. 2001a. "Phonotactic cues for segmentation of fluent speech by infants." *Cognition* 78: 91–121.

Mattys, S. and Jusczyk, P.W. 2001b. "Do infants segment words or recurring contiguous patterns?" *Journal of Experimental Psychology: Human Perception and Performance* 27: 644–55.

McLennan, S. 2005. "A dynamic adaptive model of linguistic rhythm." In *Proceedings of the I.S.C.A. Workshop on Plasticity in Speech Perception* 130. London, U.K., June 15–17 2005.

McQueen, J.M., Norris, D. and Cutler, A. 1994. "Competition in spoken word recognition: Spotting words in other words." *Journal of Experimental Psychology: Learning, Memory and Cognition* 20: 621–38.

Mehler, J., Dommergues, J. Y., Frauenfelder, U. and Segui, J. 1981. "The syllable's role in speech segmentation." *Journal of Verbal Learning and Verbal Behavior* 20: 298–305.

Mehler, J., Dupoux, E., Nazzi, T. and Dehaene-Lambertz, G. 1996. "Coping with linguistic diversity: The infant's viewpoint." In *Signal to syntax* J.L. Morgan and K. Demuth (eds.), 101–16. Mahwah, NJ: Lawrence Erlbaum Associates.

Mills, D.L., Coffey-Corina, S. and Neville, H.J. 1997. "Language comprehension and cerebral specialization from 13 to 20 months." *Developmental Neuropsychology* 13: 397–445.

Mills, D.L., Prat, C., Zangl, R., Stager, C.L., Neville, H.J., Werker, J.F. 2004. "Language experience and the organization of brain activity to phonetically similar words: ERP evidence from 14- and 20-month-olds." *Journal of Cognitive Neuroscience* 16: 1452–64.

Morgan, J.L. and Saffran, J.R. 1995. "Emerging integration of sequential and suprasegmental information in preverbal speech segmentation." *Child Development* 66: 911–36.

Nazzi, T. 1997. Du rythme dans l'acquisition et le traitement de la parole. [Rhythm in the acquisition and processing of speech]. PhD dissertation, Ecole des Hautes Etudes et Sciences Sociales, Paris.

Nazzi, T., Bertoncini, J. and Mehler, J. 1998. "Language discrimination by newborns: Toward an understanding of the role of rhythm." *Journal of Experimental Psychology: Human Perception and Performance* 24: 756–66.

Nazzi, T., Dilley, L.C., Jusczyk, A.M., Shattuck-Hufnagel, S. and Jusczyk, P.W. 2005. "English-learning infants' segmentation of verbs from fluent speech." *Language and Speech* 48: 279–98.

Nazzi, T., Iakimova, I., Bertoncini, J., Frédonie, S. and Alcantara, C. 2006. "Early segmentation of fluent speech by infants acquiring French: Emerging evidence for crosslinguistic differences." *Journal of Memory and Language* 54: 283–99.

Nazzi, T., Jusczyk, P.W. and Johnson, E.K. 2000. "Language discrimination by English learning 5-month-olds: Effects of rhythm and familiarity." *Journal of Memory and Language* 43: 1–19.

Nazzi, T. and Ramus, F. 2003. "Perception and acquisition of linguistic rhythm by infants." *Speech Communication* 41: 233–43.

Pannekamp, A., Toepel, U., Alter, K., Hahne, A. and Friederici, A.D. 2005. "Prosody-driven sentence processing: An event-related brain potential study." *Journal of Cognitive Neuroscience* 17: 407–21.

Peretz, I., Lussier, I. and Béland, R. 1998. "The differential role of syllabic structure in stem completion for French and English." *European Journal of Cognitive Psychology* 10: 75–112.

Perruchet, P. and Vinter, A. 1998. "PARSER: A model for word segmentation." *Journal of Memory and Language* 39: 246–63.

Pike, K. 1945. *The intonation of American English.* Ann Arbor, MI: University of Michigan Press.

Polka, L. and Sundara, M. 2003. "Word segmentation in monolingual and bilingual infant learners of English and French." *Proceedings of the 15th International Congress of Phonetic Sciences*, 1021–4. Barcelona, Spain.

Ramus, F., Hauser, M. D., Miller, C., Morris, D. and Mehler, J. 2000. "Language discrimination by human newborns and by cotton-top tamarin monkeys." *Science* 288: 349–51.

Ramus, F., Nespor, M. and Mehler, J. 1999. "Correlates of linguistic rhythm in the speech signal." *Cognition* 73: 265–92.

Rivera-Gaxiola, M., Silva-Pereyra, J. and Kuhl, P.K. 2005. "Brain potentials to native and non-native speech contrasts in 7- and 11-month-old American infants." *Developmental Science* 8: 162–72.

Saffran, J.R., Aslin, R.N. and Newport, E.L. 1996. "Statistical learning by 8-month-old infants." *Science* 274: 1926–8.

Sanders, L.D. and Neville, H.J. 2003a. "An ERP study of continuous speech processing. I. Segmentation, semantics, and syntax in native speakers." *Cognitive Brain Research* 15: 228–40.

Sanders, L.D. and Neville, H.J. 2003b. "An ERP study of continuous speech processing. II. Segmentation, semantics, and syntax in non-native speakers." *Cognitive Brain Research* 15: 228–40.

Sanders, L.D., Newport, E.L. and Neville, H.J. 2002. "Segmenting nonsense: An event-related potential index of perceived onsets in continuous speech." *Nature Neuroscience* 5: 700–3.

Sebastián-Gallés, N. and Bosch, L. 2002. "Building phonotactic knowledge in bilinguals: Role of early exposure." *Journal of Experimental Psychology: Human Perception and Performance* 28: 974–89.

Sebastián-Gallés, N., Dupoux, E., Segui, J. and Mehler, J. 1992. "Contrasting syllabic effects in Catalan and Spanish." *Journal of Memory and Language* 31: 18–32.

Shafer, V. L., Shucard, D. W. and Jaeger, J.J. 1999. "Electrophysiological indices of cerebral specialization and the role of prosody in language acquisition in three-month-old infants." *Developmental Neuropsychology* 15: 73–109.

Thierry, G. 2005. "The use of event-related potentials in the study of early cognitive development." *Infant and Child Development* 14: 85–94.

Thiessen, E.D. and Saffran, J.R. 2003. "When cues collide: Use of stress and statistical cues to word boundaries by 7- to 9-month-old infants." *Developmental Psychology* 39: 706–16.

Turk, A.E., Jusczyk, P.W., Gerken, L. 1995. "Do English-learning infants use syllable weight to determine stress?" *Language and Speech* 38: 143–58.

van de Weijer, J. 1998. Language input for word discovery. PhD dissertation, University of Nijmegen (MPI Series in Psycholinguistics 9).

Vroomen, J., van Zon, M. and de Gelder, B. 1996. "Metrical segmentation and inhibition in spoken word recognition." *Journal of Experimental Psychology: Human Perception and Performance* 21: 98–108.

Weber, C., Hahne, A., Friedrich, M. and Friederici, A.D. 2004. "Discrimination of word stress in early infant perception: Electrophysiological evidence." *Cognitive Brain Research* 18: 149–61.

Wioland, N., Rudolf, G., Metz-Lutz, M.N., Mutschler, V., Kurtz, D. and Marescaux, C. 1996. "An electrophysiological dichotic syllable test: Normative data for a right-handed population." *Functional Neuroscience* (EEG suppl.) 46: 277–86.

Wioland, N., Rudolf, G., Metz-Lutz, M.N., Mutschler, V. and Marescaux, C. 1999. "Cerebral correlates of hemispheric lateralization during a pitch discrimination task: An ERP study in dichotic situation." *Clinical Neurophysiology* 110: 516–23.

CHAPTER 4

Reflections on reflections of infant word recognition*

Valesca Kooijman, Elizabeth K. Johnson and Anne Cutler

1   Introduction: Reflecting the development of speech perception

The history of experimental psychology is a progression of ever more ingenious attempts to capture reflections of the processes of the mind. No mental operations can ever be observed directly. Since experimental psychology began in earnest – in Wilhelm Wundt's Leipzig laboratory in the late nineteenth century – the principal concern of experimental psychologists has been to devise methods which allow mental operations to be observed indirectly. Most commonly, these methods record the speed or accuracy of behavior for which certain mental processes are a prerequisite; more recently, the electrophysiological signals or the blood flow in the brain can be measured as mental processing occurs. Although only such indirect reflections can ever be available to us, experimental psychology has contrived to amass substantial knowledge about the processes which go on in the human mind.

Particularly challenging has been the study of the beginnings of cognitive processing. Infants in the first year of life cannot command the overt behavioral responses required in the most common adult testing procedures; it is obviously laughable to imagine nine-month-olds signaling recognition of a word by pressing a response button or giving a verbal answer. Nonetheless, as will become clear, we do now know that nine-month-olds can indeed recognize word forms. This is because the challenge of capturing reflections of early cognition has also been met: in the past four decades, highly effective covert-behavioral methodologies have been devised for studying mental operations in the infant brain.

In the area of early speech perception and the beginnings of vocabulary development, the commonest testing methodologies have used the rate or duration of simple behavioral responses, such as sucking on a pacifier or looking at a visual stimulus associated with an auditory signal, as the indirect measures of developing speech perception and processing abilities. Creative use of these testing methodologies has uncovered remarkably sophisticated speech perception skills in preverbal infants. The High Amplitude Sucking Paradigm, for example, which uses sucking rate as a dependent measure of speech preferences and discriminatory abilities, works well with infants up to two months of age (Jusczyk 1985; Sameroff 1967). Research using this paradigm has demonstrated that infants begin laying a foundation for language acquisition even before birth. Newborns prefer to listen to their mother's native tongue over other languages (e.g. English-learning infants prefer to listen to English over Spanish; Moon, Cooper and Fifer 1993). They also show recognition of voices (DeCasper and Fifer 1980) and of stories heard before birth (DeCasper and Spence 1986), and they discriminate phoneme contrasts (Eimas, Siqueland, Jusczyk and Vigorito 1971).

Of course, newborns are still far removed from linguistic competence. Their phoneme discrimination skills reflect their auditory abilities, not their use of linguistic experience; they can discriminate phonetic contrasts which do not appear in their maternal language as well as those that do (Aslin, Jusczyk and Pisoni 1998; Werker and Tees 1984; 1999). At two months of age, likewise, English-learning infants cannot yet perceive the difference between their own language and the rhythmically similar Dutch (Christophe and Morton 1998). However, speech processing skills develop rapidly during the first year of life, as research using other procedures more suited to testing older infants, such as the Conditioned Headturn Procedure and the Headturn Preference Procedure, has demonstrated. By four months, infants recognize their own name (Mandel, Jusczyk and Pisoni 1995) and discriminate between their native language and other rhythmically similar languages (Bosch and Sebastián-Gallés 1997). By five months, infants are so familiar with the prosodic structure of their native language that they can even discriminate between two dialects of their native language – thus American infants can discriminate between American and British English (Nazzi, Jusczyk and Johnson 2000). Sensitivity to language-specific vowel patterns emerges by six months of age (Kuhl, Williams, Lacerda, Stevens and Lindblom 1992), and language-specific consonant perception is well in place before infants reach their first birthday (Werker and Tees 1984; 1999). First evidence of rudimentary word segmentation and comprehension skills has been observed between six and seven and a half months of age (Bortfeld, Morgan, Golinkoff and Rathbun 2005; Jusczyk and Aslin 1995; Tincoff and Jusczyk 1999), and these skills continue to develop at an impressive rate throughout the first year of life (Hollich, Hirsch-Pasek and Golinkoff 2000; Jusczyk, Houston and Newsome 1999). In short, infant testing methodologies using simple behavioral measures such as sucking rate and looking time have revealed that the infant's world is a far cry from the "*blooming, buzzing confusion*" envisioned by William James (James 1911). Infants in fact amass considerable linguistic knowledge long before they begin to communicate with language.

Thus despite the fact that the processes of speech perception are not directly observable, indirect reflections of these processes in infancy have proven highly informative. As the title of this chapter suggests, we compare and evaluate the various methods in current use; we also argue that new (electrophysiological) methods in combination with older (behavioral) methods open the way to further insights. We draw our examples from research on the segmentation of continuous speech into its component words.

2   The word segmentation problem

Hearing speech as a string of discrete words seems so effortless to adults listening to their native language that it is tempting to suspect that the speech signal unambiguously informs us where one word ends and the next begins. However, listening to an unfamiliar language or examining a spectrogram easily dispels this illusion. When we listen to an unfamiliar language, words seem to run together in an impossibly fast manner; it is only in our own language that segmenting streams of speech into their component words is so easy. But in fact words run together in any language. Nazzi, Iakimova, Bertoncini and de Schonen, this volume, make this point with a French example; our Figure 1 illustrates it with a Dutch eight-word sentence: *Die oude mosterd smaakt echt niet meer goed* 'that old mustard really doesn't taste good any more'. There are several silent portions in the speech stream, but even where these happen to occur between words, they have not arisen from pauses between the words: each such point just represents the closure of the speaker's mouth as a stop consonant (/d/, /t/, /k/, or the glottal stop separating successive vowels) has been uttered. The eight words are not demarcated by recurring word-boundary signals of any kind. This utterance was in fact spoken slowly and carefully in a manner associated with infant-directed speech; most utterances in our everyday experience, however, proceed even faster and weld the separate words even more closely together than we see here.

Why is it so easy to hear words in our native language? As it turns out, there are a myriad of cues to word boundaries which listeners can call upon, but these cues are probabilistic rather than fully reliable; furthermore, and most importantly, they are language-specific. Adults therefore exploit multiple cues for identifying word boundaries in fluent speech, and the cues they use are determined by their native language experience (Cutler 2001). An example of a language-specific cue for word segmentation is lexical stress in English. Since the majority of English content words begin with a stressed syllable (Cutler and Carter 1987), English listeners are biased towards perceiving stressed syllables as word onsets (Cutler and Butterfield 1992). English listeners who tried to apply this strategy towards the segmentation of spoken French, Polish or Japanese, however, would have little luck extracting words from the speech stream.

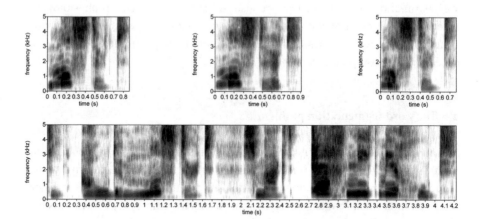

Figure 1. Above, three spectrograms of the Dutch word *mosterd* 'mustard', produced in isolation in a manner associated with infant-directed speech; below, a sentence *Die oude mosterd smaakt echt niet meer goed* 'That old mustard really doesn't taste good any more', produced in the same manner. The displays represent frequency on the vertical axis against time on the horizontal axis, with greater energy represented by darker color. It can be seen that the three word tokens differ in duration, from about 750 ms to about 900 ms, and also differ in spectral quality. The word *mosterd* in the sentence begins at about 0.78 on the time line and finishes at about 1.75

Segmenting words from speech is a trivial task for adults because they have had years of experience listening to their native language. Learning how to find words for the first time, however, presents a much bigger challenge. Moreover, it is a very important skill to learn in the first year of life, as is clear from Newman, Bernstein Ratner, Jusczyk, Jusczyk, and Dow's (2006) demonstration that relative ability to recognize discrete words in continuous speech before age one is directly predictive of vocabulary size at age two. It has been proposed that infants might solve the word segmentation problem by first learning words in isolation, and then subsequently recognizing these words in fluent speech (Bloomfield 1933; Brent 1999). But the speech which infants hear in the first year of life consists predominantly of multiword utterances (Morgan 1996; van de Weijer 1998; Woodward and Aslin 1990), so it seems unlikely that hearing words in isolation could constitute the full explanation for how language learners first begin segmenting words from speech. It seems more likely that the onset of word segmentation is fueled by developing knowledge about the typical sound pattern of words, i.e., by exploitation of language-specific probabilistic cues like typical stress patterns. As the next section describes, there is now a good deal of evidence supporting this account.

3   The headturn preference procedure and early word segmentation

The development of the Headturn Preference Procedure (HPP) brought about great advances in understanding of when infants begin segmenting words from speech. Before the HPP was in widespread use, evidence from language production led researchers to conclude that four-year-olds still had not completely solved the word segmentation problem (Chaney 1989; Holden and MacGinitie 1972; Huttenlocher 1964; Tunmer, Bowey and Grieve 1983). At the same time, however, most studies of early syntactic development assumed that two- and three-year-olds were perceiving speech as a string of discrete words. In retrospect, this assumption does not seem unwarranted, especially since it seems only logical that children would need to learn to segment words from speech before they could build a large enough vocabulary to communicate their thoughts verbally. In other words, research on infant word segmentation lagged behind research on, for instance, phoneme and language discrimination.

One reason for the relative lag is that studying word segmentation presents methodological challenges. First, long stretches of speech must be presented. Second, there must be a measure of recognition rather than simply of discrimination or preference. The earliest widely-used infant testing methodologies, such as the High Amplitude Sucking Procedure and the Visual Fixation Procedure, were unsuited to the study of word segmentation because they offered no recognition measure.

The first use of HPP was in a test of four-month-olds' preferences concerning adult- versus infant-directed speech (Fernald 1985). In Fernald's experiment, infants sat facing forward on a parent's lap in the middle of a three-sided booth. A light was mounted at eye level in the center of each of the three walls of the booth. Speakers were hidden behind the lights on the two side walls; infant-directed speech (IDS) was played from one speaker and adult-directed speech (ADS) from the other. The green light on the front panel blinked at the onset of each trial. Once infants oriented towards the green light, it would immediately stop blinking and both of the side lights would begin blinking. Depending on which light the infants turned towards, they would hear either IDS or ADS. Headturns were observed by an experimenter out of view of the infant. Fernald *et al.* found that infants turned to the side from which IDS was played more often than they turned to the side from which ADS was played. Accordingly, they inferred that four-month-olds preferred to listen to IDS over ADS.

In this version of HPP, the dependent measure was how often infants turned to the left versus right. In the first HPP study of word segmentation (Myers, Jusc-zyk, Kemler Nelson, Luce, Woodward and Hirsch-Pasek 1996), the procedure was modified so that all stimulus types were played equally often from the left and right speaker, and the dependent measure was length of orientation time to speech from one side versus the other. The contrast in this study was between passages containing pauses inserted within words versus pauses inserted between words. Eleven-month-olds listened longer to the latter type of speech. Based on the as-sumption that infants prefer to listen to natural- over unnatural-sounding speech samples (see Jusczyk 1997, for review), this study suggested that 11-month-olds have some concept of where word boundaries belong in speech. But this is not the best test of word segmentation abilities, since it is possible that the infants had simply noticed the unnatural disturbance of the pitch contour.

A better test of infants' word segmentation skills was devised by Jusczyk and Aslin (1995), who further modified HPP by adding a familiarization phase prior to the test phase (see also Kemler Nelson, Jusczyk, Mandel, Myers, Turk and Gerken 1995). During the familiarization phase of Jusczyk and Aslin's study, 7.5-month-olds listened for 30 seconds to isolated repetitions of each of two words: *dog* and *cup* or *bike* and *feet*. In the test phase immediately following this familiarization, infants' length of orientation to test passages containing *dog, cup, bike,* and *feet* was measured. Infants familiarized with *bike* and *feet* listened longer to test passages containing *bike* and *feet*, while infants familiarized with *cup* and *dog* listened long-er to passages with *cup* and *dog*. Six-month-olds tested with the same procedure and stimuli failed to demonstrate any listening preferences.

Jusczyk and Aslin accordingly concluded that infants begin segmenting words from speech some time between six and 7.5 months of age. Numerous subsequent segmentation studies with the two-part version of HPP have supported this find-ing (see Jusczyk 1999, and Nazzi *et al.*, this volume, for reviews).

In combination, these HPP studies have provided clear evidence that produc-tion studies underestimate the rate of development of infants' word segmentation ability. Production studies were inadequate to study early word segmentation for several reasons. First, they required a verbal response, which limited researchers to testing children who could already speak. Second, the tasks used to test children's ability to hear word boundaries were often quite complicated (e.g. repeating the words in an utterance in reverse order). The difficulty of these tasks is very likely to have masked younger children's ability to segment words from speech. Word segmentation abilities develop in the course of initial vocabulary building, and studies with the HPP have allowed us to see that.

4   Advantages and disadvantages of behavioral word segmentation measures

The HPP has many strengths as a testing methodology for research on word segmentation. First, it allows long stretches of speech to be presented in either the
familiarization or test phase of the experiment; this is obviously an essential prerequisite for studying fluent speech processing. Indeed, recent studies have shown
that HPP also works well with fluent speech in <u>both</u> familiarization and test phases (Soderstrom, Kemler Nelson and Juscyk 2005; Seidl and Johnson, forthcoming). Second, the dropout rate in HPP is relatively low compared to other testing
methodologies. Third, HPP yields less variable data than some other methods,
since looking-time measures are often based on 12 to 16 trials, rather than the two
or four test trials commonly used, for example, in the Visual Fixation Procedure
(however, see Houston and Horn 2007, for discussion of an adapted version of the
Visual Fixation Procedure allowing multiple test trials and providing results which
are arguably suitable for individual subject analysis). Fourth, HPP is widely ap-
plicable; although it may be best suited for testing children between six and nine
months of age, it has been shown to work well with children as young as four
months or as old as 24 months. This is certainly useful, considering the protracted
development of word segmentation abilities (e.g., see Nazzi, Dilley, Jusczyk, Shattuck-Hufnagel and Jusczyk 2005). Fifth and finally, HPP does not require that infants be trained to focus on any particular aspect of the speech signal. Rather, in
contrast to procedures like the Conditioned Headturn Procedure (CHT), it provides a measure of what infants naturally extract from the speech signal.

Like all infant testing methodologies, HPP has a few disadvantages too. As
with other methods, it is hard to say whether performance in the laboratory is ac-
curately representative of performance in the real world, where visual and auditory distractions are plentiful (see however, Newman 2005). HPP is ill-suited to
the study of individual variation, because a typical HPP study requires multiple
subjects. Infants can become bored with the HPP procedure, and re-testing a child
with the same procedure is not advisable. Finally, HPP looking times do not reflect
the temporal nature of the processing involved. This is of particular importance to
the case of word segmentation.

In adult word segmentation research, the temporal course of word processing
has played an important role in understanding how words are recognized. Reaction time studies have revealed that many word candidates are simultaneously activated, and then compete for recognition (Norris, McQueen and Cutler 1995).
The competition process is further modulated by explicit segmentation procedures
which can be language-specific (e.g., attention to rhythmic structure; Cutler and
Butterfield 1992) or universal (e.g., rejection of activated words which would leave
isolated consonants unaccounted for in the signal; Norris, McQueen, Cutler and

Butterfield 1997; Cutler, Demuth and McQueen 2002). But HPP effectively only tells us whether word segmentation has occurred, not how rapidly it has occurred. Evidence for the temporary activation of spurious word candidates, or information about the precise timing of online segmentation, cannot be found with HPP. Thus although we know that twelve-month-olds also fail to segment word candidates which would leave isolated consonants unaccounted for (Johnson, Jusczyk, Cutler and Norris 2003), the results of this study – summarized in Figure 2 – tell us only that segmentation has occurred in one condition and not in the other; they tell us nothing about the relative speed of word recognition which was addressed in the adult studies, let alone about the relative segmentation success for individual words in the passages or the performance of individual listeners.

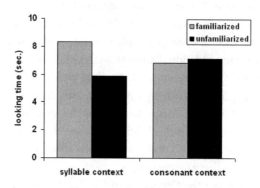

Figure 2. Mean looking times for 12-month-old infants in the HPP study of Johnson *et al.* (2003) to passages containing embedded words which were familiarized versus unfamiliarized, separately for conditions where the embedding context was a whole syllable (e.g., *win* in *winsome* or *window, rest* in *caressed* or *fluoresced*) versus an isolated consonant (e.g., *win* in *wind* or *whinge, rest* in *dressed* or *breast*). Each test passage contained five occurrences of the crucial word in five different embedding contexts. Each mean is an average over 40 participants

It would certainly be advantageous if the fine-grained temporal course of word segmentation could also be studied in younger infants, who are just beginning to use their newly acquired knowledge about the sound structure of their native language to extract word forms from speech. Two procedures which appear more temporally sensitive than HPP each have limitations. First, eye-tracking procedures (Fernald, Pinto and Swingley 2001; Swingley, Pinto and Fernald 1999) certainly offer a window onto the temporal course of children's processing; however, these procedures can only be used with children who already have a lexicon in place, which makes them unsuitable for early segmentation research. Second, the Conditioned Headturn (CHT) Procedure, in which infants are trained to turn to a puppet box for reinforcement each time they hear a target word, can also be used to test infants' extraction of words from fluent speech. In CHT studies on phoneme discrimination, target words or syllables were embedded in a list of other words, all spoken in isolation (Werker, Polka and Pegg 1997), but more recently, infants have been trained to respond to target words embedded in utterances (Dietrich 2006; Gout, Christophe and Morgan 2004), and Gout *et al.* have claimed that CHT provides a more sensitive measure of word segmentation capabilities than HPP.

Although the dependent measure in CHT is usually not the speed of initiating a headturn but the probability of making one, this method almost approaches an online measure, and it clearly has the potential to provide a useful convergent measure of early word segmentation. But CHT has a notoriously high dropout rate, and it typically requires two highly experienced experimenters to run the procedure. Given the skills needed to run CHT, procedural differences between laboratories could affect results. Moreover, while HPP's familiarization phase is arguably a laboratory instantiation of natural parental repetitions, CHT's phase of training infants to attend to a specific word could be seen as less ecologically valid.

Online reflection of infant speech perception is, however, available from non-behavioral methods; in particular, electrophysiological methods have been used to study infant speech processing for over 30 years (Molfese, Freeman and Palermo 1975). As we argue in the following section, these methods now offer new insights into word segmentation in infancy too.

5   ERPs as a reflection of early word segmentation

Kooijman, Hagoort and Cutler (2005) recently adapted infant Event-Related Brain Potential (ERP) measures to the study of word segmentation. Compared with the behavioral techniques just reviewed, a much clearer case can be made that this measure succeeds in reflecting the temporal course of infant word processing. In contrast to HPP and CHT, the dependent measure in ERP studies is not a behavioral response, but an electrophysiological signal produced by the brain. There are both pros and cons to the use of a brain response rather than an explicit behavior as a measure of word recognition. On the one hand, behavioral measures may be rather conservative reflections of word segmentation. When a predicted behavior is not observed in HPP or CHT, researchers can conclude that word recognition has not occurred. But it is conceivable that the infant may have recognized the word but just failed to indicate so in the way we expect. This is why null results can be so difficult to interpret in behavioral studies such as HPP (see Aslin and Fiser 2005, for discussion). Although ERP measures are also only an indirect reflection of the mental operations we wish to reveal, the behavioral measures require that neural activity be translated to behavior while ERPs arguably tap the neural activity on which the behavior is founded. On the other hand, note that it is possible that the neural activity underlying a measured behavioral response may go undetected in a particular ERP measurement situation (Kutas and Dale 1997).

Electroencephalography (EEG) measures the electrical signals generated by cortical, and to a lesser degree subcortical, areas of the brain. In a typical cognitive ERP experiment, a task is presented to the participant during continuous EEG recording. A marker, usually time-locked to the onset of stimulus presentation (but sometimes also to the offset, or to the participant's response) is linked to the EEG signal. Recorded EEG signals given different stimulus types are extracted and averaged for each condition to calculate ERPs. (For a detailed description of EEG, see Luck 2005). Although there are different ways to use the EEG signal as a measure of cognitive processes, ERP measurement is currently the most commonly used testing method.

Significant increases in knowledge of the pros and cons of ERP measurement have been achieved in the past decade. Many laboratories use ERPs to investigate language processing, and quite a few have now turned to the use of ERPs to study language development. In adults, ERPs have been used for a considerable number of years as a measure of language processing and several ERP components have been well described. For example, the N400 has been shown to be related to semantic information processing (Federmeier and Kutas 1999; Kutas and Federmeier 2000), and grammatical information processing has been shown to be reflected by the Early Left Anterior Negativity (Friederici, Hahne and Mecklinger 1996) and the SPS/P600 (Hagoort, Brown and Osterhout 1999). Studies on adult ERP reflections of word segmentation are limited: Sanders and Neville (2003) tested N100 modulation as a signature of adult word boundary recognition, and proposed this early component as an index of word segmentation; Snijders, Kooijman, Hagoort and Cutler (in press) studied word segmentation in Dutch with an ERP repetition paradigm, and found significant segmentation delay in foreign listeners with no knowledge of Dutch, as compared to adult native speakers of Dutch.

Although we as yet know relatively little about the ERP components of language processing in infants, this field of research is developing rapidly (for recent reviews, see Friederici 2005; Kuhl 2004). Note that EEG is particularly suitable for use with difficult subject groups such as young children because it is an easy noninvasive procedure and does not require the subject to perform an overt task. The use of so-called EEG caps, i.e. caps containing a number of electrodes on fixed positions, has further increased the utility of EEG with infants. Some research has already addressed the development of ERP components. Pasman, Rotteveel, Maassen and Visco (1999) investigated the development of the N1/P2 complex in children, and showed that this response to tones does not reach mature levels until about

14–16 years of age. The Mismatch Negativity response (Cheour, Alho, Ceponiené, Reinikainen, Sainio, Pohjavouri, Aaltonen and Näätänen 1998) has been claimed to be a stable component that can be found in both adults and very young infants (though see Dehaene-Lambertz and Pena 2001); considerable changes do however occur during development (Cheour *et al.* 1998). More recently, in some laboratories the development of the N400 component has been investigated as a representation of early word meaning; for example, Friedrich and Friederici (2004; 2005) observed an N400-like semantic incongruity effect in 14- and 19-month-olds.

Kooijman *et al.*'s (2005) study on early word segmentation was the first to use an ERP paradigm to test infants under a year of age on continuous speech input. Kooijman *et al.* devised an ERP-compatible adaptation of the familiarization-and-test HPP procedure of Jusczyk and Aslin (1995), described above. Since no headturns or other behavioral responses are required in an ERP study, or even desired because of possible movement artifact, Kooijman *et al.*'s study involved no lights, and speech signals did not change source location. Infants heard, in a familiarization phase, ten tokens of the same bisyllabic word. Immediately following the familiarization, infants listened to eight randomized sentences making up the test phase. Four of these sentences contained the familiarized word, while the other four contained an unfamiliar bisyllabic word. Comparison of the ERP to the familiar and unfamiliar target words in the test phase sentences is then the measure of word segmentation. The words and sentences were spoken in a lively manner typical of infant-directed speech; the speech samples in Figure 1 are three examples of the word *mosterd* 'mustard' from a familiarization phase in this study, and one of the sentences containing this word from a test phase. There were 20 blocks of familiarization plus test phase; ERP requires such a high number of experimental blocks because an acceptable signal-to-noise ratio can only be attained with many trials per condition, and the dropout of trials per infant can be quite high due to movement artifacts. Table 1 shows an example block.

Table 1. Example of an experimental trial in the ERP study of Kooijman *et al.* (2005)

Familiarization: Ten repetitions of _mosterd_

Test:
Die oude _mosterd_ smaakt echt niet meer goed.
    That old mustard really doesn't taste so good any more.
Voor soep is de dikke _mosterd_ ook te gebruiken.
    The thick mustard can also be used for soup.
De oude _pelgrim_ maakt een reis naar Lourdes.
    The old pilgrim is travelling to Lourdes.
De _pelgrim_ is niet blij met de openbaring.
    The pilgrim is not happy about the revelation.
Bij de jonge _mosterd_ past een goed stuk kaas.
    A nice piece of cheese is good with with the young mustard.
Met verbazing keek de dikke _pelgrim_ naar het beeld.
    The fat pilgrim looked at the statue in amazement.
Dankzij die jonge _pelgrim_ kon de vrouw toch mee.
    Thanks to the young pilgrim, the woman came along after all.
De _mosterd_ wordt verkocht bij elke slager.
    The mustard is sold at every butcher's.

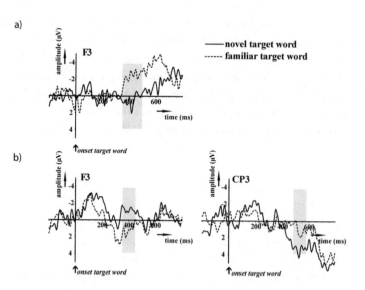

Figure 3. Mean ERPs to familiarized and unfamiliarized words in sentences; (a) 10-month-old listeners, electrode position F3; (b) seven-month-olds listeners, electrode positions F3 and CP3. Negativity is plotted upwards. The grey areas indicate the time windows showing a statistically significant difference between the two conditions

Twenty-eight normally developing ten-month-old Dutch-learning infants were tested using this procedure. The results, shown in the upper panel of Figure 3, revealed a clear difference between the waveforms generated by the familiar and the unfamiliar words in the form of a negative-going ERP response to the familiar words only, with a left lateral distribution. This effect occurred about 350 ms after word onset, indicating that word segmentation has begun as early as halfway through the word. That is, infants do not need the whole word to initiate word segmentation. These results nicely show how ERP methodology can be used to complement and extend earlier findings of word segmentation (specifically, demonstrations of word segmentation by Dutch-learning infants with the Jusczyk and Aslin procedure by Kuijpers, Coolen, Houston and Cutler 1998, and Houston, Jusczyk, Kuijpers, Coolen and Cutler 2000). The millisecond level of precision of this measure gives insight into online processes and offers a new window on developmental word segmentation.

In addition to the study with ten-month-old infants, Kooijman and colleagues also used the same ERP paradigm to test for word segmentation in seven-month-old infants (Kooijman, Hagoort and Cutler, submitted). The results of this study are summarized in the lower panel of Figure 3. Two ERP effects differentiating familiar and unfamiliar words were found with this younger age group: an early positive effect with a frontal distribution, starting at about 350 ms; and a later negative effect with a left lateral distribution, starting at about 480 ms. The words in the sentences had an average duration of 720 ms; so even about halfway into the word, seven-month-olds too show some indication of word recognition.

It is particularly interesting to compare the seven-month-old and the ten-month-old ERP data. The differential responses to familiar versus unfamiliar words, as well as the early onset of the ERP effect, show the groups to be responding similarly: both seven- and ten-month-olds initiate an early response of word segmentation. But the distribution of the effects shows the groups to be different. It could thus be that the effect has different underlying sources in the two age groups. This is a tempting conclusion to draw, since cognitive development has obviously progressed between seven and ten months of age. But such a conclusion could be premature, as physical and neural development has to be considered as well. Neural development is not complete at birth; it continues for years, indeed well into the second decade of life. Especially dendritic growth and pruning, and cortical folding, continue into the first year of life (Mrzljak, Uylings, Van Eden and Judas 1990; Uylings 2006). To what extent these changes affect the EEG is as yet unknown. In addition, physical changes in the skull, that is, the closing of the fontanels, continues until well into the second year of life. Flemming, Wang, Caprihan, Eiselt, Haueisen and Okada (2005), in a simulation study, found that a hole in the skull would have a large effect on the EEG signal. All these changes in neural and physical development may thus have an effect on the distribution and polarity of ERP results, so that caution is warranted in interpreting differences between different age groups. Nonetheless, the timing information of ERPs, and the comparison between different conditions, allow us to be confident that the similarity between groups – the clear evidence of early segmentation by both seven- and ten-month-olds – is real.

6   Parallel measures: A preliminary account

Both HPP and ERP, it is clear, provide valuable views of word segmentation in preverbal infants. HPP delivers a behavioral reflection of segmentation even at this young age, and ERP offers an online measure of segmentation skills with high temporal precision. In an attempt to combine the advantages of these differing techniques, Kooijman et al. (submitted) undertook a first study putting the two methodologies together.

Previous HPP data from Dutch-learning infants showed evidence of segmentation by nine-month-olds (Kuijpers et al. 1998; Houston, Jusczyk, Kuijpers, Coolen and Cutler 2000) but no trace of segmentation responses with 7.5-month-olds (Kuijpers et al. 1998). The ERP data which Kooijman et al. (2005; submitted) collected showed clear evidence of segmentation by ten-month-olds and likewise clear, but in some respects different, evidence of segmentation by seven-month-olds. However, it could be that the materials used in the ERP and HPP studies with seven-month-olds were dissimilar; some aspect of the materials used in the ERP study – for instance, the particular speaker's voice, the slow rate of speech (see Figure 1 for an example), the pitch contour of the child-directed speech – may have particularly encouraged word recognition by seven-month-olds. Note that the degree of mismatch between familiarization token and test token is known to affect the ease with which infants segment words from speech (Houston 2000; Singh, Morgan and White 2004). Kooijman et al. therefore undertook an HPP study directly parallel to their ERP experiment with seven-month-olds.

To achieve close comparability between the two data sets, they made certain modifications to the standard HPP paradigm. First, the two-stage familiarization-and-test procedure was replaced with a cycling testing design that more closely resembled the design of the ERP study. Instead of one familiarization phase and one test phase as in the version of HPP used by Jusczyk and Aslin, there were multiple consecutive phases of familiarization and test. Second, and again to make the HPP and ERP studies as similar as possible, the familiarization phase consisted of ten tokens of the same word, instead of the 30 seconds of speech used by Jusczyk and Aslin (1995). The test phase most closely resembled the original word segmentation

HPP studies. In each test phase, four trials of four sentences were presented, of which two trials contained sentences with the familiarized word, while two contained sentences with an unfamiliar word. From the speech stimuli used in the ERP study, ten blocks of familiarization and test were constructed for this HPP design; an example block is given in Table 2. The two test conditions (familiar, unfamiliar) were played to the infant equally often from the right and left speaker.

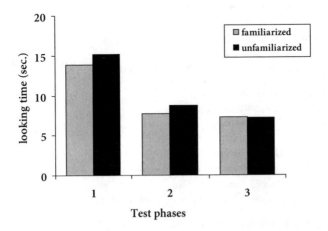

Figure 4. Mean looking times for seven-month-old infants in the first three Test phases in an adjusted HPP design to sentences containing familiarized and unfamiliarized words. The same materials were used in the ERP study.

Twenty-eight seven-month-old infants were tested in this study. As in the ERP study, familiarization and order of presentation of the blocks was counterbalanced across subjects. Figure 4 shows results of the first three blocks (one block consists of a familiarization and a test phase): there was no significant preference for one type of sentence over the other. This finding is fully in line with the results of Kuijpers *et al.*'s (1998) study with 7.5-month-olds using standard HPP. Dutch seven-month-olds do not show a behavioral indication of word segmentation, even though the ERP results suggest that their brain is capable of the cortical responsiveness which necessarily underlies such behavior.

Table 2. Example of an experimental trial in the adjusted HPP study of Kooijman *et al.* (forthcoming) with seven-month-olds

---

Familiarization: Ten repetitions of _mosterd_

Test:
Die oude _mosterd_ smaakt echt niet meer goed.
    That old mustard really doesn't taste so good any more.
Voor soep is de dikke _mosterd_ ook te gebruiken.
    The thick mustard can also be used for soup
De _mosterd_ wordt verkocht bij elke slager.
    The mustard is sold at every butcher's.
Bij de jonge _mosterd_ past een goed stuk kaas.
    A nice piece of cheese is good with with the young mustard

De oude _pelgrim_ maakt een reis naar Lourdes.
    The old pilgrim is travelling to Lourdes.
De _pelgrim_ is niet blij met de openbaring.
    The pilgrim is not happy about the revelation.
Met verbazing keek de dikke _pelgrim_ naar het beeld.
    The fat pilgrim looked at the statue in amazement.
Dankzij de jonge _pelgrim_ kon de vrouw toch mee.
    Thanks to the young pilgrim, the woman came along after all.

Die oude _mosterd_ smaakt echt niet meer goed.
    That old mustard really doesn't taste so good any more.
Voor soep is de dikke _mosterd_ ook te gebruiken.
    The thick mustard can also be used for soup
De _mosterd_ wordt verkocht bij elke slager.
    The mustard is sold at every butcher's.
Bij de jonge _mosterd_ past een goed stuk kaas.
    A nice piece of cheese is good with with the young mustard.

De oude _pelgrim_ maakt een reis naar Lourdes.
    The old pilgrim is travelling to Lourdes.
De _pelgrim_ is niet blij met de openbaring.
    The pilgrim is not happy about the revelation.
Met verbazing keek de dikke _pelgrim_ naar het beeld.
    The fat pilgrim looked at the statue in amazement.
Dankzij de jonge _pelgrim_ kon de vrouw toch mee.
    Thanks to the young pilgrim, the woman came along after all.

---

7   What does it mean when behavior and brain activity fail to line up?

As we pointed out above, difficulties do arise in interpreting ERP data. So how do we interpret ERP data and behavioral data which do not line up? Kooijman *et al.*'s

(2005) report of an ERP response to familiarized words in 10-month-olds fits well with the HPP literature; studies with both English- and Dutch-learning infants have demonstrated that infants begin segmenting words from speech before this age. However, Kooijman *et al.*'s (submitted) evidence from ERPs that seven-month-olds too can segment words from speech contrasts starkly with their own finding of no HPP effect in the same age group, and with other earlier findings. In fact, no HPP study with infants learning any language has found evidence that infants as young as seven months can segment words from fluent natural speech (though see Bortfeld, Morgan, Golinkoff and Rathbun 2005, for an exceptional situation with English-learning six-month-olds). English-learning infants have been shown to segment speech by 7.5 months of age (Jusczyk and Aslin 1995), but the HPP studies have suggested that Dutch infants are slightly delayed compared to English-learning infants in their ability to segment words from speech (this has been attributed to phonological differences in word boundary salience in English vs. Dutch; Kuijpers *et al.* 1998). Kooijman *et al.*'s result with seven-month-olds now reveals that the absence of an effect in HPP does not imply the absence of any relevant processing in the infant brain.

As also discussed above, the ERP and HPP are very different measures. Thus, it is easy to construct different explanations for the observed patterns of results that they yield. Such explanations can involve different levels of processing, in the same way as, for instance, explanations at different levels have been proposed for the fact that mastery of linguistic abilities often appears earlier in perception than in production: that perception is a more sensitive behavioral test than production, that the behavioral response required in perception tasks is less cognitively demanding than the responses required in production studies, or that there is a difference in the levels of knowledge tapped by the tasks. The mismatch between the HPP and ERP findings we have described allows a similar range of accounts.

First, it is possible that the ERP measure is simply more sensitive than the HPP measure. Thus the difference between ERP and HPP data could be analogous to differences between two behavioral paradigms requiring different types of response. There are differences in task sensitivity even between different perceptual measures, often depending on how engaging the task is or how metabolically expensive the response is (Gout *et al.* 2004; McMurray and Aslin 2004). Second, the difference between ERP and HPP data could be due to different levels of processing being tapped. Third, the discrepancy could be due to theoretically uninteresting differences between experiments, such as differences in speech stimuli or in test phase length. More studies collecting parallel ERP and HPP data with the same speech stimuli, as Kooijman *et al.* did, will help clarify these issues.

A fourth possibility, however, and the one which we favor in the interpretation of Kooijman *et al.*'s results, is that the brain response observed in seven-month-olds is a precursor of an overt behavior which is to come. Certainly overt behaviors cannot appear overnight without some drastic changes first taking place in the mind of an infant. The suggestion that the ERP component found in the seven-month-olds is a precursor of overt behavior is comparable to the interpretation which McLaughlin, Osterhout, and Kim (2004) offered of their findings with adults learning a second language; modulation of the N400 appeared after only 14 hours (on average) of classroom instruction, but the same participants still performed at chance level on a word discrimination task, thus showing no behavioral evidence of increased knowledge of the second language. Cortical responsiveness to a difference in stimuli is one essential prerequisite for a differential behavioral response to the same stimuli, but it need not be the only precondition on which the behavior depends.

8   Simultaneous measures: Future goals

The use of ERP and HPP measures in parallel is, as we have seen, clearly possible, and it can prove highly informative; the asymmetry in the appearance of ERP and HPP reflections of lexical segmentation sheds light not only on how infants learn to segment speech but also on how behavioral responses should be explained. In other areas of processing, simultaneous measures have been collected that allow alternative views of the same individual's speech processing at the same time. Thus Berger, Tzur and Posner (2006) have successfully demonstrated infant sensitivity to arithmetic errors in ERP in combination with looking-time methods. In our view, simultaneous ERP and behavioral reflections of infant word segmentation should be equally feasible

Obviously there are practical difficulties: dependent measures such as headturns cause artifacts in the EEG signal (Luck 2005), so standard HPP would be incompatible with EEG measures. Abrupt eye movements can also disrupt the EEG signal, so that it would similarly be difficult to run an eye-tracking study at the same time as recording ERPs. Given these issues, it is clear that combinations of behavioral and brain measures need to be very creative. Thus even if simultaneous HPP and ERP measures seem to be ruled out, partially simultaneous measures involving a modified familiarization phase should be perfectly possible. HPP studies have succeeded in familiarizing infants to fluent passages through passive listening to speech accompanied by a visual stimulus on a TV screen, with infants moved to a HPP booth after familiarization for the behavioral test of segmentation (Hollich, Newman and Jusczyk 2005). These experiments kept children's attention to the speech signal by showing a video of a woman speaking, but attention could also be held by a colorful image on a small screen, as Kooijman *et al.* (2005) used in their ERP study. With this procedure, ERPs could be measured while children passively listened to passages. Following exposure, the ERP cap could be removed and infants could be moved to the headturn booth for behavioral testing.

This design assumes that the ERP measurement will pick up evidence of segmentation of a word without exposure to that word in isolation. This seems justified, given that, as we noted above, HPP works well with fluent speech in both familiarization and test (Seidl and Johnson, forthcoming). This suggests that passive exposure to words in passages will result in evidence of segmentation. However, ERP requires multiple measurements for evidence of segmentation, because ERP signals are quite noisy. Thus, if ERP measurements were made during the familiarization phase, this phase might need to be lengthened, or the stimuli adjusted such that sentences contained multiple target words. Given the limited attention span of young children, it is possible that by the end of a lengthy familiarization phase infants might be too fatigued to successfully complete a further test phase. This potential problem can, however, be overcome. Infants familiarized with a word one day will easily recognize the word the next day (Houston and Jusczyk 2003). In fact, there is evidence that children continue to recognize words for at least two weeks after familiarization (Jusczyk and Hohne 1997). These considerations thus motivate the hope that partially simultaneous measures of word segmentation could be obtained by slightly modifying the classic HPP design, and collecting ERP measurements during the familiarization phase of the experiment.

Fully simultaneous measurements would require that a dependent measure other than headturns be used in the test phase. One possible candidate behavioral measure requiring no headturns might be a modified version of the Visual Fixation Procedure, in which infants' looking time to a single visual display is measured as a function of different auditory inputs. Although the paradigm has chiefly been used to test discrimination, it is not unrealistic to imagine that it could be adapted to study word segmentation. As in the ERP study of Kooijman et al. (2005), a single visual stimulus is fixated, so that no eye movements between multiple stimuli will cause interference with EEG measurement. With this procedure, infants could be familiarized to isolated words using the passive exposure method described above. They could then be presented with passages containing familiar and unfamiliar words, and their fixation time to the screen would serve as the dependent measure to gauge word recognition. The prediction would be that infants would fixate the screen longer for familiar than for unfamiliar words. At the same time, ERP data could be collected and ERP signals to the familiar and unfamiliar words could be compared.

Candidates therefore seem to exist for the next generation of methodologies; in particular, we predict that comparison of simultaneously measured behavioral and ERP response will constitute a powerful tool for a better understanding of both behavioral and brain responses to familiar words. Longitudinal studies, i.e., testing infants three or four times between the ages of six and ten months, could also provide an informative window into the development of word segmentation abilities. We see a bright future for the continuing attempts to capture the elusive reflections of infant word recognition.

Notes

Preparation of this chapter, and the research reported here, were supported by the NWO-SPINOZA project "Native and Non-native Listening" awarded to the third author. We thank Dennis Pasveer for making Figure 1, and Holger Mitterer for helpful comments on the text.

References

Aslin, R.N. and Fiser, J. 2005. "Methodological challenges for understanding cognitive development in infancy." *Trends in Cognitive Science* 9: 92–8.
Aslin, R.N., Jusczyk, P.W. and Pisoni, D.B. 1998. "Speech and auditory processing during infancy: Constraints on and precursors to language." In *Handbook of child psychology*, 5th edn, Volume 2: *Cognition, perception and language*, D. Kuhn and R. Siegler (eds.), 147–98. New York NY: Wiley.
Berger, A., Tzur, G. and Posner, M.I. 2006. "Infants detect arithmetic errors". *Proceedings of the National Academy of Sciences of the United States of America* 103: 12649–53.
Brent, M.R. 1999. "Speech segmentation and word discovery: A computational perspective." *Trends in Cognitive Science* 3: 294–301.
Bloomfield, L. 1933. *Language*. New York, NY: Holt.
Bortfeld, H., Morgan, J.L, Golinkoff, R.M. and Rathbun, K. 2005. "Mommy and me: Familiar names help launch babies into speech stream segmentation." *Psychological Science* 16: 298–304.
Bosch, L. and Sebastián-Gallés, N. 1997. "Native-language recognition abilities in four-month-old infants from monolingual and bilingual environments." *Cognition* 65: 33–69.
Chaney, C.F. 1989. "I pledge a legiance tothe flag: Three studies in word segmentation." *Applied Psycholinguistics* 10: 261–81.
Cheour, M., Alho, K., Ceponiené, R., Reinikainen, K., Sainio, K., Pohjavouri, M., Aaltonen, O. and Näätänen, R. 1998. "Maturation of mismatch negativity in infants." *International Journal of Psychophysiology* 29: 217–26.
Christophe, A. and Morton, J. 1998. "Is Dutch native English? Linguistic analysis by 2-month-olds." *Developmental Science* 1: 215–19.
Cutler, A. 2001. "Listening to a second language through the ears of a first." *Interpreting* 5: 1–23.
Cutler, A. and Butterfield, S. 1992. "Rhythmic cues to speech segmentation: Evidence from juncture misperception." *Journal of Memory and Language* 31: 218–36.
Cutler, A. and Carter, D.M. 1987. "The predominance of strong initial syllables in the English vocabulary." *Computer Speech and Language* 2: 133–42.

Cutler, A., Demuth, K. and McQueen, J.M. 2002. "Universality versus language-specificity in listening to running speech." *Psychological Science* 13: 258–62.

Dehaene-Lambertz, G. and Pena, M. 2001. "Electrophysiological evidence for automatic phonetic processing in neonates." *Neuroreport* 12: 3155–8.

DeCasper, A.J. and Fifer, W.P. 1980. "Of human bonding: Newborns prefer their mothers' voice." *Science* 208: 1174–6.

DeCasper, A.J. and Spence, M.J. 1986. "Prenatal maternal speech influences newborns' perception of speech sounds." *Infant Behavior and Development* 9: 133–50.

Dietrich, C. 2006. The acquisition of phonological structure: Distinguishing contrastive from non-contrastive variation. PhD dissertation, Radboud University Nijmegen. (*MPI Series in Psycholinguistics* 40).

Eimas, P.D., Siqueland, E.R., Jusczyk, P.W. and Vigorito, J. 1971. "Speech perception in infants." *Science* 171: 303–6.

Federmeier, K. D. and Kutas, M. 1999. "A rose by any other name: Long-term memory structure and sentence processing." *Journal of Memory and Language* 41: 469–95.

Fernald, A. 1985. "Four-month-old infants prefer to listen to motherese." *Infant Behavior and Development* 8: 181–95.

Fernald, A., Swingley, D., and Pinto, J.P. (2001). "When half a word is enough: Infants can recognize spoken words using partial phonetic information." *Child Development* 72: 1003–1015.

Flemming, L., Wang, Y.Z., Caprihan, A., Eiselt, M., Haueisen, J. and Okada, Y. 2005. "Evaluation of the distortion of EEG signals caused by a hole in the skull mimicking the fontanel in the skull of human neonates." *Clinical Neurophysiology* 116: 1141–52.

Friederici, A.D. 2005. "Neurophysiological markers of early language acquisition: From syllables to sentences." *Trends in Cognitive Sciences* 9: 481–8.

Friederici, A.D., Hahne, A., and Mecklinger, A. 1996. "Temporal structure of syntactic parsing: Early and late event-related brain potential effects." *Journal of Experimental Psychology: Learning, Memory, and Cognition* 22: 1219–48.

Friedrich, M. and Friederici, A.D. 2005. "Lexical priming and semantic integration reflected in the event-related potential of 14-month-olds." *Neuroreport* 16: 653–6.

Friedrich, M. and Friederici, A.D. 2004. "N400-like semantic incongruity effect in 19-month-olds: Processing known words in picture contexts." *Journal of Cognitive Neuroscience* 16: 1465–77.

Gout, A., Christophe, A. and Morgan, J.L. 2004. "Phonological phrase boundaries constrain lexical access II. Infant data." *Journal of Memory and Language* 51: 548–67.

Hagoort, P., Brown, C.M. and Osterhout, L. 1999. "The neurocognition of syntactic processing." In *The neurocognition of language*, C.M. Brown and P. Hagoort (eds.), 273–316. New York, NY: OUP.

Holden, M.H. and MacGinitie, W.H. 1972. "Children's conception of word boundaries in speech and print." *Journal of Educational Psychology* 63: 551–7.

Hollich, G., Hirsh-Pasek, K. and Golinkoff, R.M. 2000. "Breaking the language barrier: An emergentist coalition model for the origins of word learning." *Monographs of the Society for Research in Child Development* 65 (3, Serial No. 262).

Hollich, G., Newman, R.S. and Jusczyk, P.W. 2005. "Infants' use of synchronized visual information to separate streams of speech." *Child Development* 76: 598–613.

Houston, D.M. 2000. The role of talker variability in infant word representations. PhD dissertation, Johns Hopkins University, 2000. *Dissertation Abstracts International* 60 (11-B): 5802.

Houston, D.M., Horn, D.L., Qi, R., Ting, J. and Gao, S. 2007. Submitted. "Assessing speech discrimination in individual infants." *Infancy*, 12, 1-27.

Houston, D.M., Jusczyk, P.W., Kuijpers, C., Coolen, R. and Cutler, A. 2000. "Cross-language word segmentation by nine-month-olds." *Psychonomic Bulletin and Review* 7: 504–9.

Houston, D.M. and Jusczyk, P.W. 2003. "Infants' long term memory for the sound patterns of words and voices." *Journal of Experimental Psychology: Human Perception and Performance* 29: 1143–54.

Huttenlocher, J. 1964. "Children's language: Word-phrase relationship." Science 143: 264–5.

James, W. 1911. *Some problems of philosophy*. Cambridge, MA: Harvard University Press.

Johnson, E.K., Jusczyk, P.W., Cutler, A. and Norris, D. 2003. "Lexical viability constraints on speech segmentation by infants." *Cognitive Psychology* 46: 65–97.

Jusczyk, P.W. 1997. *The discovery of spoken language*. Cambridge, MA: The MIT Press.

Jusczyk, P.W. 1999. "How infants begin to extract words from fluent speech." *Trends in Cognitive Science* 3: 323–8.

Jusczyk, P.W. 1985. "The high-amplitude sucking technique as a methodological tool in speech perception research." In *Measurement of audition and vision in the first year of postnatal life: A methodological overview*, G. Gottlieb and N.A. Krasnegor (eds.), 195–222. Norwood, NJ: Ablex.

Jusczyk, P.W. and Aslin, R.N. 1995. "Infants' detection of the sound patterns of words in fluent speech." *Cognitive Psychology* 29: 1–23.

Jusczyk, P.W. and Hohne, E.A. 1997. "Infants' memory for spoken words." *Science* 277: 1984–6.

Jusczyk, P.W., Houston, D.M. and Newsome, M. 1999. "The beginnings of word segmentation in English-learning infants." *Cognitive Psychology* 39: 159–207.

Kemler Nelson, D.G., Jusczyk, P.W., Mandel, D.R., Myers, J., Turk, A. and Gerken, L.A. 1995. "The headturn preference procedure for testing auditory perception." *Infant Behavior and Development* 18: 111–6.

Kooijman, V., Hagoort, P. and Cutler, A. 2005. "Electrophysiological evidence for prelinguistic infants' word recognition in continuous speech." *Cognitive Brain Research* 24: 109–16.

Kooijman, V., Hagoort, P. and Cutler, A. submitted. "Word recognition at seven months: Mismatching behavioral and electrophysiological evidence."

Kuhl, P. K. 2004. "Early language acquisition: Cracking the speech code." *Nature Reviews Neuroscience* 5: 831–43.

Kuhl, P.K., Williams, K.A., Lacerda, F., Stevens, K.N. and Lindblom B. 1992. "Linguistic experience alters phonetic perception in infants by six months of age." *Science* 255: 606–8.

Kuijpers, C., Coolen, R., Houston, D. and Cutler, A. 1998. "Using the head-turning technique to explore cross-linguistic performance differences." In *Advances in Infancy Research*, C. Rovee-Collier, L. Lipsitt and H. Hayne (eds.), 12: 205–20. London: Ablex.

Kutas, M. and Dale, A. 1997. "Electrical and magnetic readings of mental functions." In *Cognitive neuroscience*, M.D. Rugg (ed.), 197–237. Hove: Psychology Press.

Kutas, M. and Federmeier, K.D. 2000. "Electrophysiology reveals semantic memory use in language comprehension." *Trends in Cognitive Sciences* 4: 463–70.

Luck, S. 2005. *An introduction to the Event-Related Potential technique*. Cambridge, MA: The MIT Press.

Mandel, D.R., Jusczyk, P.W. and Pisoni, D.B. 1995. "Infants' recognition of the sound patterns of their own names." *Psychological Science* 6: 314–7.

McLaughlin, J., Osterhout, L. and Kim, A. 2004. "Neural correlates of second-language word learning: Minimal instruction produces rapid change." *Nature Neuroscience* 7: 703–4.

McMurray, B. and Aslin, R.N. 2004. "Anticipatory eye movements reveal infants' auditory and visual categories." *Infancy* 6: 203–29.

Molfese, D.L., Freeman, R.B. Jr, and Palermo. D.S. 1975. "The ontogeny of brain lateralization for speech and nonspeech stimuli". *Brain and Language* 2: 356–68.

Myers, J., Jusczyk, P.W., Kemler Nelson, J., Charles-Luce, J., Woodward, A.L. and Hirsch-Pasek, K. 1996. "Infants' sensitivity to word boundaries in fluent speech." *Journal of Child Language* 23: 1–30.

Moon, C., Cooper, R.P. and Fifer, W.P. 1993. "Two-day-olds prefer their native language." *Infant Behavior and Development* 16: 495–500.

Morgan, J.L. 1996. "Prosody and the roots of parsing." *Language and Cognitive Processes* 11: 69–106.

Mrzljak, L., Uylings, H.B.M., Van Eden, C.G. and Judas, M. 1990. "Neuronal development in human prefrontal cortex in prenatal and postnatal stages." *Progress in Brain Research* 85: 185–222.

Nazzi, T., Dilley, L.C., Jusczyk, A.M., Shattuck-Hufnagel, S. and Jusczyk, P.W. 2005. "English-learning infants' segmentation of verbs from fluent speech." *Language and Speech* 48: 279–98.

Nazzi, T., Jusczyk, P.W. and Johnson, E.K. 2000. "Language discrimination by English-learning 5-month-olds: Effects of rhythm and familiarity." *Journal of Memory and Language* 43: 1–19.

Newman, R.S. 2005. "The cocktail party effect in infants revisited: Listening to one's name in noise." *Developmental Psychology* 41: 352–62.

Newman, R., Bernstein Ratner, N., Jusczyk, A.M., Jusczyk, P.W. and Dow, K.A. 2006. "Infants' early ability to segment the conversational speech signal predicts later language development: A retrospective analysis." *Developmental Psychology* 42: 643–55.

Norris, D., McQueen, J.M. and Cutler, A. 1995. "Competition and segmentation in spoken-word recognition." *Journal of Experimental Psychology: Learning, Memory and Cognition* 21: 1209–28.

Norris, D., McQueen, J.M., Cutler, A. and Butterfield, S. 1997. "The Possible-Word Constraint in the segmentation of continuous speech." *Cognitive Psychology* 34: 191–243.

Pasman, J.W., Rotteveel, J.J., Maassen, B. and Visco, Y.M. 1999. "The maturation of auditory cortical evoked responses between (preterm) birth and 14 years of age." *European Journal of Paediatric Neurology* 3: 79–82.

Sameroff, A.J. 1967. "Nonnutritive sucking in newborns under visual and auditory stimulation." *Child Development* 38: 443–52.

Sanders, L.D. and Neville, H.J. 2003. "An ERP study of continuous speech processing I. Segmentation, semantics, and syntax in native speakers." *Cognitive Brain Research* 15: 228–40.

Seidl, A. and Johnson, E.K. Forthcoming. "Utterance boundaries and infants' extraction of words from fluent speech."

Singh, L., Morgan, J.L. and White, K.S. 2004. "Preference and processing: The role of speech affect in early spoken word recognition." *Journal of Memory and Language* 51: 173–89.

Snijders, T.M., Kooijman, V., Hagoort, P. and Cutler, A. in press. "Neurophysiological evidence of delayed segmentation in a foreign language." *Brain Research*.

Soderstrom, M., Kemler Nelson, D.G. and Jusczyk, P.W. 2005. "Six-month-olds recognize clauses embedded in different passages of fluent speech" *Infant Behavior and Development* 28: 87–94.

Swingley, D., Pinto, J.P. and Fernald, A. 1999. "Continuous processing in word recognition at 24 months." *Cognition* 71: 73–108.

Tincoff, R. and Jusczyk, P.W. 1999. "Some beginnings of word comprehension in 6-month-olds." *Psychological Science* 10: 172–5.

Tunmer, W.E., Bowey, J.A. and Grieve, R. 1983. "The development of young children's awareness of words as a unit of spoken language." *Journal of Psycholinguistic Research* 12: 567–94.

Uylings, H.B.M. 2006. "Development of the human cortex and the concept of 'critical' or 'sensitive' period." *Language Learning* 56 (s1): 59–60.

Van de Weijer, J. 1998. Language input for word discovery. PhD dissertation, Radboud University Nijmegen. (*MPI Series in Psycholinguistics* 9).

Werker, J.F., Polka, L. and Pegg, J.E. 1997. "The Conditioned Head Turn Procedure as a method for testing infant speech perception." *Early Development and Parenting* 6: 171–8.

Werker, J.F. and Tees, R.C. 1984. "Cross-language speech perception: Evidence for perceptual reorganization during the first year of life." *Infant Behavior and Development* 7: 49–63.

Werker, J.F. and Tees, R.C. 1999. "Influences on infant speech processing: Toward a new synthesis." *Annual Review of Psychology* 50: 509–35.

Woodward, J.Z. and Aslin, R.N. 1990. "Segmentation cues in maternal speech to infants." Paper presented at the meeting of the International Conference of Infant Studies, Montreal, Quebec, Canada.

CHAPTER 5

The onset of word form recognition

A behavioural and neurophysiological study

Guillaume Thierry and Marilyn May Vihman

1 Introduction

It has long been known that word learning under natural circumstances is characterised by a slow start followed by a steeply rising curve (Lewis 1936; Oviatt 1980). The studies that we report here were designed to provide an exhaustive exploration, in two language groups, of the timing of the earliest word form recognition based on frequent exposure in the course of the infant's daily life and the neurophysiological mechanisms involved. Use of Event-Related Potentials (ERPs) with infants, alongside the Headturn Preference Procedure (HPP), makes it possible to detect implicit attentional responses to words heard frequently in the home at an age when word knowledge is not yet widely reported and novel form-meaning pairings are not yet readily trained.[1] Our primary goal was to map the interaction between infant response to word form over the course of the 'slow start' and to explore language group differences in the onset of word form recognition.

1.1 Early advances in linguistic knowledge as revealed by the headturn preference procedure

Experimental studies of infant speech perception have taught us a great deal about changes in infant responses to speech over the course of the first year of life (Jusczyk 1997; Vihman 1996). We know that at birth or within the first one or two

---

1.   In this chapter we use the abbreviation HPP to designate the Headturn Preference Procedure, in conformance with common usage in this volume and elsewhere. However, we take the view that head turns as initiated and sustained by infants need not be fully voluntary or intentional and we therefore consider that the use of the term 'preference' may not be appropriate (see Thierry et al. 2003 for discussion).

months of life infants already respond to both the rhythms of the native language and the affective meanings they express (Fernald 1992; Mehler, Jusczyk, Lambertz, Halsted, Bertoncini and Amiel-Tison, 1988; Ramus 2002). Furthermore, it is only in the second half of the first year that infants begin to respond with greater attention (as measured through longer head turns toward a sound source) to the typical prosody of native language content words over less typical prosody (Jusczyk, Cutler and Redanz 1993), to narrative passages incorporating words trained in the laboratory (Jusczyk and Aslin 1995; Polka and Sundara 2003; cf. chapters by Nazzi *et al.* and Kooijman *et al.*, this volume), and to phonotactic patterns typical of their language (Jusczyk, Friederici, Wessels, Svenkerud and Jusczyk 1993; Jusczyk, Luce and Charles-Luce 1994; Mattys and Jusczyk 2001). We also know that by the end of the first year infants no longer discriminate consonantal contrasts not found in the native language, although this capacity is seen up to age 8 or 10 months (Werker and Tees 1984; Best 1994); the change is generally interpreted as a narrowing of attention (Werker and Pegg 1992). Finally, work with 'artificial languages', or sequences of syllables strung together according to an invented 'grammar', has shown that infants, like adults, are able to learn the distributional patterns of such sequences (Saffran, Aslin and Newport 1996). Those findings shed new light on infant phonological and lexical learning in the first year, suggesting a critical distinction between the *rapid advances in implicit knowledge* of different aspects of ambient language sequential patterning (prosodic, segmental, phonotactic), in the absence of either voluntary attention or an intent to learn, and the *more gradual learning of particular form-meaning correspondences* in the second year, when infants actively seek to know the 'names of things' (Macnamara 1982, Vihman and McCune 1994).

The 'preferential' head-turn procedure, on which most of the experimental findings mentioned above are based, has also been used to elicit an attentional response to untrained 'familiar words' (or phrases), lexical units whose form is retained from infants' everyday experiences. Experimentally, these words are tested in contrast with phonotactically matched rare words, or words no infant would be expected to have heard with any regularity (Hallé and Boysson-Bardies 1994). In our laboratory in North-Wales, using the same paradigm with infants exposed to British English, we replicated Hallé and Boysson-Bardies' finding that 11-month-olds recognize such untrained words in the absence of any situational cues but we failed to elicit the response in 9-month-olds (Vihman, Nakai, DePaolis and Hallé 2004). In a parallel study with Welsh infants we found word form recognition at 12 but not at 11 months (Vihman and DePaolis 1999). We interpret the differential response to familiar words at 11 (English) or 12 months (Welsh) as evidence for word form recognition but not necessarily for comprehension. Such dawning awareness of particular word forms might constitute a bridge between the implicit knowledge of linguistic patterning reviewed above and the explicit demand for words, communicated through pointing, grunting, or phrases such as 'whazis?', which accompanies the lexical spurt often seen by 17–18 months (Mc-Cune, Vihman, Roug-Hellichius and Delery 1996).

Werker and her colleagues (Stager and Werker 1997; Werker, Cohen, Lloyd, Casasola and Stager 1998; Werker, Fennell, Corcoran and Stager 2002) have used a preferential looking paradigm to explore the onset of children's ability to 'fast-map' or rapidly learn arbitrary form-meaning relationships. They found that although both 8- and 14-month-old infants can *discriminate* minimal pairs (as can younger infants as well: Jusczyk 1997), infants can learn to *link arbitrary nonword forms with meanings* (based on training with novel objects) only at 14 months – and then only if the nonsense stimuli are *non-minimal pairs*. Infants can associate *minimally distinct* word forms (*bih-dih*) to meanings by 17 months. Furthermore, Nazzi (2005) has shown that even at 20 months infants learning French can learn minimal pairs which differ by a single consonant but not those which differ by a *single vowel*. Clearly the word learning trajectory changes rapidly over this period.

Finally, as early as 7.5 months infants can be trained by repeated exposure to word forms presented in isolation to segment those words out of a brief narrative (Jusczyk and Aslin 1995), but the recognition of *untrained word forms* presented in isolation emerges only between 9 and 11 months. Furthermore, the ability to segment familiar words from a brief passage without training also emerges later, at 11–12 months (De Paolis and Vihman 2006). Holistic form-meaning association is seen experimentally at 15 months (Schafer and Plunkett 1998 – but see Schafer 2005, for evidence that focused training in the home over the last three months of the first year can result in precocious generalised word comprehension) and the learning of more finely distinguished novel form-meaning pairings only by 17 months. Earlier experimental work investigating the origins of word comprehension has suggested a similar trajectory, with considerably more rapid new word learning in the period from 15 to 17 months (Oviatt 1980).

1.2   Word recognition as revealed by ERPs

In an attempt to gain complementary insight at the neurophysiological level we designed a first ERP study to identify the neural time-course of the familiarity effect found in the HPP (Thierry, Vihman and Roberts 2003). Based on previous studies by Mills, Coffey-Corina and Neville (1997), we expected to see familiar words elicit negative shifts of amplitude relative to rare words ca. 200 ms after stimulus onset. We presented 18 English 11-month-olds with 56 familiar words (based on The MacArthur Communicative Development Inventory [CDI] adapted for British English: Hamilton, Plunkett and Schafer 2001) and 56 phonotactically matched rare words. We observed a succession of four peaks labelled P1, N2, P3 and N4 for descriptive purposes (Figure 1). The main result from this study was an increase in amplitude of the N2 peak which extended into the P3 window, resulting in a familiarity main effect significant between 170 and 248 ms after stimulus onset (based on ms-by-ms t-tests).

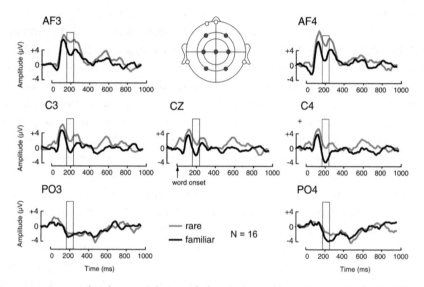

Figure 1. Event-related potentials recorded at 7 electrodes in 11-month-old English infants exposed to familiar (black line) and rare words (grey line). The N2 window in which a main effect of familiarity was found is framed

We interpreted the N2 modulation as a Mismatch Negativity (MMN; see Näätänen 2001, for a review). The MMN is an ERP modulation typically observed between 100 and 250 ms after the onset of a stimulus of low local probability presented within a stream of stimuli of high local probability (Näätänen, Paavilainen, Alho, Reinikainen and Sams 1989). The MMN requires no involvement of conscious attention; it is thought to be wholly automatic and reliant on the spontaneous evaluation of perceptual cues by the auditory system. Furthermore, the MMN has been reliably identified using simple harmonic tones in newborns and can be found throughout the first year of life (Kushnerenko, Ceponiene, Balan, Fellman and Naatanen 2002; see also Thierry 2005). Here we interpreted the N2 modulation as an MMN because any one infant tested was unlikely to be familiar with all of the stimuli selected as 'familiar'. Since the subset of word stimuli that were actually familiar to a given child would thus have been of low local probability for individual infants, these words would have elicited an MMN which survived the averaging process and emerged in the form of an N2 modulation. To account for the remarkable speed of the discrimination observed, we proposed that the time-course of the familiarity effect (peaking at ca. 200 ms) was dependent upon the degree of statistical phonological overlap between familiar and rare words. Indeed, while fully 72% of the familiar words shared their initial phoneme with a rare word, only 36% shared their second phoneme and 5% their third.[2] Thus it is plausible that the infants showed automatic familiarity responses within the period of the first few phonemes. This interpretation should be kept in mind when we discuss the response pattern seen in Welsh infants.

Taken together, the HPP and ERP results suggest that familiar words are recognised at around 11 months in English, i.e., not long before the typical onset age for word production (ca. 12 months). Furthermore, the basis for the HPP effect appears to be an automatic involvement of attention based on the implicit detection of familiar perceptual cues rather than a voluntary orientation mechanism. The difference in the HPP results for English vs. Welsh is interesting since it indicates that not all languages yield the familiarity response on the same developmental time-course. However, since the samples used in the HPP studies were small (12 infants) and the relative familiarity of the stimuli used in the HPP studies of English, French and Welsh was uncontrolled, we planned more systematic experimentation over a longer period and with larger samples of infants. Furthermore, the disparity between the HPP results in English vs. Welsh had yet to receive validation at the neurophysiological level.

2   Onset of word recognition in English and Welsh

Here we sought to determine the age at which the first neurophysiological and behavioural signs of untrained familiar word form recognition can be found in English and Welsh. In these studies we replicated and expanded previous findings with English-learning infants recruited from the bilingual community of North Wales by testing cross-sectional samples of 9-, 10-, 11- and 12-month-olds on their response to familiar and rare words. In addition, we tested 9-, 10-, 11- and 12-month-old Welsh infants from the same community, using the same technique and the same paradigm. 'Monolingual' infants were defined as those whose parents indicated more than 80% use of one language with the child (completely

---

2.   So, for example, *again* could immediately be distinguished from all of the rare words, since no rare word began with unstressed schwa, while *blanket* vs. *blindfold, bottle* vs. *balmy* or *car* vs. *carnal* (in an English dialect that lacks post-vocalic /r/) could only be distinguished after the occurrence of the second segment.

monolingual usage cannot always be found in this community; both children learning English and children learning Welsh sometimes produce one or two early words from the other language).

New stimuli were developed in both the English and Welsh studies, with the goal of arriving at a selection of familiar words well matched for relative frequency of use according to previous parental reports, so that age of onset of word recognition could be reliably equated across language groups. A list of 33 familiar and 33 rare words was recorded by three female native speakers for each language. Based on 158 CDIs returned for English-hearing infants participating in previous studies in our laboratory and 113 CDIs returned for Welsh-hearing infants, for each of the words used as 'familiar' stimuli in the experiments an average of 36% of the parents of English infants and 35% of the parents of Welsh infants words reported that the words were understood at ages 9, 10, 11 or 12 months.[3] Testing consonants and vowels separately, we ascertained that the input frequency of the phonemes found in the familiar word stimuli was not different from that of those found in the rare word stimuli in either language.[4] Acoustic analysis showed that there were no significant differences in loudness, pitch or duration between familiar and rare words.

2.1   English infants

Overall we tested 128 English-hearing infants. A total of 101 infants (25 9-, 27 10-, 23 11-, and 26 12-month olds) completed the HPP test successfully and were included in the final analysis. A total of 81 infants (15 9-, 21 10-, 26 11-, and 19 12-month olds) completed the ERP test successfully and had enough artefact free trials to be included in the final analysis.

In the HPP, the difference in looking times to familiar vs. rare words reached significance only at 11 months (Figure 2). This 11-month effect is robust in English, as we have found it repeatedly in experiments using different stimuli. In the present experiment the stimuli were increased from 12 (repeated across 6 trials in Vihman, Nakai, DePaolis, and Hallé 2004) to 33, with 11 stimuli in each of three trials, repeated once each; the increase in number of stimuli was due to the need to use the same words in the HPP as we used in ERPs, which require larger numbers (while minimizing repetition). Additionally, all of the words were recorded by three different female speakers, although in the HPP each child heard only one:

---

3.   The CDI for Welsh was originally created by Margaret Bell, a postgraduate in the Bangor Psychology School; we have adapted it on the basis of our data and in consultation with our Welsh-speaking researchers. It has no official status or title; it has not been normed.

4.   For English phoneme frequencies we used Mines, Hanson and Shoup (1978). For Welsh we used 30-minute transcripts of mothers' speech recorded in previous studies in our laboratory.

This made it possible to present the stimuli in two blocks in the ERPs, one with each of two voices; the third voice was used for the HPP, with counterbalancing to ensure that no child heard any voice more than once in the two procedures and that all three voices were used in both procedures. Hence, in the ERP sessions infants heard 33 familiar words repeated once (66 trials, 50%) and 33 rare words repeated once (66 trials, 50%). We found that the variability in voice in the HPPs led to variability in familiarity effects across infants, although the subgroups of infants hearing each of the voices were not large enough to test for significance independently of the larger group. Furthermore, we found that the effect size at 11 months was smaller than in previous studies (Vihman, Thierry, Lum and Keren-Portnoy, in press). This is likely due to the fact that there were more words presented in this case, with fewer opportunities for infants to hear words they knew.

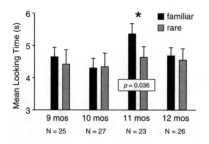

Figure 2. Summary of the HPP results in English

Interestingly, after its robust appearance at 11 months the familiarity effect was no longer seen at 12 months, suggesting that exposure to the form of words alone no longer held the infants' attention at this age, when word meanings have begun to be learned more generally (Oviatt 1980; Schafer 2005). The latter explanation is substantiated by the decrease in overall looking time at 12 months to both familiar and rare words.

The pattern of HPP results was strongly corroborated and supplemented by the ERP data (Figures 3 and 4). First, we replicated Thierry *et al.* (2003), since a significant main effect of familiarity on N2 mean peak amplitudes[5] was found at 11 months. In addition, we found a new main effect of familiarity on N2 mean peak amplitude at 10 months. Furthermore, a significant familiar vs. rare N2 amplitude difference was found at electrode AF4 (right anterior frontal) already in 9-month-olds (a difference that survived correction for multiple comparisons).

---

5.   As in Thierry *et al.*, we label the peaks according to their order of appearance and polarity. N2 is therefore a descriptive label for the second peak with a negative polarity.

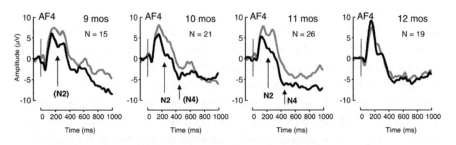

Figure 3. ERPs elicited by familiar (black wave) and rare (grey wave) words at electrode AF4. Peak labels in parentheses indicate peaks that were significantly affected by familiarity at electrode AF4 and not across the scalp. Peak labels without parentheses indicate the peaks that were affected by a main effect of familiarity across the scalp

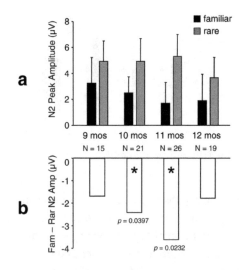

Figure 4. N2 familiarity effects in English infants. a. Mean amplitudes of the N2 peak at electrodes AF3 and AF4 (electrodes of maximal sensitivity) in the familiar (back bars) and rare (grey bars) conditions. b. Mean N2 amplitude difference between familiar and rare conditions at electrodes AF3 and AF4 (electrodes of maximal sensitivity)

On Figure 4 the N2 effect can be seen to increase steadily in size from 9 to 11 months (see Figure 4b, where the difference between familiar and rare words reaches its maximum at 11 months). The N2 effect then disappears entirely at 12 months. As in Thierry et al. (2003), we interpret the N2 effect as an MMN-like event, showing automatic orientation of the auditory system to (low-probability) recognizable stimuli presented amongst (high probability) unknown stimuli.

The progressive emergence of the familiarity effect shows that implicit word recognition commences well before 11 months over the right frontal hemi-scalp (Thierry *et al.* 2003; see Mills *et al.* 1997 and Thal, Marchman, Stiles, Aram, Trauner, Nass and Bates 1991 for discussion of the lateralisation of word familiarity effects in this age range). At 10 and 11 months the familiarity effect spreads broadly across the scalp, which suggests wider involvement of underlying cortical networks.

Interestingly, the N2 effect was accompanied by a developing N4 effect. No such effect was reported in Thierry *et al.* (2003). The immediate explanation for this apparent inconsistency comes from the data processing methods applied to the new monolingual dataset. Whereas the high pass digital filter used in Thierry *et al.* (2003) was set at 0.5 Hz, the filter used in the present experiments was set at 0.3 Hz. The higher the cut off frequency of the filter, the cleaner the data, given that the wide amplitude waves which characterize infant EEG are greatly reduced by filtering in this frequency range. We chose to downgrade the filter to 0.3 Hz based on Friedrich and Friederici (2004, 2005), where use of such a filter allowed variations of the scale of the N400 to be measured and analyzed.

In the present study the N4 modulation became a significant main effect at 11 months and then – like the N2 –disappeared at 12 months. Furthermore, the size of the familiarity effect in the N2 range was significantly correlated with the size of the familiarity effect in the N4 range ($r = 0.69$, $p < 0.001$) across all age groups. The emergence of the N4 modulation at 11 months can be interpreted as reflecting increased infant familiarity with the second syllable (or the later part of the word more generally), a kind of pervasive N2 modulation. This view is supported by the significant correlation between N2 and N4 familiarity effects.[6]

At 12 months the N2 and N4 disappear together. It is unlikely that words that sound familiar to a group of 11-month-olds suddenly become unfamiliar to a group of 12-month-olds. In the framework of our MMN-based interpretation of the N2-N4 complex we speculate that by 12 months a sufficient number of the intended 'familiar' words presented in the experiment have actually become familiar (to a sufficiently large number of infants) to eliminate the 'oddball' effect. That is, the probability of occurrence of familiar and rare words now becomes roughly equal, since we did actually present equal numbers of familiar and rare words.

---

6.   It should be noted again that N4 is a purely descriptive label; the N4 peak should not be confounded with the classical N400, which refers to a theoretical ERP modulation observed in experiments in which semantic context is manipulated. The N400, first reported by Kutas and Hillyard (1980), is particularly large when a word (or other meaningful stimulus) violates the semantic context in which it is presented (e.g., a sentence or a preceding picture). In infants, the N400 has not been observed before 14 months (Friedrich and Friederici 2005) and its maximal sensitivity as measured in the picture-word priming paradigm is typically between 500 and 800 ms after word onset (see chapter by Manuela Friedrich in this volume).

Under these conditions the MMN effect should no longer be expected – and it is not observed; this would explain why the two waveforms overlap so closely at 12 months. A critical test of this hypothesis would involve using a 'true' oddball paradigm at 12 months, i.e., by presenting a small number of familiar words amidst a large number of phonotactically matched rare words.

Finally, in 12-months-olds we also noted a significant modulation between rare and familiar words beyond 400 ms, i.e., between 450 and 600 ms. In this time window the rare words elicited a broader negativity than familiar words over left-sided electrodes (i.e., F3, C3) and Cz. It is possible that this wave is a precursor of the N400, peaking later than in adults (Friedrich and Friederici 2005) and attaining greater amplitude for rare words which, even in the absence of contextual cues, require more semantic search. This was not a main effect, however, which is consistent with Friedrich and Friederici (2005), who report that reliable N400 modulations are first observed at 14 months. In summary, the onset of word form recognition is robust at 11 months in English but the first neurophysiological signs of word recognition can be seen already at 10 months, and no clear signs of lexical-semantic activity are yet identified at 12 months.

2.2   Welsh infants

Overall we tested 79 Welsh-hearing infants. A total of 74 infants (14 9-, 12 10-, 27 11-, and 21 12-month-olds) completed the HPP test successfully and were included in the final analysis. A total of 52 infants (13 9-, 13 10-, 13 11-, and 13 12-month-olds) completed the ERP test successfully and had a sufficient number of artefact free trials to be included in the final analysis.

In the HPP we found no significant effect of familiarity in any of the age groups (see Figure 5). Mean looking times to familiar words were nevertheless marginally longer at 11 and 12 months (p <.096 and p <.071, respectively).

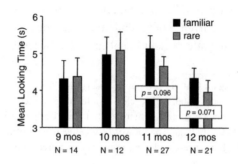

Figure 5. Summary of the HPP results in Welsh

The pattern of results seen in ERPs was again consistent overall with the HPP results (Figure 6). No main effect of familiarity was found in any of the age groups,
whether we looked at the N2 or the N4 windows (Figure 7). At 11 months, however, we found signs of the familiarity effect in the form of a localised N2 amplitude difference at electrode AF4 ($p < 0.05$, uncorrected) and a difference in the N4
range at electrodes AF4 and Cz (both $p < 0.05$, uncorrected). The absence of a
main effect in Welsh infants in both the HPP and ERPs and in both 11- and 12-
month-olds suggests that the differentiation between familiar and rare words is
less efficient in Welsh than in English.

Close examination of the N2 amplitude pattern at electrode AF4 (Figure 7a)
shows that the N2 amplitudes elicited by *rare words* tend to closely follow the pattern of N2 amplitudes elicited by *familiar words* (an effect not seen in English infants). It is therefore possible that in Welsh automatic orientation of attention is
elicited not only by familiar words but also by rare words. The lack of a familiarity
effect could then be seen as reflecting not a lack of interest (or a failure of those
words to elicit a sense of familiarity) but rather a more balanced attentional response to both familiar and rare words.

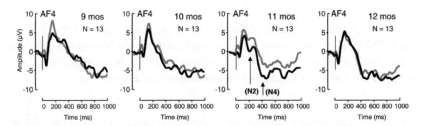

Figure 6. ERPs elicited by familiar (black wave) and rare (grey wave) words at electrode
AF4. The amplitude of the peaks labelled in parentheses was significantly affected at AF4
but not elsewhere

A number of possible explanations could be invoked to explain the absence of a
familiarity effect in Welsh infants at 11 months. It is important to note, first, the
difference in sample sizes between the Welsh-hearing and English-hearing groups.
Even in North-Wales, a region in which Welsh is still in common use everyday,
monolingual Welsh infants (i.e. infants exposed to more than 80% Welsh at home)
are rare compared to English monolinguals. Consequently, we were able to test
only 13 infants in each of the Welsh-hearing groups. In adults, a group of 12 to 15
individuals constitutes a good sample to identify amplitude and latency differences of the same order of magnitude as behavioural effects. In infants, however, the
considerable extent of baseline noise means that more participants and many more

trials per condition are required in order to achieve the same level of confidence as can routinely be obtained with adults.

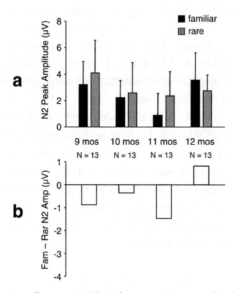

Figure 7. N2 familiarity effects in Welsh infants. a. Mean amplitudes of the N2 peak at electrodes AF3 and AF4 (electrode of maximal sensitivity) in the familiar (black bars) and rare (grey bars) conditions. b. Mean N2 amplitude difference between familiar and rare conditions at electrodes AF3 and AF4 (electrodes of maximal sensitivity)

Other explanations relate to the nature of the Welsh language itself. First, although Welsh, like English, is considered to be primarily trochaic (strong-weak accentual pattern), the accent in Welsh is manifested differently: The vowel of the first (accented) syllable is short, the medial consonant is lengthened, and the vowel of the final syllable is also long (Vihman, Nakai and DePaolis 2006). Thus the second part of a word is more salient than the first part – the reverse of English, in which stress has the effect of lengthening the first syllable as well as adding both intensity and a pitch change. As a consequence, the first part of the word is more salient in English than in Welsh.

Differences in accentuation have been shown to play a role in word form recognition: A change to the first consonant blocks it in English but not in French, while the reverse is true of the medial consonant in a disyllable (Vihman *et al.* 2004). Welsh infants could be expected to rely more on later parts of a word, as French children do, despite the classification of most Welsh disyllables as 'trochaic'. Since ERPs are time-locked to the word onset, ERP modulations discriminating familiar from rare words will be offset in Welsh and the relative increase in amplitude of the N2/N4 will be delayed and blurred. Secondly, Welsh, like all Celtic languages, has several prevalent mutation processes, by which the initial consonant of a word changes under particular grammatical conditions (e.g., feminine *cath* 'cat' becomes *gath* when preceded by the definite article *y*, whereas masculine *car* 'car' undergoes no consonant change). Depending on their grammatical gender and other aspects of the syntactic context, then, words can take different forms.[7] As a consequence the initial consonant in Welsh words serves as a relatively less reliable lexical cue than do onset consonants in English. Word recognition in Welsh thus appears to require more attention to later parts of the phonotactic string, possibly delaying and blurring any familiarity effect.

Finally, it is worth bearing in mind the sociolinguistic situation of Welsh as a minority language in North-Wales: Welsh speakers are also generally fluent in English while English speakers in the same community are frequently not bilingual. We will return to this issue after considering our findings with bilingual infants.

2.3   Welsh-English bilingual infants

Because bilingualism is so prevalent in North-Wales it was natural to test a sample of bilingual infants alongside our two monolingual groups; since the numbers are small, however, we tested only at 11 months, the age at which word form recognition has been found most consistently.[8] Using as the criterion for bilingual status exposure to more than 20% but less than 80% of either language in the home we were able to test 28 11-month-old infants. Any infant whose exposure to the two languages fell outside of these boundaries was included in the monolingual studies described previously. Of the infants categorised as bilingual 20 provided usable data in the HPP and 16 had a sufficient number of artefact-free trials (i.e., > 30) to be included in the final ERP analysis.

The stimuli in this study were different from those used in the monolingual experiments because infants had to be tested in both of their languages, which

---

7.   Of the familiar words used in the study about 75% were subject to mutation, and so will likely have been regularly heard by our infant participants both with and without the initial consonant of the base form we used, within sentential contexts. However, as noted earlier, infants at this age do not readily 'segment' or identify familiar words within a longer discourse without specific training. Consequently the familiar words will in most cases have been heard as isolated words or in short phrases; this means that, more realistically, the form of about one third of the words will have been registered by our infant participants both with and without the onset consonants of the base forms used as stimuli.

8.   Welsh-English bilingual infants formed an opportunity sample constructed across the span of the 3-year monolingual project described in the "English infants" and "Welsh infants" sections of this chapter.

greatly increased experimental time. For the HPP the infants were tested on both the English and the Welsh stimuli. In the ERP procedure we used 30 familiar words (selected from the 33 used in the HPP) pseudo-randomly inter-mixed with 90 rare words of similar phonotactic structure. This experiment therefore conformed to a fairly standard oddball paradigm with 25% familiar and 75% rare words (unlike the 50–50 ratio used in the monolingual study). We made this choice to reduce the number of trials needed in each language, given the goal of testing infants in their two languages. All words were produced in both English and Welsh by a single high-ly proficient bilingual female speaker with no detectable accent in either of the two languages. Words from the two languages were presented in two different blocks.

In the HPP, we found significantly longer looks to English familiar words and a marginally significant difference in Welsh (Figure 8). In ERPs, we found signifi-cant N2 modulation for both English and Welsh (Figure 9). We also found a main effect of familiarity in the N4 time window.

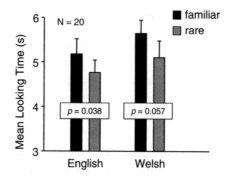

Figure 8. HPP results of 11-month-old Welsh-English bilingual infants

Indeed, there was a main effect of familiarity on mean ERP amplitude between 180 and 310 ms and between 360 and 490 ms after word onset. There was, however, no main effect of language on the amplitude of the N2 and N4 peaks and no interac-tion between familiarity and language. In addition, both the N2 and N4 peaked later in Welsh (276 and 560 ms, respectively) than in English (228 and 477 ms, respectively) as indicated by a main effect of language on N2 and N4 latencies. Here again there seems to be good agreement between the behavioural data de-rived from the HPP and the neurophysiological data derived from ERPs. It is strik-ing that a word form recognition effect is found in both languages, in both proce-dures, for bilinguals but not for Welsh monolinguals from the same community. We will consider the implications of this unexpected finding below.

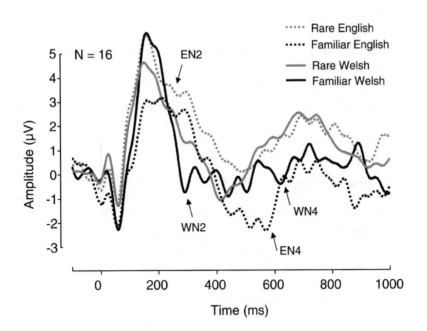

Figure 9. ERP results of 11-month-old Welsh-English bilingual infants

3   General discussion

We have presented the findings of our studies of infant word form recognition using the HPP and ERPs in parallel. In the cross-sectional study with English infants we have replicated and extended the earlier finding of the emergence of word form recognition at 11 months, using a somewhat more difficult experimental procedure (33 rather than 11 familiar word stimuli); as in the earlier HPP study of Vihman *et al.* 2004, we found no effect at 9 months and we established further that 10-month-olds do not yet show the effect in the HPP. We have also now shown that the first generalised neurophysiological sign of word form recognition is found at 10 months in English, even though the first behavioural response can be detected only at 11 months. Furthermore, we were able to show the gradual developmental emergence of the N2 and N4 familiarity effects, the latter offset by one month. In addition, we have shown that by 12 months the familiarity effect vanishes in English, probably for one reason in the HPP (a lack of interest in decontextualised words) and another in ERPs (balanced proportion of familiar and rare words cancelling the oddball effect underlying the MMN). In Welsh infants we failed to see clear familiarity effects in either procedure, although signs of N2 and

N4 modulations were found within the expected time window at the predicted electrode sites. Finally, we reported results from Welsh-English bilingual infants, showing an effect of familiarity in both English and Welsh and in both the HPP and ERPs. The components affected by word familiarity tended to be delayed in Welsh as compared to English. In the discussion below we address the two main 'surprises' presented by these studies: The absence of a word form familiarity effect in infants addressed only in Welsh in the home and the unique pattern of familiarity effects in infants addressed in both English and Welsh.

3.1   The absence of a main familiarity effect in Welsh

In agreement with a previous study we failed to find an HPP familiarity effect in 11-month-old Welsh infants. However, given the fact that we found a main effect of familiarity on N2 mean amplitudes in English 10-month-olds, we expected to find an N2 modulation in Welsh at 11 months, i.e., a precursor of the behaviourally measurable familiarity effect expected at 12 months. However, neither the N2 ERP effect at 11 months nor the HPP familiarity effect at 12 months were found in infants being raised with monolingual exposure to Welsh in the home (but it is worth bearing in mind the fact that the use of 33 stimuli in this study made the HPP experiment relatively more difficult, resulting in smaller effect sizes in both languages at 11 months). Close observation of the pattern of N2 amplitudes at electrode AF4 (Figures 4a and 7a) makes for an interesting comparison: Whereas the pattern of N2 amplitude in response to familiar words was very similar between the two languages and across age groups, the pattern of N2 elicited by rare words was radically different. In English, N2 amplitudes tended to be large and stable (at least for ages 9, 10 and 11 months), while N2 amplitudes for familiar words tended to become more negative with age (up to 11 months). In the case of Welsh, however, N2 amplitudes elicited by rare words closely followed the general pattern elicited by familiar words, as if rare words induced almost as much processing as familiar words. Although this provides no clear explanation as to what the difference underlying the response of infants exposed only to English or to Welsh in the home may be, this observation highlights fundamental differences in the way rare words are processed in the two languages.

It is likely that the difference is related to the imbalance in use of the two languages in the community of North-Wales. Despite the fact that the two counties of Anglesey and Gwynedd, from which our participants are drawn, boast the largest proportion of Welsh speakers anywhere in the world[9], all of the 'monolingual Welsh' infants must be regularly exposed to some English in the home (through television, radio, and visitors) as well as in the community (through overheard conversations in shops and other public places; see Gathercole, Mueller and Thomas 2005; Deuchar 2005). This situation of dual language exposure does not obtain for English infants, most of whose parents do not know Welsh. A consequence of heavy exposure to a language in which the infant is seldom if ever directly addressed may be the requirement of a secondary level of discrimination for the minority language monolingual infants: Not only do they need to tease apart familiar from rare word forms; they also need to distinguish Welsh from English, without the kind of consistent opportunity to hear and thus gain familiarity with English that obtains for infants being raised as bilinguals.

3.2   The familiarity effect in bilinguals

Does learning English induce 'neo-familiarity' in Welsh? In other words, is the bilingual infant more sensitive to the onset consonant in Welsh words, because the onset is important in English words? Might the strong bilingual N4 response to English at 11 months be amplified by the same infants' N4 response to Welsh? All the characteristics of the monolingual responses to Welsh and English can be seen in the bilinguals. It is notable that bilingual 11-month-olds show a pattern that falls in between those observed in the English and Welsh monolinguals. Furthermore, there seems to be no cost for the on-line processing of English: the N2 peaks at roughly the same time in bilinguals and monolinguals.[10] It appears that developing a system compatible with the phonotactic structure and accentual pattern of both English and Welsh supports word form recognition in both languages, since the overt HPP response is obtained for both English and Welsh in bilinguals whereas 11 month-old Welsh infants fail to show it.

It must be kept in mind, however, that the paradigm used in the bilingual study involved a 'true' oddball paradigm since the familiar/rare ratio in words was 1:3. Since there were only 25% familiar words in total, the familiar condition was more likely to elicit not only an MMN-like response but also a P300-like response. Some authors have speculated that the P300 may be inverted in infants and peak

---

9.   In the 2001 census 76% of adults in Gwynedd and 70% in Anglesey reported an ability to read, write, speak or understand Welsh. However, all of these adults are also fluent in English, which is the dominant language for many of them.

10.   Since different paradigms were used for testing monolingual and bilingual infants, direct comparison of N2 latencies between groups is not statistically feasible. In both the English and the Welsh monolingual infants the N2 peaked at 228 ms and in the Welsh-English bilingual infants the N2 peaked at 222 ms in English and 276 ms in Welsh.

later (i.e., between 400 and 700 ms, see Thierry 2005). Therefore the significant N4 effect that we obtained might have been facilitated by a paradigm prone to inducing a P3 modulation. Such a hypothesis depends on making the assumption that infants were 'overtly conscious' of the low local probability of familiar words in the experiment, since the P300 is observed only when the participant is aware of the oddball context. The N2 modulation, on the other hand, might have been more pronounced due to the low local probability of familiar words. However, in retrospect, with only 30 familiar words in each of two blocks, each testing recognition in one language, it is quite surprising that the N2 effect has emerged as significant. Indeed, if only half of the familiar words included were recognized by the infants as familiar, say, the N2 modulation will have been induced by only 15 trials. A replication of this study using a balanced number of familiar and rare words will be needed to allow direct comparison with the pattern of results found in monolinguals. In any case, it is not plausible to interpret the significant N2/N4 effect as a sign of greater vocabulary size in the bilinguals, as bilingual children are known to have smaller lexicons (in each of their languages taken separately) than their monolingual peers (Pearson 1998).

The N2 and N4 peak latency difference between English and Welsh in bilingual infants suggests that English recognition effects are observed systematically earlier in the time-course of the underlying neural events. This effect very likely relates to the prosodic and morphophonological characteristics of Welsh mentioned earlier with regards to the ERPs obtained from Welsh monolinguals: the accentual pattern, which lends less salience to the initial consonant than does English (Vihman *et al.* 2006) and the pervasive mutation system, which greatly lessens the cue validity of the onset consonant. An HPP familiarity effect has been found in French and English at the same age, despite the fact that the initial consonant is demonstrably less salient in French than in English, for prosodic reasons (Vihman *et al.* 2004). Testing French monolingual infants using ERPs with the same word recognition paradigm as reported above would therefore provide an ideal way to test the relative importance of accentual pattern in delaying the N4 in the bilingual infants.

4   Conclusion

Our results establish the age of onset of implicit word form recognition in English at 10 months, followed by behaviourally measurable effects one month later. We also demonstrate that the developmental course of word form recognition is not universal but is, instead, highly dependent upon the characteristics of the language(s) of exposure as well as the sociolinguistic context in which learning takes place. The complementary nature of the HPP and ERPs is clearly evident throughout this chapter even though the actual underlying neural mechanisms of either remains to be understood. We believe that combining traditional behavioural methods and neurophysiological techniques can provide fundamentally new insight into the mechanisms of language development in terms of both the cognitive processes involved and their neural time-course.

Notes

*   We gratefully acknowledge funding from the ESRC (RES 00230095). We would also like to thank Jarrad Lum, who carried out the statistical analysis of the HPP data, Satsuki Nakai, who helped to design the study and developed the stimuli, Kat Barker, Naomi Craig, Fran Garrad-Cole and Pam Martin, who ran the ERP and HP procedures, and Tamar Keren-Portnoy, who contributed insightful interpretations.

References

Best, C.T. 1994. "The emergence of language-specific phonemic influences in infant speech perception." In *The development of speech perception*, J.C. Goodman and H.C. Nusbaum (eds.). Cambridge, MA: The MIT Press.

De Paolis, R. and Vihman, M.M. 2006. "A cross-sectional study of infant segmentation of familiar words from connected speech." Presented at the International Conference on Infancy Studies, Kyoto.

Deuchar, M. 2005. "Real-life language practices in the home: Observations and reported use." In *Language Transmission in Bilingual Families in Wales*, V.C.M. Gathercole (ed.). Welsh Language Board.

Fernald, A. 1992. "Human maternal vocalizations to infants as biologically relevant signals: An evolutionary perspective." In *The Adapted Mind: Evolutionary Psychology and the Generation of Culture*, J.H. Barkow, L. Cosmides and J. Tooby (eds.). Oxford: OUP.

Friedrich, M. and Friederici, A.D. 2004. "N400-like semantic incongruity effect in 19-month-olds: Processing known words in picture contexts." *Journal of Cognitive Neuroscience* 16: 1465–77.

Friedrich, M. and Friederici, A.D. 2005. "Lexical priming and semantic integration reflected in the ERP of 14-month-olds." *NeuroReport* 16: 653–6.

Gathercole, V.C. Mueller and Thomas. E.M. 2005. "Factors contributing to language transmission in bilingual families." In *Language Transmission in Bilingual Families in Wales*, V.C.M. Gathercole (ed.). Welsh Language Board.

Hallé, P. and Boysson-Bardies, B. de. 1994. "Emergence of an early lexicon." *Infant Behavior and Development* 17: 119–29.

Hamilton, A., Plunkett, K. and Schafer, G. 2001. "Infant vocabulary development assessed with a British CDI." *Journal of Child Language* 2: 689–705.

Jusczyk, P.W. 1997. *The Discovery of Spoken Language*. Cambridge, MA: The MIT Press.

Jusczyk, P.W. and Aslin, R.N. 1995. "Infants' detection of the sound patterns of words in fluent speech." *Cognitive Psychology* 29: 1–23.

Jusczyk, P.W., Cutler, A. and Redanz, N.J. 1993. "Infants' preference for the predominant stress patterns of English words." *Child Development* 64: 675–87.

Jusczyk, P.W., Friederici, A.D., Wessels, J., Svenkerud, V.Y. and Jusczyk, A.M. 1993. "Infants' sensitivity to the sound patterns of native language words." *Journal of Memory and Language* 32: 402–20.

Jusczyk, P.W., Luce, P.A. and Charles-Luce, J. 1994. "Infants' sensitivity to phonotactic patterns in the native language." *Journal of Memory and Language* 33: 630–45.

Kushnerenko, E., Ceponiene, R., Balan, P., Fellman, V., Naatanen, R. 2002. "Maturation of the auditory change detection response in infants: A longitudinal ERP study." *Neuroreport* 13: 1843–8.

Kutas, M. and Hillyard, S.A. 1980. "Reading senseless sentences: Brain potentials reflect semantic inconguity." *Science* 207: 203–5.

Lewis, M.M. 1936. *Infant Speech: A study of the beginnings of language.* New York, NY: Harcourt, Brace. (Reprint edn, 1975. New York, NY: Arno Press).

McCune, L., Vihman, M.M., Roug-Hellichius, L., Delery, D.B. and Gogate, L. 1996. "Grunt communication in human infants (Homo sapiens)." *Journal of Comparative Psychology* 110: 27–37.

Macnamara, J. 1982. *Names for things.* Cambridge, MA: The MIT Press.

Mattys, S.L. and Jusczyk, P.W. 2001. "Phonotactic cues for segmentation of fluent speech by infants." *Cognition* 78: 91–121.

Mehler, J., Jusczyk, P. Lambertz, G., Halsted, N., Bertoncini, J. and Amiel-Tison, C. 1988. "A precursor of language acquisition in young infants." *Cognition* 29: 143–78.

Mills, D.L., Coffey-Corina, S.A. and Neville, H.J. 1997. "Language comprehension and cerebral specialization from 13 to 20 months." *Developmental Neuropsychology* 13: 397–445.

Mines, M., Hanson, B. and Shoup, J. 1978. "Frequency of occurrence of phonemes in conversational English." *Language and Speech* 21: 221–41.

Näätänen, R. 2001. "The perception of speech sounds by the human brain as reflected by the mismatch negativity (MMN) and its magnetic equivalent (MMNm)." *Psychophysiology* 38: 1–21.

Näätänen, R., Paavilainen, P., Alho, K., Reinikainen, K., and Sams, M. 1989. "Do event-related potentials reveal the mechanism of the auditory sensory memory in the human brain?" *Neurosci Lett* 98: 217–21.

Nazzi, T. 2005. "Abstract use of phonetic specificity during the acquisition of new words: differences between consonants and vowels." *Cognition* 98: 13–30.

Oviatt, S. 1980. "The emerging ability to comprehend language." *Child Development* 50: 97–106.

Pearson, B.Z. 1998. "Assessing lexical development in bilingual babies and toddlers." *The International Journal of Bilingualism* 2: 347–72.

Polka, L. and Sundara, M. 2003. "Word segmentation in monolingual and bilingual infant learners of English and French." In *Proceedings of the 15th International Congress of Phonetic Sciences, Barcelona*, M.J. Solé, D. Recasens and J. Romero (eds.). Barcelona: Causal Productions.

Ramus, F. 2002. "Language discrimination by newborns." *Annual Review of Language Acquisition* 2: 85–115.

Saffran, J.R., Aslin, R.N. and Newport, E.L. 1996. "Statistical learning by 8-month-old infants." *Science* 274: 1926–8.

Schafer, G. 2005. "Infants can learn decontextualized words before their first birthday." *Child Development* 76: 87–96.

Schafer, G. and Plunkett, K. 1998. "Rapid word learning by fifteen-month-olds under tightly controlled conditions." *Child Development* 69: 309–20.

Stager, C.L. and Werker, J.F. 1997. "Infants listen for more phonetic detail in speech perception than in word-learning tasks." *Nature* 388: 381–2.

Thal, D.J., Marchman, V., Stiles, J., Aram, D., Trauner, D., Nass, R. and Bates, E. 1991. "Early lexical development in children with focal brain injury." *Brain and Language* 40: 491–527.

Thierry, G. 2005. "The use of event-related potentials in the study of early cognitive development." *Infant and Child Development* 14: 85–94.

Thierry, G., Vihman, M. and Roberts, M. 2003. "Familiar words capture the attention of 11-month-olds in less than 250 ms." *Neuroreport* 14: 2307–10.

Vihman, M.M. 1996. *Phonological development: The origins of language in the child.* Oxford: Blackwell.

Vihman, M.M. and DePaolis, R.A. 1999. "The role of accentual pattern in early lexical representation." End of Award Report, ESRC grant R000222266.

Vihman, M.M. and McCune, L. 1994. "When is a word a word?" *Journal of Child Language* 21: 517–42.

Vihman, M.M., Nakai, S. and DePaolis, R.A. 2006. "Getting the rhythm right: A cross-linguistic study of segmental duration in babbling and first words." In *Varieties of Phonological Competence*, L. Goldstein, D. Whalen and C. Best (eds.), Laboratory Phonology 8: 341–66. Berlin: Mouton de Gruyter.

Vihman, M.M., Nakai, S., DePaolis, R.A. and Hallé, P. 2004. "The role of accentual pattern in early lexical representation." *Journal of Memory and Language* 50: 336–53.

Vihman, M.M., Thierry, G., Lum, J. and Keren-Portnoy, T. 2007. "Onset of word form recognition in English, Welsh and English-Welsh bilingual infants." *Applied Psycholinguistics.* 28: 475-93.

Werker, J.F., Cohen, L.B., Lloyd, V.L., Casasola, M. and Stager, C.L. 1998. "Acquisition of word-object associations by 14-month-old infants." *Developmental Psychology* 34: 1289–309.

Werker, J.F. and Pegg, J.E. 1992. "Infant speech perception and phonological acquisition." In *Phonological development*, C.A. Ferguson, L. Menn and C. Stoel-Gammon (eds.), 285–311. Timonium, MD: York Press.

Werker, J.F., Fennell, C.T., Corcoran, K.M. and Stager, C.L. 2002. "Infants' ability to learn phonetically similar words: Effects of age and vocabulary size." *Infancy* 3: 1–30.

Werker, J.F. and Tees, R.C. 1984. "Cross-language speech perception: Evidence for perceptual reorganization during the first year of life." *Infant Behavior and Development* 7: 49–63.

CHAPTER 6

Neurophysiological correlates of picture-word priming in one-year-olds

Manuela Friedrich

1   Introduction

Word learning does not only consist in the segmentation of the acoustic speech stream into separate words and the acquisition of their phonological forms, but also in the acquisition of relevant meanings and the mapping of phonological forms onto meaningful representations. When investigating children's word learning and comprehension abilities it is therefore necessary to separately assess these aspects of language processing. While extensive research has been conducted on the phonological and prosodic aspects of early language acquisition, only little is known about children's early conceptual development and about its interaction with word form acquisition. Moreover, virtually nothing is known about the neural mechanisms involved in early word comprehension.

2   Behavioural and ERP research: Complementary methodological approaches

During the last few decades researchers have developed a variety of elaborated behavioural paradigms such as the high-amplitude sucking method, the head-turn preference procedure, preferential looking paradigms, and object examination tasks. These methods have provided intriguing insight into the early language related abilities of infants and young children (e.g., Eimas, Siqueland, Jusczyk and Vigorito 1971; Jusczyk 1997; Kemler-Nelson, Jusczyk, Mandel, Myers, Turk and Gerken 1995; Kuhl, Williams, Lacerda, Stevens and Lindblom 1992; Mandler and McDonough 1993; for recent reviews see Kuhl 2004; Werker and Yeung 2005). However, all of these paradigms rely on attention-based changes in children's behaviour, that is, they use children's habituation and novelty responses to assess their language abilities. For this reason, such behavioural methods are limited for investigating those abilities that do not affect the children's attention, abilities for which the attentional response changes with development, and abilities that involve several interacting mechanisms, which together affect attention and therefore cannot be dissociated based on the observed behaviour.

The method of event-related brain potentials (ERPs) is a well established neurophysiological measure in medical, psychological, and linguistic research in adults. The ERP maps represent average temporal changes in the activity of different brain regions during the processing of external stimuli. Because of its high temporal resolution the ERP is particularly suitable for separating different pre-attentive and attention-dependent mechanisms involved in stimulus processing. A certain ERP component can be associated with a specific neural mechanism that underlies a specific cognitive or linguistic ability. Since, in principle, the non-invasive ERP method does not require attention or active behaviour from subjects, it can successfully be applied to infants and young children (for a recent review see Friederici 2005). Several ERP paradigms have been developed for investigating specific neural mechanisms in adults and they can be adapted to the particular requirements for use with children of various ages. By means of these paradigms a variety of early language-related abilities can be assessed. Moreover, the complementary interpretation of ERP and behavioural measures may provide first insights into the relation between maturing brain mechanisms and developing behavioural skills during early childhood.

In the present chapter, the results of ERP studies of word comprehension in one-year-olds (Friedrich and Friederici 2004; 2005a; 2005b; 2006) are reviewed, to illustrate how the ERP method contributes to the study of early language acquisition. It is shown that perceptual and semantic facilitation effects can be dissociated in the ERP of one-year-olds when they process words or word-like stimuli in the context of pictures of familiar objects. The studies reviewed here indicate different developmental trajectories for the observed perceptual and semantic facilitation effects and allow conclusions about the successive development of lexical-semantic priming and semantic integration mechanisms in 12- to 19-month-olds. Post-hoc analyses based on children's behavioural language skills further show that ERP indices might be predictive of later language development.

3   The N400: An electrophysiological correlate of semantic processing

In adults, word comprehension is mainly associated with the N400 component of the ERP. The N400 is a negative wave with a centro-parietal distribution which is maximum at about 400 ms post stimulus onset. An N400 was first observed in response to semantically incorrect sentence endings, for example in response to the word *socks* in the sentence *He spread the warm bread with socks* (Kutas and Hillyard 1980). Based on this early work, the N400 has been interpreted as reflecting the ease of lexical search and access (Fischler and Raney 1991). However, a number of subsequent studies have shown that the N400 is not uniquely observed in response to words, but also in response to pictures when they do not match an expectation established by a word, a sentence, another picture, a picture story, or even by an odour prime (Barrett and Rugg 1990; Federmeier and Kutas 2001; Ganis, Kutas and Sereno 1996; Holcomb and McPherson 1994, Nigam, Hoffman and Simons 1992; Pratarelli 1994; Sarfarazi, Cave, Richardson, Behan and Sedgwick 1999; West and Holcomb 2002). Environmental sounds also elicit an N400 when they do not match a sound expectation corresponding to a word (Van Petten and Rheinfelder 1995). Moreover, pseudowords, i.e., nonsense words that are regular according to the phonetic, prosodic, and phonotactic rules of a given language elicit substantial N400 responses, whereas nonwords, i.e., nonsense words that violate the regularities of the language, do not (Bentin, McCarthy and Wood 1985; Bentin, Mouchetant-Rostaing, Giard, Echallier and Pernier 1999; Holcomb 1993; Holcomb and Neville 1990; Nobre and McCarthy 1994; Rugg and Nagy 1987). Based on these more recent findings, the N400 is now considered to reflect a default response to potential referents for meaning, which can be reduced by semantic predictability. It has been proposed that N400 amplitude reflects the cognitive effort involved in integrating a stimulus into a given semantic context (Holcomb 1993), such as the effort required to semantically integrate a word into a sentence, or a picture into a picture-story. A relative reduction in the amplitude of the N400 indicates that the expectation triggered by a prime, a sentence, or any other context, has facilitated semantic processing of a target stimulus. Thus, although the N400 does not reflect the priming process itself, it indicates the effect of semantic priming on the subsequent process of semantic integration.

The N400 priming effect depends on the specific expectation derived from semantic memory of an individual subject. This means that the integration of a stimulus into semantic working memory is mainly affected by the individual organization of semantic knowledge in long-term memory (for a recent review see Kutas and Federmeier 2000) which varies between and within individuals during development. This property makes the N400 of special interest for developmental researchers, because only little is known about the development of semantic memory as well as about the interactions of perceptual and semantic memory during early language acquisition. For example, we still do not really understand the nature of semantic overgeneralizations in development. Why is a *cat* referred to as a *dog* – a behaviour that is often observed in young children? Do children think that a *cat* is the same thing as a *dog*? Or do they think that the word *dog* refers to a *cat* as well as a *dog*? Or, is this overextension a speech production error due to the fact that the word cat has not yet been acquired? Although behavioural measures have already provided some evidence for the influence of shape, taxonomical related-ness, and prior lexical knowledge on specific overextensions in children (Gelman, Croft, Fu, Clausner and Gottfried 1998), ERPs have the additional potential to dis-sociate semantic from perceptual processing stages. If an N400 priming effect is present in the ERP then it can be attributed to the presence of appropriate seman-tic memory structures.

Besides semantic development per se, the interactions of children's phono-logical, prosodic, and phonotactic knowledge with semantic memory can be ex-plored using N400 paradigms. What infants consider to be potential words, for instance, is an unsolved question. Although environmental sounds might be as-sociated with meaning, one would intuitively not assume that infants consider them to be word-like referents for meaning. But what are the features that make a complex acoustic stimulus a candidate to become a word? And how does children's knowledge of the phonetic, prosodic, and phonotactic properties of their native language affect which features are necessary for children to consider a word-like stimulus to in fact be a word?

There are a lot of further questions that could be tackled by means of N400 studies. If the N400 is shown to be generally present during the early stages of development, then it can be used as a tool for investigating the acquisition of con-ceptual representations and their organization into semantic memory as well as the development of a variety of specific cognitive and linguistic abilities in infants and toddlers (for an example see Friedrich and Friederici 2005c).

4   The cross-modal picture-word priming paradigm

In order to determine whether the N400 is already present at the time when chil-dren learn their first words, we designed a picture-word priming paradigm that is suitable even for one-year-olds (Friedrich and Friederici 2004; 2005a; 2005b; 2006). We not only explored whether the N400 is present on words, but also how children's early phonotactic knowledge affects their processing of nonsense words. Behavioural studies had suggested that children are sensitive to major phonotactic regularities of their target language by the age of 9 months (Friederici and Wessels 1993; Jusczyk, Friederici, Wessels, Svenkerud and Jusczyk 1993; for a review see Jusczyk and Luce 2002). Using the picture-word priming paradigm we investigat-ed whether such probabilistic phonotactic knowledge is stable enough in one-year-olds to produce the adult rule-like pattern of N400 responses to legal pseu-dowords but not to phonotactically illegal nonwords.

4.1 Participants

Children at 12, 14, and 19 months of age participated in the studies. Children were continuously observed via a video-monitor while the electroencephalogram (EEG) was recorded. Their behaviour and average attention to the visual stimuli were rated at one-minute intervals. In the ERP averages of the different age groups we included only those children who attended to the stimuli on at least 70% of the trials and had at least 20 artefact-free trials per condition. The final analyses included a total of 46 children tested at the age of 12 months (27 boys, 19 girls, 12 month ± 7 days), 30 children at the age of 14 months (13 boys, 17 girls, mean age 14 months 11 days), and 47 children at the age of 19 months (26 boys, 21 girls, 19 month ± 7 days). A control group consisting of 20 adults (10 men, 10 women, mean age 23.7 years) was tested on the same paradigm.

4.2 Stimuli

In our picture-word priming paradigm, pictures of known objects represented a simple, early acquired and easily accessible context for words. Pictures were brightly coloured, clearly identifiable illustrations of single objects. The objects were selected in such a way that one-year-old children already know most of them, i.e., children had either some experience of their own with the objects (e.g., apple, banana, bed, baby bottle, cookie, spoon), or the objects are commonly illustrated in picture books (e.g., ball, car, dog, duck, flower, tree). In order to capture the children's attention, all pictures had a bright background colour.

The acoustic stimuli were 44 words and 44 mono-and disyllabic nonsense words. They were spoken very slowly by a young woman, digitized at a rate of 44100 Hz, and presented via loudspeaker with an intensity of approximately 65 dBSPL. Words were names of basic level concepts, the most inclusive concepts for which concrete images can be formed (Rosch, Mervis, Gray, Johnson and Boyes-Braem 1976), which are known to be the earliest acquired by infants (e.g., *ball, car, dog, flower*). All words were selected from the ELFRA-1 (Grimm and Doil 2000), the German analogue of the MacArthur Communicative Development Inventory (Fensen, Dale, Reznick, Bates, Hartung, Pethick and Reilly 1993), and had a mean item difficulty of 78% (based on the percentage of 18-month-olds reported to comprehend each item). Words were either correct basic level names of the pictured objects or basic level names of other objects, i.e. either congruous or incongruous to the picture meanings. Both incongruous and nonsense words always differed in their first phoneme from the congruous words presented with the same pictures. That is, information about their incongruity was already available on the first phoneme. Nonsense words were either pseudowords or nonwords.

Pseudowords were prosodically, phonologically, and phonotactically legal in German (e.g., *fless* or *traune*). Nonwords had a word-onset that is phonotactically illegal in German (e.g., *rlink* or *sranto*). Information about the phonotactic irregularity of nonwords was available at the second phoneme, on average 174 ms post word onset. The mean word length was 1083 ms for words, 1084 ms for pseudowords, and 1085 ms for nonwords.

Each acoustic stimulus was presented twice. Each word occurred once as congruous and once as incongruous word such that the acoustic stimuli were exactly the same in the two word conditions. The picture-word pairs were combined such that there was no obvious semantic relation between an object and its incongruous word or between an object and a word that was phonologically similar to its nonsense word (e.g., a rhyming word). Each picture was presented four times, once with a congruous word, once with an incongruous word, once with a pseudoword, and once with a nonword to ensure that the effect of the visual stimuli was the same in each condition. Thus, each child saw each of the 44 pictures four times, but a specific picture-word combination occurred only once. The order of these combinations was balanced by presenting a fixed randomization in which no systematic repetition effects occurred between conditions.

4.3 Procedure

In each trial a coloured picture of a single object appeared on the screen for 4000 ms. After an interval of 900 ms from picture onset, a German indefinite article with a word length of about 700 ms was acoustically presented to refer to the pictured object in a natural way and to increase the children's attention to the subsequent acoustic stimulus. Congruous and incongruous words for a certain picture always had the same gender, and pseudo- and nonwords were presented with the same article as well, so that incongruity was not detectable at the position of the article. After a natural pause of about 300 ms, while the picture was still on the screen, the article was followed by a word or nonsense word (Figure 1). Thus, the target acoustic stimulus occurred at 1900 ms post picture onset, at the time when the primary visual and semantic processing of the picture had most likely already completed. Words and nonsense words were mixed within each block. The experimental session lasted about 12 minutes overall. It was divided into two blocks with a short break between the blocks.

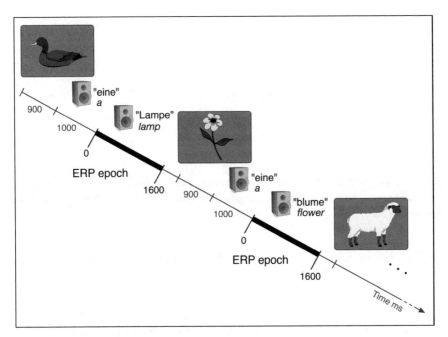

Figure 1. The picture-word priming paradigm

5   The comparison of congruous and incongruous words

5.1   The early priming effect

Rather unexpectedly, in all age groups of 12-, 14-, and 19-month-old children studied so far, we found very early ERP differences between congruous and incongruous words over lateral frontal regions (Friedrich and Friederici 2004; 2005a; 2005b; 2006). In the temporal range from about 100 to 500 ms post word onset, congruous words elicited significantly more negative responses than incongruous words (Figure 2).[1] Obviously, this effect does not represent an N400 priming effect, as all of its characteristics are different from the classical N400 reported in studies with adults. More specifically, its onset latency is shorter than that of the N400, its spatial distribution is lateral frontal instead centro-parietal, and the direction of the modulation is inverted, that is, congruous words elicited more negative responses than incongruous words, whereas an N400 priming effect would consist in larger negativities to incongruous than congruous words.

1.   The letter-number combinations in Figures 2-9 (F7, F3, FZ, F4, F8, T3, C3, CZ, C4, T4, CP5, CP6, P3, PZ, P4) indicate the electrode positions according to the 10-20 International System of Electrode Placement.

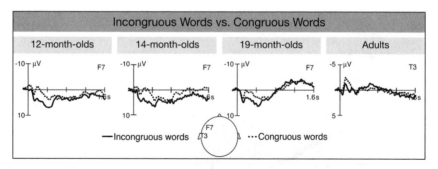

Figure 2. The early phonological-lexical priming effect for the comparison of congruous and incongruous words in different age groups. Figures are modified from Friedrich and Friederici (2005a; 2005b)

Similar early negative effects have been observed in unimodal studies, i.e. studies in one sensory modality (here, the auditory modality) with 11- to 20-month-olds (Conboy and Mills 2006; Mills, Coffey-Corina and Neville 1993; 1997; Mills, Prat, Zangl, Stager, Neville and Werker 2004; Thierry, Vihman and Roberts 2003). In one study by Mills and her colleagues, 20-month-old children listened to known words, unknown words, and words presented backwards. Sensitivity to the different word types was indicated by two negative components that the authors called N200 and N350. Both components were more pronounced in response to known than unknown words, and nearly absent in response to words presented backwards (Mills *et al.* 1993). In another study (Mills *et al.* 2004) mean ERP amplitude in the 200 to 400 ms range already differentiated between known and unknown words in 14-month-old children, but not yet between known words and "phonemic contrast" nonsense words that differed from known words only in their initial phoneme (e.g, *bear-gare*). In 20-month-olds this 200–400 ms negativity also differentiated between known words and the phonemic contrast words (Mills *et al.* 2004). Moreover, Thierry *et al.* (2003) compared ERPs elicited by familiar and unfamiliar words in 11-month-old children. In this young age group familiar words already elicited more negative responses than that found for unfamiliar words between 170 and 240 ms post word onset.

From the results of these studies we conclude that the early negativities in infants around one year of age reflect some kind of familiarity with native language word forms. The more negative the components for a certain stimulus type the more familiar children are with that stimulus type. This conclusion is consistent with results of a recent study in which 10-month-olds were repeatedly presented with low frequency nouns. During the process of experimentally controlled familiarization a slow positive wave initially present over frontal and fronto-temporal regions decreased gradually and after about eight presentations, a negativity emerged (Kooijman, Hagoort and Cutler 2005).

In this context, the more negative response to congruous words in our cross-modal picture-word priming studies might indicate that congruous words were processed as more familiar than incongruous words. However, congruous and incongruous words could not have differed in their familiarity as they were exactly the same words. That is, the early lateral frontal negativity differentiated between congruous and incongruous words even though they were physically identical. The only factor that could have caused the effect is the different picture contexts in which the two word conditions were presented. This leads to the conclusion that, similar to the adult N400, this early negativity in the cross-modal study indicates the *presence* of lexical-semantic priming, even though it might not directly reflect the *process* of lexical-semantic priming. The priming process itself should have already occurred in response to the picture before the word was presented. The lexical-semantic priming by the picture context then has the same effect on the subsequent word processing of congruous words as enhanced familiarity caused by past experience or repeated experimental presentations. As the effect started as early as 100–150 ms post word onset, it most likely reflects differences in the early acoustic-phonological processing stage rather than eased lexical access or semantic processing routines. These acoustic-phonological processing differences between physically identical words must be caused by top-down generated expectations of the perceptual features of those words that were semantically primed by the picture. That is, if German one-year-old children see a picture of a car, and hear the German article *ein (a)*, then they expect the phonemes of the German word *Auto (car)* to follow the indefinite article. This possibly unconscious expectation affects the efficiency of subsequent word processing. Thus, the enhanced early lateral frontal negativity elicited by congruous words reflects the facilitation of acoustic-phonological processing by lexical-semantic priming. More generally, we suggest that the enhanced negativity over infants' lateral frontal brain regions reflects improved phonological processing caused by the use of memory representations that have either been strengthened by increased familiarity or have been pre-activated by lexical-semantic priming (Friedrich and Friederici 2004; 2005a; 2005b).

Interestingly, adults also displayed early ERP differences similar to the phonological-lexical priming effect observed in infants (Friedrich and Friederici 2004). The adult effect, however, was mainly present over the left temporal region, instead of the rather bilateral more anterior effect in one-year-olds. A few studies with adults have reported left fronto-temporal ERP components that were more negative following semantic or word-fragment priming (Friedrich, Kotz, Friederici and Gunter 2004; Matsumoto, Iidaka, Nomura and Ohira 2005; Nobre and McCarthy 1994), but these components had longer latencies than that found in our study and were interpreted to reflect lexical access. Since these studies used visually present-ed words as targets they cannot be directly compared with our study, although visually presented words might also activate phonological representations (Blum and Yonelinas 2001). However, the question is why the phonological-lexical prim-ing effect observed in our study has not yet been reported in adult N400 priming studies using acoustic stimuli. One important aspect of our studies that contrasts with other adult priming studies is that the congruous words were basic level names of unambiguously identifiable objects and were therefore clearly predicta-ble. Moreover, since words were spoken very slowly the online acoustic-phonolog-ical processing was also slow such that the facilitation effect was longer and might only in this case become visible in the ERP. And finally, the fixed relative long in-terval between the article and the following word stimulus had possibly induced an additional expectation about the exact temporal occurrence of certain pho-nemes, which was confirmed only by congruous words.

5.2   The later N400 priming effect

In addition to the phonological-lexical priming effect, incongruous words elicited more negative responses than congruous words from about 300 ms post word on-set (Figure 3). This broadly distributed and long-lasting effect with a centro-pari-etal maximum was present in 19- and 14-month-old children, but not in 12-month-olds (Friedrich and Friederici 2004; 2005a; 2005b). The similarity of the spatio-temporal distribution of this later negativity in infants to that of the adult N400 observed in the same paradigm strongly suggests that it is the expected in-fant N400 priming effect. However, this infant N400 was not present in the young-est group. One possible explanation for the absence of the N400 in 12-month-olds is that these children did not yet comprehend the meanings of the presented words. However, similarly to the two older age groups, children at 12 months of age al-ready showed the early phonological-lexical priming effect. As the same words were presented in congruous and incongruous conditions, this effect cannot be explained merely by familiarity effects, but rather, it must originate from the se-mantic processing of the picture content that affects subsequent word processing via the activation of a lexical element. Therefore, we reason that the 12-month-old children already had some, at least implicit, lexical knowledge about the presented words. This in turn suggests that the N400 mechanisms generally, or at least the mechanisms of the N400 reduction by semantic priming are not yet mature in children at 12 months of age.

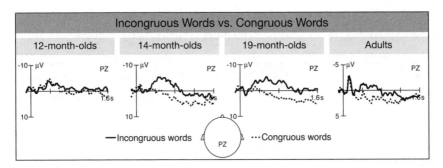

Figure 3. The N400 semantic priming effect for the comparison of congruous and incongruous words in different age groups. Figures are modified from Friedrich and Friederici (2005a; 2005b)

5.3   Summary of the comparison of congruous and incongruous words

From the results of the word stimuli in our picture-word studies it can be concluded that even the first lexical-semantic knowledge established in memory affects the acoustic-phonological processing of words in one-year-olds. The facilitation of these perceptual processing stages indicates the presence of lexical-semantic priming preceding word processing. However, although pictures already prime words semantically in 12-month-olds, N400 mechanisms of semantic integration were either not yet present, or not yet affected by semantic priming at that age. The presence of an N400 priming effect in 14-month-olds suggests that the full functionality of these mechanisms develops between 12 and 14 months of age.

6   The comparison of legal and phonotactically illegal nonsense words

6.1   The early phonotactic familiarity effect

Early processing differences were also observed in the comparison between phonotactically legal and illegal nonsense words (Figure 4). In all age groups, legal nonsense words (pseudowords) elicited more negative responses than illegal nonsense words (nonwords) primarily over the left lateral frontal brain region. Again, the spatio-temporal characteristics of this effect suggest that it is not an N400-like response but rather a familiarity effect similar to that observed in unimodal studies with infants (Kooijman *et al.* 2005; Mills *et al.* 1993; 1997; Mills *et al.* 2004; Thierry *et al.* 2003). This phonotactic familiarity effect indicates that acoustic-phonological processing is facilitated for phonotactically legal phoneme clusters that children have perceived in real word contexts previously and for which phonological representations are already established in memory (Friedrich and Friederici 2005b).

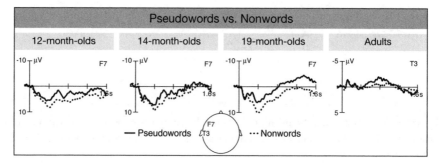

Figure 4. The phonotactic familiarity effect for the comparison of legal pseudowords and phonotactically illegal nonwords in different age groups. Figures are modified from Friedrich and Friederici (2005b)

When comparing the lateral-frontal ERP's elicited by words with those elicited by nonsense words, a gradual differentiation can be seen in the amplitudes of the responses in 19-month-olds (Figure 5). Phonotactically illegal nonsense words, which contain phoneme combinations that were unfamiliar to the children, elicited the most positive responses. The responses to phonotactically legal pseudowords and incongruous words, which both consisted of familiar phoneme combinations but were unprimed by the pictures, were moderately positive and very similar to one another. And finally, congruous words that were both familiar and primed by pictures elicited the smallest positivity. In this condition, the N200 was most pronounced. These results fit well with the finding of Kooijman *et al.* (2005) that the positivity is reduced with increasing familiarity. The similarity of the early responses to known incongruous words and unknown legal pseudowords supports the view that the enhanced early negativity (or the reduced positivity) over the lateral frontal brain region does not reflect eased lexical access but facilitated acoustic-phonological processing. Moreover, because phonotactic legality was not detectable until the second phoneme, whereas phonological incongruity to the expected lexically primed word was already detectable by the first phoneme, the difference between the two types of nonsense words started slightly later than the difference between congruous and incongruous real words.

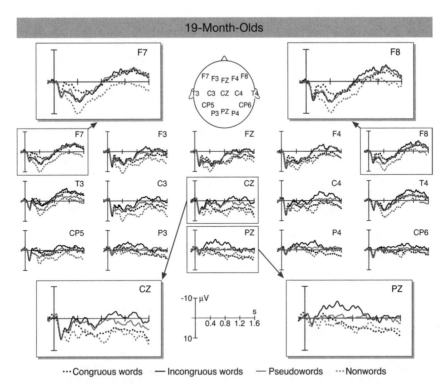

Figure 5. ERPs for congruous words, incongruous words, legal pseudowords, and phonotactically illegal nonwords in 19-month-old children (n=47). Figures are modified from Friedrich and Friederici (2005b)

In 12-month-olds, only primed congruous words showed facilitated responses over the lateral frontal brain region in the early temporal ranges (Figure 6 below). The same responses to unprimed incongruous words as to both nonsense word types suggest that the 12-month-old children are not able to provide additional resources for the adequate processing of unfamiliar phoneme combinations during this early processing stage. During later stages, however, the processing of both incongruous words and phonotactically legal pseudowords was facilitated as indexed by their reduced positivity in comparison to phonotactically illegal nonsense words.

Interestingly, adults failed to show a phonotactic familiarity effect. This may result from the fact that adults commonly have some acoustic experience with foreign languages. Moreover, the phonotactically illegal phoneme clusters of nonwords were built from phonemes of the adults' native language. These phonemes are highly learned and have very well established memory representations so that they may be easily processed even in phonotactically illegal combinations.

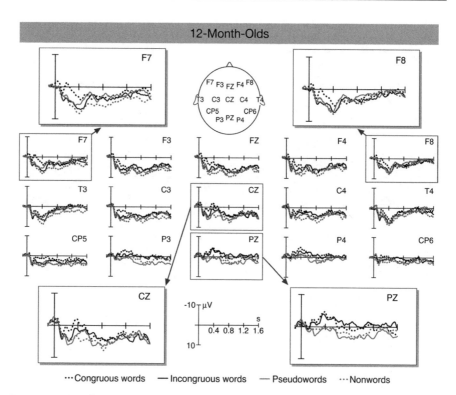

Figure 6. ERPs for congruous words, incongruous words, legal pseudowords, and phono-tactically illegal nonwords in 12-month-old children (n=46). Figures are modified from Friedrich and Friederici (2005b)

6.2   The later semantic integration effect

In both 19- and 14-month-olds the negative difference between legal and illegal nonsense words was sustained, and similar to the N400 elicited by legal pseudo-words in adults over centro-parietal regions, mainly from about 400 ms post word onset (Figure 7). This shift in the spatial distribution of the negativity appears to reflect an overlap of the phonotactic familiarity effect with the N400 on legal pseu-dowords. Indeed, phonotactically legal pseudowords but not phonotactically ille-gal nonwords were processed more negatively than congruous words from about 500 ms which indicates the elicitation of an N400 by legal pseudowords in 19-month-olds (Figure 5). The presence of the N400 on pseudowords suggests that mechanisms of semantic integration are triggered in response to these legal non-sense words. The different N400 responses to pseudo- and nonwords indicate the brain's ability to differentiate those nonsense words that are potential lexical elements of the children's target language and thus potential referents for meaning from those that are not potential words of the language because of their illegal phonotactic structure (Friedrich and Friederici 2005b).

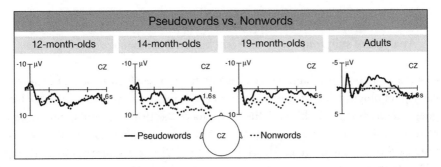

Figure 7. The N400 semantic integration effect for the comparison of legal pseudowords and phonotactically illegal nonwords in different age groups. Figures are modified from Friedrich and Friederici (2005b)

Similar to what was found for words, an N400 difference between legal pseudowords and illegal nonwords was not present in 12-month-olds. Since the N400 neither occurred in the difference between pseudo- and nonwords nor between incongruous and congruous words, the N400 mechanisms appear to be immature at 12 months, although the lexical priming effect of that age group indicates the presence of appropriate lexical-semantic knowledge. However, negative differences between words and nonsense words observed over the parietal region in the N400 time range (Figure 6) could possibly be an N400 that emerges in response to known words but is not yet reduced by semantic priming of congruous words. In any case, the results support the view that the N400 develops as a response to potential words at a time when children have become sensitive to native language regularities, rather than being already present at birth and declining in response to nonwords during the acquisition of native language regularities (Friedrich and Friederici 2005b).

6.3   Summary of the comparison of legal and illegal nonsense words

From the results of the nonsense word comparison in our picture-word studies it can be concluded that the early experience of one-year-olds with the phonotactic regularities of their native language affects their acoustic-phonological processing of unknown words. Moreover, the initiation of semantic integration mechanisms depends on the regularity of the phonotactic properties of nonsense words. Whereas

semantic mechanisms indexed by the N400 are triggered in response to legal pseudowords, these mechanisms are not present in response to phonotactically illegal
nonwords. This result indicates that one-year-old children treat phonotactically legal pseudowords but not phonotactically illegal nonwords as potential words.

7   Analyses of subgroups with different behavioral language development

Using a longitudinal design we investigated how the ERP correlates of children's
early phonological, lexical and semantic processing are related to their later language development. To this end, the ERP data of the 19-month-old children were
retrospectively grouped according to the children's verbal language skills as measured by the German language development test SETK-2 (Grimm 2000) at the age
of 30 months.

7.1   The language test SETK-2

The SETK-2 was designed to measure both receptive and expressive language skills
in two- to three-year-old German children, and to identify children with a potential risk for developmental language impairments early. In the expressive subtests
that were used to group the children post-hoc, the production of 30 words (e.g
Ball/ball, Schlüssel/key, Kuchen/cake, Bär/bear) and 16 sentences (e.g., *Der Vogel
fliegt/The bird is flying. Der Mann putzt die Fenster/The man is cleaning the windows*) was elicited by presenting the children with objects and pictures and asking
them standardized questions about these stimuli.

7.2   Participants

Children who successfully performed both expressive subtests of the SETK-2, defined by scores higher than one standard deviation below the mean for their age,
and who had no family history of any developmental language disorder were as-
signed to the group with age-adequate later language skills. This group included 22
children (11 male, 11 female). Children with very low scores in the production
subtests, defined as lower than one standard deviation below the mean, formed the
group with later poor language skills. A total of 18 children (11 male, 7 female)
were included in this group. The groups differed significantly in their SETK-2
scores at 30 months for both word and sentence production. The groups also differed in the number of words produced at 24 months as reported by parents in the
ELFRA-2 questionnaire (Grimm and Doil 2000), but not in their word comprehension, which was assessed by a parental questionnaire at the time of the ERP

session. The groups did not differ in parental education, type of care persons, child care activities, level of household income, and parents' contentment with personal life circumstances.

7.3   Results

The ERPs at 19 months of the children with age-adequate later language skills displayed both the phonological-lexical priming effect (i.e. a more negative response to congruous words from 150 to 400 ms which was restricted to the left lateral frontal region, Figure 8) and the N400 priming effect (i.e. a more negative response to incongruous words from 250 to 1200 ms, broadly distributed but maximal over centro-parietal midline sites, Figure 9). In contrast, the ERPs of 19-month-old children with poor later language skills displayed a more negative response to congruous words only. Their broadly distributed phonological-lexical priming effect started at about 150 ms and lasted until 700 ms (Figures 8 and 9, Friedrich and Friederici 2006).

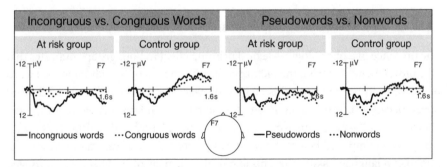

Figure 8. The phonological-lexical priming effect and the phonotactic familiarity effect in the post-hoc defined subgroups of 19-month-old children with different later language development. At risk group: children with poor later language skills (n=18). Control group: children with age-adequate later language skills (n=22). Figures are modified from Friedrich and Friederici (2006)

In addition, 19-month-old children with age-adequate later language skills displayed more negative responses to legal pseudowords than to phonotactically illegal nonwords (Figure 8). The phonotactic familiarity effect started early and was most pronounced over lateral frontal and temporal regions. In this group with normal later language skills, an N400 followed the phonotactic familiarity effect (Figure 9). In contrast, the group with poor later performance did not show any significant difference between the processing of legal and phonotactically illegal nonsense words although correlation analyses indicated that within this group, more negative responses on legal as compared to illegal nonsense words were present for those children who had better scores in the language test later on (Figures 8 and 9, Friedrich and Friederici 2006).

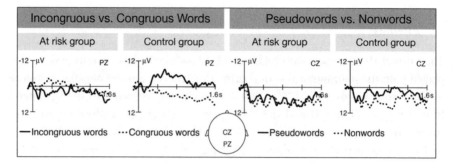

Figure 9. The N400 semantic integration effect in the post-hoc defined subgroups of 19-month-old children with different later language development. At risk group: children with poor later language skills (n=18). Control group: children with age-adequate later language skills (n=22). Figures are modified from Friedrich and Friederici (2006)

7.4   Discussion of the subgroup comparisons

The presence of a phonological-lexical priming effect in both groups indicates that all children benefited from the picture context in their acoustic-phonological word processing. In both groups, this facilitation was effective immediately after word onset, because semantic assignment, lexical choice, and pre-activation of the expected phonological forms were triggered by the picture and had most likely already been completed before the word was presented. However, in the group with poor later language skills the phonological-lexical priming effect was stronger, more broadly distributed, and more prolonged in its duration than that of the group with age-adequate later language skills. This indicates that 19-month-old children with poor language performance later on relied more extensively on the facilitation created by the picture context and seemed to need more effort to adequately process unexpected words than peers who performed better on the language test later on.

The results of the post-hoc analyses clearly demonstrate that the early emergence of the N400 in development is related to differences in children's later language skills. Since at the time of the ERP measures children of both groups had sufficient lexical knowledge to elicit the phonological-lexical priming effect, the absence of the N400 in the group with poor language performance later on could not have been caused by a lack of comprehension due to non-existing vocabulary. Interestingly, the 19-month-olds in the lower language group displayed a similar pattern to 12-month-olds who also showed early phonological-lexical priming without significant N400 modulation (Friedrich and Friederici 2005a). This finding and the fact that 14-month-olds already show an N400 priming effect (Friedrich and Friederici 2005b) strongly suggest an early developmental delay in the children with poor expressive language skills at the age of 30 months. More specifically, these children are delayed for at least about half a year in their maturation of the semantic integration mechanisms indexed by the N400.

Normally developing children also displayed the phonotactic familiarity effect and the N400 effect to legal pseudowords. This indicates that they are sensitive to the phonotactic regularities of their native language. This sensitivity was not present in children with poor later language skills. However, significant correlations between language scores and ERP response patterns suggest that those children for whom phonotactic knowledge was emerging at 19 months had relatively better later language skills by 30 months. The absence of the phonotactic familiarity effect in the group as a whole might be due to weaker memory representations for legal phoneme clusters in these children or to their inability to provide additional resources for the adequate processing of illegal phoneme clusters.

Overall, the results from the post-hoc analyses of the 19-month-old children indicate that variability in expressive language development observed at 30 months has precursors in children's ERP patterns obtained about one year earlier. The presence of the N400 in children with better expressive language development and its absence in children with poorer expressive language development suggest a direct relationship between children's early development of specific word comprehension mechanisms and their later production abilities.

8   The importance of N400 mechanisms for word learning

Although the post-hoc analyses of subgroups have shown that the early development of the N400 is related to children's success in language acquisition, we do not know *how* the presence of N400 mechanisms affects word acquisition and further language development. In order to answer this question, we would have to know what the N400 mechanisms actually reflect. How are these mechanisms realized on a neural level? And what exactly does semantic integration mean? At the moment, we can only speculate about how semantic integration of a stimulus into the current context might be realized. One possibility is that processing a semantically inappropriate target stimulus modifies or resets the semantic representation of the context held in working memory. Another alternative is that either the actual phonological representation or the momentarily activated semantic representation of the target stimulus is rejected and the search for other existing representations that better fit into the current semantic context is initiated. Finally, both the stimulus representation and the contextual representation might be rejected, and a new integrated representation might be built from the episodic co-occurrence of the stimulus within a certain context. In all of these cases, the changed or newly established representation might be strengthened so that the next time the stimulus and context co-occur, the strengthened representation is accessed more easily and semantic integration is thus facilitated.

All these hypothetical mechanisms are assumed to be important for word learning during early language acquisition when meaning has to be extracted from the context and linked to a new phonological word representation. Suppose a child already knows a certain word for an object just seen, but hears a word that differs from the one he or she is expecting. In this case the integration mechanisms described above would enable the child to correct the phonological word representation, to change the semantic representation of either the word or the context, or to modify both phonological and semantic word representations. In either case, a new object-word association would be learned, resulting in the successive expansion and refinement of the lexicon. Such mechanisms of "rejecting" or "resetting" momentarily activated representations held in working memory have the potential to override inadequate or underspecified memory representations which would otherwise be constantly activated by a particular external stimulus or event (for a possible neural implementation of such mechanisms see Carpenter and Grossberg 1987).

The presence of these mechanisms seems not necessary during very early language development when children begin to acquire lexical knowledge. During this early stage, a slow learning mechanism that increases both stimulus familiarity and associations between visual (object) and auditory (word) stimuli may be sufficient for establishing first lexical representations. However, as children become able to rapidly learn new words for new objects, they may initially establish inappropriate representations or wrong associations, and mechanisms for correcting them would need to develop. As described above, the resetting of such inappropriate representations activated by incoming stimuli enables the establishment of new memory representations and thus facilitates the learning of new words with new meanings instead of only allowing for slow modifications of already stored knowledge (for a discussion of this issue see also Friedrich and Friederici 2006).

Interestingly, the first appearance of the N400 during development is temporally closely related to the first appearance of the fast mapping ability, that is, the capacity of children to rapidly learn new words for new objects after only a few presentations. This ability has been shown to be behaviourally established in 13-, 14-, and 15-month-olds, but 12-month-olds fail to show it even in favourable experimental conditions (Schafer and Plunkett 1998; Werker, Cohen, Lloyd, Casasola and Stager 1998; Woodward, Markman and Fitzsimmons 1994). The fast mapping ability might be seen as a qualitative shift from slow associative learning based on many repetitions to rapid learning within a few presentations. Alternatively, it might indicate the maturation of a new, rather explicit learning mechanism supplementing implicit associative learning mechanisms already present at birth (for the development of explicit and implicit memory, see for example, Naito and Komatsu 1993). The temporal co-occurrence of the maturation of the N400 and the development of the fast mapping ability might reflect a causal relationship between N400 neural mechanisms and children's word learning capacity.

Another important milestone in children's early language acquisition is the vocabulary spurt, a dramatic increase in word learning rate which starts between 14 and 24 months of age and is assumed to be related to the fast mapping ability (Benedict 1979; Goldfield and Reznick 1990; Reznick and Goldfield 1992). From the suggestions of the present chapter, the vocabulary spurt should not occur before the N400 to words has been developed. This would mean that the presence of N400 mechanisms is a necessary precondition for the onset of the vocabulary spurt. The further investigation of this hypothesized relationship between N400 mechanisms and children's learning capacities is an interesting topic for future research using a combined behavioural-ERP approach.

Notes

*   This research was supported by the Deutsche Forschungsgemeinschaft (German Research Foundation, DFG) (FR-519/18–1), the Schram Foundation (T278/10824/2001) and the EU (EC12778/NEST-CALACEI Project).

References

Barrett, S.E. and Rugg, M.D. 1990. "Event-related potentials and the semantic matching of pictures." *Brain and Cognition* 14: 201–12.
Benedict, H. 1979. "Early lexical development: Comprehension and production." *Journal of Child Language* 6: 183–200.
Bentin, S., McCarthy, G. and Wood, C.C. 1985. "Event-related potentials, lexical decision and semantic priming." *Electroencephalography and Clinical Neurophysiology* 60: 343–55.
Bentin, S., Mouchetant-Rostaing, Y., Giard, M.H., Echallier, J.F. and Pernier, J. 1999. "ERP manifestion of processing printed words at different psycholinguistic levels: Time course and Scalp distribution." *Journal of Cognitive Neuroscience* 11: 235–60.
Blum, D. and Yonelinas, A.P. 2001. "Transfer across modality in perceptual implicit memory." *Psychonomic Bulletin & Review* 8 (1): 147–54.

Carpenter, G.A. and Grossberg, S. 1987. "A massively parallel architecture for a self-organizing neural pattern recognition machine." *Computer Vision, Graphics, and Image Processing* 37: 54–115.

Conboy, B.T. and Mills, D.L. 2006. "Two languages, one developing brain: Event-related potentials to words in bilingual toddlers." *Developmental Science* 9 (1): 1–12.

Eimas, P.D., Siqueland, E.R., Jusczyk, P. and Vigorito, J. 1971. "Speech perception in infants." *Science* 171: 303–6.

Federmeier, K.D. and Kutas, M. 2001. "Meaning and modality: influence of context, semantic memory organization, and perceptual predictability on picture processing." *Journal of Experimental Psychology: Learning, Memory, and Cognition* 27 (1): 202–24.

Fensen, L., Dale, P.S., Reznick, J.S., Bates, D., Hartung, J.P., Pethick, S. and Reilly, J.S. 1993. *MacArthur communicative development inventories.* San Diego, CA: Singular.

Fischler, I. and Raney, G.E. 1991. "Language by eye: Behavioural and psychophysiological approaches to reading." In *Handbook of cognitive psychophysiology: Central and autonomic nervous system approaches.* J.R. Jennings and M.G.H. Coles (eds.), 511–61. New York, NY: John Wiley & Sons.

Friederici, A.D. 2005. "Neurophysiological markers of early language acquisition: From syllables to sentences." *Trends in Cognitive Sciences* 9 (10): 481–8.

Friederici, A.D. and Wessels, J.M.I. 1993. "Phonotactic knowledge of word boundaries and its use in infant speech perception." *Perception & Psychophysics* 54: 287–95.

Friedrich, M. and Friederici, A.D. 2006. "Early N400 development and later language acquisition." *Psychophysiology* 43: 1–12.

Friedrich, M. and Friederici, A.D. 2005a. "Lexical priming and semantic integration reflected in the ERP of 14-month-olds." *NeuroReport* 16 (6): 653–6.

Friedrich, M. and Friederici, A.D. 2005b. "Phonotactic knowledge and lexical-semantic processing in one-year-olds: Brain responses to words and nonsense words in picture contexts." *Journal of Cognitive Neuroscience* 17 (11): 1785–802.

Friedrich, M. and Friederici, A.D. 2005c. "Semantic sentence processing reflected in the event-related potentials of one- and two-year-old children." *NeuroReport* 16 (16): 1801–4.

Friedrich, M. and Friederici, A.D. 2004. "N400-like semantic incongruity effect in 19-month-olds: Processing known words in picture contexts." *Journal of Cognitive Neuroscience* 16: 1465–77.

Friedrich, C.K., Kotz, S.A., Friederici, A.D. and Gunter, T.C. 2004. "ERPs reflect lexical identification in word fragment priming." *Journal of Cognitive Neuroscience* 16: 4, 541–52.

Ganis, G., Kutas, M. and Sereno, M. 1996. "The search for "Common Sense": An electrophysiological study of the comprehension of words and pictures in reading." *Journal of Cognitive Neuroscience* 8: 89–106.

Gelman, S.A., Croft, W., Fu, P., Clausner, T. and Gottfried, G. 1998. "Why is a pomgranate an apple? The role of shape, taxonomical relatedness, and prior lexical knowledge in children's overextensions of apple and dog." *Journal of Child Language* 25: 267–91.

Goldfield, B.A. and Reznick, J.S. 1990. "Early lexical acquisition: Rate, content and vocabulary spurt." *Journal of Child Language* 17: 171–84.

Grimm, H. 2000. *SETK-2: Sprachentwicklungstest für zweijährige Kinder (2.0–2.11). Diagnose rezeptiver und produktiver Sprachverarbeitungsfähigkeiten.* Göttingen: Hogrefe.

Grimm, H. and Doil, H. 2000. *ELFRA: Elternfragebögen für die Früherkennung von Risikokindern (ELFRA-1, ELFRA-2).* Göttingen: Hogrefe.

Holcomb, P.J. 1993. "Semantic priming and stimulus degradation: Implications for the role of the N400 in language processing." *Psychophysiology* 30: 47–61.

Holcomb, P.J. and Neville, H.J. 1990. "Auditory and visual semantic priming in lexical decision: A comparison using event-related brain potentials." *Language and Cognitive Processes* 5: 281–312.

Holcomb, P.J. and McPherson, W.B. 1994. "Event-related brain potentials reflect semantic priming in an object decision task." *Brain and Cognition* 24: 259–76.

Jusczyk, P.W. 1997. *The discovery of spoken language.* Cambridge, MA: The MIT Press.

Jusczyk, P.W., Friederici, A.D., Wessels, J.M.I., Svenkerud, V. and Jusczyk, A.M. 1993. "Infants' sensitivity to the sound pattern of native language words." *Journal of Memory and Language* 32: 402–20.

Jusczyk, P.W. and Luce, P.A. 2002. "Speech perception and spoken word recognition: Past and present." *Ear and Hearing* 23: 2–40.

Kemler-Nelson, D., Jusczyk, P.W., Mandel, D.R., Myers, J., Turk, A. and Gerken, L. 1995. "The head-turn preference procedure for testing auditory perception." *Infant Behavior and Development* 18: 111–6.

Kooijman, V., Hagoort, P. and Cutler, A. 2005. "Electrophysiological evidence for prelinguistic infants' word recognition in continuous speech." *Cognitive Brain Research* 24 (1): 109–16.

Kuhl, P.K. 2004. "Early language acquisition: Cracking the speech code." *Nature Neuroscience Reviews* 5: 831–43.

Kuhl, P.K., Williams, K.A. Lacerda, F., Stevens, K.N. and Lindblom, B. 1992. "Linguistic experience alters phonetic perception in infants by 6 months of age." *Science* 255: 608.

Kutas, M. and Federmeier, K.D. 2000. "Electrophysiology reveals semantic memory use in language comprehension." *Trends in Cognitive Sciences* 4: 463–70.

Kutas, M. and Hillyard, S.A. 1980. "Reading senseless sentences: Brain potentials reflect semantic incongruity." *Science* 207: 203–5.

Mandler, J.M. and McDonough, L. 1993. "Concept formation in infancy." *Cognitive Development* 8: 291–318.

Matsumoto, A., Iidaka, T., Nomura, M. and Ohira, H. 2005. "Dissociation of conscious and unconscious repetition priming effect on event-related potentials." *Neuropsychologia* 43: 1168–76.

Mills, D.L., Coffey-Corina, S.A. and Neville, H.J. 1993. "Language acquisition and cerebral specialization in 20-month-old infants." *Journal of Cognitive Neuroscience* 5: 317–34.

Mills, D.L., Coffey-Corina, S.A. and Neville, H.J. 1997. "Language cmprehension and cerebral specialization from 13 to 20 months." *Developmental Neuropsychology* 13.

Mills, D.L., Prat, C., Zangl, R., Stager, C.L., Neville, H.J. and Werker, J.F. 2004. "Language experience and the organization of brain activity to phonetically similar words: ERP evidence from 14-and 20-month-olds." *Journal of Cognitive Neuroscience* 16: 1452–64.

Naito M., Komatsu S. 1993. "Processes involved in childhood development of implicit memory." In *Implicit memory: New directions in cognition, development, and neuropsychology,* P. Graf and M.E.J. Masson (eds.), 231–60. Hillsdale, NJ: Lawrence Erlbaum Associates.

Nigam, A., Hoffman, J.E. and Simons, R.F. 1992. "N400 to semantically anomalous pictures and words." *Journal of Cognitive Neuroscience* 4: 15–27.

Nobre, A.C. and McCarthy, G. 1994. "Language related ERPs: Scalp distributions and modulation by word-type and semantic priming." *Journal of Cognitive Neuroscience* 6: 233–55.

Pratarelli, M.E. 1994. "Semantic processing of pictures and spoken words: Evidence from event-related brain potentials." *Brain & Cognition* 24: 137–57.

Reznick, J.S. and Goldfield, V.A. 1992. "Rapid change in lexical development in comprehension and production." *Developmental Psychology* 28: 406–13.

Rosch, E., Mervis, C.B., Gray, W.D., Johnson, D.M. and Boyes-Braem, P. 1976. "Basic objects in natural categories." *Cognitive Psychology* 8: 382–439.

Rugg, M.D. and Nagy, M.E. 1987. "Lexical contribution to nonword-repetition effects: Evidence from event-related potentials." *Memory and Cognition* 15: 473–81.

Sarfarazi, M. Cave, B. Richardson, A., Behan, J. and Sedgwick, E.M. 1999. "Visual event related potentials modulated by contextually relevant and irrelevant olfactory primes." *Chemical Senses* 24: 145–54.

Schafer, G. and Plunkett, K. 1998. "Rapid word learning by fifteen-month-olds under tightly controlled conditions." *Child Development* 69: 309–20.

Thierry, G., Vihman, M. and Roberts, M. 2003. "Familiar words capture the attention of 11-month-olds in less than 250 ms." *NeuroReport* 14: 2307–10.

Van Petten, C. and Rheinfelder, H. 1995. "Conceptual relationships between spoken words and environmental sounds: Event-related brain potential measures." *Neuropsychologia* 33 (4): 485–508.

Werker, J.F., Cohen, L.B., Lloyd, V.L., Casasola, M. and Stager, C.L. 1998. "Acquisition of word-object associations by 14-month-old infants." *Developmental Psychology* 34: 1289–309.

Werker, J.F. and Yeung, H.H. 2005. "Infant speech perception bootstraps word learning." *Trends in Cognitive Sciences* 9 (11): 519–27.

West, W.C. and Holcomb, P.J. 2002. "Event-related potentials during discourse-level semantic integration of complex pictures." *Cognitive Brain Research* 13: 363–75.

Woodward, A.L., Markman, E. and Fitzsimmons, C.M. 1994. "Rapid word learning in 13- and 18-month-olds." *Developmental Psychology* 30: 553–66.

CHAPTER 7

The effects of early word learning on brain development

Elizabeth A. Sheehan and Debra L. Mills

1   Introduction

The first three years of life are characterized by rapid changes in language development: from the perception of prosodic and phonological cues of the infant's native
language, mapping meaning onto sounds in understanding their first words, to
speaking in words and sentences. Yet the development of the underlying brain
systems that precede, accompany, or follow these achievements is not well understood. Different theoretical positions offer opposing views on the initial state of
cerebral specializations for different aspects of language and the extent to which
experience influences the subsequent organization of the brain for these functions.
In this chapter, we review literature and research suggesting specific experiences
with language influence how the brain responds to spoken language. We are interested in how the process of learning language shapes the organization of language-
relevant brain activity.

It is well known that for the vast majority of typically developing adults, most
aspects of "language" are processed in the left hemisphere. Although it is commonly thought that the preferential status of the left hemisphere for language is
apparent from birth, research will be discussed in this chapter indicating that the
left hemisphere does not exclusively process all aspects of language, but there are
changes in the organization of brain activity over development. We will demonstrate how the lateralization of language-relevant brain activity changes with experience and increased proficiency with language.

The trajectory of language development throughout the period of infancy has
been extensively studied using a variety of behavioral techniques. These techniques
have provided us with a wealth of information concerning cognitive development
but they cannot inform us on how language is processed within the brain. The
technique discussed in this chapter is event-related potentials (explained below).

This technique is non-invasive and ideally suited for studying development over the lifespan and is particularly good for testing infants.

The measure of experience with language adopted here is operationalized as the child's receptive/comprehensive and expressive/productive vocabulary size. In the studies presented here, vocabulary size is measured using the MacArthur-Bates Communicative Development Inventory (MCDI, Fenson, Dale, Reznick, Bates, Thal and Pethick 1994). This is a parental report measure from which a child's percentile ranking and raw scores can be calculated on a number of variables including vocabulary comprehension, vocabulary production, and the use of word combinations and syntax.

Of interest in the set of studies discussed is how the highly distinct neural systems used to process language during adulthood arise and how acquiring a spoken language influences brain development. We posit that the development of lateralization is not static or linked to pre-programmed genetic changes in maturation. Rather, changes in the organization of language-relevant brain activity are dynamic and linked to a variety of domain-specific and domain-general processes as well as influenced by task-specific demands on these cognitive resources. The methodology employed to investigate these questions is the event-related potential technique.

2   Event-related potentials

Event-related potentials (ERPs) are used to measure brain activity elicited by a specific set of stimuli. The electrical activity elicited by populations of neurons firing simultaneously can be recorded at the scalp. This ongoing electrical activity can be recorded using electroencephalogram (EEG) millisecond-by-millisecond. A participant's EEG is segmented into epochs corresponding to the onset of a particular stimulus event and these epochs are grouped by condition. ERPs are created when the epochs of EEG for trials in a particular condition are averaged to construct one waveform that is time-locked to the onset of that particular stimulus set. The latter waveform is a series of positive and negative deflections; some of which over time have been associated with various sensory and psychological processes and are called components.

ERP components are commonly named from their polarity (P for positive or N for negative) and their peak latency. That is the convention used here. For example, one negative component elicited by semantic processing typically peaks around 400 ms and is labeled the N400. Components are also often named for the order in which they occur in the waveform. For example, the first positive component in a waveform is often labeled the P1. Typically, illustrations of ERPs are plotted with the latency, measured in milliseconds, along the X-axis and the peak amplitude, measured in microvolts, along the Y-axis. Measurements of the ERP are taken to reflect the peak latency (the time in milliseconds at which the maximum positive or negative activity occurred), peak amplitude (the maximal positive or negative going activity in microvolts), and distribution of the activity across the scalp (at which electrode sites the activity occurred).

In the studies presented in this chapter, ERPs were recorded using an electrocap with 16, 22, or 32 electrodes. See Figure 1 for an illustration of the electrode locations. The nylon electrocap has electrodes sewn into it at specific locations. It is designed to sit securely on the participant's head. Once the cap is placed, a small amount of conductive gel is inserted into each electrode to ensure that the electrical activity generated by the brain on the scalp is conducted to the electrodes on the cap. Fixation of the cap takes 10 to 15 minutes and serves as an opportunity to acquaint children with their surroundings and the experimenters.

Electrode Sites

Left Hemisphere

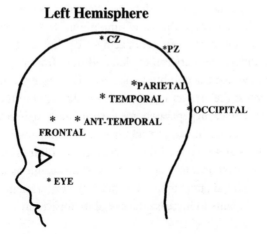

Figure 1. Electrode placements for infant studies using 16 channels

This technique is ideal for use with infants because it is safe, non-invasive, and does not require an overt behavioral response. In some behavioral paradigms (e.g. habituation, preferential looking) used to study language development with infants and toddlers, the child needs to make a response such as a head turn or a specific eye movement. ERPs are beneficial because the child does not need to make a pre-specified response to collect data. They simply need to sit relatively still and attend to the stimulus presented. The ERP technique can also be used to study development across the lifespan with very limited modifications to the paradigm. For two comprehensive reviews on this technique see Luck (2005) and Rugg and Coles (1995).

One limitation of this technique is that it is sensitive to movements made by the child. To reduce this type of artifact in the data, efforts are made to keep the child still and attending to a specified location. The child is given periodic breaks throughout testing during which they are positively reinforced for sitting still. Additionally, special artifact rejection techniques are used on a trial-by-trial basis. For example, the experimenter presses a button to mark trials on which the child did not see the stimuli or was not paying attention. These trials are eliminated from the analyses. Because infants produce large frontal brain potentials, the practice of eliminating trials that exceed a set threshold (e.g. +/- 100 µv) across all electrodes can reject true brain activity. Moreover, blinks and other eye movements can fall below this level and would be included in the average. Additionally, thresholds can vary person to person and by age (see Luck 2005 for other problems with this common approach). Therefore, we adopt a more customized approach. Eye blinks and vertical eye movements elicit potentials that are opposite in polarity over and under the eye. Our computer program detects differences in the slopes of the potentials over and under the eye at the same time points. Separate criteria are set for determining a variety of different types of artifact, e.g. horizontal eye artifact based on peak to peak differences between the left and right frontal electrodes, and amplifier blocking in which the amplitude of the activity exceeds the capacity of the amplifiers. We adjust the artifact rejection thresholds used in the computer algorithms for artifact detection separately for each infant based on visual inspection of each trial. These procedures have increased the number of artifact-free trials retained for analysis and increased the percentage of children successfully tested. Of course even the best artifact rejection procedures cannot substitute for clean data. Therefore, maximal effort is spent to make the experiments short and interesting for the participants to increase the signal to noise ratio.

3   Single word processing from 13 to 20 months

One of the first questions addressed was how brain activity to words whose meaning the child understood differed from that to unknown words (Mills, Coffey-Corina and Neville 1993, 1994, 1997; see also Molfese 1989, 1990). Mills and colleagues examined brain activity to known and unknown words for infants of 13 to 17 months and 20 months of age. These ages were chosen to investigate the brain bases of the rapid change in vocabulary size often occurring during this period called the vocabulary burst. In addition to investigating age-related differences in brain activity, this was one of the first investigations of changes in the organization of brain activity based on language abilities. Word comprehension was measured in three ways, the MCDI, a parental rating scale, and a picture-pointing task. During the picture-pointing task, each child's comprehension of the words used in the study was tested. The children were presented with two pictures and asked to choose which picture went with a particular word. To ensure that the words played during testing were comprehended by the child, the word must be correctly identified by the child during the picture-pointing task and be rated by the parents as highly comprehended (3 or 4 on a 4-point scale).

ERPs to both known and unknown words elicited four components differing in functional significance across the experimental conditions: the first positivity peaking at approximately 100 ms, P100, two negative components peaking at 200 and 350 ms, N200 and N350, and a frontally distributed slow wave from 600–900 ms N600–900. The P100 has been associated with auditory sensory processing by the primary auditory cortex within the superior temporal gyrus (Huotilainen, Winkler, Alho, Escera, Virtanen and Ilmoniemi 1998; Thoma, Hanlon, Moses, Edgar, Huang, Weisend 2003). This component is influenced by both endogenous and exogenous factors and increases in amplitude are linked to increased stimulus intensity and attention (Hillyard, Mangun, Woldorff and Luck 1995). The amplitude of the P100 did not differ for known vs. unknown words. However, the left greater than right P100 asymmetry to known words was correlated with higher percentile rankings on vocabulary size in both age groups. The amplitudes of the N200 and N350 were larger for known than unknown words, suggesting that the functional significance of these two components was linked to word meaning or semantic processing. Evidence to support the semantic interpretation of the N200 and N350, rather than alternative explanations such as recognition of phonology or word form, will be addressed in the series of studies throughout the rest of the chapter. This issue will be revisited later after all of the studies have been presented. The lateral distribution of the N200 and N350 amplitude difference between known vs. unknown words showed marked developmental differences. At 13 to 17 months, the effect was broadly distributed across the scalp but was slightly larger over the right hemisphere. At 20 months, the amplitude difference was restricted to temporal and parietal regions of the left hemisphere. The authors raised the working hypothesis that the shift in the lateral distribution of this effect was linked to changes in brain organization underlying the marked changes in vocabulary development. That is, as children become more experienced with word learning, the neural systems underlying language processing become more specialized (and lateralized).

This hypothesis was the basis of several subsequent studies reviewed in this chapter. The later N600–900 was larger to known than unknown words over anterior regions of the right hemisphere for 13- to 17-month-olds but did not differ between the word types for the older age group. This component may be similar to the Nc component commonly found for infants (de Haan and Nelson 1997) and is thought to index attention and integration of the stimulus. Differences in N600–900 amplitude at 13–17 months may be related to continued attention and semantic processing in the younger group.

To examine the effects of vocabulary size independent of chronological age, ERPs were examined based on a median split of the groups for the number of words comprehended at 13–17 months, and number of words produced at 20 months. These analyses suggested that the ERP effects were linked to vocabulary size rather than chronological age. Similar findings were observed with a group of late talkers, i.e. older children who were matched on vocabulary size to the two groups described above.

4   Measuring language experience:
Overall Language Exposure or Individual Words?

A theoretical question raised by the studies (Mills *et al.* 1993, 1997) described above is whether the reorganization of language-relevant brain activity between 13 and 20 months was linked to a qualitative change in the mechanisms underlying language processing as a function of overall exposure to language and achievement of language milestones such as the vocabulary spurt. However, the 20-month-olds had several months more experience with the words presented in the study than did the younger children. Therefore, an alternative explanation is that the bilateral to left lateralized pattern of activity is a function of experience with individual words as evidenced by the strength of the word-referent association. Mills, Plunkett, Prat and Schafer (2005) investigated these competing hypotheses for 20-month-olds (n = 22) with high and low productive vocabularies (n = 10 and 12, respectively) by examining their ERPs to novel words and familiar words. The authors reasoned that if the left lateralized ERP distribution was linked to the amount of experience with individual words, then newly learned words should show a bilateral "newly learned" vs. unknown difference, similar to the 13- to 17-month-olds in the earlier study. However, if the vocabulary burst was associated with a qualitative reorganization in the way 20-month-olds process words, then the ERP differences to "newly learned" vs. unknown words should be lateralized to temporal and parietal regions of the left hemisphere. ERPs were recorded while the infants listened to novel words (e.g., *bard, wug, gaf,* and *sarl*) and familiar words (e.g., *dog* and *cat*) at three time points: before training, during training, and after training. The infants experienced training with half of the novel words. Training consisted of pairing the word with an object. A puppet was used to hold the object to be labeled as the computer generated the words with infant-directed speech intonation, e.g. "Look, look at the cat"). For the other half of the novel stimuli the words were repeated the same number of times but not paired with an object. To control for directing attention to the words, the same puppet was moved in front of the child as the computer generated the words, also in infant-directed speech, "Listen, hear the word *dog*". Infants were videotaped to examine differences in looking behavior as a measure of attention in the two conditions. Because the functional significance of the N200 and N350 peaks in response to known vs. unknown words did not differ in the previous studies, a mean amplitude measurement was taken from 200–500 ms to control for latency jitter across participants in this time window as recommended by ERP methodology publications (e.g., Luck 2005; Picton, Bentin, Berg, Donchin, Hillyard, Johnson, Miller, Ritter, Ruchkin, Rugg and Taylor 2000).

Prior to training, no ERP differences were found between the novel words that were to be trained and those that were not to be trained. This showed that ERP differences observed after training were due to the experimental manipulations. After training, the N200–500 to the novel words that received training was significantly larger than the N200–500 to the untrained novel words. Consistent with the individual word-learning hypothesis, this effect was bilaterally distributed. This effect is linked to training of word meaning because prior to testing the trained novel words were paired with an object whereas the untrained novel words were simply repeated. If the increase in the N200–500 shown here for the trained novel words was due only to training of word forms, we would also expect the untrained novel words to show the same pattern from being repeated prior to testing.

When the ERPs were analyzed separately for the groups of infants with high and low vocabulary size, interesting differences in distribution were revealed. Although the ERP effects for both groups were significant over both the left and right hemispheres, for the high production group the effect was asymmetrical and larger over the left hemisphere. The results were interpreted as suggesting that the left hemisphere asymmetry in the high production group is linked to faster learning rates rather than a qualitative reorganization in cognitive processing. In a current study, we are expanding on these findings by following children longitudinally to examine naturally occurring differences in the distribution of ERPs to words that 20-month-old children have known since they were 13 months of age vs. words they learned more recently. The preliminary results with 10 children replicate these findings, thus suggesting a bilateral activation for newly learned words and a left lateralized pattern for words the children have known for several months.

5   Different levels of experience: Evidence from bilingual children

One way to test the role of amount of experience and exposure is to examine children who are learning two languages. This population presents a unique opportunity in that one can examine differential amounts of experience with two languages in the same child, i.e. the same developing brain. If the child is exposed to and uses the languages in differing amounts and the two languages show distinct distributions of brain activity, then this can be taken as evidence supporting the role of experience in brain organization.

Conboy and Mills (2006) investigated the role of experience with a particular language in brain maturation with bilingual infants (19 to 22 months; see also the chapter by Conboy, Rivera-Gaxiola, Silva-Pereyra and Kuhl, this volume). These infants were learning both English and Spanish and their first exposure to both languages occurred prior to six months of age. They were grouped by their dominant language (English dominant = 16 infants, Spanish dominant = 14 infants, as determined by relative vocabulary scores from the English and Spanish versions of the MCDI, and a 3-point parent rating of comprehension and use for each language. ERPs were recorded while infants listened to known and unknown words in Spanish and English. Based on the MCDI (English and Spanish versions), infants were divided into two groups: high Total Conceptual Vocabulary size (TCV; combined scores from both languages that take into account meaning overlap between the different language lists) and low TCV.

Of particular interest was whether the dominant and nondominant languages would elicit two different patterns of organization. Based on the studies with monolingual children from the same lab, the authors predicted that a more focal pattern of activity for ERP differences to known vs. unknown words would be observed for the dominant vs. the nondominant language. Similar to the results from the monolingual children, the N200–400 was larger to known than unknown words in both languages. Consistent with the predicted results, the effect was more focally distributed for the dominant language. However, this effect was limited to anterior regions of the right hemisphere. The right hemisphere activation may be linked to switching back and forth between languages. A pilot study confirmed that presentation of the stimuli in blocks elicited a left lateralized pattern of ERP differences more consistent with the monolingual data (Conboy 2002).

There were also differences in ERP patterns for the high vs. low TVC groups. The high TVC group showed the N200–400 differences for both the dominant and nondominant language, but the effect was more focally distributed for the dominant language. In contrast, the low TVC group only showed an N200–400 effect for their dominant language. Additionally, the two groups differed in the earlier P100 left greater than right asymmetry to known words. Similar to the 20-month-old monolingual children (Mills *et al.* 1993), the high TVC group showed a left greater than right asymmetry to known words but only for the dominant language. The low TVC group did not show this asymmetry to either language.

Because the ERPs in this study differed by both dominant and nondominant language as well as vocabulary size, these findings provide strong support for the role of experience in brain organization. The authors posit that even in children with exposure to two languages prior to 6 months of age, non-identical brain systems mediate processing for each language according to differences in exposure as well as differences in rates of learning, i.e., a faster rate of vocabulary development for the dominant vs. nondominant language.

6 Cross-modal semantic priming

The rate of word acquisition changes over the first two years of life. When infants are first learning to produce words, the process is very slow and it appears that they are making simple associations between words and objects that are context dependent (Bates, Benigni, Bretherton, Camaioni and Volterra 1979; Vihman and McCune 1994). Around 18 to 20 months, infants typically show a dramatic increase in word production and they begin adding words to their vocabulary at a much higher rate (Benedict 1979; Goldfield and Reznick 1990; Nelson 1973). This period of change is often called the vocabulary spurt and different theories have been posited to account for this change, suggesting that infants undergo a reorganization in the cognitive processes that underlie language, such as symbolic representation (McCune 1995; McCune-Nicolich 1981; Nazzi and Bertoncini 2003; Werner and Kaplan 1963), changes in categorization (Gopnik and Meltzoff 1986, 1987), and increases in memory abilities (Gershkoff-Stowe 2002). If such reorganization does occur, we might expect to see related changes in the organization of brain activity before and after this period of accelerated acquisition.

Many ERP studies of adults and older children have examined semantic processing of words in a particular context. The component of interest in these studies is called the N400. The N400 is a negative going component that is elicited when meaningful stimuli violate a preceding semantic context. For example, there is a violation when the final word of a sentence is incongruent with the rest of the sentence, as in "Cows like to eat <u>shoes</u>", as opposed to "Cows like to eat <u>grass</u>". In this case, one would see a larger N400 to "shoes" relative to "grass". This can also be done using word-picture pairings. For example, a participant would see a picture of a cow and then hear the word "cow" (congruent condition) or see a picture of a hat and then hear the word "cow" (incongruent condition). Again, we would expect to see a larger N400 response to the incongruent condition relative to the congruent condition. This type of paradigm has been used to see if infants who are learning their first words show the same patterns of brain activity when processing word meaning as shown by adults and older children. If there were a reorganization of brain activity associated with the vocabulary spurt, we would expect infants younger than 18–20 months to show a different pattern of brain activity when processing word meaning than older infants and children. If a reorganization of brain activity is associated with normal brain development and not the vocabulary spurt, we would expect changes in the patterns of brain activity to be related to only age and not vocabulary size.

Thirteen- and 20-month-olds were tested in a word-picture pairing paradigm, as well as 3-year-olds and adults (Mills, Conboy and Paton 2005). An individualized stimulus set was created for each participant according to words that their parents rated as "known" in conjunction with performance on a picture-pointing task. Comprehension was assessed using a parental rating scale in which parents rated words from 1 (child does not understand) to 4 (certain that the child understands the word). For a word to be used during testing, it had to receive a "4" for comprehension on the parental rating scale and the child had to have identified the word in the pointing task. During testing, each picture was presented on the screen for 1500 ms. At 500 ms after the picture appeared, a word was played that was either congruent or incongruent with the picture (while the picture was still on the screen). Each picture and word were played twice, once as a match and once as a mismatch. ERPs were examined for the presence of the N400 component.

The results for the adults, 3-year-olds, 20- and 13-month-olds showed an N400-like response that was larger to the incongruent relative to the congruent condition and was broadly distributed across the scalp. The onset of the incongruity effect was 200 ms after the beginning of the word for all age groups. The role of vocabulary size was examined by conducting a median split for vocabulary size. The onset, duration, and distribution of the N400 effect did not differ for the high and low producers. This paradigm is similar to that reported in a series of studies by Friedrich and Friederici (2004, 2005a,b, 2006). However, the results differed somewhat in the onset of the N400 effect according to age and vocabulary size. Most importantly, the 13-month-olds in our studies did show an N400-like effect whereas the 12-month-olds in the studies by Friedrich and Friederici did not (Friedrich and Friederici 2005b). It is important to note that the period of 12 to 13 months is one of rapid change, meaning that the infants from the two studies may have been at different stages of development. Furthermore, our studies and the Friedrich and Friederici studies were conducted in different languages that may have slightly varied developmental time courses. Both of these explanations might account for the inconsistency of the results. One additional difference in the results is that the 19-month-olds in the studies show an N400 that occurs 400 ms later than the adult N400 response (Friedrich and Friederici 2004) whereas in our studies the latency of the N400 is similar to the latency for adults by 20 months of age. There were also some important variations in the methodology that may account for the distinct patterns of results. In the studies by Friedrich and Friederici (2004, 2005a,b, 2006) the infants, especially the low comprehenders, did not understand the meanings of all of the words according to parental report. For example, the parents rated the words after testing and the average proportion of word comprehension was 76–81% of 44 words (Friedrich and Friederici 2004). In addition, participants were only required to attend to 70% of the trials to be included and missed an averaged of 15-17% of the trials. These were not excluded from the final analysis unless they contained other movement or eye artifact. In our studies the word lists were tailored to each child to include only those words whose meanings were understood by the child. Also, trials were not included if the infant did not see the picture. Our results suggest that if the infants understand the meanings of all of the words and see all of the pictures, the onset of the N400 response is at the same latency as the adult N400, even for 20-month-olds. These findings suggest that from the time they understand the meaning of words, infants process semantic relations using similar neural systems as adults as evidenced by an N400 response that is similar in latency to the adult N400 and is broadly distributed across the scalp.

Another hypothesis is that the marked changes in vocabulary size during the vocabulary burst are related to increasing memory abilities (Gershkoff-Stowe 2002). Increases in the flexibility of memory abilities and working memory capacity could be related to word acquisition in that they allow the infant to hold the association in mind longer and make more connections to prior knowledge. In addition, with strong word-object associations, a decrease in memory load required to process the word is expected, allowing for more in depth processing of related associations. Preliminary studies in our lab (e.g., Larson, Lewis, Horton, Addy and Mills 2005) have begun to examine the role of working memory in the processing of word meaning. The paradigm is similar to the word-picture pairing presented above. The difference was that the word is presented first. At 500 ms after the onset of the word, a picture is presented that is congruent or incongruent with the preceding word. This introduces a delay in processing and requires the infant to hold the word in mind until the picture is presented. Again, the N400 response should be larger to the incongruent condition relative to the congruent condition. If there were deficits in working memory early in language development such that the infant cannot hold the word in mind, we would not expect to see an N400 for the 13-month-olds but would expect to see an N400 for the older age groups.

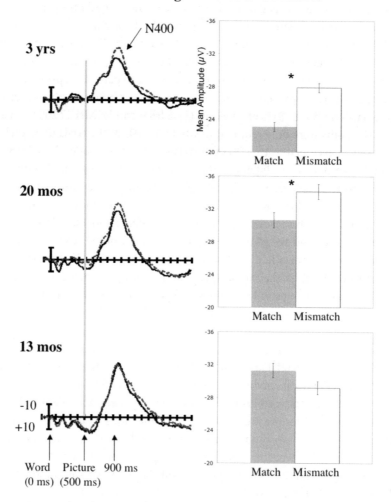

Figure 2. Bar graphs of mean amplitudes from 400–600 ms and the ERPs (recorded at at the vertex electrode Cz) to word-picture pairs that did (solid line) or did not match (dashed line) for 3-year-olds (n = 20), 20-month-olds (n = 17), and 13-month-olds (n = 21). * p < 0.05. The error bars indicate standard error

Adults, 3-year-olds, and 20-month-olds showed an N400 response to the anoma- lous word – picture pairs, but unlike the simultaneous picture-word paradigm there were clear developmental differences in the latency and distribution of the N400 effect. With increasing age, the N400 response decreased in latency. The adults showed an N400 response that was broadly distributed across the scalp from 200–600 ms after the picture appeared. N400 latency and distribution for the

3-year-olds was similar. The 20-month-olds had an N400 response that peaked later and was only significant at medial and central sites. The 13-month-olds as a group did not show a significant N400 response at any sites. Figure 2 shows a visual display of the ERPs and a bar graph of the mean amplitude measurements for 3-year-olds, 20-month-olds, and 13-month-olds. However, when 13-month-olds were divided into high and low comprehension groups, the high comprehenders (>100 words) showed an N400 response similar to the 20-month-olds. In contrast, the low comprehenders (<100 words) did not show a significant N400 response. This suggests that infants with small vocabularies (and weaker word-object associations) may have had interference when the picture was presented on the screen after a delay. Recall that 13-month-old low producers showed the N400 effect when the picture was present with simultaneous presentation. These findings are consistent with Gershkoff-Stowe's (2002) position that memory abilities are important in vocabulary development between 13 and 20 months. More generally, the findings lend further support to the idea that domain-general processes influence patterns of language-relevant brain activity. The extent to which the neural systems mediating semantic processing are specific to language is examined in the next section on processing meaning for words and gestures.

6.1   Semantic processing of words and gestures

Another approach to studying the role of domain-general processes in language development is to examine the extent to which non-verbal modes of communication use similar or distinct neural systems to those used by words. Gestures convey meaningful information in both adult and infant communication; however, there are important developmental differences in the way gestures are used. Prior to 20 months of age, when infants are first learning to speak, they use gestures and words in very similar ways (Acredolo and Goodwyn 1988). For example, infants may label a cup using the word "cup" but may also use a representational gesture for cup (e.g., the action of drinking) in the same contexts to label or request objects or actions.

Later in development words and gestures take on divergent communicative functions reflecting the communicative conventions observed in the input the child receives. Infants show a gradual change in the use of gestural communication as they gain experience with language, with words replacing symbolic gestures over time (Acredolo and Goodwyn 1988; Bates and Dick 2002; Bretherton, Bates, McNew, Shore, Williamson and Beeghly-Smith 1981; Iverson, Capirci and Caselli 1994; Namy, Campbell and Tomasello 2004; Namy and Waxman 1998, 2002) and infants show a decrease in the use of representational gestures and an increase in deictic gestures (such as pointing) paired with a word (Iverson, Capirci and Caselli 1994).

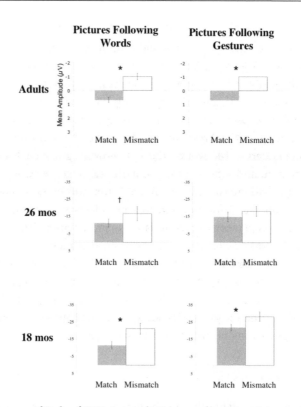

Figure 3. Mean amplitude of ERPs to word-picture and gesture-picture pairs that did and did not match from 400–600 ms. * $p < 0.05$, † only significant at specific electrode sites: anterior temporal, temporal, and parietal sites. The error bars indicate standard error

Similarities in the communicative functions and developmental trajectories of words and gestures have led developmentalists to posit that shared domain-general neural processes mediate both functions (Bates and Dick 2002). Adult neuroimaging studies have found many similarities in the organization of brain activity linked to processing words and different types of gestures (Buccino, Binkofski, Fink, Fadiga, Fogassi, Gallese, Seitz, Zilles, Rizzolatti and Freund 2001; Kelly, Kravitz and Hopkins 2004; Wu and Coulson 2004). Sheehan, Namy and Mills (2007) employed event-related potentials to compare patterns of brain activity linked to processing of words and gestures using a cross-modal priming task similar to the word-picture paradigm described in the section above. Infants of 18 and 26 months of age were presented with a movie clip of an actor either saying a word or producing a gesture. A picture that matched or did not match the preceding word or gesture followed this movie. An example of a matching trial would be the gesture for phone (holding hand to ear) followed by a picture of a phone. The distribution of the N400 effect across the scalp to these stimuli was examined. If the distribution of the N400 effect differed for the trials beginning with a word and trials beginning with a gesture, this would indicate that processing these differing stimuli is mediated by nonidentical neural systems. Of particular interest were developmental changes in the patterns of brain activity linked to semantic processing of words and gestures.

A congruency effect was found for 18-month-olds (n = 17) for pictures preceded by words and pictures preceded by gestures for the time window 400–600 ms that started by 200 ms. This effect was broadly distributed across the scalp for both symbol types. At 26 months (n = 17), the congruency effect was limited to pictures preceded by words for the time window 400–600 ms. This effect was only significant at anterior temporal, temporal, and parietal sites, replicating Mills *et al.*'s findings of increased lateralization with increasing experience with language. Figure 3 shows bar graphs of the mean amplitudes for match and mismatch trials for both trial types (pictures preceded by words and pictures preceded by gestures) for each age group.

Namy and colleagues (Namy, Campbell and Tomasello 2004; Namy and Waxman 1998) suggest that the reason children readily accept a gesture to name a novel object at 18 but not 26 months is due to children's developing appreciation of the conventional roles of words and gestures in communication. This position is supported by the ERP findings indicating that 26-month-olds show an N400 congruency effect for pictures preceded by words but not pictures preceded by gestures.

The N400 congruency effect in 18-months-olds is the first neurobiological evidence showing that semantic processing of words and gestures is associated with similar patterns of neural activity during the period of development when children are using words and gestures in the same way. Our data from 26-month-old infants are consistent with the hypothesis that children's use of gestures takes on less of a symbolic and more of a deictic function over the course of early development (Iverson, Capirci, Longobardi and Caselli 1999; Masur 1982). We argue that the gesture-object pairings children have learned at this age have taken on a different status from words, perhaps as conventionalized associations that are not semantic or symbolic in nature.

For 26-month-olds *only* words, and not gestures, provided a strong enough semantic context to elicit an N400 effect. One possible explanation, and the one we believe is most likely, is that the association between the gesture and the object is not as strong as the association between the word and the picture. Thus, gestures are not as predictive of the matching picture as a word may be and result in greater neural activity on the match trials (similar to what is seen in a mismatch trial). In future research, it will be important to further explore how symbolic gestures are being processed by 26-month-olds, perhaps by comparing children's processing of symbolic gestures with other non-symbolic gesticulation (e.g. pointing). Although in adulthood the N400 response can be elicited by other non-symbolic stimuli, such as odors (Grigor, Van Toller, Behan and Richardson 1999; Sarfarazi, Cave, Richardson, Beha and Sedgwick 1999), it is unclear whether or not the same response would be shown for infants.

Data from adults employing the same paradigm (Sheehan, Namy and Mills 2006) show an N400 response to violations of the semantic context set up by both words and gestures. That is, with increased cognitive resources and flexibility adults are not limited to only the most common symbol form and can process both modalities as semantic symbols. These findings illustrate how dynamic changes in the use of communicative symbols across development shape the organization of neural activity linked to semantic processing. Further research needs to be conducted to ascertain the mechanism of recovery of the N400 response to gesture-picture pairings from 26 months to adulthood. Namy, Campbell and Tomasello (2004) demonstrated that by 4 years children are able to map both iconic and arbitrary gestures like their 18-month-old counterparts. We would predict that by this age, children would show an adult-like N400 response to pictures preceded by words *and* pictures preceded by gestures.

In the sections below we examine how other more domain-specific aspects of language processing such as phonology and linguistic prosody interact with semantic processing in the development of language-relevant brain activity.

7   Influences of phonological information on word comprehension

Prior to representing the meanings of words, infants become familiar with the phonology of their native language. We know from past work that even neonates can discriminate different speech sounds as evidenced by behavioral research (Eimas, Siqueland, Jusczyk and Vigorito 1971) and more recent ERP research (Molfese 2000; Molfese, Molfese and Modgline 2001). Although even very young infants can discriminate fine differences in phonetic detail, the task appears to become more difficult when combined with semantic processing. At 14 months of age, infants show difficulty in distinguishing phonetically similar words when they map those words onto meaning (Stager and Werker 1997; Werker, Cohen, Lloyd, Casasola and Stager 1998; Werker, Fennell, Corcoran and Stager 2002). Werker, Fennell, Corcoran and Stager (2002) explored the developmental trajectory of the integration of the processing of meaning and phonology. They demonstrated that when mapping a word to an object, 14-month-old infants would confuse phonetically similar words. By 20 months of age, infants could reliably distinguish between similar sounding words and map them correctly. Seventeen-month-old infants' performance fell in between that of 14- and 20-month-olds. Important for this chapter, 14-month-old infants with a larger vocabulary were able to correctly map similar sounding words than their same age peers with a lower vocabulary size. At this age, measures of both vocabulary comprehension and production positively correlated with performance in the task.

Mills, Prat, Zangl, Stager, Neville and Werker (2004) investigated developmental changes in infants' use of phonetic detail from 14 to 20 months[1]. ERPs were recorded to words the children understood (e.g. Bear), nonce words that were phonologically similar to the known words (e.g. Gare), and nonsense words that were phonologically unrelated (e.g. Kobe). The known and phonemic contrasts were balanced for the types of initial consonants and the number of stop consonants, nasal and fricatives, and did not differ in their phonological neighbors for other words frequently understood by children in this age range. The lateral distribution of the ERP effects to known vs. phonologically dissimilar nonsense words replicated previous findings, i.e., from bilateral at 14 months to left lateralized at 20 months. The results for the comparisons with phonologically similar stimuli were consistent with behavioral findings showing that at 14 months, brain activity did not differ to known words and phonologically similar nonce words. This suggested that for inexperienced word learners, minimal pair mispronunciations were processed as known words. In contrast, more proficient word learners at 20 months showed ERP differences between known words and both types of nonsense words. The findings suggested that language experience is an important factor in the organization of brain activity linked to processing phonetic detail. These results taken in conjunction with the study above showing the role of working memory in semantic processing lend further support to the position that resource allocation of both language-specific and domain-general processes contribute to facilitating vocabulary development.

In the following section, we examine how even younger infants use prosody to break into the word learning game.

8   Influences of prosodic information on word comprehension

When speaking to an infant, people of all ages and in most cultures use a modified form of speech called infant-directed speech (IDS; also called baby talk, motherese, parentese, or child-directed speech). Infant-directed speech is characterized by higher pitch, more expanded pitch range, more repetitions, elongated vowels, and a slower tempo when compared to adult-directed speech (ADS; Garnica 1977;

---

1.   According to parental report, these infants only had monolingual exposure to English.

Grieser and Kuhl 1988; Fernald, Taeschner, Dunn, Papousek, Boysson-Bardies and Fukui 1989). This special speech register has been credited with helping children focus attention on meaningful information, facilitate word segmentation from continuous speech, and even aid in word learning (Fernald 1992). To examine the neural underpinnings of how young infants process IDS, Zangl and Mills (2007) conducted an ERP study with typically developing infants at ages 6 and 13 months. In this study, ERPs were recorded while infants listened to both familiar and unfamiliar words in both IDS and ADS. Two components of interest were identified: the N200–400 (an index of word meaning), and the N600–800 (similar in latency to the Nc component and may index attention). The latter component may be similar to the Nc component commonly found for infants (de Haan and Nelson 1997) and is thought to index attention and integration of the stimulus. The amplitude of the Nc component is positively correlated with the allocation of attention (Nelson and Monk 2001). Zangl and Mills tested two hypotheses. First, if IDS serves to increase attention to speech, then we would expect the N600–800 to be larger to IDS than ADS. Second, if infants also use IDS to facilitate word comprehension, we may expect the amplitude of the N200–400 to be modulated by the use of IDS and ADS. The use of IDS may be particularly salient for the 13-month-olds who are at an age where they are not only showing evidence of comprehending words but are also beginning to produce them.

In support of their first hypothesis, Zangl and Mills found that for 6- and 13-month-olds, the N600–800 component was larger to IDS relative to ADS for familiar words. This suggests that at both ages IDS serves to boost neural activity linked to attention to familiar words for which the child may already have some phonological representation. At 13 months, the increased N600–800 IDS/ADS effect was also observed for unfamiliar words. That is, with increased experience with words, the older infant can take advantage of the special properties of IDS for both familiar and novel acoustic-phonetic representations. Additionally, at 13 months, but not 6 months, the N200–400 was larger to familiar words in IDS relative to unfamiliar words in IDS. Although we did not directly examine the effect of IDS on word learning, this result has some implication for the role of prosody in processing familiar phonological representations. The N200–400 has been linked to word learning in our earlier studies. Therefore, we propose that the special properties of IDS may be beneficial in early word learning by increasing neural activity in this time window to highly familiar and potentially meaningful words, thus increasing the strength of the neural association between the word and its referent. The results are consistent with the plausibility hypothesis put forward by Bates and her colleagues (Bates, Bretherton, Beeghly-Smith and McNew 1982), which assumes that IDS has evolved as an aid for the language-learning infant because of its exaggerated form.

8.1   Effects of altered experience with infant-directed speech

One approach to investigating the effects of experience on language development is to examine the effects of altered early language exposure. Maternal depression is an example of such a case. Ten to twelve percent of mothers suffer from postpartum maternal depression over the first year of their infants' life (O'Hara and Swain 1996). Depression is characterized by low mood, apathy, helplessness, irritability, and hostility (Weissman, Paykel and Klerman 1972). It is well established that mothers who have been diagnosed with depression interact differently with their infants than healthy mothers. Depressed mothers use less IDS and their IDS deviates less from their ADS than that of healthy mothers. In addition, they talk less to their infants overall and are more likely to show negative affect, particularly to sons (Murray, Kempton, Woolgar and Hooper 1993; Radke-Yarrow, Nottlemann, Belmont and Welsh 1993). Depressed mothers are less responsive, have flat affect, less expanded intonation, and express more negative emotions overall (Bettes 1988; Frankel and Harmon 1996; Righetti-Veltema, Conne-Perreard, Bousquet and Manzano 2002).

Consequentially, the developmental outcomes for children of depressed mothers are worse than for infants of healthy mothers. By the age of 3, they talk less than their same-aged peers (Breznitz and Sherma 1987) and show numerous other social and emotional problems (Cummings and Davies 1994; Downey and Coyne 1990; Gelfand and Teti 1990). These findings suggest that abnormal language and affective input may affect not only infants' early language development but also their social and emotional development.

Larson, Mills, Huot, Stowe and Walker (2006) recorded ERPs while 6-month-old infants of healthy mothers and infants of depressed mothers listened to IDS and ADS produced by a healthy female speaker. They tested three hypotheses. First, as a result of less experience with IDS, infants of depressed mothers will show less activity to IDS and greater activity to ADS. Second, if humans have an innate response to the acoustic properties of IDS, IDS will increase neural activity independent of the infant's experience with different speech registers. Third, increased cortisol levels, which have frequently been reported in infants of depressed mothers, will be associated with decreased activity to both IDS and ADS. Saliva samples were taken at three time points during the study (during capping, after capping, and after testing) to measure cortisol levels for infants of depressed mothers and infants of healthy mothers.

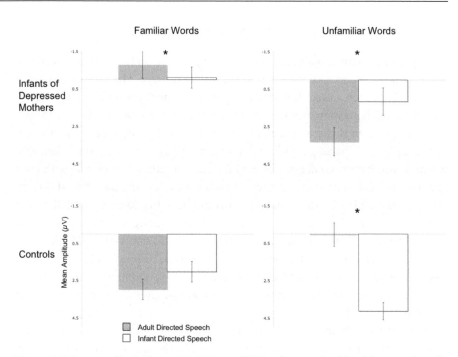

Figure 4. Mean amplitude from 600–800 ms of ERPs of 6-month-olds of depressed mothers (n = 16) and controls (n = 16) to familiar and unfamiliar words presented in adult-directed and infant-directed speech. The error bars indicate standard error. * p < 0.05

Infants of healthy mothers showed an increase in amplitude for the N600–800 component for familiar words spoken in IDS relative to ADS, thus replicating the results of Zangl and Mills (2007). Interestingly, infants of depressed mothers showed increased activity to words spoken in ADS. Figure 4 shows a bar graph of the mean amplitude measurements for both groups from 600–800 ms. These results supported the authors' hypothesis that exposure to IDS is the critical factor in neural responsiveness to IDS. That is, infants of depressed mothers hear more ADS so they attend more to this type of speech compared to IDS. The cortisol levels did not differ across time points or across groups. A follow-up study is currently being conducted with these infants once they turn 13 months.

9   Single word processing from 3 to 11 months

Although research on brain activity indexing word comprehension with infants aged 12 to 20 months is limited, even less work has been conducted with younger children as they first segment words from continuous speech and begin to associate words with meanings. We examined the development of brain activity linked to word meaning by recording ERPs to familiar, unfamiliar, and backward words in infants from 3 to 11 months of age. The backward words consisted of the "known" words played backwards. This provided a non-speech control that shared some of the same physical characteristics as the word stimuli. Note that in this section we employed "familiar" words whose meanings were not necessarily understood by the child. Word familiarity was determined by parental rating based on the number of times the child had heard a word (this is in contrast to the "known" words that were based on correct identification of the objects in a picture-pointing task). A word was considered familiar if the parent reported that the infant had heard the word several times a day or several times per week. In contrast, an unfamiliar word was reported as rarely or never heard by the child. The stimuli consisted of 10 words in each condition presented six times each in a random order. Preliminary ERP data from infants 3 to 4, 6 to 8, and 9 to 11 months are presented in Figure 5 (Addy and Mills 2005).

Single Word Processing

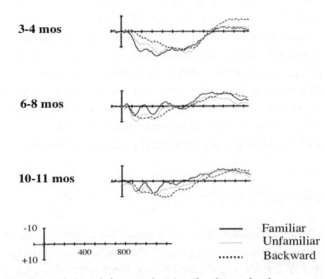

Figure 5. ERPs (recorded at a left parietal site) to familiar and unknown words for infants 3 to 4 (n = 27), 6 to 8 (n = 22), and 9 to 11 months (n = 21)

For 3- to 4-month-olds, all three types of stimuli elicited a large positivity between 175 and 550 ms. This positivity was significantly larger for familiar than unfamiliar or backward words. For infants 6 to 8 months of age, two large negative peaks were shown from 200 to 500 ms but only for the familiar words. For infants 9 to 11 months of age, both familiar and unfamiliar words elicited a negative-going component from 200–500 ms, but the backward words did not. For 9 to 11-month-old children whose parents said they understood the meanings of the familiar words, the N200–500 was larger for the familiar (known) than unfamiliar words. No such differences were observed in the children whose parents said the children did not understand the meanings of the familiar words. Thierry, Vihman and Roberts (2003) report similar findings for 11-month-olds who show an N200 component for familiar words (see also Thierry and Vihman, this volume).

In contrast to older infants, 3-month-olds show a similar positive-going wave for all three word types suggesting immature neural responsiveness even to familiar speech. By 6 months of age, patterns of brain activity to speech start to look more like those for older infants, but only for familiar words. Because there are no behavioral indices of comprehension for the 6-month-olds, we assume that the children are recognizing the word forms and do not index meaning at this age. However, these findings are consistent with behavioral data (Tincoff and Jusczyk 1999) suggesting that the onset of language comprehension may begin earlier than previously thought. In contrast to older children, 6-month-olds, like 3-month-olds, do not show ERP differences to unfamiliar and backward words. It is not until 11 months of age that infants show the N200–400 to both familiar and unfamiliar words. This suggests that the infant brain is beginning to recognize unfamiliar words as potentially meaningful information. However, only 9- to 11-month-olds whose parents said that the children understood the familiar words showed N200–400 differences to known vs. unknown words that were similar to 13-month-olds in our previous studies. The results from the current study are consistent with and expand upon previous findings showing that experience with language shapes the organization of neural activity to language stimuli.

10   Discussion

Based on the findings from the studies reviewed in this chapter we offer the following conclusions to be discussed in turn: 1) the amplitude of the negative going wave between 200–500 ms is modulated by word meaning and not simply by phonological word form, and 2) the organization of brain activity during early vocabulary development is dynamic, depends on both domain general and language specific processes, and is shaped by the experience of learning language.

10.1   N200–400 indexes word meaning

One argument against the interpretation that the N200–500 indexes word meaning is that the single-word paradigm, employed in the Mills *et al.* studies, is not a "semantic paradigm" because there are no objects or pictures associated with the words. This argument is easily countered in that adults, children, and infants could not understand speech if content words spoken in isolation did not invoke meanings. In fact, it is very difficult to suppress accessing meaning to spoken content words. There is no reason to believe that once infants understand a word as defined in our paradigms, i.e. as understood with a variety of different exemplars in a variety of different contexts, that they do not access meaning when they hear the word in isolation.

In adults, ERPs within the 200 to 500 ms window are sensitive to a variety of linguistic and domain general processes including attention, phonology, syntax, meaning, and different types of priming effects. Therefore, modulation of the amplitude of brain activity in this time window in infants could be interpreted on many levels. For example, developmental ERP studies have shown that a negative peak at around 200 ms is sensitive to acoustic cues in nonspeech stimuli (Dehaene-Lambertz 2000; Simos and Molfese 1997), phonetic variation in place of articulation (Dehaene-Lambert and Dehaene 1994; Molfese, Burger-Judisch and Hans 1991), and voice onset time (Molfese and Molfese 1988; Simos and Molfese 1997). One interpretation is that the observed ERP differences between the known and unknown words in our studies actually indexes acoustic or phonological features of the different word-types, showing recognition of word form rather than indexing word meaning. Although these factors can modulate the amplitude of the N200 in specific paradigms, it is not necessarily the only factor that modulates the amplitude of this component. Here (see also Mills *et al.* 2004, and Mills, Conboy and Paton 2005), we argue that a top-down process linked to word meaning is the dominant factor modulating the amplitude of the N200–500 in our studies.

First, if ERP differences between conditions were due solely to phonological factors then ERP differences should have been observed when the word lists were phonologically dissimilar regardless of word meaning, but this was not the case. For example, in our study of bilingual toddlers (Conboy and Mills 2006), if the N200–400 indexed the phonological aspects of the words, amplitude differences would be expected between Spanish and English. In contrast, the results showed that although phonological differences between Spanish and English influenced the latency of the P100, the amplitude of the N200–400 did not differ between Spanish and English for either the known or unknown words as compared across children for the dominant language. The same was true for the nondominant language. Moreover, balanced bilinguals with the same number of words in English and Spanish did not show N200–400 differences for the two languages. In contrast, word meaning (known vs. unknown) did modulate the amplitude of this component, whereas language dominance and total conceptual vocabulary size influenced the distribution of this effect. In another study specifically manipulating phonology (Mills *et al.* 2004), 20-month-olds but not 14-month-olds showed N200–400 amplitude differences to known words vs. phonologically similar nonce words. It is difficult to explain why the phonemic contrasts patterned with the known words at 14 months and the nonsense words at 20 months based solely on acoustical and phonemic differences. If phonology alone was responsible for these effects then both age groups would have displayed N200 amplitude differences between the known words and phonetic contrasts. Instead, from the combined results of the ERP (Mills *et al.* 2004) and behavioral studies (Stager and Werker 1997; Werker *et al.* 2002), it appears that when phonology and meaning are pitted against each other, early word learners focus more attention on word meaning than precise phonetic detail in the word form.

Another line of evidence comes from the training study (Mills, Plunkett, Prat and Schafer 2005) showing that when phonological form was held constant, word meaning modulated the amplitude of the N200–500. Pairing an object with the novel word increased the amplitude of the N200–500, whereas repetition without being paired with a meaningful stimulus resulted in increased positivity. Because the stimuli were counterbalanced across participants, the increased amplitude of the N200–500 to the newly learned words was modulated by its association with a meaningful stimulus and cannot be explained by phonological differences between word-types. This position is also strengthened by the results from 9- to 11-month-old infants (Addy and Mills 2005) showing that there were N200–400 differences to familiar vs. unfamiliar words only for children whose parents said their children understood the words. Familiarity alone in terms of amount of exposure did not elicit N200–400 amplitude differences. Finally, in the study on gesture processing (Sheehan, Namy and Mills 2007), both words and gestures preceding a picture elicited an ERP mismatch effect starting at 200 ms after the onset of the picture. The ERPs in this time window to cross-modal (word-picture and picture-word paradigms) in adults has been interpreted as a phonological mismatch negativity that precedes the onset of semantic processing (e.g. Connolly, Service, D'Arcy, Kujala and Alho 2001). However, in the gesture–picture paradigm the presence of this component for non-verbal primes (for which there is no phonological explanation) provides further support to Mills and colleagues' position that the N200–400 in infants may also be modulated by meaning rather than word form.

10.2 Experience and the organization of language-relevant brain activity

Across several studies, developmental changes in the lateralization of brain activity were observed that show the link between increasing language proficiency and a more focal pattern of activity. However, we do not mean to suggest that these finding are consistent with a pattern of progressive lateralization that occurs as a function of brain maturation or age-related synaptic pruning. In our earlier studie, we proposed that the change in ERP differences to known vs. unknown words, from bilateral to left lateralized, reflected a qualitative shift in the way children process words before and after the vocabulary spurt. These results have been interpreted in some secondary sources (text books and television media) as evidence supporting the notion that "language" becomes lateralized at 20 months. This was not how we interpreted the findings in either of the original studies (Mills *et al.* 1993, 1997), nor do we concur with that interpretation. To be clear, although the observed changes in the distribution of ERP differences to known vs. unknown words, from bilateral to left lateralized, have been observed reliably across several studies reported here, it is important to note that these changes reflect a) differences between two word types, b) group effects and not necessarily individual data, and c) a pattern of brain activity that is different from that observed in adults to spoken words. First, the bilateral to left lateralized changes are observed in amplitude *differences* between known and unknown words. These data do not characterize changes in the distributions of the N200–500 to known words specifically. For children 3 to 13 months, the N200–500 displays a right hemisphere asymmetry and is symmetrical at 20 to 30 months (Mills and Sheehan, 2007). At 20 months, the left greater than right asymmetry to ERP differences is due in large part to a right hemisphere asymmetry to unknown words. The mature left greater than right asymmetry for the first negative component is not evident until quite late in development, that is, 9 to 13 years of age (Neville *et al.* 1993). In comparisons of ERPs across the life-span from 3 months to 76 years of age, asymmetries to the first three ERP components elicited to auditory words fluctuate across development. They often switch from one side to the other from left to right or right to left and are influenced by levels of proficiency with language (Mills and Sheehan, 2007).

In contrast, our more recent studies suggest that increasing lateralization to different types of words depends in part on the amount of exposure to individual words and the rate of learning, reflecting a more continuous developmental process. Additionally, these studies showed that patterns of brain activity that varied with vocabulary size also interacted with prosody, phonology, the conventional use of a given symbolic form, and manipulating task demands on working memory. Recent evidence from healthy adults suggests that the timing, amplitude, and distribution of ERPs, specifically the N400 congruency effect, can be manipulated to resemble that observed in atypical populations and the elderly by filtering the context of the sentence (Aydelott, Dick and Mills 2006). This suggests that processing demands rather than developmental changes in brain structure can influence the observed patterns of brain activity.

In the course of language development, there are many different influences on language processing that act independently and interact with word meaning and familiarity. When brain development is considered in the context of multiple neural systems interacting, the reasons we see changes in patterns of brain activity over development become more evident. As neural systems are developing independently over the lifespan, they are also forming connections with other neural systems. Taken together, these findings lead us to conclude that the organization of language-relevant brain activity during the first two years of life is shaped by experience with the process of learning language and emerges as a function of dynamic interactions between language-specific and domain-general processes.

References

Acredolo, L.P. and Goodwyn, S.W. 1988. "Symbolic gesturing in normal infants." *Child Development* 59: 450–66.

Addy, D.A. and Mills, D.L. 2005, April. "Brain activity to familiar, unfamiliar, and backward words in infants 3 to 10 months of age." Poster presented at the Biennial Meeting of the Society for Research in Child Development, Atlanta, GA.

Aydelott, J., Dick, F. and Mills, D. 2006. "Effects of acoustic distortion & semantic context on event-related potentials to spoken words." *Psychophysiology* 43: 454–64.

Bates, E. and Dick, F. 2002. "Language, gesture, and the developing brain." *Developmental Psychobiology* 40: 293–310.

Bates, E., Bretherton, I., Beeghly-Smith, M. and McNew, S. 1982. "Social bases of language development: A reassessment." In *Advances in child development and behavior*, H. Reese and L. Lipsitt (eds.), 16: 8–68. New York, NY: Academic Press.

Bates, E., Benigni, L., Bretherton, I., Camaioni, L. and Volterra, V. 1979. *The emergence of symbols: Cognition and communication in infancy*. New York, NY: Academic Press.

Benedict, H. 1979. "Early lexical development: Comprehension and production." *Journal of Child Language* 6: 183–200.

Bettes, B. 1988. "Maternal depression and motherese: Temporal and intonational features." *Child Development* 59: 1089–96.

Bretherton, I., Bates, E., McNew, S., Shore, C., Williamson, C. and Beeghly-Smith, M. 1981. "Comprehension and production of symbols in infancy: An experimental study." *Developmental Psychology* 17 (6): 728–36.

Breznitz, Z. and Sherman, T. 1987. "Speech patterning of natural discourse of well and depressed mothers and their young children." *Child Development* 58: 395–400.

Buccino, G., Binkofski, F., Fink, G.R., Fadiga, L., Fogassi, L., Gallese, V., Seitz, R.J., Zilles, K., Rizzolatti, G. and Freund, H.J. 2001. "Action observation activates premotor and parietal areas in a somatotopic manner: An fMRI study." *European Journal of Neuroscience* 13: 400–4.

Conboy, B. 2002. "Patterns of language processing and growth in early English-Spanish bilingualism." PhD dissertation, UCSD and San Diego State University, 2000. *Dissertation Abstracts International, B: The Sciences & Engineering.* 63 (11-B), (UMI No. 5193).

Conboy, B. and Mills, D.L. 2006. "Two languages, one developing brain: Event-related potentials to words in bilingual toddlers." *Developmental Science* 9: F1-F12.

Connolly, J.F., Service, E., D'Arcy, R.C.N., Kujala, A. and Alho, K. 2001. "Phonological aspects of word recognition as revealed by high-resolution spatio-temporal brain mapping." *Neuroreport* 12: 237–43.

Cummings, E.M. and Davies, P.T. 1994. "Maternal depression and child development." *Journal of Child Psychology and Psychiatry* 35: 73–112.

de Haan, M. and Nelson, C.A. 1997. "Recognition of the mother's face by six-month-old infants: A neurobehavioral study." *Child Development* 68: 187–210.

Dehaene-Lambertz, G. 2000. "Cerebral specialization for speech and non-speech stimuli in infants." *Journal of Cognitive Neuroscience* 12: 449–60.

Dehaene-Lambert, G. and Dehaene, S. 1994. "Speed and cerebral correlates of syllable discrimination in infants." *Nature* 370: 292–4.

Downey, G. and Coyne, J.C. 1990. "Children of depressed parents: An integrative review." *Psychological Bulletin* 108: 50–76.

Eimas, P.D., Siqueland, E.R., Jusczyk, P. and Vigorito, J. 1971. "Speech perception in infants." *Science* 171: 303–6.

Fenson, L., Dale, P.S., Reznick, J.S., Bates, E., Thal, D.J. and Pethick, S.J. 1994. "Variability in early communicative development." *The MacArthur communicative development inventories: User's guide and technical manual.* San Diego, CA: Singular.

Fernald, A. 1992. "Human maternal vocalizations to infants as biologically relevant signals: An evolutionary perspective." In *The adapted mind: Evolutionary psychology and the generation of culture,* J.H. Barkow, L. Cosmides and J. Tooby (eds.), 391–428. New York, NY: OUP.

Fernald, A., Taeschner, T., Dunn, J., Papousek, M., Boysson-Bardies, B. and Fukui, I. 1989. "A cross-language study of prosodic modifications in mothers' and fathers' speech to preverbal infants." *Journal of Child Language* 16: 477–501.

Frankel, K.A. and Harman, R.J. 1996. "Depressed mothers: They don't always look as bad as they feel." *Journal of American Academy of Child and Adolescent Psychiatry* 9: 205–17.

Friedrich, M. and Friederici, A.D. 2004. "N400-like semantic incongruity effect in 19-month-olds: Processing known words in picture contexts" *Journal of Cognitive Neuroscience* 16 (8): 1465–77.

Friedrich, M. and Friederici, A.D. 2005a. Lexical priming and semantic integration reflected in the event-related potential of 14-month-olds. *Neuroreport* 16: 653–6.

Friedrich, M. and Friederici, A.D. 2005b. "Phonotactic knowledge and lexical-semantic processing in one-year-olds: Brain responses to words and nonsense words in picture contexts." *Journal of Cognitive Neuroscience* 17: 1785–802.

Friedrich, M. and Friederici, A.D. 2006. "Early N400 development and later language acquisition." *Psychophysiology* 4: 1–12.

Garnica, O. 1977. "Some prosodic and paralinguistic features of speech to young children." In *Talking to children: Language input and acquisition.* Snow, C.E. and Ferguson, C.A. (eds.), 63–88. Cambridge: CUP.

Gelfand, D.M. and Teti, D. 1990. "The effects of maternal depression on children." *Clinical Psychology Review* 10: 329–53.

Gershkoff-Stowe, L. 2002. "Object naming, vocabulary growth, and the development of word retrieval abilities." *Journal of Memory and Language*, 46: 665–87.

Goldfield, B.A. and Reznick, J.S. 1990. "Early lexical acquisition: Rate, content and the vocabulary spurt." *Journal of Child Language* 17: 171–83.

Gopnik, A. and Meltzoff, A.N. 1986. "Words, plans, things and locations: Interactions between semantic and cognitive development in the one-word stage." In *The development of word meaning*, S. Kuczaj and M. Barrett (eds.), 199–223. New York, NY: Springer.

Gopnik, A. and Meltzoff A. 1987. "The development of categorization in the second year and its relation to the other cognitive and linguistic developments." *Child Development* 58: 1523–31.

Grieser, D.L. and Kuhl, P. 1988. "Maternal speech to infants in a tonal language: Support for universal features in motherese." *Developmental Psychology* 24: 14–20.

Grigor, J., Van Toller, S., Behan, J. and Richardson, A. 1999. "The effect of odour priming on long latency visual evoked potentials of matching and mismatching objects." *Chemical Senses* 24 (2): 137–44.

Hillyard, S.A., Mangun, G.R., Woldorff, M.G. and Luck, S. 1995. "Neural systems mediating selective attention." In *The cognitive neurosciences*. M.S. Gazzaniga (ed.), 665–81. Cambridge, MA: The MIT Press.

Huotilainen, M., Winkler, I., Alho, K., Escera, C., Virtanen, J. and Ilmoniemi, R.L. 1998. "Combined mapping of human auditory EEG and MEG responses." *Electroencephalography & Clinical Neurophysiology* 108: 370–9.

Iverson, J.M., Capirci, O. and Caselli, M. 1994. "From communication to language in two modalities." *Cognitive Development* 9: 23–43.

Iverson, J.M., Capirci, O., Longobardi, E. and Caselli, M.C. 1999. "Gesturing in mother-child interactions." *Cognitive Development* 14: 57–75.

Kelly, S.D., Kravitz, C. and Hopkins, M. 2004. "Neural correlates of bimodal speech and gesture comprehension." *Brain and Language* 89: 253–60.

Larson, M., Lewis, E., Horton, C., Addy, D. and Mills, D. 2005, March. "Working memory and early language development." Poster at Biennial Meeting of the Society for Research in Child Development, Atlanta, Georgia.

Larson, M.K., Mills, D.L., Huot, R.L., Stowe, Z.N and Walker, E. 2006, January. "Neural activity to infant- and adult-directed speech in infants of depressed mothers." Poster presented at Latsis Conference, Geneva, Switzerland.

Luck, S.J. 2005. *An introduction to the event-related potential technique*. Cambridge, MA: The MIT Press.

Masur, E.F. 1982. "Mothers' responses to infants' object-related gestures: Influences on lexical development." *Journal of Child Language* 9 (1): 23–30.

McCune, L. 1995. "A normative study of representational play in the transition to language." *Developmental Psychology* 31: 198–206.

McCune-Nicolich, L. 1981. "The cognitive bases of relational words in the single word period." *Journal of Child Language* 8: 15–34.

Mills, D.L., Coffey-Corina, S.A. and Neville, H.J. 1993. "Language acquisition and cerebral specialization in 20-month-old infants." *Journal of Cognitive Neuroscience* 5: 317–34.

Mills, D.L., Coffey-Corina, S.A. and Neville H.J. 1994. "Variability in cerebral organization during primary language acquisition." In *Human behavior and the developing brain*, G. Dawson and K. Fischer, (eds.), 427–55. New York, NY: Guilford Press.

Mills, D.L., Coffey-Corina, S.A. and Neville, H.J. 1997. "Language comprehension and cerebral specialization from 13 to 20 months." *Developmental Neuropsychology* 13: 397–445.

Mills, D.L., Conboy, B. and Paton, C. 2005. "Do changes in brain organization reflect shifts in symbolic functioning?" In *Symbol use and symbolic representation*, L. Namy (ed.), 123–53. Mahwah, NJ: Lawrence Erlbaum Associates.

Mills, D., Plunkett, K., Prat, C. and Schafer, G. 2005. "Watching the infant brain learn words: Effects of language and experience." *Cognitive Development* 20: 19–31.

Mills, D., Prat, C., Stager, C., Zangl, R., Neville, H. and Werker, J. 2004. "Language experience and the organization of brain activity to phonetically similar words: ERP evidence from 14- and 20-month olds." *Journal of Cognitive Neuroscience*. Special Issue on Developmental Cognitive Neuroscience, Charles A. Nelson (ed.), 16: 1452–64.

Mills, D.L. and Sheehan, E.A. (2007). Experience and developmental changes in the organization of language-relevant brain activity. In *Human Behavior, Learning, and the Developing Brain, 2nd Ed*, Coch, D., Dawson, G. and Fischer K.W. (Eds), 183–218. New York, NY: Guilford Press.

Molfese, D.L. 1989. "Electrophysiological correlates of word meanings in 14-month-old human infants." *Developmental Neuropsychology* 5: 79–103.

Molfese, D.L. 1990. "Auditory evoked responses recorded from 16-month-old human infants to words they did and did not know." *Brain and Language* 38: 345–63.

Molfese, D.L. 2000. "Predicting dyslexia at 8 years of age using neonatal brain responses." *Brain and Language* 72: 238–45.

Molfese, D.L., Burger-Judisch, L.M. and Hans, L.L. 1991. "Consonant discrimination by newborn infants: Electrophysiological differences." *Developmental Neuropsychology* 7: 177–95.

Molfese, D.L. and Molfese, V.J. 1988. "Right hemisphere responses from preschool children to temporal cues contained in speech and nonspeech materials: Electrophysiological correlates." *Brain and Language* 33: 245–59.

Molfese, V.J., Molfese, D.L. and Modgline, A.A. 2001. "Newborn and preschool predictors of second-grade reading scores: An evaluation of categorical and continuous scores." *Journal of Learning Disabilities* 6: 545–54.

Murray, L., Kempton, C., Woolgar, M. and Hooper, R. 1993. "Depressed mothers' speech to their infants and its relation to infant gender and cognitive development." *Journal of Child Psychology and Psychiatry* 34: 1083–101.

Namy, L., Campbell, A. and Tomasello, T. 2004. "The changing role of iconicity in non-verbal symbol learning. A U-shaped trajectory in the acquisition of arbitrary gestures." *Journal of Cognition and Development* 5 (1): 37–57.

Namy, L. and Waxman, S. 1998. "Words and gestures: Infants' interpretations of different forms of symbolic reference." *Child Development* 69: 295–308.

Namy, L. and Waxman, S. 2002. "Patterns of spontaneous production of novel words and gestures within an experimental setting in children ages 1:6 and 2:2." *Journal of Child Language* 29: 911–21.

Nazzi, T. and Bertoncini, J. 2003. "Before and after the vocabulary spurt: Two modes of word acquisition?" *Developmental Science* 6: 136–42.

Nelson, C.A. and Monk, C.S. 2001. "The use of event-related potentials in the study of cognitive development." In *Handbook of developmental cognitive neuroscience*, C. Nelson and M. Luciana (eds.), 125–36. Cambridge, MA: The MIT Press.

Nelson, K. 1973. "Structure and strategy in learning to talk." *Monographs of the Society for Research in Child Development* 38: 1–135.

Neville, H.J., Coffey, S.A., Holcomb, P.J., & Tallal, P. (1993). The neurobiology of sensory and language processing in language impaired children. *Journal of Cognitive Neuroscience 5*: 235–334.

O'Hara, M.W. and Swain, A.M. 1996. "Rates and risk of postpartum depression-a meta-analysis." *International Review of Psychiatry* 8: 37–54.

Picton, T.W., Bentin, S., Berg, P., Donchin, E., Hillyard, S.A., Johnson, R. Jr., Miller, G.A., Ritter, W., Ruchkin, D.S., Rugg, M.D. and Taylor, M.J. 2000. Guidelines for using human event-related potentials to study cognition: Recording standards and publication criteria. *Psychophysiology* 37: 127–152.

Radke-Yarrow, M., Nottlemann, E., Belmont, B. and Welsh, J. 1993. "Affective interactions of depressed and nondepressed mothers and their children." *Journal of Abnormal Child Psychology* 21: 683–95.

Righetti-Veltema, M., Conne-Perreard, E., Bousquet, A. and Manzano, J. 2002. "Postpartum depression and mother-infant relationship at 3 months old." *Journal of Affective Disorders* 70: 291–306.

Rugg, M. and Coles, M. 1995. *Electrophysiology of mind: Event-related brain potentials and cognition.* Oxford: OUP.

Sarfarazi, M., Cave, B., Richardson, A., Behan, J. and Sedgwick, E.M. 1999. "Visual event related potentials modulated by contextually relevant and irrelevant olfactory primes." *Chemical Senses* 24 (2): 145–54.

Simos, P. G and Molfese, D.L. 1997. "Electrophysiological responses from a temporal order continuum in the newborn infant." *Neuropsychologia* 35: 89–98.

Stager, C. and Werker, J. 1997. Infants listen for more phonetic detail in speech perception than in word-learning tasks." *Nature* 388: 381–2.

Sheehan, E.A., Namy, L.L., Mills, D.L. 2007. "Developmental changes in neural activity to familiar words and gestures." *Brain and Language* 101 (3): 246–59

Sheehan, E.A., Mills, D.L., & Namy, L.L. (2006). Semantic processing of spoken words and meaningful gestures. Manuscript in preparation.

Thierry, G., Vihman, M. and Roberts, M. 2003. "Familiar words capture the attention of 11-month-olds in less than 250 ms." *Neuroreport* 14: 2307–10.

Thoma, R.J., Hanlon, F.M., Moses, S.N., Edgar, J.C., Huang, M., Weisend, M. P. 2003. "Lateralization of auditory sensory gating and neurophysiological dysfunction in schizophrenia." *American Journal of Psychiatry* 160: 1595–605.

Tincoff, R. and Jusczyk, P.W. 1999. "Some beginnings of word comprehension in 6-month-olds." *Psychological Science* 10: 172–175.

Vihman, M.M. and McCune, L. 1994. "When is a word a word?" *Journal of Child Language.* 21, 517–42.

Weissman, M.M., Paykel, E.S. and Klerman, G.L. 1972. "The depressed woman as a mother." *Social Psychiatry* 7: 98–108.

Werker, J.F., Cohen, L., Lloyd, V., Casasola, M. and Stager, C. 1998. "Acquisition of word-object associations by 14-month-old infants." *Developmental Psychology* 34: 1289–309.

Werker, J.F., Fennell, C.T., Corcoran, K.M. and Stager, C.L. 2002. "Infants' ability to learn phonetically similar words: Effects of age and vocabulary size." *Infancy* 3 (1): 1–30.

Werner, H. and Kaplan, B. 1963. *Symbol formation.* New York, NY: Wiley.

Wu, Y.C. and Coulson, S. 2005. "Meaningful gestures: Electrophysiological indices of iconic gesture comprehension." *Psychophysiology* 42: 654–69.

Zangl, R. and Mills, D. L. 2007. "Increased brain activity to infant-directed speech in 6- and 13-month-old infants." *Infancy* 2 (1): 31–62.

CHAPTER 8

From perception to grammar

Jacques Mehler, Ansgar Endress, Judit Gervain and Marina Nespor

Tosto sarà ch'a veder queste cose
non ti fia grave, ma fieti diletto
quanto natura a sentir ti dispuose[1]

1 Biological perspectives on language acquisition

The early writings of Chomsky (1957, 1959), and Lenneberg's *The Biological Foundations of Language* (1967) are two examples of how a biological perspective should
be incorporated in the explanation of how language is acquired and why other
higher vertebrates do not acquire grammatical systems. In this chapter we defend
the view that neither of the two favorite views of language acquisition–the "all rule
learning" or the "all distributional regularity extraction"–are explanatory when one
is conceived without the other. Moreover, as we discuss below, we have worked
extensively on another mechanism that we call "perceptual primitive", comple-
menting the former two. By "perceptual primitives", we mean more than just basic
perceptual mechanisms that transduce to the brain the stimuli reaching the sensorium. Rather, we try to capture those Gestalt-like organizations of elements or the
natural highlighting of certain properties, which then determine many of the properties that can influence or be used by the other two computational mechanisms. In
the later sections, we explain how we conceive of these three mechanisms.

Before we do that, let us review just a few salient properties of language that an
adequate theory of language acquisition needs to explain:

– *Productivity*: "there are indefinitely many propositions the system can encode" (Fodor and Pylyshyn 1988). Given knowledge of the lexicon, humans can

---

1. Soon will it be, that to behold these things
Shall not be grievous, but delightful to thee
As much as nature fashioned thee to feel.
(Dante: *Divine Comedy*, Purgatory, Canto XV; English translation by H.W. Longfellow)

comprehend any sentence in their language, even those never heard before, and can produce an equivalent sentence whenever the thought process renders it necessary. That is, human grammar is indefinitely productive, but, crucially, it relies on a finite set of structural elements (Chomsky 1957) to achieve this.

– *Partial input*: Humans can learn language on the basis of partial information. The input learners receive comes without explicit indications of structure. Yet, learners extract the regularities that generated the input sequences (which is in itself remarkable given that any finite set of data can be described by indefinitely many different sets of rules) even under very impoverished conditions, such as when deaf children create their own sign language.

– *Acquiring multiple systems*: Humans can simultaneously learn more than one language if the input data obliges them to do so. This requires, firstly, that they discover that the input was generated by two (at least partially) different sets of rules and, secondly, that they consistently process and store the rules from the two sets distinctly. Interestingly, the acquisition of multiple languages follows a particular ontogenetic path. Namely, young learners in the phase of first language acquisition learn several languages with almost equal ease and can achieve roughly the same proficiency as their monolingual peers. However, at later ages, learners have more difficulty picking up a new language and, typically, master it less proficiently. Although there is significant individual variation as to how proficient a second language learner may get, the general pattern that late language learning is not, in most cases, native-like is unequivocal, and arguably derives from how the faculty of language is implemented biologically in the human phylogenetic endowment and its ontogenetic unfolding.

The above traits of language suggest that a theory of language acquisition will be both computational and biological. Undeniably, some species acquire complex song or vocalization patters that have structures remotely reminiscent of some syntactic constraints. But the range of expressions these allow are poor. In fact, no animal communication system has the flexibility to serve purposes other than those programmed to secure the needs of the species, i.e., collecting food, mating, grooming, and so forth. Obviously, humans also use language to secure the same basic needs. Yet, in addition, they frequently use language to express propositions that have nothing to do with either survival or basic needs. They express their states of mind, their beliefs and their desires. They also have many uses for language which allows us to express theoretical ideas, elaborate abstract constructions that make it possible to expand primitive social and cultural settings into ever more detailed social contracts and laws, science and the arts. This suggests that, to obtain a realistic account of language acquisition, one should acknowledge that our brain/mind is different from that of non-human creatures.

Hauser, Chomsky and Fitch (2002, HCF henceforth) proposed that it is convenient to view language as a collection of two components: the first, which they call the faculty of language in the broad sense (FLB), is a collection of abilities we share with other animals; the second is the faculty of language in the narrow sense (FLN) and it is still a conjecture whether it contains a single or multiple components or conceivably even an empty set. Yet the authors' hypothesis (HCF, 2002: 1751) is that it is likely to contain only recursion or more precisely,

> "a computational system that generates internal representations and maps them into the sensory-motor interface by the phonological system, and into the conceptual-intentional interface by the semantic system...the core property of FLN is recursion, attributed to narrow syntax".

HCF believe that their comparative approach will lead to new insights and will generate new hypotheses about how the language faculty came to adopt grammatical systems like those now present in all natural languages. In their view the ability to use recursion is an essential ingredient to explain the grammatical systems used by all natural languages. HFC's thesis might turn out to be correct, although we are not certain that the attempt to demonstrate this (Fitch and Hauser 2004) is convincing (see below).

In this paper we take the stance that there are two informative ways to explore the biology of language, namely, a *synchronic* and a *diachronic* perspective. The diachronic approach is the one HFC espouse; it tries to establish how human faculties arose during evolution from precursors supposedly present also in nonhuman animals.

Putatively, precursors evolved to become parts of the language we observe in present day humans. As students of animal cognition, we can inspect the bolts and notches with which humans have been bestowed in possibly phylogenetically distant animals. Unfortunately, there are many aspects of language that we can observe now but whose precursors (except for the shallowest aspects) do not leave traces, as for instance, speech, proto-languages, etc.

Almost four decades ago, Lenneberg (1967: 255) already foresaw the growing popularity, as well as the concomitant pitfalls of this approach:

> There were days when learned treatises on the origin of language were based on nothing more than imagination. The absence of ascertainable facts rendered these essays disreputable early during the rise of empirical sciences. For some time the topic became taboo in respectable scientific circles. But recently it seems to have acquired new probity by adumbration of the speculations with empirical data.

This is why a synchronic perspective may contribute to our understanding of the language faculty. Such a perspective focuses on language acquisition and the neural underpinning of language performance. It conceives of our linguistic capacity as a kind of Chomskyan I(nternal)-language. Like Lenneberg in his seminal work, it considers evidence from a broad variety of sources within the same species, ranging from data about neuronal maturation to properties of the perceptual system, to particularities of the respiratory system to evidence from speakers/hearers at all ages to abnormalities in patients with brain lesions or who suffer from developmental impairments. In other words, we think that exploring data without having to rely only on conjectures seems a more promising route to understand how languages are acquired, how the performance apparatus works and how grammar is represented in the brain. In this context, novel brain imaging methods may provide particularly informative data for a better understanding of long-debated issues. For example, Peña *et al.* (2002) used optical topography (OT) to investigate the question whether the lateralization of language is prior to or the consequence of exposure and acquisition. Testing neonates, they have found a left hemisphere advantage in brain activity for speech stimuli as compared to the same speech stimuli played backwards (impossible or non-language) and to silence, suggesting that this hemispheric advantage may not rely on extensive experience. Although it is not clearly established why backward speech functions as non-linguistic material, most probably it is because the human vocal tract is unable to produce backward speech. This is most obvious for stop consonants, whose production is not direction-independent, i.e. requires first a closure, and a burst-like release of the closure, the opposite order is not possible.

For all those reasons we believe that the synchronic route is more promising, although there is no denying that these days the synchronic route is not as popular as the diachronic one.

2   Setting the stage: earlier thoughts on language acquisition

In the last four decades, linguists and cognitive scientists studying language acquisition have made tremendous progress, as we shall see below. Today we tend to forget how hard it was to change the dominant paradigm most psychologists espoused in the first half of the twentieth century. Indeed, the classical picture was that of psychologists who overlooked whether their theories were biologically tenable or not. Skinner went as far as to teach and write that he did not believe that studying the brain was of much use. He used to claim that the best way to conceive of the abbreviation CNS was as meaning "conceptual nervous system".

A variety of theories supported the notion that conditioning of various sorts was the essential mechanism underlying language acquisition. In parallel, psychologists also argued that sensitivity to distributional regularities in the environment remains an essential mechanism to acquire language. Information theorists and structural linguists championed this view. Notice, however, that this manner of describing language acquisition avoids mentioning that only the human mind/ brain has the disposition to take advantage of such cues to acquire grammar. Moreover, most psychologists working in the early 1920s viewed lexical learning as being the crux of language acquisition, ignoring syntax, semantics, phonology and morphology. This view is still not uncommon today.

In contrast to classical learning psychologists, contemporary students of language acquisition try to focus on syntax without ignoring either the lexicon or phonology. They explore how the complex and abstract structure of syntax arises in the brain of every healthy child who grows up in an environment in which language is utilized. They examine how infants learn to produce and comprehend the sentences of the language they are exposed to, while other organisms that share many of the cognitive abilities humans also posses fail to do so. Synchronic studies also highlight how important it is to study which impairments do and do not result in problems for the pre-lexical infant. Such research has uncovered conditions (such as Specific Language Impairment; see e.g. Gopnik 1990; Vargha-Khadem, Watkins, Alcock, Fletcher and Passingham 1995) that specifically affect language acquisition, without (or with rather minor) impairments of other cognitive capacities.

The contemporary view of language acquisition tends to merge theoretical and experimental studies of the problem. The formal and computational models of language acquisition influence how empirical scientists couch their research. Moreover, methods to study infants have made great progress, making it possible to use neuroscience-inspired methods to expand our understanding of the cortical mechanisms of the changes we observe in early language acquisition. In particular, cognitive scientists have explored systematically both how the child converges to the basic properties of the target language, and the brain changes that accompany acquisition. For example, when children make production mistakes, these may remain constrained by syntactic possibilities attested in some actual natural language (Baker 2005). Such findings fit well with Chomsky's proposal that, on the one hand, we are born with Universal Principles and, on the other, that we acquire a large range of natural languages. Crucially, these are not arbitrarily variable, but seem to be organized such that different parametric choices account for variations among languages.

In this chapter, we outline a model of language acquisition that follows the integrative approach introduced above. We thus propose an account that seeks psychological and biological plausibility, while considering the logical problem of language acquisition in its full complexity.

3   Learning language: rule-based and statistics-based approaches

Inspired by Chomsky's rule-based approach to language, early psycholinguistic work strove to understand how humans learn language. Artificial grammars were devised and presented to participants in order to test their ability to extract underlying regularities and generalize them to novel items. The rationale behind these studies was to investigate the learnability of syntax, conceived of as autonomous from other aspects of language. In other words, the question was whether and, if yes, what structures can be learned "in isolation", i.e. in a situation in which participants are deprived of the usual concomitant cues, such as meaning/reference, prosody etc.

Early work in this tradition (Chomsky and Miller 1958; Reber 1967, 1969 among several others) suggested that participants who had been familiarized with letter strings generated by an underlying finite-state grammar were able to discriminate between grammatical and ungrammatical sequences that were both novel, despite the fact that they were not consciously aware of the generative rules responsible for the grammatical sequences. In later work, however, it was suggested that success in these tasks relies on learning about bigrams and trigrams, i.e. immediately adjacent sequences of elements, rather than about the more complex underlying pattern that characterizes the string as a whole (e.g. Cleeremans and McClelland 1991; Dienes, Broadbent and Berry 1991; Kinder 2000; Kinder and Assmann 2000). However, Reber (1969) also provided experiments that are immune to such criticisms: in these experiments, participants were again familiarized with consonant strings conforming to a finite state grammar—but then tested on strings from a *new* consonant "vocabulary". As the consonants during familiarization and during test were distinct, successful classification as grammatical or ungrammatical could not be explained by simple statistical computations on the consonants (e.g., Altmann, Dienes and Goode 1995; Brooks and Vokey 1991; Gómez, Gerken and Schvaneveldt 2000; Knowlton and Squire 1996; Meulemans and van der Linden 1997; Reber 1969; Tunney and Altmann 2001).

Another one of the early influential studies was work by Braine (1963, 1966), who approached the learnability issue from the point of view of the structure of natural languages. Specifically, he conjectured that the universal presence of frequent functors (e.g., articles, prepositions/postpositions, pronouns etc.) in the world's languages is a design feature aimed at facilitating learning. These functional elements, easy to track because of their high frequency and their phonological properties, act as anchor points relative to which content words (e.g., nouns, verbs, adjectives etc.) can be positioned. Braine (1963, 1966) tested this hypothesis with 8–10-year-old children in artificial grammar experiments, and found that participants readily learn the position of a non-frequent element relative to a frequent marker (e.g., first, second after the marker), as opposed to the absolute position of the element. Moreover, Green (1979) and later Morgan, Meier and Newport (1987) showed that artificial languages in which there are no such markers, or in which the 'content words' are not contingent upon the markers, which thus become bad predictors of structure, are hard or impossible to learn, while a language with reliable markers is fully learnable.

A large body of subsequent work (for example, Morgan and Newport 1981, Mori and Moeser 1983; Valian and Seana 1988; Valian and Levitt 1996, among others) was concerned with questions similar to Braine's, i.e., how certain features, especially the presence of function words and the existence of larger constituent units such as phrases, contribute to learning. In addition, some of these studies also asked the question how the organization of language in terms of function and content words interacts with other basic properties such as reference (Mori and Moeser 1983) or prosody (Morgan *et al.* 1987; Valian and Levitt 1996). They found that these additional features facilitate learning, but are not mandatory for learning to take place, and without the function words, they are not sufficient in themselves to induce structure.

In spite of their differences, the quoted studies all have a common feature. They share the interpretation that participants' success in these artificial grammar learning tasks is attributable to their ability to (implicitly) extract rules from the input, an ability that the authors also believe to underlie first language acquisition.

About a decade ago, a new view emerged, reviving pre-generativist ideas about language acquisition. Proponents of this view argue, firstly, that the input to language learners is richer in (statistical) information than previously argued by the generativists, and, secondly, that learners can use their domain-general learning abilities to pick this information up. In an influential paper, Saffran, Aslin and Newport (1996) showed that participants are able to segment a continuous (artificial) speech stream into its constituent word forms solely on the basis of the statistical information contained in the signal. This proposal is based on the intuition, described among others by Shannon (1948) and Harris (1955), that elements (segments, syllables etc.) building up a larger unit are statistically more coherent than elements across unit-boundaries. For instance, in the expression *pretty baby*, the syllable *pre-* predicts the syllable *-tty* with a greater probability than this latter predicts *ba-*, which is part of another word. Following this idea, Saffran and colleagues (1996) constructed a monotonous, synthetic speech stream by concatenating consonant-vowel syllables in such a way that syllables belonging to the same word predicted each other with a higher transitional probability (TP)[2] than those

---

2.   (Forward) transitional probability is a conditional probability statistics defined as: $TP(A \rightarrow B)$ = $F(AB)/F(A)$, where A and B are syllables, and $F(X)$ is the frequency of element X.

spanning a word boundary. Specifically, they created four trisyllabic nonsense words (e.g., *bidaku, golabu* etc.), which were repeated in random order to make up a 2-minute-long speech stream (*bidakupadotigolabubidaku…*), lacking all phonological or prosodic information about word boundaries. The only cues about the words were the TPs, set to be 1.0 between syllables within a word (e.g., *bi-da*), and 0.33 across word boundaries (e.g., *ku-pa*). This stream served as the material to which 8-month-old infants were familiarized. Following familiarization, infants were tested on whether they were able to discriminate between the trisyllabic words of the language and other trisyllabic sequences (called "part-words") that also appeared in the stream, but contained a syllable pair with low transitional probabilities, i.e. that spanned a word boundary (e.g., *kupado*). Indeed, infants attended longer to part-words than to words, indicating that they could discriminate between the familiar words and the statistically illicit part-words. The authors argued that the computation of statistical measures of coherence, such as transitional probability, is a mechanism that potentially plays a very important role in early language acquisition, especially in word segmentation, since it does not require language-specific knowledge on the part of the learner. It has to be noted, however, that it is not equally useful in all languages. Languages that are predominantly monosyllabic, such as Mandarin or (possibly) child-directed English, might pose a problem, since irrespective of TPs, most syllable boundaries are also word boundaries at the same time (Yang 2002, also about other cross-linguistic issues about TP-based segmentation).

This initial study was followed by a series of others that aimed at exploring different aspects of the statistical learning (SL) mechanism. Thus, it was shown that SL is not specific to linguistic stimuli and operates equally well over tones (Saffran, Johnson, Aslin and Newport 1999) or visual patterns (Fiser and Aslin 2002). Neither is it restricted to humans, since cotton top tamarins and rats also succeed in the segmentation experiments (Hauser, Newport and Aslin 2001; Toro and Trobalón 2005).

More importantly, some recent studies have tried to clarify the actual role and scope of SL in language acquisition. Several questions have been raised, including what distance TPs are computed at (only over adjacent element pairs or also over element pairs at a distance), and whether SL also allows rule extraction and generalization. We will address these problems in turn below.

The question of whether TPs can also be computed between non-adjacent elements has arisen because in natural languages the relevant structural dependencies that infants need to learn are not only local as in Saffran *et al.* (1996), but also distant. Dependencies at a distance are universally present in many syntactic structures: e.g. in a sentence like *The children of my brother are coming tonight, are* does not refer to the nearest noun, that is *brother*, but to the subject of the sentence, i.e. *the children*. Similarly, in *John promised his kids to buy a new boat*, the subject of *buy* is not the nearest noun *kids*, but *John*.

Similarly, at the level of morphology, many languages have processes of compound formation or inflection, so called parasynthesis or circumfixing, that simultaneously attach a prefix and a suffix to a stem: neither the prefix plus the stem nor the stem plus the suffix are existing words. For example, *demarcate* in English is a verb derived from the noun *mark*, but neither *demark*, nor *marcate* exist (at least, in British English). Or in Hungarian, the superlative of adjectives is formed by adding the circumfix *leg-Adj-bb*, e.g. *jó* 'good', *legjobb* 'best'.

Therefore, Peña *et al.* (2002) devised an adult experiment similar to Saffran *et al*'s (1996), except that TPs were made to be predictive between the first and the last syllables of the trisyllabic nonsense words (AXC, e.g., *puliki, puraki, pufoki*, where *pu* predicts *ki* with a TP of 1.0). Three such distant syllable pairs were defined (*pu-* X *-li, ta-* X *-du, be-* X *-ga*), and for each distant pair, the same middle items were used (X: *-li-, -ra-, -fo-*). Consequently, the adjacent TPs, as well as the TPs across word boundaries were uniformly 0.33, and thus were not informative of word boundaries. For 10 minutes, participants were familiarized with a monotonous stream of synthetically produced words that were placed one after the other. When tested with the words versus part-words of the language, participants succeeded in recognizing the words, indicating that they could keep track of and use non-adjacent TPs in order to establish constituent boundaries in the input.[3]

As mentioned before, another crucial question is whether TP computations, and SL in general, allow generalizations or not. Peña *et al.* (2002) explored this by testing whether participants who were familiarized with the artificial AXC language learn not only the actually attested AXC words, but also the generalization that A predicts C, whatever X comes in between. To answer this question, they used the same familiarization stream as in the simple non-adjacent TP experiment described above, but they modified the test items in such a way that the part-words were pitted against what they called "rule-words", i.e. trisyllabic words in which the first and the last syllables were provided by one of the language's word frames (*pu-* X *-be*), but the intervening X was a syllable that never appeared in that position

---

3.   Interestingly, in a very similar experiment, Newport and Aslin (2004) have not found better than chance performance on the same word vs. part-word discrimination task. These authors also used trisyllabic nonsense words defined by a TP of 1.0 between the first and the third syllable, but instead of three word frames and three middle syllables as in Peña *et al.* (2002), they used five word frames and four intermediate syllables. The resulting adjacent TPs were thus 0.25 between the first and the second syllables, and 0.20 between the second and the third syllables. The adjacent TPs over word boundaries were also 0.25. It remains to be clarified what is the exact reason for the difference in performance obtained by the two groups of researchers, but the details of the material might play an important role.

during familiarization (it was, for instance, the initial syllable of another frame, e.g. *pubeki*, where be was the first syllable of the frame *be...ga*). Peña *et al.* found that participants do not generalize, as evidenced by their lack of preference for the rule-words over the part-words. However, once 25 ms subliminal pauses were inserted between the words during familiarization, solving the task of segmentation for the participants, they readily generalized, choosing rule-words over part-words. The authors interpreted these findings as indications that very subtle differences in the properties of the input might induce different processing mechanisms. When TPs are the only cues available, participants compute them to chunk the speech stream into words. However, when other cues are also present, cutting up the stream into constituents, learners engage in different computations and generalize the AXC pattern.

It later turned out that the generalization participants extract seems to be a class-based dependency. They learn that the first syllable of each word has to belong to one syllable class, and the final syllable to another one (Endress and Bonatti, under review). However, also under this interpretation of Peña *et al.*'s (2002) results, very subtle cues trigger entirely different processes: When the speech stream is segmented even by subliminal silences, participants generalize the structure of the words; in contrast, when no such segmentation cues are given, participants only perform the statistical computations that allow them to segment the stream and do not show any evidence for generalizations.

The question of rule learning was also addressed by Marcus *et al.* (1999), although from a slightly different perspective, testing directly for generalization in experiments where SL could not take place at all, given that the items used in the test were all novel tokens. Thus no TPs could be computed for them during familiarization. Marcus and colleagues familiarized two groups of 7-month-old babies with synthesized languages in which the trisyllabic "sentences" had an ABA (*ga ti ga*) or an ABB (*ga ti ti*) structure, respectively. Then they tested the infants on sentences that were consistent with their familiarization grammar (e.g., ABB for the ABB group) and on sentences that were inconsistent (e.g., ABA for the ABB group). Crucially, however, the items themselves were all made up of novel syllables (e.g., *wo fe fe*), so the only feature that made the test items consistent or inconsistent with the familiarization material was the underlying structure. The authors found that babies looked longer for the inconsistent items, indicating that they discriminated them from the consistent ones. This implies that they had extracted the underlying pattern. As a control, the authors also ran an experiment in which the structure of the two grammars was more similar, i.e., AAB vs. ABB, which both contain immediate repetitions. The rationale was to make sure that the babies did not distinguish the two grammars on the basis of cues that were simpler than the structure of the sentences, such as the sheer presence or absence of a repetition. The results showed discrimination under these conditions, too.

An important contribution to our understanding of how generalizations happen comes from a series of artificial grammar experiments done by Gómez and Gerken (1999) with 1-year-old infants. In the first experiment, the authors exposed infants to an artificial language generated by a finite state grammar similar to that of Reber (1967), except that they used word strings ("sentences") pronounced by a female speaker instead of letters strings. After a less than two-minute familiarization with grammatical strings deriving from the grammar (e.g., PEL TAM RUD, VOT PEL PEL JIC, VOT JIC RUD TAM etc.), infants were tested on their discrimination between novel grammatical and ungrammatical sentences (e.g., **VOT** PEL PEL **TAM** and **TAM** JIC RUD **VOT**, respectively). The latter were obtained by interchanging the first and the last words of the grammatical sentences. Infants successfully discriminated the two kinds of sentences, as indicated by their significantly longer looking time to the grammatical strings. In a second experiment, using the same familiarization as before, participants were tested on the same grammatical sentences as before, but this time these sentences were contrasted with ungrammatical sentences that contained licit words in the initial and final positions, but illicit word pairs in the internal slots (e.g., VOT*RUD*PEL JIC, where * marks transitions not allowed by the grammar). Babies, once again, looked longer at the grammatical strings, suggesting discrimination. As a third step, the authors asked whether infants are able to discriminate between two grammars that used the same vocabulary and the same sentence-initial and sentence-final words, but had different "word orders", i.e. different transitions. Two groups of infants were tested. Each group was familiarized with one of the grammars. Then both groups were tested on sentences generated by both grammars. For each group, the sentences produced by the grammar they were not exposed to constituted the "ungrammatical" strings. As before, participants showed evidence of learning by looking longer to sentences deriving from their familiarization grammar. Finally, the authors also tested infants' ability to generalize their knowledge about the grammar by familiarizing them to the grammar using one vocabulary (JED, FIM, TUP, DAK, SOG, e.g. JED FIM FIM FIM TUP was a possible sentence), and then testing them on sentences coming from the same grammar, but using a new vocabulary (VOT, PEL, JIC, RUD, TAM; e.g., VOT PEL PEL PEL JIC was a corresponding test sentence). This precludes the use of simple transition probabilities between pairs of words to solve the task. Using the same procedure as in the previous experiment (except for the change of vocabulary between training and test), the authors found that infants can still tell apart their discrimination grammar from the other one, concluding that these results constitute evidence in favor of the learning of abstract linguistic knowledge not reducible to statistics.

In sum, the bulk of the work about the basic aspects of language acquisition has subscribed to one of two interpretations. Participants' performance is either attributed to rule extraction and generalization, or to statistical learning. Although proponents of both views claim that the two processes are not mutually exclusive (Marcus *et al.* 1999; Newport and Aslin 2004), there is disagreement as to how labour is shared between the two during acquisition.

4   A new perspective: perceptual primitives in artificial grammar experiments and language

As mentioned in the introduction, the specificity of language is nowadays studied essentially from a diachronic perspective. For example, researchers compare human computational capacities with those of other animals (mostly primates) in order to draw conclusions about the origins of different aspects of language. However, a synchronic perspective may also yield important insights into language-specificity. In the last section, we reviewed how simplified artificial grammars have been used to explore the kinds of structures that can be learned from simple exposure to exemplars. We will now suggest that two simple–and potentially perceptually based–mechanisms in conjunction with statistical learning can explain the findings of most of the previous artificial grammar learning experiments. Then we will argue that these mechanisms may also explain more abstract linguistic observations.

As mentioned before, in artificial grammar learning, participants are presented with sequences of linguistic units that conform to a finite state grammar, and then have to judge whether *new* sequences are grammatical or not. They can judge the grammaticality of sequences even when tested on strings from a *different* consonant "vocabulary" than the one used during training (e.g., Altmann, Dienes and Goode 1995; Brooks and Vokey 1991; Gómez, Gerken and Schvaneveldt 2000; Knowlton and Squire 1996; Meulemans and van der Linden 1997; Reber 1969; Tunney and Altmann 2001). While the successful classification with the same vocabulary during the familiarization and test phases can be explained by exclusively statistical cues (e.g., Cleeremans and McClelland 1991; Dienes, Broadbent and Berry 1991; Kinder 2000; Kinder and Assmann 2000), it turns out that a different mechanism is responsible when the vocabulary changes between familiarization and test. Indeed, "loops" in the finite state grammars give rise to characteristic patterns of *repetitions*. For example, if strings containing repetitions such as "MTTVT" or "VXVRXRM" are licensed by a grammar, then the pattern of repetitions will also appear when the grammar is instantiated over a *new* consonant set–since this repetition pattern is a property of the grammar and not of the "vocabulary." Subsequent research has shown that the transfer depends on these repetition patterns; no transfer occurs when the grammars avoid such repetition patterns (see e.g. Gómez *et al.* 2000; Tunney and Altmann 2001; see also Brooks and Vokey 1991).

A repetition-based mechanism may also explain other research. Recall for instance that Marcus *et al.* (1999) used seven-month-olds' capacity to generalize repetition-based structures such as ABA, ABB and AAB to argue that these infants can use symbol-manipulation capacities to infer the structure of the stimuli. However, as the grammars entailed repetitions, the infants may simply have detected the repetition-patterns in the stimuli. Indeed, Endress, Dehaene-Lambertz and Mehler (under review) showed that even adults readily learn repetition-based structures but not other structures that are formally equally simple; in particular, using piano tones to carry the structures, they showed that participants readily generalize the structures ABA and ABB (that is, two repetition-based structures), but that they perform poorly for the structures Low Tone–High Tone–Middle Tone and Middle Tone–High Tone–Low Tone.

A mechanism detecting identity relations can also explain results that have been used to draw strong conclusions about specifically human linguistic computations. In particular, HCF (2002) suggested that "recursion" may be a uniquely human capacity that is at the core of the language faculty.[4] To test this hypothesis, Fitch and Hauser (2004) asked whether humans and monkeys could learn a phrase-structure grammar that required "recursion" or a finite state grammar. The finite state grammar entailed an alternation of a female and a male voice, while the phrase structure grammar entailed *n* syllables pronounced by a male speaker followed by another *n* syllables pronounced by a female speaker (or vice-versa). Human adults learned both types of grammars, while monkeys learned only the finite state grammars. Recent fMRI results by Friederici *et al* (2005) have rendered the debate about the status of "recursion" in human language even more interesting. These authors have found that local structural computations that are sufficient for learning a finite-state but not a phase-structure grammar recruit the left frontal operculum, while computing hierarchical structures necessary for phrase-structure grammars activates Broca's area. The authors interpret this differential activity as further evidence for the separation of local and hierarchical structures, with the latter localized in a brain area especially developed in humans.

While it is certainly possible to cast these stimuli in terms of phrase-structure grammars versus finite-state grammars, a simpler possibility is to assume that participants simply learned the alternations between male and female voices. This

---

4.   "Recursion" is used by HCF in a way that is more general than how it is most often understood in linguistics. These authors employ the notion of recursion to refer to embedding in general, and not only to embedding of a constituent in a constituent of the same category.

204 Jacques Mehler, Ansgar Endress, Judit Gervain and Marina Nespor

seems indeed to be the case: When exposed to strings conforming to the phrase-structure grammar, most participants did not discriminate between strings with equal numbers of male and female syllables and strings with unequal numbers of male and female syllables (which violate the phrase-structure grammar but conform to the pattern of alternations; see Hochmann et al., submitted), and performance decreased dramatically when the saliency of the alternation was reduced (using a contrast between Consonant-Vowel-Consonant (CVC) and Consonant-Vowel (CV) syllables instead of the male vs. female contrast).

The importance of repetitions has also been implicitly acknowledged by researchers studying statistical learning. Indeed, when preparing speech streams for such experiments, care is always taken to avoid immediate repetitions of words (e.g., Saffran et al. 1996); such repetitions seem to make the words pop out. In line with this possibility, speech streams are segmented only if words are "repeated" closely enough, but not when two occurrences of the same word are separated by too many intervening items (Shukla, in preparation).

The arguments reviewed above suggest that a mechanism detecting identity relations can explain a wide range of data. Other experiments can be explained by another, equally simple, mechanism. One can illustrate this mechanism again with Marcus et al's experiments. In their experiments, repetitions always occurred at the *edges* of sequences; that is, repetitions occurred either sequence-initially or sequence-finally. Of course, it has been known since Ebbinghaus (1885) that edges are salient, and remembered better. (We will discuss below how the edges may favor generalizations.)

The importance of edges in language acquisition was first stressed in corpus-based studies. For example, grammatical constructions such as auxiliaries or root infinitives are more frequent in child language if the corresponding constituents appear in sentence-edges (e.g., Gleitman, Newport and Gleitman 1984; Wijnen, Kempen and Gillis 2001). It is thus possible that the structures in Marcus et al's (1999) experiments were particularly easy to extract because the repetitions were at the edges, unlike what Marcus et al's (1999) more general interpretation would suggest. Endress, Scholl and Mehler (2005) tested this hypothesis by asking whether participants would generalize repetition-based grammars where the repetitions were either in sequence-edges (e.g., ABCDEFF) or in sequence-middles (e.g., AB-CDDEF). Indeed, participants readily generalized the edge-repetitions but were close to (or at) chance for the middle-repetitions. Still, the advantage for edge-repetitions was not simply due to participants remembering syllables better in edges than in middles; indeed, when asked to *discriminate* the same syllable sequences (that is, they still had to process the sequences but they no longer had to generalize their structures), participants performed at ceiling for both edge- and middle-repetitions, suggesting that the generalization ability is specifically constrained by the place in the sequence where the relevant structure occurs.

Edges proved to be important also for other experiments. For example, Chambers, Onishi and Fisher (2003) showed that infants can learn phonotactic-like constraints from brief exposure; in particular, the infants learned that in Consonant-Vowel-Consonant (CVC) words the initial and the final consonants had to come from distinct sets (see also Onishi, Chambers and Fisher 2002, for experiments with adults). As the crucial consonants were the word-edges, one can ask whether this feature was crucial to the generalizations. Later studies observed such phonotactic-like generalizations when the crucial syllables were at word edges, but not when they were in word-middles (Endress and Mehler, under review). Again, a control experiment showed that the edge advantage was not due to a brute impairment for processing consonants in word middles, but that these edge-based constraints seem to affect more the generalization ability than the ability to process consonants.

Yet another example comes from Peña *et al*'s (2002) experiments. Recall that these authors showed that when participants are familiarized with a quasi-continuous speech stream, the inclusion of subliminal 25 ms silences between words triggers generalizations that are not available otherwise. Under these conditions, participants seem to extract a class-based dependency: They learn that the first syllable of each word has to belong to one syllable class, and the final syllable to another one (Endress and Bonatti, 2007). Again, the crucial syllables occurred at the edges, so one may ask whether this feature of the experiment was crucial to the generalizations. As in the other experiments, the class-based generalizations were observed when the crucial syllables occurred at word edges, but not when they were in the middle syllables (Endress and Mehler, unpublished). It thus seems that the class-based generalizations were triggered by the edges in which the crucial syllables were placed. This explanation also accounts for previous experiments studying how word classes can be learned, as also in these experiments the crucial elements occurred at edges (Braine 1963, 1966; Smith 1966, 1967, 1969).

These results suggest that two mechanisms may be important for structures used in Artificial Grammar Learning experiments: an operation sensitive to repetitions, and a second operation specifically attending to word edges.

We first turn to repetitions. Using optical imaging, Gervain and Mehler (in preparation) have recently shown that a sensitivity to repetitions may arise very early in ontogenesis. The authors found that the neonate brain readily distinguishes between sequences containing repetitions at the edges of items (similar to Marcus *et al*'s ABA and ABB sequences) and matched controls that do not contain such repetitions (ABC sequences), as evidenced by larger and longer-lasting activation for the former type of stimuli. Thus, we might hypothesize that edges and

repetitions act as perceptual primitives that infants can detect from the very beginning of language acquisition and might use as basic building blocks towards learning some aspects of more abstract structures.

These results also suggest that identity relations may not be a peculiarity of
Artificial Grammar Learning experiments, but rather that they may be more widespread. Indeed, a basic operation sensitive to identity relations may also explain a
range of linguistic observations. Reduplication is a widespread phenomenon in
morphology that entails the repetition of (part of) a word root (McCarthy and
Prince 1999). It can either create new words through derivation or composition, or
new forms of a word through inflection. Though total reduplication is sometimes
attested, partial reduplication is more frequent. For example, in Marshallese, a
Malayo-Polynesian language spoken in the Marshall Islands, reduplication of the
syllable at the right edge of a word is used to derive verbs from nouns. For example, *takinkin* ('to wear socks') is derived from *takin* ('sock'; Moravcsik 1978). In
Classical Greek, left edge reduplication is used in verbal inflection: λείπω [leipo] 'I
leave', λέλοιπα [leloipa] 'I left'. Although medial reduplication is attested, it is rare
compared to either initial or final reduplication.

Other examples of reduplications found in languages are rhyming reduplications as in *abracadabra, boogie-woogie, hocus-pocus*, total reduplication as in *bon-
bon, bye-bye, couscous* or reduplication with a vowel change as in *flip-flop, hippety-
hoppety, kitcat, zig zag, ping-pong*.

Edge-based regularities may be even more widespread in linguistics. The data
reviewed above is already suggestive of the generality of such phenomena: edge-
based phenomena could be observed at sequence edges, sentence edges, word
edges, and probably still under other conditions; the crucial items could be phonemes, syllables or words. It thus seems that edge-based regularities may be exploited by natural languages at different levels of description.

Before discussing the linguistic phenomena that may appeal to edges, however, it is worthwhile discussing what the role of edges might actually be. In the first
demonstrations of an edge advantage, Ebbinghaus (1885) observed that items in
edge positions are remembered better than items in non-edge positions. Later research found that this is not the only role of the edges. Indeed, participants do not
only have to learn *that* particular items occur in a sequence, but also *where* the
items occur. For example, one type of error in sequence recall consists of sequentially correct *intrusions*, where an intruder is recalled in its correct sequential position but in a sequence that it has never appeared in (e.g., Conrad 1960; Henson
1998, 1999; Ng and Maybery 2002). Such results can only be explained if participants learn *positional codes* for each item that are independent of the sequence that
the item appeared in; such positional codes seem to undergo their own serial position effect, such that it is easier to remember that a particular item occurred in the

first or the last position than to remember that it occurred in a middle position (e.g., Conrad 1960; Henson 1998, 1999; Hicks, Hakes and Young 1966; Ng and Maybery 2002; and many others). As the edges may be the most reliable positional code, it seems plausible that many different processes use them to define regularities. Indeed, most contemporary models of positional codes in sequences assume, in some form or the other, that *only* the edges have proper positional codes, and that the other positions are encoded with respect to the edges (e.g., Henson 1998; Hitch, Burgess, Towse and Culpin 1996; Ng and Maybery 2002). Such results also suggest that edges may not be "hard" limits to generalizations, but that it is probably possible to draw generalizations "close to" edges and to observe a graceful degradation afterwards[5].

Linguistic regularities extensively appeal to edges. In phonology, for example, word stress rules make reference to either the left or to the right edge. Stress may be initial (e.g., in Hungarian) or final (e.g., in Turkish) or on a different syllable defined starting from the right edge. For example, in Latin (as well as many other languages), stress is defined on the basis of a word's right edge: it is penultimate (i.e. second from the right) if the penultimate syllable is heavy, antepenultimate (i.e., third from the right) otherwise. No language makes reference to the middle of words, e.g. by stating that stress falls in the middle syllable (Halle and Vergnaud 1987; Hayes 1995; Kager 1995). Interestingly, if word stress does not fall at the same position within the word, it is computed from the right, but not from the left edge (Hayes 1995; Kager 1995).

Phenomena of phrasal phonology often apply to one edge of a constituent or across two constituents to signal their syntactic cohesion, by eliminating their edges. An example of the first type is the final devoicing of voiced stop consonants in Dutch (be[t] vs. be[d:]en 'bed' vs. 'beds'). An example of the second type is *liaison* in French, the resyllabification of the final consonant of a word with a vowel-initial following word; this process has the effect of eliminating the edges that separate the words. It occurs for example between articles and nouns (as in *les enfants*, le[z]enfants 'the children') or between auxiliaries and verbs (as in *je suis allé*, jesui[z]allé 'I have gone'), but it does not apply between a subject and verb (as in *les enfants ont mangé*, les enfants[Ø]ont mangé 'the children have eaten') to signal that the two constituents have a low level of cohesion (Nespor and Vogel 1986).

The morphological process of affixation also clearly privileges edges: languages are rich in suffixes and prefixes, while infixes are rare (Greenberg 1957). In addition, suffixes are more frequent than prefixes (Sapir 1921; Dryer 2005; Cutler *et al.* 1985; Hawkins and Cutler 1988); in a cross-linguistic database of grammatical

---

5.   Similarly, identity may not be an all-or-none relation, but may be the extreme case of similarity of two items (see e.g., Frisch, Pierrehumbert and Broe 2001).

markers 74.4% are suffixes (Bybee, Pagliuca and. Perkins 1990). While there are languages such as Turkish, Basque, Burmese or Hindi that have only suffixes, language with only prefixes, like Thai, are quite rare (Greenberg 1963). This asymmetry between prefixes and suffixes would seem to suggest, as the phenomenon of stress assignment seen above, that the right edge is perceptually more salient than the left edge.

Edges are not only privileged positions for various types of linguistic processes; they are also crucial for the mapping of different levels of representation. Morphosyntactic and phonological representations are both hierarchical in nature, but the two hierarchies are distinct: while *dis* is a morpheme in *disillusion*, it is not a syllable. Constituents of the two hierarchies often coincide, but when they do not, they are never totally mismatched: at least one of the edges –either left or right– must be aligned. For example, the left edge of a syntactic phrase is aligned with the left edge of a phonological phrase in right recursive languages, that is, languages with subordinate clauses after main clauses and complements after heads (as English or Spanish); in contrast, the right edge is not necessarily so aligned. The reverse is true in left recursive languages, that is, in languages with subordinate clauses before main clauses and complements before heads (as Turkish or Japanese): In such languages, the right edges of the two constituents are necessarily aligned, but not the left edges (Nespor and Vogel 1986).

For example, the sentence [*John*] [*bought*] [*some nice land*] contains three phonological phrases, as indicated by the brackets (for a technical definition of phonological phrases, see Nespor and Vogel 1986). In all three cases, the left edge of the phonological phrase is aligned with the left edge of a syntactic phrase: the subject noun phrase, the verb phrase and the object noun phrase. In the first and third phonological phrase, the right edge is also aligned with the corresponding syntactic phrases, but in the second phonological phrase, it is not: the syntactic phrase does not end after the verb. The opposite is true in a Turkish phrase, such as [*Mehmet*] [*cam*] [*kIrdI*] (Mehmet–window–broke) 'Mehmet broke a window'. In the two noun phrases, both edges are aligned with the edges of a phonological phrase. Not so for the verb phrase, where only the right edge is aligned. The left edge is not the beginning of the verb phrase, which also includes the object *cam*.

It thus appears that although there is not necessarily a one-to-one correspondence between the constituents of the two hierarchies, at least one of the edges of the two must coincide. This capacity of edges to mediate between different hierarchies and levels of representation is a surprisingly powerful notion for an operation as simple as edges. Indeed, hierarchical processing has long been thought to be a fundamental property of human (and presumably other animals') cognition (e.g., Fodor 1983; Gallistel 1990; Gallistel 2000; Marr 1982; Marr and Nishihara 1992); this gives rise to the need for mechanisms through which different levels of representation can be matched to each other. If different hierarchies independently define their edges, the edges may in some cases be the common currency through which these hierarchies can be coordinated (McCarthy and Prince 1993; Nespor and Vogel 1986).

In sum, many Artificial Grammar Learning experiments can be explained by two simple mechanisms: a mechanism sensitive to identity relations, and another one attending specifically to edges. Both mechanisms seem to be shared by other animals: Non-human primates both are sensitive to positional codes (e.g., Orlov, Yakovlev, Hochstein and Zohary 2000) and generalize identity relations (e.g., Hauser, Weiss and Marcus 2002; Wallis Anderson and Miller 2001), a capacity that is shared even with honeybees (Giurfa, Zhang, Jenett, Menzel and Srinivasan 2001). Nevertheless, the language faculty seems to use such "perceptual primitives" extensively for its structural computations, which may shed some light on at least parts of its origins using purely synchronic investigations.

5   Conclusion

In this paper, we have presented two views on the specificity of language. While the currently more popular view is based on a diachronic perspective and compares the capacities of different animals, we have suggested that also synchronic observations may yield crucial insights. We have illustrated this approach first by considering a wide variety of experiments in Artificial Grammar Learning. We showed that much of this work can be explained by two simple "perceptual primitives" specifically tuned to certain salient patterns and configurations in the input: An operation sensitive to identity relations, and another operation specifically sensitive to edges. We then reviewed linguistic observations suggesting that the language faculty makes extensive use of these very same perceptual primitives. These primitives suggest a new way in which people may learn from their environment: In addition to ubiquitous statistical mechanisms, such Gestalt-like primitives may allow individuals to extract particular structures from the input. Both statistical computations and perceptual primitives may then interact and feed into more abstract computations; in this way, they may also contribute to learning parts of morphosyntax. On the basis of purely synchronic investigations we may thus have identified two psychological mechanisms that could be used by the language faculty (but were presumably present before language arose), namely, an operation sensitive to identity relations and one that is sensitive to edges. It may thus be possible to understand some linguistic computational principles by considering principles of perceptual organization.

References

Altmann, G.T., Dienes, Z. and Goode, A. 1995. "Modality independence of implicitly learned grammatical knowledge." *Journal of Experimental Psychlogy:l Learning, Memory and Cognition* 21 (4): 899–912.

Baker, M. 2005. "The innate endowment for language: Overspecified or underspecified?" In *The innate mind: Structure and contents*. P. Carruthers, S. Laurence and S. Stitch (eds.). Oxford: OUP.

Braine, M. 1963. "On learning the grammatical order of words." *Psychological Review* 70: 323–48.

Braine, M. 1966. "Learning the positions of words relative to a marker element." *Journal of Experimental Psychology* 72 (4): 532–40.

Brooks, L.R. and Vokey, J.R. 1991. "Abstract analogies and abstracted grammars: Comments on Reber" (1989) and Mathews *et al.* (1989). *Journal of Experimental Psychology General* 120 (3):316–23.

Bybee, J., Pagliuca W. and Perkins, R.D. 1990. "On the asymmetries in the affixation of grammatical material." *Studies in typology and diachrony*, William Croft (ed.), 1–42. Amsterdam: John Benjamins.

Chambers, K.E., Onishi, K.H. and Fisher, C. 2003. "Infants learn phonotactic regularities from brief auditory experience." *Cognition* 87 (2): B69–77.

Chomsky, N. and Miller, G. 1958. "Finite state languages." *Information and Control* 1: 91–112.

Chomsky, N. 1957. *Syntactic structures*. The Hague: Mouton.

Chomsky, N. 1959. "A review of B. F. Skinner's Verbal Behavior." *Language* 35: 26–58.

Cleeremans, A. and McClelland, J.L. 1991. "Learning the structure of event sequences." *Journal of Experimental Psychology General* 120 (3): 235–53.

Conrad, R. 1960. "Serial order intrusions in immediate memory." *British Journal of Psychologyl* 51: 45–8.

Cutler, A., Hawkins, J.A. and G. Gilligan 1985. "The suffixing preference: A processing explanation." *Linguistics* 23: 723–58.

Dienes, Z., Broadbent, D. and Berry, D. 1991. "Implicit and explicit knowledge bases in artificial grammar learning." *Journal of Expreimental Psychology: Learning, Memory and Cognition* 17 (5): 875–87.

Dryer, M.S. 2005. "Position of case affixes." In *World atlas of language structures*, M. Haspelmath, M.S. Dryer, D. Gil and B.Comrie (eds.) 210–13. Oxford: OUP.

Ebbinghaus, H. 1885/1913. "Memory: A contribution to experimental psychology." New York, NY: Teachers College, Columbia University. (http://psychclassics.yorku.ca/Ebbinghaus/)

Endress, A.D., Scholl, B.J. and Mehler, J. 2005. "The role of salience in the extraction of algebraic rules." *Journal of Experimental Psychology General* 134 (3): 406–19.

Endress, A.D. and Bonatti, L.L. 2007. "Rapid learning of syllable classesfrom a perceptually continuous speech stream." *Cognition* 105 (2): 247-99.

Endress, A.D. and Mehler, J. Under review. "Perceptual constraints in phonotactic learning." *Psychological Science.*

Endress, A.D., Dehaene-Lambertz, G. and Mehler, J. Under review. "Perceptual constraints and the learnability of simple grammars." *Cognition.*

Fiser, J. and Aslin, R.N. 2002. "Statistical learning of higher-order temporal structure from visual shape-sequences." *Journal of Experimental Psychology: Learning, Memory and Cognition* 28 (3): 458–67

Fitch, W.T. and Hauser, M.D. 2004. "Computational constraints on syntactic processing in a nonhuman primate." *Science* 303: 377–80

Fodor, J.A. and Pylyshyn, Z.W. 1988. "Connectionism and cognitive architecture: a critical analysis". *Cognition* 28 (1–2): 3–71.

Fodor, J.A. 1983. *The modularity of mind*. Cambridge, MA: The MIT Press.

Friederici, A., Bahlmann, J., Heim, S., Schubotz, R., Anwander, A. 2005. "The brain differentiates human and non-human grammars." *PNAS* 103 (7), 2458–63.

Frisch, S.A., Pierrehumbert, J.B. and Broe, M.B. 2004. "Similarity avoidance and the OCP." *Nat Lang Ling Theory* 22 (1): 179–228.

Gallistel, C. 1990. *The organization of learning*. Cambridge, MA: The MIT Press.

Gallistel, C. 2000. "The replacement of general-purpose learning models with adaptively specialized learning modules." In *The cognitive neurosciences*, 2nd edn, M. Gazzaniga (ed.), 1179–91. Cambridge, MA: The MIT Press.

Gervain, J., Mehler, J. In preparation. "Ready for structure? The neonate brain's ability to detect linguistic structure."

Giurfa, M., Zhang, S., Jenett, A., Menzel, R. and Srinivasan, M.V. 2001. "The concepts of 'sameness' and 'difference' in an insect." *Nature* 410 (6831): 930–3.

Gleitman, L.R., Newport, E.L. and Gleitman, H. 1984. "The current status of the motherese hypothesis." *Journal of Child Language* 11: 43–79.

Gómez, R. and Gerken, L. 1999. "Artificial grammar learning by 1-year-olds leads to specific and abstract knowledge." *Cognition* 70: 109–35.

Gómez, R.L., Gerken, L. and Schvaneveldt, R. 2000. "The basis of transfer in artificial grammar learning." *Memory & Cognition* 28 (2): 253–63.

Gopnik, M. 1990. "Feature-blind grammar and dysphasia." *Nature* 344: 715.

Green, T. 1979. "The necessity of syntax markers: Two experiments with artificial languages." *Journal of Verbal Learning and Verbal Behavior* 18: 481–6.

Greenberg, J.H. 1957. *Essays in linguistics*. Chicago IL: University of Chicago Press.

Greenberg, J.H. 1963. "Some universals of grammar with particular reference to the order of meaningful elements." In *Universals of Language*, J.H. Greenberg (ed.), 92–6. Cambridge, MA: The MIT Press.

Halle, M. and J.R. Vergnaud 1987. *An Essay on Stress*. Cambridge, MA: The MIT Press.

Harris, Z. 1955. "From phoneme to morpheme." *Language* 31:190–222.

Hauser, M.D., Newport, E.L. and Aslin, R.N. 2001. "Segmentation of the speech stream in a nonhuman primate: Statistical learning in cotton-top tamarins." *Cognition* 78: B53-B64

Hauser, M.D., Chomsky, N. and Fitch, W.T. 2002. "The faculty of language: What is it, who has it, and how did it evolve?" *Science* 298 (5598):1569–79.

Hauser, M.D., Weiss, D. and Marcus, G. 2002. "Rule learning by cotton-top tamarins." *Cognition* 86 (1): B15–22.

Hawkins, J.A. and A. Cutler 1988 "Psycholinguistic factors in morphological asymmetry." In *Explaining Language Universals*, J.A. Hawkins (ed.), 280–317. Oxford: Blackwell.

Hayes, B. 1995 *Metrical stress theory: Principles and case studies*. Chicago, IL: University of Chicago Press.

Henson, R. 1998. "Short-term memory for serial order: The Start-End Model." *Cognitive Psychology* 36 (2): 73–137.

Henson, R. 1999. "Positional information in short-term memory: Relative or absolute?" *Memory & Cognition* 27 (5): 915–27.

Hicks, R., Hakes, D. and Young, R. 1966. "Generalization of serial position in rote serial learning." *Journal of Experimental Psychology* 71 (6): 916–7.

Hitch, G.J., Burgess, N., Towse, J.N. and Culpin, V. 1996. "Temporal grouping effects in immediate recall: A working memory analysis." *Quarterly Journal of Experimental Psychology* 49A (1): 116–39.

Hochmann, J-R, Azadpour, M. and Mehler, J. Submitted. "Specific language abilities lost in a methodological labyrinth." *Science*.

Kager, R 1995. "Consequences of Catalexis." In *Leiden in last: HIL phonology papers I*, H. van der Hulst and J. van de Weijer (eds.), 269–98. The Hague: HAG.

Kinder, A. 2000. "The knowledge acquired during artificial grammar learning: Testing the predictions of two connectionist models." *Psychological Research* 63 (2): 95–105.

Kinder, A. and Assmann, A. 2000. "Learning artificial grammars: No evidence for the acquisition of rules." *Memory & Cognition* 28 (8): 1321–32.

Knowlton, B.J. and Squire, L.R. 1996. "Artificial grammar learning depends on implicit acquisition of both abstract and exemplar-specific information." *Journal of Experimental Psychology: Learning, Memory and Cognition* 22 (1): 169–81.

Lenneberg, E. 1967. *The biological foundations of language*. New York, NY: Wiley.

Marcus, G.F., Vijayan, S., Rao, S.B. and Vishton, P. 1999. "Rule learning by seven-month-old infants." *Science* 283 (5398): 77–80.

Marr, D. and Nishihara, H.K. 1992. "Visual information processing: Artificial intelligence and the sensorium of sight." In *Frontiers in cognitive neuroscience*, S.M. Kosslyn and RA. Andersen (eds.), 165–86. Cambridge, MA: The MIT Press. (Reprinted from *Technology Review* 81: 2–23 (1978))

Marr, D. 1982. *Vision*. San Francisco, CA: W.H. Freeman and Company

McCarthy, J.J. and Prince, A. 1993. "Generalized alignment." In *Yearbook of morphology 1993*, G. Booij and J. van Marle (eds.), 79–153. Dordrecht: Kluwer.

McCarthy, J.J. and Prince, A.S. 1999. "Faithfulness and identity in prosodic morphology." In *The prosody morphology interface* R. Kager, H. van der Hulst and W. Zonneveld (eds.), 218–309. Cambridge: CUP.

Meulemans, T. and van der Linden, M. 1997. "Associative chunk strength in artificial grammar learning." *Journal of Experimental Psychology: Learning, Memory and Cognition* 23 (4): 1007–28.

Moravcsik, E. 1978. "Reduplicative constructions." In *Universals of human language: Word structure*, J.H. Greenberg (ed.), 3: 297–334. Stanford, CA: Stanford University Press.

Morgan, J.L. and Newport, E.L. 1981. "The role of constituent structure in the induction of an artificial language." *Journal of Verbal Learning and Verbal Behavior* 20: 67–85.

Morgan, J.L., Meier, R.P. and Newport, E.L. 1987. "Structural packaging in the input to language learning." *Cognitive Psychology* 19: 498–550.

Mori, K. and Moeser, S.D. 1983. "The role of syntactic markers and semantic referents in learning an artificial language." *Journal of Verbal Learning and Verbal Behavior* 22: 701–18.

Nespor, M. and I. Vogel. 1986. *Prosodic phonology*. Dordrecht: Foris.

Newport, E.L. and Aslin, R. N. 2004. "Learning at a distance: I. Statistical learning of non-adjacent dependencies." *Cognitive Psychology* 48: 127–62.

Ng, H.L. and Maybery, M.T. 2002. "Grouping in short-term verbal memory: Is position coded temporally?" *Quarterly Journal of Experimental Psychology: Section A* 55 (2): 391–424.

Onishi, K. H., Chambers, K. E. and Fisher, C. 2002. "Learning phonotactic constraints from brief auditory experience." *Cognition* 83 (1): B13–23.

Orlov, T., Yakovlev, V., Hochstein, S. and Zohary, E. 2000. "Macaque monkeys categorize images by their ordinal number." *Nature* 404 (6773): 77–80.

Peña, M., Bonatti, L.L., Nespor, M. and Mehler, J. 2002. "Signal-driven computations in speech processing." *Science* 298 (5593): 604–7.

Peña, M., Maki, A., Kovacic, D., Dehaene-Lambertz, G., Koizumi, H., Bouquet, F., Mehler, J. 2002. "Sounds and silence: An optical topography study of language recognition at birth." *PNAS* 100 (20): 11702–5.

Premack, D. and Premack, A. 2003. *Original intelligence*. New York, NY: McGraw-Hill.

Reber, A.S. 1969. "Transfer of syntactic structure in synthetic languages." *Journal of Experimental Psychology* 8: 115–119.

Reber, A.S. 1967. "Implicit learning of artificial grammars." *Journal of Verbal Learning and Verbal Behavior* 6 (6): 855–63.

Saffran, J., Aslin, R. and Newport, E. 1996. "Statistical learning by 8-month- old infants." *Science* 274 (5294): 1926–8.

Saffran, J., Johnson, E., Aslin, R. and Newport, E. 1999. "Statistical learning of tone sequences by human infants and adults." *Cognition* 70 (1): 27–52.

Sapir, E. 1921 *Language: An introduction to the study of speech*. New York, NY: Harcourt, Brace.

Shannon, C.E. 1948. "A mathematical theory of communication." *Bell System Technical Journal* 27: 379–423, 623–56.

Shukla, M. In preparation. An interaction between prosody and statistics in segmenting fluent speech. PhD dissertation, SISSA, Trieste.

Smith, K. 1966. "Grammatical intrusions in the recall of structured letter pairs: Mediated transfer or position learning?" *Journal of Experimental Psychology* 72 (4): 580–8.

Smith, K. 1967. "Rule-governed intrusions in the free recall of structured letter pairs." *Journal of Experimental Psychology* 73 (1): 162–4.

Smith, K. 1969. "Learning co-occurrence restrictions: Rule learning or rote learning." *Journal of Verbal Learning and Verbal Behavior* 8: 319–21.

Soto-Faraco, S. 2000. "An auditory repetition deficit under low memory load." *Journal of Experimental Psychology: Human Perception and Performance* 26 (1): 264–78.

Toro, J.M. and Trobalón, J.B. 2005. "Statistical computations over a speech stream in a rodent." *Perception & Psychophysics* 67: 867–75.

Tunney, R. and Altmann, G.T. 2001. "Two modes of transfer in artificial grammar learning." *Journal of Experimental Psychology: Learning, Memory and Cognition* 27 (3): 614–39.

Valian, V. and Levitt, A. 1996. "Prosody and adults' learning of syntactic structure." *Journal of Memory and Language* 35: 497–516.

Valian, V. and Seana, C. 1988. "Anchor points in language learning: The role of marker frequency." *Journal of Memory and Language* 27: 71–86.

Vargha-Khadem, F., Watkins, K., Alcock, K., Fletcher, P. and Passingham, R. 1995. "Praxic and nonverbal cognitive deficits in a large family with a genetically transmitted speech and language disorder." *Proceedings of the National Academy of Sciences* 92: 930–3.

Wallis, J. Anderson, K. and Miller, E.K. 2001. "Single neurons in prefrontal cortex encode abstract rules." *Nature* 411 (6840): 953–6.

Wijnen, F., Kempen, M. and Gillis, S. 2001. "Root infinitives in Dutch early child language: An effect of input?" *Journal of Child Language* 28: 629–60.

Yang, C. 2002. "Universal Grammar, statistics or both?" *Trends in Cognitive Sciences* 8 (10): 451–6.

CHAPTER 9

The development of syntactic brain correlates during the first years of life

Angela D. Friederici and Regine Oberecker

1 Introduction

Language is a rule based system. Thus, when acquiring a language, the child has to extract from the speech input the relevant rules which constitute linguistic knowledge. Due to the fact that the linguistic input children receive does not consist of single word utterances, the child needs to learn to segment out the words and extract rules from fluent speech in order to build up a vocabulary and acquire a language. Word segmentation for example seems to develop in the second half of the first year. Jusczyk and Aslin (1995) showed that 7.5-month-old English-speaking children are already able to segment monosyllabic words from fluent speech whereas 6-month-olds are not able to do so. Within the domain of rule extraction, infants as young as 8 months have been shown to keep track of transitional probabilities in the auditory input (Aslin, Saffran and Newport 1998; Saffran, Aslin and Newport 1996; Yang 2004). There is an ongoing debate about whether the child uses mechanisms reflecting statistical learning, or symbol manipulation to achieve this and about how such mechanisms change with development (for a review see Gomez and Gerken 2000; Aslin et al. 1998; Gomez and Gerken 1999; Marcus, Vijayan, Rao and Vishton 1999; Saffran et al. 1996; Saffran, Johnson, Aslin and Newport 1999). Around the same age, i.e. 7-months, infants are able to distinguish a simple three word ABA grammar from an ABB grammar in which the A category words are + voiced and B category words are – voiced (Marcus et al. 1999). As the test ‚sentences‘ consisted of novel words in this study, this finding cannot be explained by the processing of transitional probabilities for words, but must be interpreted as reflecting the ability to extract and generalize abstract rules that represent the relationship between categories. By the age of 12 months infants are able to differentiate more complex artificial grammars, which require abstraction beyond the ordering of specific words (Gomez and Gerken 1999). Santelmann and

Jusczyk (1998) investigated morphosyntactic dependencies in 15- and 18-month-old children. In this study children were exposed either to a well-formed English combination of the auxiliary verb *is* and a verb with the *-ing* ending, or to a control condition consisting of an ungrammatical dependency between the modal auxiliary *can* and the *–ing* ending. The results of this study revealed that 18-month-olds are able to track non-adjacent dependencies in English (e.g. *is –ing* across the root of the main verb) whereas 15-month-old children are not sensitive to these basic relationships; see also Gomez (2002) for a similar result. Höhle, Schmitz, Santelmann, and Weissenborn (2006) have investigated the children's ability to process discontinuous dependencies in German. They found that the 18-month-olds' ability to do so depends on the distance between the crucial elements and moreover on the ease with which the intervening material can be analyzed. This result argues for the notion that infants initially recognize discontinuous relations only when they are reducible to local ones based on the transparency of the intervening material. Behavioural studies also revealed that English-speaking children between 18 and 24 months can already identify subjects and objects in sentences (Hirsh-Pasek and Golinkoff 1996). German-learning children at about the same age, e.g., 20 months, are able to recognize the relation between the presence of a complementizer introducing a finite subordinate clause, and the resulting obligatory sentence final position of the finite verb (Weissenborn, Höhle, Kiefer and Cavar 1998). Thus, it appears that by the end of the second year of life children have acquired the basic syntactic regularities of their mother tongue.

Although there is no doubt about the fact that children acquire the basic syntactic regularities of spoken language early during development, the way children fulfil this task is still a mystery. Within the last years, the hypothesis that one crucial cue for syntax development may lie in the domain of phonology has become more and more popular. Children acquire the phonologic and prosodic regularities of their native language, which are helpful for the maturation of syntactic information, within early stages of language development (e.g., Christiansen and Dale 2001; Gleitman and Wanner 1982; Weissenborn and Höhle 2001). Furthermore, the fact that even newborns are able to distinguish their native language from a foreign language containing a different sentence melody (Mehler, Jusczyk, Lambertz, Halsted, Bertoncini and Amiel-Tison 1988; Nazzi, Floccia and Bertoncini 1998; Ramus, Hauser, Miller, Morris and Mehler 2000; Gleitman and Wanner 1982) strengthens the view that the prosodic aspects of a language play a substantial role during language acquisition. Prosody is a fundamental key to the segmentation of an endless stream of sounds into phrases. Language-specific phonotactic and stress patterns signal word boundaries and therefore permit further segmentation of the incoming stream into single words (Jusczyk, Cutler and Redanz 1993; Friederici and Wessels 1993). Mattys and Jusczyk (2001) for example showed that

9-month-old children already use these probabilistic phonotactic cues to segment words from fluent speech. At the phrasal level it has further been shown that 8- and 9-month-old infants are able to recognize syntactic phrases based on prosodic information (Hirsh-Pasek, Kemler Nelson, Jusczyk, Cassidy, Druss and Kennedy 1987; Jusczyk, Pisoni and Mullennix 1992). In addition to these behavioural findings recent studies using neurophysiological measures have considerably added to our knowledge about children's sensitivity to phonological and prosodic cues during early language development (for reviews see Kuhl 2004; Friederici 2005).

Overall, these studies suggest that distributional regularities, both with respect to local transitions as well as with respect to phonological parameters are used by the infant and young child to extract the underlying language-relevant rules from the received input. So far only a few neurophysiological studies investigating early syntactic development of natural languages have been published. These have either looked into local phrase structure building in German (Oberecker, Friedrich and Friederici 2005; Oberecker and Friederici 2006) or into morphosyntactic processes in English (Silva-Pereyra, Klarman, Lin and Kuhl 2005a; Silva-Pereyra, Rivera-Gaxiola and Kuhl 2005b). Local phrase structure building requires knowledge about major phrase types, such as determiner phrase, verb phrase, and prepositional phrase. It is conceivable that local phrase structure building is based on a mechanism which builds up local predictions. For example, when perceiving a determiner the probability that a noun follows is high (e.g. *the dog*), although an adjective-noun combination is also possible (e.g. *the small dog*). Morphosyntactic processes in turn depend on the knowledge of how phrases can be combined to build sentences. Depending on the morphosyntactic elements and/or word order in a particular language, the grammatical relations between constituents in a sentence can be worked out. The neurophysiological studies conducted in English (Silva-Pereyra *et al.* 2005a, 2005b) tested children's sensitivity to the relationship between a modal verb and the tense inflection (e.g. *will-ing* across the root of the verb).

We will first review event-related brain potential (ERP) studies of phrase structure processing conducted in German and morphosyntactic studies conducted in English between the ages of 3 and 11 years and then we present some recent studies on syntactic processing conducted with 2.0- and 2.8- year- old German children.

Before we provide this overview, however, syntax-related ERP effects observed in adult listeners need to be introduced so that they can serve as a basis for comparison with ERP patterns observed in children. Such comparison will reveal whether children show an adult-like syntactic competence and it will shed light on the issue of whether syntax development is continuous, or characterized by qualitatively different developmental stages. There are two main hypotheses regarding the mechanisms underlying language development: The discontinuity hypotheses states that the processes underlying the production and the comprehension of language differ between childhood and adulthood (Felix 1994) whereas the continuity hypothesis claims that these processes are qualitatively similar in children and adults but change in a quantitative manner over the course of development (Gleitman and Wanner 1982; Pinker 1984; Weissenborn, Goodluck and Roeper 1992). Behavioural studies have provided evidence supporting both these assumptions.

2   Phases of language processing in the adult

Within the domain of auditory language processing there are different ERP components that have been identified for the processing of phonologic, semantic, and syntactic processes in adults. Friederici (1995, 2002) proposes three syntax-related processing stages in a neurocognitive model. According to the model, in the first phase (100–300 ms) the syntactic structure is formed based on word category information. The second phase is characterized by morphosyntactic processes, in addition to semantic processes, ending in thematic role assignments (300–500 ms). In the third phase (500–1000 ms) all available information is integrated.

In adults, processes underlying the first phase are reflected in an early negativity in the ERP, distributed over left hemispheric anterior electrode positions (early left anterior negativity, ELAN). The ELAN is taken to reflect processes of early, fast and highly automatic word category detection and occurs for word category violations (Friederici, Pfeifer and Hahne 1993; Hahne and Friederici 1999). The ELAN-component was found for the processing of phrase structure violations in the visual and the auditory modalities in English (Neville, Nicol, Barss, Forster and Garrett 1991) and in German (Friederici, Pfeifer and Hahne 1993; Friederici, Hahne and Mecklinger 1996; Hahne and Friederici 1999; Hahne and Jescheniak 2001; Oberecker et al. 2005). Syntactic processes of the second phase are also reflected in a syntax-related negative ERP component. This left anterior negativity (LAN) appears between 300 and 500 ms and occurs for case marking errors (Coulson, King and Kutas 1998; Friederici and Frisch 2000) or for failure of subject-verb agreement (Gunter, Stowe and Mulder 1997; Münte, Matzke and Johannes 1997). Finally, during the third phase, the ELAN and LAN are followed by a late centro-parietally distributed positivity after 600 ms (P600). In this late stage, the system starts the processes of syntactic reanalyses — or a repair in case of a mismatch. The P600 occurs for example for the processing of phrase structure violations (Friederici, Hahne, Mecklinger 1996; Hahne, Eckstein and Friederici 2004; Oberecker, Friedrich, Friederici 2005), subjacency violations (Neville et al. 1991), and for non-preferred sentences (Osterhout and Holcomb 1992; 1993).

3   Processing of syntactic violations in children

While a lot of studies have described the processing abilities of adults, compara-
tively little is known about the processing of syntactic violations in children. There
are two sets of studies investigating the processing of syntactic violations in children. One set of studies focused on the processing of phrase structure violations in
German passive sentences in children between 6 and 13 years (Hahne, Eckstein and
Friederici 2004). The phrase structure violations were realized as a word category
error (e.g. *Das Eis wurde im gegessen. / The ice-cream was in-the eaten.*). For the
processing of these phrase structure violations, the results showed a biphasic ERP
pattern consisting of an ELAN and a P600 in children between 7 and 13 years of age,
even if the negativity observed in 7-to 10-year-old children was long lasting. In
6-year-old children only a late positivity was found for the processing of phrase
structure violations. Another set of studies investigated the processing of morphosyntactic violations in English-speaking children between 30 and 48 month of age
(Silva-Pereyra *et al.* 2005a, 2005b). In these latter studies, the morphosyntactic violation consisted of a tense violation (e.g. *my uncle will watching the movie*). These
morphosyntactic studies reported a late positivity for 3- and 4-year-old children and
a very late positivity for 30-month-olds. The findings of both studies suggest that the
processes reflected by the P600 are developed earlier than those reflected by the
ELAN. The late appearance of the ELAN in the German study may be due to the fact
that Hahne, Eckstein and Friederici (2004) used sentences in the passive mode.

4   The present study

Given the finding that automatic phrase structure building processes are not established for passive sentence constructions before the age of 7 years (Hahne, Eckstein
and Friederici 2004), we designed a study to test whether these abilities might exist
earlier for the processing of simple active sentences. Considering the two hypotheses
described above, qualitative changes would be compatible with a discontinuity view,
whereas quantitative changes could support the view of the continuity hypothesis of
language development (Gleitmann and Wanner 1982; Pinker 1984; Clahsen 1988;
Weissenborn, Goodluck and Roeper 1992). In order to investigate whether the neural implementation of syntactic procedures is established between 2 and 3 years of
age (at least for simple sentence structures) we conducted two ERP experiments using short active sentences (Oberecker, Friedrich, Friederici 2005; Oberecker and
Friederici 2006). The vocabularies we used were simple and child-appropriate in order to guarantee the children's comprehension. We created a corpus of 60 active sentences. Each sentence was realized in three conditions, i.e., two correct conditions

and one syntactically incorrect condition. Correct sentences contained a determiner-noun-verb structure (e.g. *Der Löwe brüllt/The lion roars (is roaring)*) or contained a full prepositional phrase following the subject noun. The latter were included as filler sentences (e.g. *Der Löwe im Zoo brüllt/The lion in the zoo roars (is roaring)*). Incorrect sentences contained a phrase structure violation (e.g. *Der Löwe im brüllt/ The lion in the roars (is roaring)*). The violation was realized as a word category error, i.e. the case marked preposition obligatorily required a noun or adjective-noun combination to follow whereas the actually presented verb was syntactically incorrect. Each condition (correct, incorrect, and filler) consisted of 60 sentences.

All sentences were spoken by a trained female speaker. In order to ensure that the verbs in each condition were balanced and that an equal pause prior to the critical verb was included in the spoken material, the incorrect sentences were derived from the correct filler sentences by splicing out the noun from the prepositional phrase. The correct condition with the article-noun-verb structure was also derived from the filler sentences, but by splicing out the entire prepositional phrase. The aim of using only one sentence to create the critical conditions was to make sure that the critical words were equal in their physical features. In order to guarantee that the splicing would not be impaired by coarticulation phenomena, and to ensure that the material was interesting to the children, all sentences were spoken in a modified child-directed way. That is, sentences were spoken slowly with long pauses in between each word (about 150 ms). The length of the critical verb was about 700 ms. All sentences were digitized at 22 kHz and 16 bit (mono). Lastly, three independent experts were asked to listen to the sentences and reported that they sounded normal.

We investigated two groups of children: 2.0-year-olds and 2.8-year-olds as well as adults using the same paradigm. The 2.0- and the 2.8-year-olds were recruited within the German Language Development Study. The adult participants were between 20 and 30 years of age. All of the participants were healthy and had no neurological or developmental abnormalities.

Before the experiment started, a screening test was conducted in order to check the children's hearing. During the experiment, the children were seated comfortably on their parent's lap in an EEG cabin. The parents were instructed not to speak. The children listened to the sentences that were presented via loudspeaker. While the adults had to focus on a red cross, children were watching a silent aquarium video on a small video-screen placed approximately one meter in front of them.

The video, which merely showed fish, was presented to prevent extreme eye movements. The whole experimental session was divided into two blocks, each containing 90 sentences. Each block lasted about eight minutes. A break was included between the blocks if necessary. Between each sentence, there was an inter-stimulus-interval of 3000 ms. In total, one complete experimental session took around 16 minutes.

5   Adult ERP pattern

The ERPs of adults showed a typical N1-P2 complex, correlated with auditory stimuli presentation. This complex appeared for the correct as well as the incorrect sentences. Furthermore, a more negative response to the incorrect than correct condition was observed over the left anterior brain regions. In later time windows, a positivity occurred during the processing of the incorrect sentences (see Figure 1).

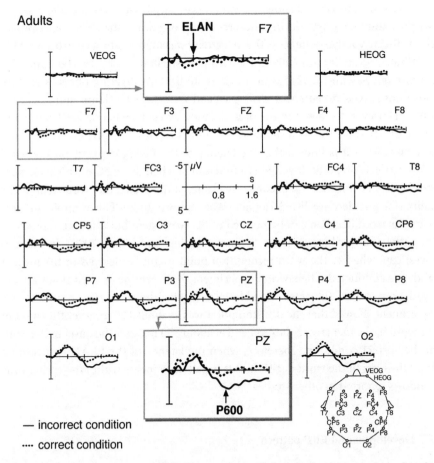

Figure 1. Grand average event-related brain potential of adults for the critical word in the syntactically correct (dotted line) and incorrect condition (solid line). The vertical line indicates the onset of the critical word. Negative voltage is plotted upwards. Modified from Oberecker *et al.* (2005).

Left anterior negativity. Between 300 to 500 ms, we observed a more negative response to the condition containing a phrase structure violation compared to the correct condition. This negativity was more pronounced over left anterior brain regions and was interpreted as an ELAN effect.

P600. In later time windows, from about 700 to 1500 ms, a positivity occurred for the processing of the incorrect condition compared to the correct one. This late positivity was distributed over centro-parietal brain regions and was interpreted as a P600 effect.

To summarize, adults showed a left anterior negativity between 300 and 500 ms post-stimulus onset during the processing of phrase structure violations in child-directed active sentences. This negativity was followed by a centro-parietally distributed positivity from 900 to 1500 ms post-stimulus onset. This biphasic ERP pattern agrees with the results of previous studies investigating phrase structure violations in passive sentences (Friederici and Wessels 1993; Hahne and Friederici 1999). However, the effect in the present study was somewhat delayed compared to the ELAN and P600 pattern that other studies reported involving phrase structure violations. It is known that the latency of the ELAN depends on the word category decision point. It varies as a function of when during the critical element word category information becomes available, in the prefix, the word stem or the suffix (for a review see Friederici and Weissenborn 2006). For example, in German, the word decision can be marked in the word stem but also in the prefix or the suffix of a word (see Friederici, Gunter, Hahne and Mauth 2004). In order to investigate whether the word recognition point might be delayed in the present study we conducted a behavioral experiment to determine at what point during word presentation subjects were able to recognize the word. The results of this experiment showed that the decision point was at about 190 ms after the onset of the word in the incorrect condition and at about 150 ms after the onset of the word in the correct condition. Therefore, when the latency of the ELAN is measured from the time of the word decision, this negativity appears within the earlier time windows reported in other studies.

6   Developmental ERP pattern

The ERPs of the 2.0- and 2.8-year-old children also revealed clear differences between the processing of the syntactically correct and incorrect sentences (see Figure 2 and 3). A left anterior negativity starting around 350 ms occurred for the processing of the incorrect condition compared to the correct condition in the 2.8-year-old children. Furthermore, in later time windows, the incorrect condition elicited a pronounced positivity over right centro-parietal brain regions. Two-year-olds demonstrated a late positivity, but no left anterior negativity. However, in both groups a very early positivity was observed for the correct condition.

6.1   Early positivity

The positive-negative pattern observed in the early time window is characteristic of young children. It generally represents an auditory evoked response (e.g., Friedrich and Friederici 2004; Morr, Shafer, Kreuzer and Kurtzberg 2002; Kurtzberg, Stone and Vaughan 1986; Kushnerenko, Ceponiene, Balan, Fellman, Huotilainen and Näätänen 2001; Mills, Coffey-Corina and Neville 1993; 1994). In contrast to other studies reporting this positive-negative pattern, however, it was more pronounced for the processing of incorrect than correct sentences in the present study/ies. There is one study also reporting an early positivity for syntactic violations in children. Silva-Pereyra *et al.* (2005a) found such a positivity in their investigation of morphosyntax. The authors argued that this positivity might be a child-specific counterpart of the expected LAN in adults, which normally occurs for morphosyntactic violations.

In the present studies the early positivity occurred not instead of another component but in addition to a LAN in the 2.8-year-olds. Unfortunately, we are not yet able to give a functional explanation of this early positivity but we are nevertheless able to show that the positivity not only occurs in the violating condition, but also in the filler condition containing a full prepositional phrase. More importantly, we show that the syntax-related components we found in children occur independently of this early positivity. Additional analyses of the data of the 2.0-year-old children indeed revealed that the early positivity occurred for the processing of the verb not only in the incorrect condition but also in the filler condition. Even though there were no differences between the incorrect and the correct filler conditions in early time windows, a late positivity was observed for the processing of the phrase structure violation in later time windows. Therefore, we argue that the early positivity is independent of the syntax-related ERP components and vice versa.

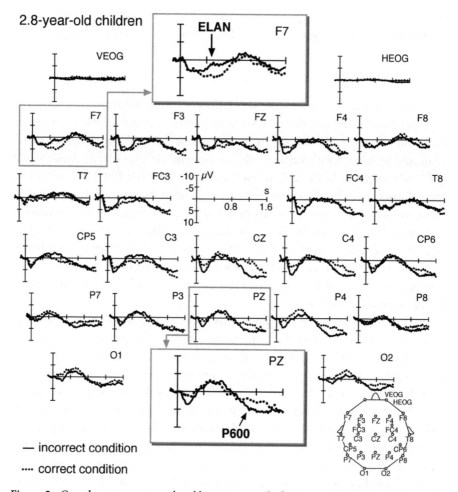

Figure 2. Grand average event-related brain potential of 2.8-year-old children for the critical word in the syntactically correct (dotted line) and incorrect condition (solid line). The vertical line indicates the onset of the critical word. Negative voltage is plotted upwards. Modified from Oberecker *et al.* (2005).

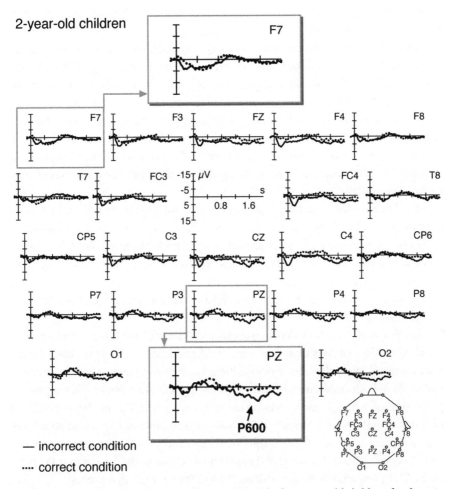

Figure 3. Grand average event-related brain potential of 2.0-year-old children for the critical word in the syntactically correct (dotted line) and incorrect condition (solid line). The vertical line indicates the onset of the critical word. Negative voltage is plotted upwards. Modified from Oberecker and Friederici, (2006).

6.2 Syntax-related components

Left anterior negativity. Following the early positivity, the 2.8-year-old children displayed a negativity in response to the incorrect condition compared to the correct condition. This negativity was distributed over left anterior brain regions and started at about 350 ms.

P600. In later time windows, the 2.0- and the 2.8-year-old children showed a late positivity for the processing of the incorrect condition. As it becomes clear from the figures, this positivity showed up later in the 2.0-year-old children compared to the 2.8-year-olds.

To summarize, in the present studies, we investigated on-line syntactic processes in 2.0- and 2.8-year-old children and in adults by means of ERPs. For the adults and the 2.8-year-old children we found clear differences between the processing of syntactically correct and incorrect sentences within early time windows in the form of an early left anterior negativity elicited by the incorrect condition. This component peaked earlier in adults (ca. 400 ms) than in children (ca. 513 ms). As the word category decision point in the present sentence material was between 150–190 ms this left anterior negativity in the adults was interpreted as an ELAN component.

The left anterior negativity found in the 2.8-year-olds occurred about 130 ms later than the ELAN observed in the adults. There is evidence that the latency of components decrease with age (Hahne, Eckstein, and Friederici 2004). Because of this and because of the fact that the ELAN represents the stage of initial structure-building based on word category information (Friederici 2002), the left anterior negativity in children can be seen as a child-specific equivalent to the ELAN we found in adults.

Furthermore, we found a P600 in adults and a late P600 in both 2.0- and 2.8-year-old children. This late positivity was interpreted as a child-specific P600. Even though it was delayed in children, we found a P600 for the processing of phrase structure violations in both children and adults. This component is known to show up for the processing of syntactic violations (Friederici, Pfeifer and Hahne 1993; Neville *et al.* 1991; Osterhout and Mobley 1995) and for non-preferred syntactic structures, such as garden-path sentences (Hagoort, Brown and Groothusen 1993; Osterhout and Holcomb 1993). The fact that 24-month-old children show a delayed P600 but no ELAN in response to phrase structure violations indicates that processes reflected by the P600 develop earlier than those reflected by the early left anterior negativity (ELAN) observed in the 2.8-year-olds. Although the 2.0-year-old children did not display an ELAN, the observed late P600 indicates that they can already differentiate between syntactically correct and syntactically incorrect sentences.

7   General Discussion

The developmental ERP pattern observed in the German studies of phrase structure building processes indicates a developmental shift between the age of 2.0 years and 2.8 years. In 2.0-year-old children, the observation of a (late) P600 suggests that principles of syntax —at least in the case of simple sentences— are established early during development. In adults, the P600 component is taken to reflect late controlled syntactic processes (Hahne and Friederici 1999) related to syntactic integration (Kaan, Harris, Gibson and Holcomb 2000). According to this interpretation the presence of a P600 effect in 2-year-olds would mean that late integration processes are already at work at this age even though highly automatic syntactic processes reflected in the ELAN are not yet effective. The biphasic ELAN-P600 pattern observed in 2.8-year-olds indicates that local phrase structure building processes are already established by that age in addition to late integration processes at least for the processing of simple active sentences. A similar developmental shift from a P600-only to a biphasic ELAN-P600 pattern was reported for the processing of phrase structure violations in passive sentences between the age of 6 and 7 years (Hahne, Eckstein. and Friederici 2004).

Similarly, in English ERP studies investigating morphosyntactic, i.e. tense, violations, a late positivity was observed in 3- and 4-year-olds, but no left anterior negativity (Silva-Pereyra et al. 2005a, 2005b). Given that no adult group was tested in these studies, we do not know whether the stimulus material used had a propensity to elicit a LAN component at all. In order to interpret the children's data, however, acquiring control adult data seems of crucial importance since not all ERP studies in English have shown a LAN component for the processing of morphosyntactic violations (for a review see Friederici and Weissenborn 2006). We have argued that this may be due to the fact that English is a weakly inflected language. With respect to our own findings in German 2.0-year-olds, the presence of the P600 indicates that they do possess knowledge of a particular phrase structure, in this case knowledge of the structure of prepositional phrases. The absence of the ELAN could mean either that the mechanism of using this knowledge to make strong predictions for the next incoming element (the mechanism of building up a template) is not yet established or that the mechanism of checking the input against the prediction in a fast template matching procedure is not yet at work.

What insight can these data give us with respect to the debate concerning the continuity or discontinuity of syntactic knowledge development? The continuity hypothesis states that universal grammar principles are present straight from the beginning whereas the discontinuity hypothesis claims that these principles change over time.

Even though a clear answer to this question does not follow from our data, the results indicate that the brain responses mature over time. These findings could be taken to support the discontinuity hypothesis. However, the brain responses of 2.0-year-olds are not entirely different from those of older children and adults. Rather than seeing qualitatively different ERP components at different ages we find one ERP component missing. But, in order to assess the absence of an ERP component as compared to categorically different ERP pattern, the question is whether it is possible that the processing of phrase structure violations can elicit an ERP pattern of a categorically different type? The answer is yes. In one other study we investigated 5-year-old children with specific language impairment (SLI) using the same stimulus material as in the studies with the 2.8- and 2.0-year-old children reported here. The results revealed an N400 modulation for the processing of phrase structure violations instead of the expected ELAN-P600 in the late time window pattern (Oberecker 2006). In addition, it has been shown that adults with cochlear implants show an N400 response when processing phrase structure violations (Wolf 2004). Given that the N400 is thought to reflect semantic integration difficulties (Kutas and Hillyard 1984), this finding suggests that cochlear implanted listeners process phrase structure violations in a qualitatively different manner. Moreover, second language learners also show a qualitatively different ERP pattern when processing phrase structure violations: They do not show a P600 in the late time window but a right anterior negativity between 500 and 1000 ms instead (Hahne and Friederici 2001).

In the context of these findings, the present results may be taken to indicate that syntactic rule knowledge does not change between 2.0 and 2.8 years, but that the processing mechanisms dealing with these rules become more and more automatic over the course of 8 months. This leads to the conclusion that the developmental shift is best described as a continuous maturation process rather than a qualitative change over time.

References

Aslin, R.N., Saffran, J.R. and Newport, E.L. 1998. "Computation of conditional probability statistics by 8 month-olds-infants." *Psychological Science* 9: 321–4.

Christiansen, M.H. and Dale, R.A.C. 2001. "Integrating distributional, prosodic and phonological information in a connectionist model of language acquisition." In *Proceedings of the 23rd Annual Conference of the Cognitive Science Society*, 220–5. Mahwah, NJ: Lawrence Erlbaum Associates.

Clahsen, H. 1988. *Normale und gestörte Kindersprache*. Amsterdam: John Benjamins.

Coulson, S., King, J. and Kutas, M. 1998. "Expect the unexpected: event-related brain response to morphosyntactic violations." *Language and Cognitive Processes* 13: 21–58.

Felix, S. 1994. "Maturational aspects of universal grammar." In *Interlanguage*, A. Davis, C. Criper and A. Howatt (eds.), 133–61. Edinburgh: EUP.

Friederici, A.D. 1995. "The time course of syntactic activation during language processing: A model based on neuropsychological and neurophysiological data." *Brain and Language* 50: 259–81.

Friederici, A.D. 2002 "Towards a neural basis of auditory sentence processing." *Trends in Cognitive Sciences* 6: 78–84.

Friederici, A.D. 2005. "Neurophysiological markers of early language acquisition: From syllables to sentences." *Trends in Cognitive Sciences* 9: 481–8.

Friederici, A.D. and Frisch, S. 2000. "Verb-argument structure processing: The role of verb-specific and argument-specific information." *Journal of Memory and Language* 42: 476–507.

Friederici, A.D., Gunter, T.C., Hahne, A. and Mauth, K. 2004. "The relative timing of syntactic and semantic processes in sentence comprehension." *NeuroReport* 15: 165–9.

Friederici A.D., Hahne A., Mecklinger A. 1996. "The temporal structure of syntactic parsing: Early and late event-related brain potential effects elicited by syntactic anomalies." *Journal of Experimental Psychology: Learning, Memory and Cognition* 22: 1219–48.

Friederici, A.D., Pfeifer, E. and Hahne, A. 1993. "Event-related brain potentials during natural speech processing: Effects of semantic, morphological and syntactic violations." *Cognitive Brain Research* 1: 183–92.

Friederici, A.D. and Weissenborn, J. 2007. "Mapping sentence form onto meaning: The syntax-semantic interface." *Brain Research* 46: 50–8.

Friederici, A.D. and Wessels, J.M.I. 1993. "Phonotactic knowledge of word boundaries ant its use in infant speech perception." *Perception & Psychophysics* 54: 287–95.

Friedrich, M. and Friederici, A.D. 2004. "N400-like semantic incongruity effect in 19-months-old infants: Processing known words in picture contexts." *Journal of Cognitive Neuroscience* 16: 1465–77.

Gleitmann, L. and Wanner, E. 1982. "Language acquisition: The state of the art." In *Language acquisition: The state of the art*, E. Wanner and L. Gleitman (eds.), 3–48. New York, NY: CUP.

Gunter, T.C., Stowe, L.A. and Mulder, G. 1997. "When syntax meets semantics." *Psychophysiology* 34: 660–76.

Gomez, R.L. 2002. "Variability and detection of invariant structure." *Psychological Science* 13: 431–6.

Gomez, R.L. and Gerken, L.A. 1999. "Artificial grammar learning by one-year-olds leads to specific and abstract knowledge." *Cognition* 70: 109–35.

Gomez, R.L. and Gerken, L.A. 2000. "Infant artificial language learning and language acquisition." *Trends in Cognitive Sciences* 4: 178–86.

Hagoort, P., Brown, C. and Groothusen, J. 1993. "The syntactic positive shift (SPS) as an ERP measure of syntactic processing." *Language & Cognitive Processes* 8: 439–83.

Hahne, A. and Friederici, A.D. 1999. "Electrophysiological evidence for two steps in syntactic analysis: Early automatic and late controlled processes." *Journal of Cognitive Neuroscience* 11: 194–205.

Hahne, A. and Friederici, A.D. 2001. "Processing a second language: Late learners' comprehension strategies as revealed by event-related brain potentials." *Bilingualism: Language and Cognition* 4: 123–41.

Hahne, A. and Jescheniak, J.D. 2001. "What´s left if the Jabberwock gets the semantics?" An ERP investigation into semantic and syntactic processes during auditory sentence comprehension. *Cognitive Brain Research* 11: 199–212.

Hahne, A., Eckstein, K. and Friederici, A.D. 2004. "Brain signatures of syntactic and semantic processes during children's language development." *Journal of Cognitive Neuroscience* 16: 1302–18.

Hirsh-Pasek, K. and Golinkoff, R.M. 1996. *The origins of grammar. Evidence from early language comprehension*. Cambridge, MA: The MIT Press.

Hirsh-Pasek, K., Kemler Nelson, D.G., Jusczyk, P.W., Cassidy, K.W., Druss, B. and Kennedy, L. 1987. "Clauses are perceptual units for young infants." *Cognition* 26: 269–86.

Höhle, B., Schmitz, M., Santelmann, L.M. and Weissenborn, J. 2006. "The recognition of discontinuous verbal dependencies by German 19-month-olds: Evidence for lexical and structural influences on children's early processing capacities." *Language and Language Development* 2: 277–300.

Jusczyk, P.W., Pisoni, D.B. and Mullennix, J. 1992. "Some consequences of stimulus variability on speech processing by 2-month-old infants." *Cognition* 43: 253–91.

Jusczyk, P.W. and Aslin, R.N. 1995. "Infants' detection of sound patterns of words in fluent speech." *Cognitive Psychology* 29: 1–23.

Jusczyk, P.W., Cutler, A. and Redanz, N.H. 1993: "Infants preference for the predominant stress patterns of English words." *Child Development* 64: 675–87.

Kaan, E., Harris, A., Gibson, E. and Holcomb, P. 2000. "The P600 as an index of syntactic integration difficulty." *Language and Cognitive Processes* 15: 159–201.

Kuhl, P. 2004. "Early language acquisition: Cracking the speech code." *Nature Reviews Neuroscience* 5: 831–43.

Kurtzberg, D., Stone, C.L. and Vaughan, H.G., Jr. 1986. "Cortical responses to speech sounds in the infant." In *Frontiers of clinical neuroscience*, Vol. 3 *Evoked potentials*, R. Cracco and I. Bodis-Wollner (eds.), 513–20. New York, NY: Alan R. Liss.

Kushnerenko, E., Ceponiene, R., Balan, P., Fellman, V., Huotilainen, M. and Näätänen, R. 2001. "Maturation of the auditory event-related potentials during the first year of life." *NeuroReport*13: 47–51.

Kutas, M. and Hillyard, S.A. 1984. "Brain potentials during reading reflect word expectancy and semantic association." *Nature* 307: 161–3.

Marcus, G.F., Vijayan, S, Rao, S.B. and Vishton, P.M. 1999. "Rule learning by 7-month-old infants." *Science* 283: 77–80.

Mattys S.L. and Jusczyk P.W. 2001. "Phonotactic cues for segmentation of fluent speech by infants." *Cognition* 78: 91–121.

Mehler, J., Jusczyk, P., Lambertz, G., Halsted, N., Bertoncini, J. and Amiel-Tison, C. 1988. "A precursor of language acquisition in young infants." *Cognition* 29: 143–78.

Mills, D.L., Coffey-Corina, S.A. and Neville, H.J. 1993. "Language acquisition and cerebral specialization in 20-month-old infants." *Journal of Cognitive Neuroscience* 5: 317–34.

Mills, D.L., Coffey-Corina, S.A. and Neville, H.J. 1994. "Variability in cerebral organization during primary language acquisition." In *Human behavior and the developing brain*, G. Dawson and K.W. Fischer (eds.), 427–55. New York, NY: Guilford Press.

Morr, M.L., Shafer, V.L., Kreuzer, J. and Kurtzberg, D. 2002. "Maturation of mismatch negativity in infants and pre-school children." *Ear and Hearing* 23: 118–36.

Münte, T.F., Matzke, M. and Johannes, S. 1997. "Brain activity associated with syntactic incongruencies in words and pseudo-words." *Journal of Cognitive Brain Sciences* 9: 318–29.

Nazzi, T., Floccia, C. and Bertoncini, J. 1998. "Discrimination of pitch contours by neonates." *Infant Behavior and Development* 21: 779–84.

Neville, H.J., Nicol, J., Barss, A., Forster, K. and Garrett, M.F. 1991. "Syntactically based sentence processing in language-impaired children." *Journal of Cognitive Neuroscience* 5: 235–53.

Oberecker, R. 2006. "Grammatikverarbeitung im Kindesalter: EKP Studien zum auditorischen Satzverstehen." PhD dissertation, University of Potsdam.

Oberecker, R. and Friederici, A.D. 2006. "Syntactic ERP components in 24-month-olds' sentence comprehension." *NeuroReport* 17: 1017–21.

Oberecker, R, Friedrich, M, Friederici, A.D. 2005. "Neural correlates of syntactic processing in two-year-olds." *Journal of Cognitive Neuroscience* 17: 407–21.

Osterhout, L. and Holcomb, P.J. 1992. "Event-related brain potentials elicited by syntactic anomaly." *Journal of Memory and Language* 31: 785–806.

Osterhout, L. and Holcomb, P.J. 1993. "Event-related potentials and syntactic anomaly: Evidence of anomaly detection during the perception of continuous speech." *Language and Cognitive Processes* 8: 413–37.

Osterhout, L. and Mobley, L.A. 1995. "Event-related brain potentials elicited by failure to agree." *Journal of Memory & Language* 34: 739–73.

Pinker, S. 1984. *Language learnability and language development*. Cambridge, MA: Harvard University Press.

Ramus, F., Hauser, M.D., Miller, C., Morris, D. and Mehler, J. 2000 "Language discrimination by human newborns and by cotton-top tamarin monkeys." *Science* 288: 340–51.

Saffran, J.R., Aslin, R.N. and Newport, E.L. 1996. "Statistical learning by eight-month-old-infants." *Science* 274: 1926–8.

Saffran, J.R., Johnson, E.K., Aslin, R.N. and Newport, E.L. 1999. "Statistical learning of tonal structure by adults and infants." *Cognition* 70: 27–52.

Santelmann, L.M. and Jusczyk, P.W. 1998. "Sensitivity to discontinuous dependencies in language learners: Evidence for limitations in processing space." *Cognition* 69: 105–34.

Silva-Pereyra J.F, Klarman L, Lin L.J., Kuhl P.K. 2005a. "Sentence processing in 30-month-old children: an event-related potential study." *NeuroReport* 16: 645–8.

Silva-Pereyra J.F., Rivera-Gaxiola M, Kuhl P.K. 2005b "An event-related brain potential study of sentence comprehension in preschoolers: Semantic and morphosyntactic processing." *Cognitive Brain Research* 23: 247–58.

Weissenborn, J., Goodluck, H. and Roeper, T. 1992. *Theoretical issues in language acquisition. Continuity and change in development*. Hillsdale, NJ: Lawrence Erlbaum Associates.

Weissenborn, J., Höhle, B., Kiefer, D. and Cavar, D. 1998. "Children's sensitivity to word-order violations in German: Evidence for very early parameter-setting." In *Proceedings of the 22 Annual Boston Conference on Language Development*, A.Greenhill, M.Hughes, H.Littlefield and H. Walsh (eds.), 2: 756–67, Somerville, MA: Cascadilla.

Weissenborn, J. and Höhle, B. (eds.) 2001. *Approaches to bootstrapping: Phonological, lexical, syntactic, and neurophysiological aspects of early language acquisition*, Vols. I, II. Amsterdam: John Benjamins.

Wolf, A. 2004. "Sprachverstehen mit Cochlea-Implantat: EKP-Studien mit postlingual ertaubten erwachsenen CI-Trägern." PhD dissertation, Max-Planck-Institut für Kognitions- und Neurowissenschaften, Leipzig.

Yang, C.D. 2004. "Universal grammar, statistics or both?" *Trends in Cognitive Sciences* 8: 451–56.

CHAPTER 10

Language acquisition and ERP approaches

Prospects and challenges

David Poeppel and Akira Omaki

1 Interdisciplinary preliminaries

Developmental cognitive neuroscience is a vibrant and growing domain of research, and various aspects of human psychological experience are being investigated using techniques that bridge developmental psychology, developmental biology, the cognitive sciences, and non-invasive neurobiological techniques. Ranging from the growth of perceptual expertise to ontogenetic change in decision making, practically every part of human perception and cognition is being evaluated – and reevaluated – from a developmental perspective enriched by neurobiological methodologies (Nelson and Luciana 2001; Johnson 2005).

Rapidly expanding scientific fields offer grounds for optimism but also cause for healthy skepticism, and before we go on to discuss the important progress made in current work on the developmental cognitive neuroscience of language, we feel compelled to remind ourselves as well as the reader that the intellectual challenges remain daunting. For example, the general excitement and implicit promise of the new integrative approaches notwithstanding, it is worth considering some basic assumptions that, in our view, tend to remain unexpressed in the field. In particular, we take it to be a reasonable presupposition that a developmental cognitive neuroscience study will enrich our understanding of *either* how development works, *or* how cognition works, *or* how the brain works. This desideratum may sound innocent enough, but if we subject numerous cognitive neuroscience studies to this straightforward standard, the analysis can be sobering: a surprisingly large number of studies (in any branch of the cognitive neurosciences) do not, at least in any obvious way, contribute either to a deeper understanding of human cognition or human brain function. Rather, much work is at best correlative (which is, of course, not without value, but presumably not the ultimate goal) and occasionally even *sui generis*, not linking to either the cognitive or the brain sciences.

It goes without saying that the problems under investigation are quite difficult indeed, and it constitutes a formidable challenge to generate meaningful accounts that link a deeper understanding of the human language faculty with biological data. In part this difficulty stems from the strikingly different ontological commitments made by the different disciplines (or, more colloquially, the 'parts lists'). As discussed by Poeppel and Embick (2005), the fields of inquiry focused on language operate over such 'elementary representations and computations' as distinctive features, syllables, morphemes, noun phrases, semantic composition, or syntactic displacement operations. The neurobiological sciences, on the other hand, build on primitives that include synapse, neuron, cortical column, oscillation, and so on. In trying to build substantive connections between these differing domains of inquiry, notably absent are the linking hypotheses that would allow us to state in explicit terms how these sets of putative primitives are related. The challenges associated with this aspect of interdisciplinary research were called the "granularity mismatch problem" and the "ontological incommensurability problem" to highlight how complex it is to relate biological and cognitive levels of analysis in a manner that is beyond merely correlative (Poeppel and Embick 2005). For example, highlighting in an imaging study that a brain area is activated for syntactic processing, while interesting, remains remarkably underspecified and entirely uninformative with respect to mechanism. 'Syntactic processing' and 'lexical access' and 'lexical semantics' are not elementary and simplex cognitive operations; similarly, brain areas on the scale of a centimeter (say Brodmann's area 45) are not elementary and simplex biological structures. Overall, it must therefore be our (interdisciplinary) goal to decompose the cognitive science aspect and the neurobiological aspect in such a way as to permit fruitful and workable linking hypotheses.

While we are skeptics in stance, we remain relentlessly optimistic about the promise of discovering deep principles of human development and cognition, and we turn now to the prospects of this important area of growth in psychological research. Can cognitive neuroscience engage some of the hard problems, say of the type, "What are the neuronal mechanisms that form the basis for the representation of and computation with linguistic primitives?" In our view, the area of language development – while not immune to the dangers inherent in interdisciplinary research – is well poised to make serious and satisfying progress. We hold this to be true because (i) the questions associated with language acquisition and development are well characterized theoretically and connect to an extensive behavioral and computational literature. (ii) There are few issues more pressing and riveting (both for basic and clinical research) than discovering how human development works and constrains human perceptual, cognitive, and affective experience. Therefore, a lot of exciting new research is enriching our knowledge of developmental mechanisms in ways that ERP, for example, can build on effectively. (iii) New techniques promise to yield unexpected insights into brain function throughout the lifespan; hemodynamic imaging and electrophysiology are increasingly adapted to record from developing brains and will provide new vistas onto ontogenetic change in childhood.

Looking at the field of language acquisition from a historical perspective, there have been a series of influential trends, and a useful summary is provided by Mehler and colleagues (this volume). Three trends that have been particularly consequential are (i) the acquisition of language-specific rules, an area of inquiry particularly prominent in the context of generative grammar, (ii) the acquisition of the phonetic inventory and the problem of word learning, areas of research at the interface of linguistics and cognitive psychology, and (iii) statistical learning approaches, research more squarely driven by experimental psychological concerns and methodologies. While these thrust areas have generated a tremendous amount of data on language development, they have remained largely insulated from neurobiological concerns. Despite some notable exceptions, the bulk of language acquisition research has been concerned with cognitive science, in the broadest sense – but not cognitive neuroscience. The chapters presented in the current volume represent an important new trend, namely bridging theoretically motivated questions in language development with new biologically based techniques that yield innovative measures of knowledge and performance.

Here we summarize and highlight some of the major observations outlined in the chapters (Section 2), discuss the methodological and conceptual challenges (Section 3), and make some specific recommendations to further strengthen the work on the developmental cognitive neuroscience of language (Section 4).

2   Highlights

The behavioral and electrophysiological studies reported in this volume contribute critical data to our understanding of the development of psycholinguistic processes as well as the neural activity that underlies these processes. In this section, we highlight some of the unique contributions reported in each chapter. This brief review forms the basis of the subsequent sections regarding the prospects and challenges for cognitive neuroscience research on language development.

Four areas of research receive special emphasis in the chapters, in part reflecting domains of acquisition in which ERP research can be argued to yield promising insights. (1) Acquisition of the phonetic inventory (Conboy chapter). (2) Word segmentation and recognition (Nazzi, Kooijman, Thierry, Sheehan, Conboy chapters). (3) Lexical and conceptual semantics in single word processing (Friedrich, Sheehan chapters). (4) Structural learning and processing (Conboy, Mehler, Friederici chapters). Table 1 summarizes the essential attributes of the chapters that contribute child ERP data and can serve as the basis for a 'conceptual meta-analysis.'

Table 1. Areas of child ERP research thematized: Sounds to sentences, 3 months to 48

Domain of Acquisition	Chapter	Tasks	Languages tested	Age (months)	Major ERP responses
Phonetic inventory	Conboy	– Passive listening (CV oddball paradigm)	English, Spanish	7	P150–250 or N250–550 (native & nonnative contrasts)
				11	N250–550 (native contrasts)
				20	N250–550 (native & nonnative contrasts)
Word segmentation/ recognition	Kooijman	– Passive listening (sentences containing familiarized word)	Dutch	7	Early frontal positivity (~ 350 ms) Left-lateralized negativity (~ 480 ms)
				10	Left-lateralized negativity (~ 350 ms)
	Thierry	– Passive listening (familiar and unfamiliar words in isolation)*	English	9/10/11 12	N2/N4 modulation (familiar-unfamiliar) No N2/N4 modulation
			Welsh	9/10/11/12	No N2/N4 modulation
			English-Welsh bilingual	11	N2/N4 modulation in English and Welsh
	Conboy; Sheehan	– Passive listening (known and unknown words in isolation)*	English-Spanish bilingual	19–22	N200–400 (known-unknown words)
		– Passive listening to (known and unknown words in isolation)*	English	13–17, 20	N200 and N350 (known-unknown words)

Domain of Acquisition	Chapter	Tasks	Languages tested	Age (months)	Major ERP responses
	Sheehan	– Passive listening (words, infant directed speech, IDS, vs. adult directed speech, ADS)	English	6	Larger N600–800 to familiar words in IDS
				13	Larger N600–800 to all words in IDS Larger N200–400 to familiar words in IDS
		– Passive listening (familiar, unfamiliar, backwards words)	English	3–4 6–8 9–11	Positivity to all types (175–550 ms) N200–500 (familiar-backwards) N200–500 (familiar & unfamiliar-backkw.)
	Friedrich	– Picture-word matching paradigm	German	12	Early negativity (congruous/incong. words)
				14, 19	Early negativity N400 (congruous/incong.)
Lexical semantics	Sheehan	– Picture-word matching paradigm	English	13/20/36	N400 (congruous/incong. words)
		– Word-pic. matching – Gesture-pic. matching	English	18 26	N400 word-pic & gesture-pic N400 word-pic only
	Conboy	– Passive listening to sentences	English	30/36/48	N400 to semantic anomaly P600 to morphosyntactic anomaly
Sentence structure	Friederici	– Passive listening to sentences	German	24 32.5	P600 to phrase structure violation P600 and ELAN

*   (Un)familiar and (un)known are used in specific differing ways in these studies. Known is used in the context of verifiable parental report; in contrast, familiar is used when the lexical item in question is a word typical of children's vocabulary but not necessarily attested.

2.1   The inventory of speech sounds

A highly productive area of language acquisition research deals with speech sound perception and acquisition. Numerous behavioral studies have established that infants in their first year transition from being 'universal listeners' – with the ability to distinguish all phonetic contrasts in natural languages – to language-specific listeners (Kuhl 2004). Infants' discrimination ability declines (differentially for vowels and consonants) throughout the first year and adjusts to the phonetic inventory of the target language (Jusczyk 1997; Kuhl 2004; Werker and Tees 1999).

ERP research reviewed by Conboy and colleagues (this volume) builds on this rich source of behavioral data and sheds light on the associated neural activity. Two striking aspects of their findings are that (i) infants at 11 months and 20 months still demonstrate neural sensitivity to non-native consonant contrasts (unlike what previous behavioral research has suggested), and (ii) a subgroup of infants show different electrophysiological responses at certain ages, and the developmental trajectory of these responses in the first year of life can be used as a predictor of later language development. In particular, ERP responses such as an early ($\sim$150–250 ms) positivity, the MMN, as well as extended negativities ($\sim$250–550 ms) appear to be robustly measurable during the first year of life and therefore can serve as non-invasive metrics of perceptual performance. More generally, such data indicate that neurophysiological responses may provide more sensitive measures that can uncover cognitive processes that are not observable in the context of behavioral paradigms. Consequently, subtle neurocognitive processes underlying the acquisition of the speech sounds inventory can be carefully characterized using a mixture of new neurophysiological and established behavioral approaches.

2.2   Segmenting the signal and finding words

A large body of work has been devoted to the basic question of the recognition of known words, and specifically of finding words in continuous speech, an essential step for constructing a lexicon for the target language (Jusczyk 1997). This task is necessarily quite challenging, since words are produced in isolation only occasionally (Woodward and Aslin 1990), and furthermore because it requires the learners to be able to access the phonetic details necessary to retrieve the associated semantic memory.

Nazzi and colleagues (this volume) investigate whether children learning different languages use language-specific word segmentation strategies. They hypothesize that learners' initial segmentation algorithm is based on 'primary,' rhythm-based attributes characteristic of the target language that provide cues for segmentation. They predict, therefore, that L1 learners of French, unlike those of

English, will principally use syllabic-based cues for word segmentation (versus stress-based cues typical of English rhythmicity). Their behavioral results, based on the head turn preference procedure, indicate that French 12-month-olds have a syllabic segmentation procedure, but 16-month-olds do not. However, the syllabic segmentation procedure may still be present in 16-month-olds, although masked by the use of other (now salient) segmentation cues (e.g., transitional probabilities, phonotactic information) available at this later developmental stage. Nazzi and colleagues argue, rightly, we think, that the sensitivity and temporal resolution of ERP might permit investigators to observe the early syllabic segmentation as well as the intermediate representations still available. The concurrent use of behavioral and ERP data might therefore illuminate the specific hypothesis that representations of a certain type (say, the syllable) are operative during processing at different ontogenetic stages, thereby providing a richer, more psycholinguistically specified, account of the U-shaped developmental function demonstrated by purely behavioral metrics.

Kooijman and colleagues (this volume) specifically address the problem of word segmentation in continuous speech (Jusczyk and Aslin 1995) as well as the comparability of behavioral studies and ERP studies addressing this question. Their ERP experiment adopts designs similar to previous behavioral studies. This strategy strikes us as eminently reasonable, insofar as it allows the ERP data to be interpreted in the context of theoretically motivated behavioral data. Indeed, these authors provide a thoughtful commentary on the methodological challenges associated with infant and child ERP studies (see Section 3.1 below for discussion). They show that in Dutch infants, the basis for word segmentation abilities already exists in 7-month and 10-month-olds (though they give slightly different responses). In contrast, the previous behavioral studies suggested that word segmentation abilities develop around 9 months (Houston, Jusczyk, Kuijpers, Coolen and Cutler 2000). These investigators also conducted a head turn preference experiment using a design maximally similar to that of their ERP experiment, and they still found that 7-month-olds do not demonstrate word segmentation abilities. This set of studies suggests, again, that ERP measures may be more sensitive to emerging cognitive processes in infants.

A series of studies by Thierry and Vihman (this volume), Sheehan and Mills (this volume), as well as Conboy and colleagues (this volume) examined word recognition and its underlying neural mechanisms in monolingual and bilingual children. Using the N200–400 response components elicited by the presentation of words, Sheehan and Mills tested a variety of factors that affect word recognition abilities in one- and two-year-olds (age, training, vocabulary size, ability to use phonetic details, and infant vs. adult directed speech). Bilingual studies conducted by these authors demonstrate that language experience significantly affects the process of vocabulary development. For example, the influence of social environment on language input plays a crucial role in vocabulary development (the case of monolingual Welsh-speaking children and English-Welsh bilingual children reported by Thierry and Vihman), and language dominance is characterized by early emergence of (adult-like) focalization of EEG responses to known and unknown words (Sheehan and Mills; Conboy and colleagues).

An important common feature across these studies is the consistent identification of an event-related negativity ranging approximately from 200–500 ms post onset of the critical item. This negative ERP is likely to be the precursor of the N400, although a thorough cross-sectional study on N400 morphology and timing has, to our knowledge, not been conducted. Therefore, we must remain open to the possibility that the negativity seen in infant and child parietal ERPs is not entirely congruent with the adult N400. This response directly sheds light on the development of neural mechanisms that support lexical access, which could not be investigated by behavioral measures alone. In other words, this offers an additional dependent measure that can be used to assess with great sensitivity how the development of lexical access and lexical representation unfolds in the developing child.

2.3   The meaning of words

Studies reviewed in Friedrich (this volume) as well as Sheehan and Mills (this volume) investigate the development of lexical semantics using a picture-word matching paradigm. In these types of experiments, the presentation of a picture is followed by a congruous or incongruous word. Friedrich reports two ERP components: an early lateral frontal negativity that apparently reflects facilitation of word form processing, and an N400 that reflects semantic integration processes. Friedrich finds that both of these components are present in German-speaking 14-month and 19-month-olds, whereas only the early negativity is elicited in 12-month-olds. Sheehan and Mills used a similar experimental procedure with English-speaking infants, and found that even 13-month-olds showed an N400-like effect, although it differed slightly in latency and duration from that reported for older children (20-month and 36-month-olds). It is thus not clear exactly when the N400 starts to emerge in infants' lexical processing, but these studies undoubtedly show that an N400-like response is robustly elicited sometime during the second year of life, a period which is characterized by rapid vocabulary growth. An important common theme across these studies, one that resonates with much current research in sentence processing, is the concept of *prediction* in language processing. What the studies show convincingly is that the presentation of prior information systematically constrains which lexical representations are suitable candidates for a given context. The idea that a speaker/hearer entertains a detailed and grammatically sophisticated current model that is used at every processing step (*analysis-by-synthesis*) is gaining acceptance in areas of research ranging from speech perception (Poeppel, Idsardi and van Wassenhove in press) to sentence processing (Phillips and Wagers 2007) and even to visual object recognition (Yuille and Kersten 2006).

2.4   Finding and processing structure in sentences

Past decades of linguistic research have established that natural language is characterized by a computational system that manipulates abstract linguistic representations (Chomsky 1957). Although this line of inquiry has proven to be productive, it naturally raises the following two questions. First, the characterization of linguistic knowledge forces a learnability question, as such abstract rules and representations are not directly observable in the input (Pinker 1984). This issue has led to proposals of innate constraints on the hypothesis space (Crain and Thornton 1998) as well as powerful (but sufficiently constrained) learning mechanisms that allow children to induce abstract generalizations (Elman 1993; Newport and Aslin 2000). While children are learning their native language(s), they must be able to analyze and internally represent the input to enable comprehension. This raises the second question: to what extent are children capable of computing such structural representations during development?

Mehler and colleagues (this volume) present a critical survey of the recent literature on artificial language learning, a field that has generated provocative debate about the nature of children's learning mechanisms. Although the discussions tend to focus on the comparison of learning performance by a (constrained) statistical learner (Newport and Aslin 2000; Saffran, Aslin and Newport 1996) and a rule-extraction/generalization learner (Marcus, Vijayan, Rao and Vishton 1999), Mehler and colleagues argue for the importance of an alternative perspective, namely, a 'perceptual' bootstrapping mechanism that is attuned to 'perceptual primitives': they propose an operation sensitive to identity relations and an operation that detects and uses the information at the edge of a given representational unit; both of these operations are argued to be used extensively by the language learner. These authors suggest that the interaction of statistical computations and those specific perceptual primitives can feed into mechanisms dealing with more abstract structures and lead eventually to learning the relevant abstract rules and representations.

Conboy and colleagues (this volume) as well as Friederici and Oberecker (this volume) explicitly investigate, using ERP, the sentence processing mechanisms testable in 2 to 4-year-old children. Conboy and colleagues show that English-speaking children as young as 30-months show adult-like N400 responses to semantically anomalous sentences and P600 responses to morphosyntactic anomalies. Friederici and Oberecker, in turn, use a version of phrase structure violation sentences that are widely studied in adult German ERP research (for a review, see Friederici 2002; Friederici and Weissenborn 2007). They observe that 32.5-month-olds show adult-like biphasic ELAN and P600 responses, whereas only the P600 is elicited in 24-month-olds. These findings indicate that children's parsers (and, by extension, grammars) are qualitatively the same as adults'. Indeed, these authors argue that the ERP data recorded in the context of sentence processing experiments in children are most consistent with a 'continuity' perspective on language development. If such arguments are on the right track, it would suggest that these neurobiological data can be used to adjudicate between theoretical alternatives about child development.

3   Prospects and challenges: The state of the art

3.1   The technological challenge

The main feature of the present volume concerns the technical advances seen in the use of EEG with language learners. At first glance, ERP offers the best of all possible worlds: its temporal resolution (msec) is appropriate to the phenomena under investigation. Whether in the study of speech perception (Conboy, this volume), lexical processing (Nazzi; Kooijman; Thierry and Vihman; Sheehan and Mills; Friedrich; all this volume), or sentence processing (Conboy; Friederici and Oberecker; this volume), the operations that underlie perceptual and linguistic computation are extremely fast, typically transient, and follow each other at rapid intervals (see, e.g. Friederici 2002 for review). ERP is well suited to capture the relevant processes. Moreover, the task requirements are suitable, permitting passive presentation, and requiring no overt tasks of infants and toddlers. We review below some methodological concerns inherent in the use of EEG measures with children, and discuss how one might make use of behavioral and EEG measures to contribute critical data.

3.1.1   *Fine time course measure and ERP components*
Multiple cognitive processes underlying language comprehension occur within a few hundred milliseconds of stimulus presentation, and a dependent measure that records responses within an appropriate time frame may capture some of the multi-level processes, such as speech perception, word recognition, or integration of the lexical item into a syntactic structure. For this reason, using a behavioral response alone it can be difficult to pinpoint which of these underlying subroutines are responsible for observed differences between conditions. Furthermore, since

standard reaction time measures are mediated by other motor responses such as eye movements or button pressing, the temporal precision of the underlying cognitive processes is rather poor. Recording of EEG, however, allows us to inspect directly the neural activity that underlies the target cognitive processes, and hence provides us with extremely good temporal precision. Moreover, different ERP components are often associated with distinct cognitive processes, and this can facilitate distinguishing which of the multiple processes that occur in parallel were affected by the experimental manipulation. The utility of a precise time course measure was highlighted by Nazzi and colleagues (this volume). Their hypothesis regarding whether 16-month-olds still have a syllabic-segmentation strategy crucially relies on evidence from the intermediate representation being built before the whole word is recognized, and it seems very reasonable to use ERP to investigate this fast, cascaded sub-processes of word recognition.

The polarity and topographic information derived from ERP components turns out to be very informative in child ERP research as well. Conboy and colleagues (this volume) report that differential ERP responses (either P150–250 or N250–550) to non-native phonetic contrasts in the first-year of life can be a predictor of later language development. Since the discrimination behavior is presumably attested in both P-responders and N-responders, the polarity information provided by ERP has the potential of disclosing properties of child language that were not observable in behavioral measures. With respect to the scalp distribution of ERP components, Sheehan and Mills (this volume) report a word learning experiment with 20-month olds, in which the infants were exposed to novel word-object associations. They found that the bilateral N200-N500 component that is elicited in response to familiar words becomes left-lateralized after further training, although this lateralization effect was observable only in children with relatively larger vocabulary size. This suggests that lexical processing becomes more specialized and lateralized towards the left hemisphere as children become much more efficient word learners. Cumulatively, these studies demonstrate how informative ERP responses can be with respect to the underlying cognitive processes that are not directly observable in behavioral measures such as looking time, head-turn preference, or high-amplitude sucking.

3.1.2 *Higher sensitivity of ERP responses to underlying cognitive processes*

Some researchers show that ERPs can reveal evidence of stimulus discrimination even when behavioral measures indicate otherwise. For example, ERP data indicate the presence of non-native phonetic contrast discrimination at a later age than previously thought (Conboy and colleagues) or an early emergence of word segmentation and recognition (Kooijman and colleagues; Thierry and Vihman), as reviewed in Section 2.

The precise reasons for such behavioral vs. ERP differences are not clear, but one possible factor is the temporal resolution discussed above: Since ERPs can directly tap into the early stages of processing, they can reveal processes that are later concealed by other cognitive operations (cf. Nazzi, this volume). Another possible factor is the difference in task demands and cognitive load: Most of the behavioral measures are attention-dependent, namely, children must pay sufficient attention to the linguistic or visual stimuli to generate looking time differences. However, ERP recording does not require explicit attention or overt responses. This may reduce the cognitive load on children, and therefore ERP approaches may allow us to observe cognitive processes in younger children who may not yet have sufficient cognitive resources to handle the task demands.

3.1.3   *Applicability across different age groups*

Since ERP responses are automatically elicited upon exposure to linguistic stimuli, processing at various levels can be tested across different age groups. This has allowed developmental researchers to investigate the developmental time course of language comprehension mechanisms for phonetic, lexical and sentence processing (for a review, see Friederici 2005). This line of research has shown similarities and differences in children and adults' language comprehension mechanisms, which raise the well known continuity question: Does a child's language comprehension mechanism qualitatively differ from that of an adult? Even though a continuity question in language development has been addressed in investigations of linguistic competence (e.g., Crain and Thornton 1998; Pinker 1984), it has not been addressed nearly as much with respect to the performance mechanisms, mainly because it had to await the advent of on-line measures that can be adapted to children. Thus, ERP can now be used to examine the developmental trajectory of, for example, the sentence processing mechanism (as reviewed in Section 2.4).

3.1.4   *Caveats*

Despite these appealing advantages of ERP measures, the interpretation of child ERP data requires special caution. Both Kooijman, Johnson and Cutler (this volume) and Sheehan and Mills (this volume) provide thoughtful commentary on the methodological challenges. We add some considerations here. First, we are still in need of much more basic understanding of the relation between brain development and ERP components. For example, in adult ERP research, the N1-P2 complex has been shown to be a robust, automatic response to auditory stimuli, but this complex is immature and its development lasts up to mid-puberty (Pasman, Rotteveel, Maassen and Visco 1999; Pang and Taylor 2000). As Kooijman *et al* (this volume) note, this suggests the possibility that ERP findings from children and adults may not be so directly comparable, although the fact that some ERP components (e.g., mismatch negativity, N400, P600) have very similar properties in children and adults in terms of scalp distribution and latency intimates that at least some adult-like ERP components do exist early on in development.

Second, the fact that ERP experiments with children do not require attention to stimuli or overt responses does not mean that it is easier to acquire clean data – in fact, extremely careful artifact rejection procedures are necessary (see Sheehan and Mills, this volume, for valuable discussion). For example, researchers not only provide positive reinforcement for sitting still during periodic breaks, but also monitor the child during the experiment and mark trials on which the child did not pay attention, such that trial-by-trial basis artifact rejection techniques can be used. Furthermore, they adjust artifact rejection thresholds for each child by visually inspecting each trial, while also using computer programs to adjust thresholds based on the presence of blinking, etc. Thierry and Vihman (this volume) use a manual stimulus delivery procedure coupled with online infant monitoring to reduce the number of artifacts recorded. On balance, many conservative artifact rejection algorithms are necessary for child ERP data, and yet clean data are not guaranteed even with careful data reduction procedures.

Finally, despite the important advantages of ERP measures, behavioral studies will certainly remain critical as experimental techniques for language development research. Experiments using the head turn preference procedure (Kemler-Nelson, Jusczyk, Mandel, Myers and Turk 1995), preferential looking paradigms (Hirsh-Pasek and Golinkoff 1996), or truth value judgment tasks (Crain and Thornton 1998) are still much more widely available and have so far provided numerous empirical data on children's language learning between birth and age five. This database will remain important and keep increasing in size: For example, the wide range of artificial language learning studies discussed by Mehler and colleagues (this volume) in the past decade was based on various behavioral experiments, and the very fact that the experimental set-up is widely available has clearly contributed to the quick growth of the literature. Furthermore, tasks like the preferential looking paradigm or the truth value judgment task, although they do not provide as precise a time course measure as ERP, are possibly more appropriate for testing grammatical constraints on sentences with multiple interpretive possibilities (Crain and Thornton 1998; Lidz, Waxman and Freedman 2003; Thornton and Wexler 1999) than ERP measures of syntactic processing, as these experiments can establish rich discourse contexts that are needed to make the relevant interpretations felicitous.

In summary, while there are obviously serious challenges in using ERP measures with children, it is very appealing that ERPs can provide much richer information about the time course and distribution of neural activities that underlie language processing, and that they allow us to compare adults and children's neural activities at various levels of linguistic processes, ranging from sounds to sentences. The addition of a new experimental technique to the field of language development is certainly a welcome one, and we believe that choosing the appropriate methodology for a given experimental hypothesis will help the field of language acquisition to further develop in an efficient fashion.

3.2   What does one stand to learn about language development from using EEG/ERP with children?

As the title of this volume suggests, our primary goal here is to improve our understanding of early *language* development by bringing together a range of behavioral and electrophysiological data. Given the cognitive science view of language as a computational system that manipulates linguistic representations, here we briefly consider whether the use of EEG/ERP with children sheds light on children's linguistic representations and their computational capacities in development.

3.2.1   *Linguistic representation*

The hallmark of linguistic research is to identify the 'parts list' at different levels of representation – that is, what are the primitives and what are their attributes? For example, phonological research suggests that the primitives are *distinctive features*, *segments*, and *syllables*. Lexical and syntactic research suggests that *morphemes* enter into linguistic computations in particular ways, and that representational elements such as *noun phrases* or *agreement markers,* and so on, constitute the representational substrates of human language. Naturally, there is vigorous debate about the nature of such representations, and it is a significant question whether research of the type presented in these chapters can speak to these critical questions about the basics of linguistic representations.

At the level of the sound structure of language, one of the basic representational units is the *phoneme* (itself made up of bundles of distinctive features), which is argued to mediate speech sounds and meaning. Although Conboy and colleagues' ERP research examines the development of *phonetic* categories that mediate speech sounds and phonological representations, it is not clear whether infants in their first two years possess *discrete phonological representations*, nor when those representations and the relevant neural mechanisms develop. From adult research (e.g. Näätänen *et al.* 1997; Phillips *et al.* 2000) we know that speakers have access to surprisingly abstract aspects of their phonological knowledge, aspects clearly not reflected in the speech signal itself. One essential representational question is whether or not learners already show evidence of such abstract categories, or whether the representations used by language learners are graded phonetic phenomena. In the domain of sound and phonology, this is the type of question that might be engaged by innovative developmental research.

The level at which sound and meaning association is established is the lexical representation. In this domain, studies reported by Friedrich (this volume) and Sheehan and Mills (this volume) have important implications. One generalization that we can draw from their studies is that the lexical representation in the first two years of life can be noisy and require further consolidation. For example, Friedrich's finding that 12-month-olds show facilitation of phonological processing indexed by early negativity and yet lack an N400 could be interpreted to mean that the lexical representation was so noisy that the infants could not retrieve the appropriate meaning. The finding reported in Sheehan and Mills that N200–400 was elicited to known-unknown words (e.g., *bear-kobe*) as well as mispronounced known-unknown words (e.g., *gare-kobe*) in 14-month-olds but not in 20-month-olds suggests a developmental change in the 'phonetic precision' of the lexical representation between 14 and 20 months.

On the other hand, the fact that even 13 to 14-month-olds start to show N400 responses to congruous-incongruous words indicates that fairly well articulated lexical representations exist soon after the end of the first year, although we do not know how exactly the semantic memory is organized. One way to address this question is to manipulate various features of a target lexical item and test if the N400 can be modulated by how much the expected word and actual word diverge (Kutas and Federmeier 2000). If one finds that the number of features manipulated can predict differential modulation of N400 components (as in adults), this will constitute evidence for continuity in how semantic memory representations are organized from childhood to adulthood.

At the level of syntactic representation, there is a considerable amount of debate regarding whether children possess abstract structural representation early in life (see, for example, Lidz 2007 and Poeppel and Wexler 1993 arguing pro; Tomasello 2003 arguing con), but currently there is no contribution in this domain deriving from child ERP research. One way in which developmental ERP data could be useful to address this controversy is to find ERP evidence for syntactic priming effects (Ledoux, Traxler and Swaab 2007). If syntactic priming of, say, argument structure occurs across different verbs, this suggests that there is an abstract syntactic representation that was primed across trials. Some behavioral studies found structural priming in children (Thothathiri and Snedeker 2006) but others did not (Savage, Lieven, Theakston and Tomasello 2003). However, given that ERP is arguably more sensitive to some underlying cognitive operations than behavioral measures, there is a chance that ERP data could reveal the presence of abstract syntactic representations in the developing child grammar.

3.2.2 *Linguistic computation*

By analogy to questions regarding the elementary representational architecture of language, we would like to specify the elementary computations operating over those representations. For example, how, when and where (in the brain) are morphemes combined to yield structured representations? How are sentences built, specifically with respect to the widely attested operations such as displacement (movement), or expectancy-driven operations such as predicting the set of possible syntactic categories permissible in a given context? With regard to the first question, very little is known even in the adult literature. Although the characterizations of what might be the most basic linguistic operations must be considered one of the deepest and most pressing questions in experimental language research, we know virtually nothing about the neuronal implementation about the putative primitives of linguistic computation. On the other hand, with respect to a set of computational sub-routines that form the basis for predictive coding in language processing, both cognitive neuroscience and developmental research are making critical contributions. One nice example comes from the picture-word matching paradigms discussed by Friedrich (this volume) and Sheehan and Mills (this volume). Data deriving from studies described by these researchers are consistent with the claim that even early learners built remarkably rich representations of the on-going 'scene,' whether it is created by words, pictures or even gestures. These representations appear to make predictions about the space of possible lexical items in nuanced ways that are demonstrable using ERP responses akin to the adult N400. As such, one promising area of research at the interface between adult and child psycholinguistics might be the systematic investigation of predictive mechanisms or analysis-by-synthesis. ERP data such as ELAN and P600 (as discussed by Friederici and Oberecker, this volume) further support the hypothesis that the language processor uses subtle knowledge of language to constrain the incoming information in building meaningful representations.

3.3   Large-scale neurocognitive models – an opportunity for developmental research?

The literature on brain and language is occasionally summarized in the context of large-scale models that attempt to articulate neurocognitive frameworks for a broad range of issues in language processing. For language production, Levelt and colleagues have proposed a detailed model of single-word production (e.g., Indefrey and Levelt 2004) and Dell and colleagues have tackled sentence production (e.g., Dell, Burger and Svec 1997). With regard to comprehension, models include Hickok and Poeppel's dorsal-ventral pathway model for speech processing (e.g. Hickok and Poeppel 2007), Price's (2000) model focused on single-word processing, and Friederici's (2002) model emphasizing sentence processing. Ben Shalom and Poeppel (in press) evaluate the extent to which a coherent 'meta-model' can be constructed on the basis of these differing proposals; they conclude that *storage and retrieval operations* (principally temporal lobe) versus *analytic operations* (principally parietal lobe) versus *combinatoric operations* (principally frontal lobe) provide some taxonomic structure to the issues.

While these large-scale models integrate vast amounts of data, they all share an 'adult perspective.' Almost without exception, the data considered come from studies of adult language processing – and developmental data are almost entirely absent. We view this as a major opportunity for language acquisition research with a neurobiological bent. In particular, if the large-scale heuristic models of this type characterize the adult state, it goes without saying that their developmental trajectory requires study. Friederici's (2002) model focused on sentence processing, and the developmental data presented, for example, in the Friederici and Oberecker contribution (this volume), serve to bring an explicitly developmental angle to the model. However, few of the other approaches consider language acquisition data in any depth. In our view, however, data from infant and child studies could be used productively to try to 'fractionate' the models into their constituent parts. For example, functional and functional-anatomic models arguing for a tight mapping between perception and production (e.g. Indefrey and Levelt 2004; Hickok and Poeppel 2007) should be forced to spell out how such links come to be, given typical developmental trajectories. One could imagine using behavioral and neurophysiological data to rule out (or rule in) some of the boxes that constitute the boxological models that practitioners like to entertain. The substantive addition of developmental data to such models would both test and strengthen them while dramatically increasing the models' empirical coverage.

To exemplify a further specific issue of how developmental data can shed light on the neurocognitive mechanisms underlying adults' language processing, we believe that there is another interesting opportunity to exploit in this context. There is debate in the adult electrophysiology literature on the computations reflected in the N400. The interpretations of the N400 are, by and large, rather 'high-level,' referring to processes such as semantic priming, lexical access, semantic integration into sentential contexts, and so on. But it is uncontroversial that the N400, a late and complex neurophysiological deflection, reflects various underlying neuronal computations that form the basis for these higher-order processes. This must be the case, because even a *putatively* simple cognitive operation such as lexical access is demonstrably structured and complex. Therefore it might be more fruitful to think of the (neuronally inspired) subroutines that make up processes such as lexical access or semantic priming. Given that the developmental data deal by and large with lexical processing in the absence of sentential context, these data provide a window into one of the hypothesized subroutines reflected in the N400, lexical access. As such, developmental data could be used creatively and effectively to fractionate the lexical part of the N400 into its constituent operations.

4   Recommendations from some (friendly) disciplinary neighbors

1. One missing ingredient in the field that everybody can agree on is the existence of a 'normative database' of electrophysiological responses recorded from infants and children. It goes without saying that the existence of normative criteria is all too often missing in adult studies as well. Nevertheless, the existence of a large body of research using and replicating basic response properties allows research-ers to compare across studies, not just with respect to the issues under investiga-tion, but specifically with respect to the response profile obtained across studies. This may include the latency and amplitude and spatial distribution of responses, the effect size of responses in a given study, and so on.

As Table 1 illustrates, even the relatively small selection of papers illustrated in the present volume shows the heterogeneity of responses associated with linguistic stimulation. But would a more extensive database be more than a list of vaguely associated phenomena? Why might such a database even be illuminating? Con-sider from the present volume three papers that use the N400 response to test as-pects of lexical semantic processing. Conboy and colleagues (this volume) describe experimental research in which the N400 is elicited in sentential contexts. This is akin to many standard designs in adult psycholinguistic research. In contrast, Friedrich (this volume), as well as Sheehan and Mills (this volume), uses a picture-word matching paradigm and demonstrates N400 modulation. Now, the presup-position underlying this work must be that the cognitive operation or set of opera-tions underlying the generation of the N400 must be to some extent shared across these studies. In other words, although the 'lead-in' processes are quite different in a sentence-processing versus a picture matching paradigm, it stands to reason that in both cases, a specific expectation is built up for a lexical semantic representa-tion, and perhaps even a specific lexical entry. If the N400 reflects aspects of re-trieving lexical representations, then the N400 pattern—at least if we look at it within an age cohort—should look rather comparable. Obviously this can only be verified with respect to some larger database in which the many conditions that elicit the N400 are tabulated and compared in a quantitative manner. In order to build a theoretically grounded and computationally satisfying account of what is reflected in N400 responses, it seems to us that such a database would be of im-mense value. The necessity of the normative database is very clear and urgent, given that different researchers are already finding these diverse components and assigning variable interpretations to them.

A further feature of a normative database that would be extremely valuable, although not tremendously amusing to establish, would be to have extensive data for given well-known responses across development. For example, the ontogenetically conditioned modification of the N1 is known, as is the fact that the MMN response can be elicited throughout development. On the other hand, the timing, amplitude, and spatial profile of, say, the N2, or N400, or P600 is not at all understood. Some laboratory will earn lots of praise for collecting, for example, N400 and P600 responses from the cradle to the grave.

2. Because of the extraordinary variability of electrophysiological responses as a function of age, the interpretation of these components vis-à-vis cognitive models is even more challenging. One small but potentially useful modification might be the following: If, in the context of practically all experiments, a 'functional landmark' was established, then the data could be interpreted with respect to the robust landmark that in turn should be more easily comparable across studies. What we have in mind is roughly the following: Suppose that at the beginning (or middle, or end) of a psycholinguistic study a simple evoked response to a supra-threshold tone was recorded (for example, N1), then it would be possible to interpret the psycholinguistically elicited ERP responses with respect to that more well understood functional landmark. It is well known that the N1 itself undergoes a rather dramatic change from infancy to late puberty (Pang and Taylor 2000; Wunderlich and Cone-Wesson 2006), but within age groups, it would be possible to compare the responses, which would now be scaled to something rather more straightforwardly interpretable. One reason we raise this possibility is the extreme variability in timing and amplitude of responses. If it were possible to interpret, say, an N400 pattern as a relative difference to a simple tone instead of an absolute time, this opportunity would constrain the interpretation one would give language-related ERPs.

3. As is true for adult studies, one feature of such research that would enrich our understanding, both with respect to linguistic and with respect to neurobiological interpretation, is the 'radical' decomposition of the tasks used with infants and children into their constituent psycholinguistic and cognitive subroutines. It is entirely uncontroversial that an experimental task such as lexical decision or picture-word matching encompasses numerous, more elementary computational subroutines. While we tend to interpret evoked responses as somewhat monolithic (the N400 reflects "semantic integration"; the P600 reflects "repair and reanalysis"), researchers agree that these are not the elementary operations executed by neuronal circuitry. Rather, many different operations go into the composition of these complicated brain responses. A richer, more satisfying account of development

will presumably give an account of the individual operations that make up, say, lexical access or semantic composition.

5   Conclusion

Even brief historical reflection should convince the reader that it is remarkable that we are now able to record extra-cranial signals from young brains with millisecond resolution, and that these signals *can* receive a coherent interpretation in the context of theories about language development and language processing. Having solved some of the major technical obstacles, the question is now whether harnessing these new techniques and optimizing them to investigate child language will yield knowledge that goes substantially beyond what we can learn from sophisticated behavioral techniques. In our view, it is terrific news when the behavioral data and the ERP data match and correlate – in some sense that can be viewed as replication with different methods. However, while it is nice when behavior and physiology match, it is also boring. When there exists substantial parallelism between ERP data and behavioral data, what is added? The experimental situation is at its most interesting when the two types of data go against each other or complement each other. It is precisely in those cases that one gets the sense of new facets of data being available to answer questions about development at a fine-grained neurobiological and cognitive level.

Finally, there is one aspect of language acquisition research in which the developmental literature is empirically more broadly informed than most of the adult literature, and that concerns the incorporation of a cross-linguistic perspective. An explicitly multilingual angle is dictated by the need to account for cross-linguistic facts about language development. Adult cognitive neuroscience of language research could benefit from this linguistic pluralism.

Acknowledgments

Preparation of this chapter was supported by NIH R01 DC 05660 to DP. The authors thank Susannah Hoffman for help with various aspects of the manuscript.

References

Ben Shalom, D. and Poeppel, D. In press. "Functional anatomic models of language: Assembling the pieces." *The Neuroscientist*.

Chomsky, N. 1957. *Syntactic structures*. The Hague: Mouton.

Crain, S. and Thornton, R. 1998. *Investigations in universal grammar: A guide to experiments on the acquisition of syntax and semantics*. Cambridge, MA: The MIT Press.

Dell, G.S., Burger, L.K. and Svec, W.R. 1997. "Language production and serial order: A functional analysis and a model." *Psychological Review* 104: 123–47.

Elman, J.L. 1993. "Learning and development in neural networks: The importance of starting small." *Cognition* 48: 71–99.

Friederici, A.D. 2002. "Towards a neural basis of auditory sentence processing." *Trends in Cognitive Science* 6: 78–84.

Friederici, A.D. 2005. "Neurophysiological markers of early language acquisition: from syllables to sentences." *Trends in Cognitive Science* 9 (10): 481–8.

Friederici, A.D. and Weissenborn, J. 2007. "Mapping sentence form onto meaning: The syntax-semantic interface." *Brain Research* 1146: 50–8.

Hickok, G. and Poeppel, D. 2007. "The cortical organization of speech perception." *Nature Neuroscience Reviews* 8: 393–402.

Hirsh-Pasek, K. and Golinkoff, R.M. 1996. *The origins of grammar*. Cambridge, MA: The MIT Press.

Houston, D.M., Jusczyk, P.W., Kuijpers, C., Coolen, R. and Cutler, A. 2000. "Crosslanguage word segmentation by nine-month-olds." *Psychonomic Bulletin and Review* 7: 504–9.

Indefrey, P. and Levelt, W.J. 2004. "The spatial and temporal signatures of word production components." *Cognition* 92: 101–44.

Johnson, M.H. 2005. *Developmental cognitive neuroscience*, 2nd edn. Malden, MA: Blackwell.

Jusczyk, P.W. 1997. *The discovery of spoken language*. Cambridge, MA: The MIT Press.

Jusczyk, P.W. and Aslin, R.N. 1995. "Infants' detection of the sound patterns of words in fluent speech." *Cognitive Psychology* 29: 1–23.

Kemler-Nelson, D. G., Jusczyk, P.W., Mandel, D.R., Myers, J. and Turk, A.E. 1995. "The Head-turn Preference Procedure for testing auditory perception." *Infant Behavior and Development* 18: 111–16.

Kuhl, P. 2004. "Early language acquisition: Cracking the speech code." *Nature Reviews Neuroscience* 5: 831–43.

Kutas, M. and Federmeier, K.D. 2000. "Electrophysiology reveals semantic memory use in language comprehension." *Trends in Cognitive Science* 4: 463–70.

Ledoux, K., Traxler, M.J. and Swaab, T.Y. 2007. "Syntactic priming in comprehension: Evidence from event-related potentials." *Psychological Science* 18 (2): 135–43.

Lidz, J. 2007. "The abstract nature of syntactic representations: Consequences for a theory of learning." In Blackwell *Handbook of language development*, E. Hoff and M. Shatz (eds.), 277–303. Cambridge: Blackwell.

Lidz, J., Waxman, S. and Freedman, J. 2003. "What infants know about syntax but couldn't have learned: Experimental evidence for syntactic structure at 18-months." *Cognition* 89: B65-B73.

Marcus, G. F., Vijayan, S., Rao, S.B. and Vishton, P. 1999. "Rule learning by seven-month-old infants." *Science* 283 (5398): 77–80.

Näätänen, R., Lehtoskoskl, A., Lennes, M., Cheour, M., Huotilainen, M., Ilvonen, A., Vainio, M., Alku, P., Ilmoniemi, R., Luuk, A., Allik, J., Sinkkonen, J. and Alho, K. 1997. "Language-specific phoneme representations revealed by electric and magnetic brain responses." *Nature* 385: 432–34.

Nelson, C.A. and Luciana, M. (eds.). 2001. *Handbook of developmental cognitive neuroscience*. Cambridge, MA: The MIT Press.

Newport, E. and Aslin, R. 2000. "Innately constrained learning: Blending old and new approaches to language acquisition." In *Proceedings of the 24th Annual Boston University Conference on Language Development*, S.C. Howell, S.A. Fish and T. Keith-Lucas (eds.), 1–21. Somerville, MA: Cascadilla.

Pang, E.W. and Taylor M.J. 2000. "Tracking the development of the N1 from age 3 to adulthood: An examination of speech and non-speech stimuli." *Clinincal Neurophysiology* 111 (3): 388–97.

Pasman, J.W., Rotteveel, J.J., Maassen, B. and Visco, Y.M. 1999. "The maturation of auditory cortical evoked responses between (preterm) birth and 14 years of age." *European Journal of Paediatric Neurology* 3: 79–82.

Phillips, C., Pellathy, T., Marantz, A., Yellin, E., Wexler, K., Poeppel, D., McGinnis, M. and Roberts, T.P. 2000. "Auditory cortex accesses phonological categories: An MEG mismatch study." *Journal of Cognitive Neuroscience* 12 (6): 1038–55.

Phillips, C. and Wagers, M. 2007. "Relating structure and time in linguistics and psycholinguistics." In *Oxford handbook of psycholinguistics*, G. Gaskell (ed.), 739-56. Oxford: OUP.

Pinker, S. 1984. *Language learnability and language development*. Cambridge, MA: Harvard University Press.

Poeppel, D. and Wexler, K. 1993. "The full competence hypothesis of clause structure in early German." *Language* 69: 1–33.

Poeppel, D. and Embick, D. 2005. "Defining the relation between linguistics and neuroscience." In *Twenty-first century psycholinguistics: Four cornerstones*, A. Cutler (ed.), 103–18. Mahwah, NJ: Lawrence Erlbaum Associates.

Poeppel, D., Idsardi, W.J. and van Wassenhove, V. In press. "Speech perception at the interface of neurobiology and linguistics." *Philosophical Transactions of the Royal Society*.

Price, C.J. 2000. "The anatomy of language: contributions from functional neuroimaging." *Journal of Anatomy* 197 (Pt 3): 335–59.

Saffran, J., Aslin, R. and Newport, E. 1996. "Statistical learning by 8-month- old infants." *Science* 274 (5294): 1926–8.

Savage, C., Lieven, E., Theakston, A. and Tomasello, M. 2003. "Testing the abstractness of children's linguistic representations: Lexical and structural priming of syntactic constructions in young children." *Developmental Science* 6: 557–67.

Thornton, R. and Wexler, K. 1999. *Principle B, VP-ellipsis, and interpretation in child grammar*. Cambridge, MA: The MIT Press.

Thothathiri, M. and Snedeker, J. 2006. "Children's representation of verbs: Evidence from priming during online sentence comprehension." In *Proceedings of the 30th Annual Boston University Conference on Language Development*, D. Bamman, M. Tatiana and C. Zaller (eds.), 643–652. Somerville, MA: Cascadilla.

Tomasello, M. 2003. *Constructing a language: A usage-based theory of language acquisition*. Cambridge, MA: Harvard University Press.

Werker, J.F. and Tees, R. C. 1999. "Influences on infant speech processing: Toward a new synthesis." *Annual Review of Psychology* 50: 509–35.

Woodward, J.Z. and Aslin, R.N. 1990. "Segmentation cues in maternal speech to infants." Paper presented at 7th biennial meeting of the International Conference on Infant Studies, Montreal, Quebec, Canada.

Wunderlich. J.L. and Cone-Wesson B.K. 2006. "Maturation of CAEP in infants and children: a review." *Hearing Research* 212 (1–2): 212–23.

Yuille, A. and Kersten, D. 2006. "Vision as Bayesian inference?: analysis by synthesis?" *Trends in Cognitive Science* 10 (7): 301–8.

Glossary of selected terms

artefact/artifact — ongoing background EEG activity that is mainly attributable to eye/body movement, technical equipment, etc.

Conditioned Headturn Procedure (CHT): — behavioral procedure in which the infant is sat on a parent's lap and entertained by an experimenter sitting in front using colorful toys. Stimulus sounds are played via a loudspeaker located on the side. During the conditioning phase, the infant is habituated to a baseline stimulus and trained to orient to a stimulus change. When the infant produces a head turn towards the loudspeaker playing the deviant stimulus, the "correct" head turn is reinforced using for example an animated toy which makes a funny noise together with experimenter's praises and encouragements. Incorrect head turns (i.e., head turns toward baseline stimuli) are not reinforced. Once the infant is conditioned and produces reliable head turns to changing stimuli, test stimuli can be introduced which vary from the baseline stimulus in different ways.

epoch, EEG epoch: — a defined time window in the EEG raw data that is time-locked to the onset of an event of interest (e.g., word onset, sentence onset)

Headturn Preference Procedure (HPP):	behavioral procedure in which infants orient differentially towards (generally two) loudspeakers playing contrasting stimulus kinds (e.g. familiar / unfamiliar words). One trial classically involves centering of attention using flashing lights in front of the infant, followed by flashing lights on one side (left or right) accompanied by lists of stimuli played continuously. Both the direction and the duration of head turns are recorded and taken to indicate the level of attention devoted to a particular stimulus type. HPP sessions may or may not include a familiarization session.
High Amplitude Sucking Paradigm:	"uses sucking rate as a dependent measure of speech preferences and discriminatory abilities, works well with infants up to two months of age" (Kooijman et al., this volume)
left frontal operculum:	a brain region in the inferior frontal cortex positioned next to the classical language-related brain region called Broca's area
N1/P2 complex	this ERP complex covers two subsequently occurring ERP components: a negativity at around 100 ms post-stimulus onset and a positivity at around 200 ms post-stimulus onset. These early components are often labelled obligatory components since they indicate the brain's automatic response to incoming auditory or visual stimuli.
N200	N200 refers to a negative-going ERP component at around 200 ms post-stimulus onset. Note that in this time range, there is a family of subcomponents rather than one single component which occur in response to task-relevant or task-irrelevant deviating stimuli among frequent standard stimuli.

N2-N4 complex:	two negative peaks elicited in sequence around 200 and 400 ms, respectively, upon presentation of spoken words to infants. The two peaks are considered a complex because amplitudes of the N2 is highly correlated to those of the N4, suggesting that they have the same functional origin
N4 modulation:	the N4 should not be confounded with the classical N400, which refers to a ERP modulation observed in experiments in which semantic context is manipulated.
Nc component:	the Nc is a late negative component taken to reflect attentional aspects of processing nonnutritive high-amplitude sucking technique: other term for the High Amplitude Sucking Paradigm (see above)
Oddball Paradigm:	general paradigm (used both in behavioral and ERP testing) in which short-term habituation is induced by frequent repetition of a stimulus (the "standard", with a probability of, for instance, 0.8) randomly interrupted by a low probability stimulus (the "deviant", with a probability of, for instance, 0.2). This paradigm is associated with the mismatch negativity in ERPs, a negative modulation induced by the deviant between ~100 and ~250 ms after stimulus onset. This effect can be measured in the absence of selective attention.
P50	the P50 is a positive-going early ERP component that peaks at around 50 ms post-stimulus onset. It is associated with sensory gating, the automatic adjustment of the brain's response to subsequently following stimuli.
P50/N100 complex	this early ERP complex includes a positive component at around 50 ms post-stimulus onset and a negative component at around 100 ms post-stimulus onset, both reflecting preattentive stimulus processing.
Preferential looking paradigm:	other term for the Headturn Preference Procedure (see above)
Unimodal studies:	studies in one sensory modality (either visual or auditory)

Visual Fixation
Procedure:
    "infants' looking time to a single visual display is measured as a function of different auditory inputs" (Kooijman et al., this volume)

Index

In the series *Trends in Language Acquisition Research* the following titles have been published thus far or are scheduled for publication: